The Corporate Responsibility Movement

The
Corporate
Responsibility
Movement

Five Years of Global Corporate Responsibility
Analysis from Lifeworth, 2001–2005

JEM BENDELL

with

Désirée Abrahams, Mark Bendell, Tim Concannon, Paul Gibbons,
Kate Ives, Kate Kearins, John Manoochehri, Jeremy Moon, Jules Peck,
Rupesh Shah, Shilpa Shah, Wayne Visser and Mark Young

Routledge
Taylor & Francis Group

LONDON AND NEW YORK

First published 2009 by Greenleaf Publishing Limited

Published 2017 by Routledge
2 Park Square, Milton Park, Abingdon, Oxon OX14 4RN
711 Third Avenue, New York, NY 10017, USA

Routledge is an imprint of the Taylor & Francis Group, an informa business

Cover design by LaliAbril.com

British Library Cataloguing in Publication Data:
  The corporate responsibility movement : five years of
    global corporate responsibility analysis from Lifeworth,
    2001-2005
    1. Social responsibility of business
    I. Bendell, Jem II. Lifeworth (Firm)
    658.4'08

    ISBN-13: 9781906093181 (pbk)

Contents

Introduction

2001

2002

2003

2004

2005

Acknowledgements

I thank John Stuart for commissioning me in 2001 to write the World Reviews for the *Journal of Corporate Citizenship* and agreeing for them to be published as Annual Reviews by Lifeworth. I am grateful for the contributions of my co-authors Désirée Abrahams, Tim Concannon, Mark Bendell, Kate Ives, Kate Kearins, John Manoochehri, Rupesh Shah, Shilpa Shah, Wayne Visser and Mark Young. Tim Concannon and John Paul Sena designed the Annual Reviews on a very tight budget, with Dean Bargh's support. Thankfully, Paul Gibbons, Hannah Jones, Jeremy Moon, David Murphy, Jules Peck, Maggie Royston and Mark Young arranged crucial financial support from Nike, Future Considerations, New Academy of Business, University of Nottingham ICCSR and WWF. Malcolm McIntosh, Sandra Waddock and David Birch provided editorial guidance as editors of the *Journal of Corporate Citizenship*, while Dean Bargh swiftly tidied up my ramblings and oversights. Thanks also to Sandy Lin for helping me prepare the thematic index. If you would like to sponsor future issues of the Annual Reviews, please get in touch via www.lifeworth.com.

Introduction

The emergence of the corporate responsibility movement

Jem Bendell

Involved for a change

Rolling onto my back, I lay my head on a rucksack, staring into the night sky. The tarmac still pushes up through my sleeping bag, but somehow it feels more comfortable this way. I think of the few times I have slept out in the open, in fields after parties, or on beaches while travelling—times when I could revel in the sense of floating through the immensity of space, secured on the edge of a cosmic plan, or comic fluke, called planet Earth. But tonight I can't drift away with thoughts of the infinite expanse of space. Police helicopters hover above, their cones of light traversing the car park like manic stilts. Dreaming is not permitted. It's the G8 Summit in Genoa, 2001. I stretch my neck. My face feels sticky with the residue of vinegar I was told would help me during tear-gas attacks. Are we being searched for or spotlighted, I wonder? If they shine their lights on us for long enough, perhaps they'll discover what they're looking for? Perhaps we're all here to discover what we're looking for—something different, something possible? I can't sleep and turn to Rik, a guy I met on the streets during the day. 'D'you want to hear my poem?' he asks. 'Yeah, why not . . . ?'

> Possessed by possessions
> Lord and Master of all we owe
> Belonging to belongings
> It's a disaster, I know
>
> Chained to the mundane
> Our reference frame is physical
> Every day the same old same
> Nothing metaphysical
>
> And if God's not dead
> He must be mad
> Or blind
> Or deaf and dumb
> Or bad
> Still smarting over Christ, perhaps
> The way the people have been had

But in our defence
I'd like to say
We nearly chose the proper path
But lost the plot along the way
You've got to laugh

It's not our fault
It's just the toys we made
Made such a lovely noise
And girls and boys
Are high and dry
Time to bid
All this
Goodbye.

Rik Strong's *The Sermon*, which he recited to me as we 'bedded' down in a car park during the demonstrations at the G8 Summit in Genoa, July 2001, captured the emotion that drove many of us to act in what was sometimes called an 'anti-globalisation' movement by the mass media, and came to be known by many activists as the global justice movement (Korten 2006). It was a feeling of something going wrong. The modern Western world didn't relate to how we felt inside. Publicly people didn't seem to care for each other, yet we knew that deep down they must do—surely? For us there had to be more to us than working, shopping and looking out for Number One.

I was protesting in Genoa as part of The Brighton Collective—an eclectic gathering from all walks of life in Brighton, England, with various political affiliations or none. It was one of many grassroots initiatives aimed at engaging the general public about the global economic causes of the various social and environmental issues faced locally, and abroad, and helping them to campaign around meetings of international organisations.

The same year I was dodging both aggressive protesters and police, I started writing a regular review of corporate responsibility issues and initiatives, five years of which are compiled in this volume. I had been working as a corporate responsibility consultant and researcher, which involved advising on matters such as how to conduct voluntary assessments of the social and environmental performance of a company's supply chain. Terms such as 'sustainable business', 'corporate social responsibility' and 'corporate citizenship' had become popular for describing the integration of social, environmental and economic considerations into the decision-making structures and processes of business. A contemporary view of corporate responsibility had emerged as not only involving diligent compliance with national law but also aspiring to meet international standards and the expectations of society. More managers understood the importance of engaging stakeholders to more effectively manage potential corporate risks, build trust within society, stimulate innovation, and enable new business models or reach new markets. Some already understood that, ultimately, being responsible involves innovating products and business processes to provide solutions to social and environmental challenges.

Jumping between barricades and boardrooms might seem schizophrenic. Or perhaps just a manifestation of an 'opposable mind' capable of holding different worldviews at the same time (Martin 2007). But I didn't see such a difference: I was experimenting with ways to play a role in helping transform economic life to make it more supportive of . . . well . . . all life. On the one hand, work on corporate responsibility could help alleviate certain problems, and grassroots mobilisation could help maintain attention on the bigger picture. Some others I met at the time had a similar view. For instance, a number of the protesters I met at the first Global Day of Action during the G7 in Birmingham, in 1998, now work on corporate responsibility or responsible finance.

I hoped there would be a coming-together of the different fields of corporate responsibility work with a more fundamental understanding of the limits of current processes of corporate and financial globalisation. The goal is that by being citizens not only at a ballot box, but also at work and in the high street, private enterprise can deliver public ends more effectively than relying on the sum of the narrow self-interests of consumers, investors or employees. As that is a comprehensive agenda, many sections in the World Reviews dealt with trade regulation, global governance and the need to reform global finance to make it more supportive of socially and environmentally responsible enterprise. In the thematic index that we have prepared to help you navigate this volume, these sections appear under the topics of 'Political involvement' and 'Responsible investment'. This explicitly normative approach to analysis is not always how academics or business writers approach things—which, in fact, is why I kept going at it. Because, as I will argue in this introduction, corporate responsibility practitioners urgently require support in understanding how their work is evolving and can achieve greater social change while benefiting their own organisation. I will argue that they are part of a social movement that has been largely overlooked by social movements theorists, organisation theorists and specialists in corporate responsibility research. I argue there is a role for intellectuals to help inform and therefore co-create critical practice. I map out some implications for research, practice and policy that come from applying a social movement lens to what is occurring today with the contemporary corporation and its systems of financing.

A key shift that was consolidated during the five years overviewed in this volume is the change in the way many business people relate to the social and environmental performance of their companies. In the not-so-distant past, there were few executives who would accept responsibility for the social and environmental impacts of their companies beyond legal compliance, or for the impacts of their suppliers or customers, or accept that those affected by their value chain should have some say over the social and environmental performance of that chain. This changed for many industries in many parts of the world. Over half of the *Fortune* Global 500 transnational corporations produce a separate corporate responsibility report annually (Williams 2004), and most have senior executives with responsibility for social and environmental performance (*Economist* 2005).

Many commentators describe these changes as a response to various social movements and the protests they have directed at companies (Murphy and Bendell 1997; Bendell 2000; Starr 2000). However, any view of the contemporary rise of corporate responsibility as solely a professional response to external social movements is challenged by the discourse of the professionals themselves. Increasingly they speak of themselves as part of a 'corporate responsibility movement'. The Vice President of Corporate Responsibility at the clothing and sportswear firm Nike often uses this very term and speaks like a social activist when describing how her company is 'blurring the edges of what corporate social responsibility is . . . looking at business models as a force for massive social change' (Jones 2007). The founder of the Global Reporting Initiative, Allen White, explains his latest work is intended to 'build . . . a vanguard for change . . . to form the beginnings of a movement that will commit in fairly concrete ways to change. And we want that movement to involve business . . .' (White 2007). 'The corporate social responsibility movement is picking up steam . . . ,' reported the CFO magazine (Teach 2005), while the former UN Secretary-General said, 'there is a pressing need to sustain the momentum of the corporate responsibility movement' (Annan 2006). At the time of going to print, the phrase 'corporate responsibility movement' produced over 4,000 hits on Google, the phrase 'corporate social responsibility movement' 6,000 hits and 'CSR movement' 14,000. The 'global justice movement', a widely used term by social movements analysts today, produced 44,000 hits. This means that, on the English-language Internet, corporate responsibility is half as prominent a movement as the global justice movement, so should warrant at least some attention in those terms—as a movement.

'Social movement' is defined in *Encyclopaedia Britannica* (2003) as a 'loosely organized but sustained campaign in support of a social goal, typically either the implementation or the prevention of a change in society's structure or values'. I will assert that, by using a social movement lens to look at corporate responsibility work, important issues come into sharper focus, such as the goals pursued and the identities involved. I argue that during the five years reviewed in this book, we witnessed the emergence of the corporate responsibility movement as a loosely organised but sustained effort by individuals both inside and outside the private sector, who seek to use or change specific corporate practices, whole corporations, or entire systems of corporate activity, in accordance with their personal commitment to public goals and the expectations of wider society. Moreover, I argue this movement is working in diverse ways on a common agenda to democratise economic activity and conclude by offering a conceptual framework for an overarching goal of 'capital democracy' to help inform both movement adherents and analysts.

We end the chronicling of events and trends in corporate responsibility at 2005, as that year marked ten years of the contemporary phase of corporate responsibility. As the prolific Toby Webb (2005: 1) wrote, in *Ethical Corporation* magazine, 'the ten-year mark for modern corporate responsibility seems an opportune moment to reflect on how far the movement has progressed'. It compelled us at Lifeworth to offer a synopsis of the scale of the challenge confronting corporate responsibility practitioners, in the Lifeworth Annual Review of 2005, called *Serving Systemic Transformations*. We called for more work on the systems around the corporation, particularly global finance. We echoed the analysis that led me to the streets of Birmingham and Genoa, and which I explained in my last book, *Terms for Endearment*:

> [Since the end of the Cold War we have witnessed] the unveiling of a form of hypercapitalism where trillions of dollars are switched around the world in a day, where companies that have never turned a profit are worth billions, and where the future of corporations is decided by a handful of investment managers who are primarily interested in short-term share price. The collective opinion of these investment managers is the compass from which the courses of corporations are set, and in turn the course of governments seeking the favour of investors. Hypercapitalism is spiralling out of control, becoming disconnected from the people living in its midst (Bendell 2000: 240).

As a credit crisis gripped financial markets, this situation was critiqued as 'super-capitalism' by Robert Reich (2007). I would not exactly call it 'super', but the increasingly mainstream critique of global finance and calls for fundamental reform during 2008 echoed the calls of corporate responsibility practitioners, since the Enron collapse six years earlier, for a more coherent approach to fostering economic democracy. That is an economy that supports people's self-actualisation, rather than subjugating them to the insatiable logic of compound interest (Kelly 2001). John Elkington and Mark Lee (2006) from the leading corporate responsibility consultancy SustainAbility argue, 'in its current incarnation, the movement is simply not equal to global challenges like poverty and climate change'. Reflecting on the future of the corporate responsibility movement, the editor of *Business Ethics* magazine, Marjorie Kelly, wrote that 'if we wish to stop being beside the point . . . we would do well to focus on democratizing structures of power. That means imagining, and then creating, economic democracy' (Kelly 2002). In concluding I will imagine what an economic democracy agenda could mean as the goal of a corporate responsibility movement that is awakening to its shared identity and common purpose.

The context in 2001

Over the past decade theories in both organisational studies and social movements have increasingly focused on the broader economic, social and political contexts within which organisations and movements emerge (McAdam and Scott 2005). The reviews in this volume similarly chronicle a widening of focus by practitioners towards the contexts around individual companies, such as regulations, consumer awareness and investment practices. Because context matters, and it is important to recall some economic and political, as well as social and environmental, contexts surrounding the actors and organisations discussed in this volume. It was an awareness of this context that motivated many of the people working on corporate responsibility to do so, and it is the nature and scale of challenges found in this context that provide a yardstick with which to judge the significance of the activities we review.

The events on 11 September 2001 changed the global political scene. Yet more children died of diarrhoea on that fateful day than the people who died in the terrorist attacks. The same number of children died the day after, and the day after that, and so on. In the years prior to the beginning of the period chronicled in this volume, many people were becoming aware of the unnecessary nature of much of this suffering. For instance, a British NGO reported that 19,000 children were dying every day because their governments were ordered by the International Monetary Fund (IMF) to cut spending on health and basic services in order to pay back debts they had no control over (Christian Aid 1999). Then there were the one billion people struggling to survive on less than a dollar a day while their traditional means of providing for themselves through fishing or farming were undermined as time and time again their resources were expropriated by others to feed the global market (Madeley 1999). Their homelands were seen as a source of cheap products for the global North, rather than a place of diverse knowledge and wisdom. Indigenous cultures were being wiped out, along with their knowledge of flora and fauna and perspectives on the human condition. The United Nations Environment Programme (UNEP) reported that in 2001 half the world's languages were in danger of immediate extinction, so oral traditions would be lost forever (World Monitors 2001). This was an extreme example of the increasing 'consumerisation' of cultures around the world, as Western television beamed images of a consumer utopia into millions of homes, helping create demand for those consumer goods that symbolised a Western lifestyle (Saddar 2000).

Many people had their own personal experience of this situation. For instance, I began writing the first review in this volume from a hut on a beach in Nicaragua. I was there to visit a project I had set up with Marina Prieto for promoting women workers' ability to use voluntary codes to improve their situation in factories and plantations. The 12-year-old boy next to where I was staying, who couldn't read, didn't go to school and could only watch TV in the village shop, stole my one pair of Nike socks from the washing line and proudly wore them around the village. There were other socks to choose from. To me this suggested the incredible power of these symbols of fairytale lifestyles. Another family I stayed with were quite poor but had cable TV for years, installed cheaply soon after a pro-US government was elected in 1990. When I talked to the father about what he wanted for the future, he nodded towards the TV and said 'to provide a better life—more consumer goods'. He had not heard of the problems in the West with regard to pollution, insecurity and affluent diseases such as heart disease and cancer. How would he? Such things didn't feature in Hollywood films or the adverts that punctuated them.

Meanwhile, increasing numbers of people faced environmental catastrophe because of the effects of a century of growing consumerism and industrial production. Freak weather episodes were becoming more common and more devastating, such as the 1998 Hurricane Mitch in Central America, which killed approximately 20,000 people, and the 1999 floods in Venezuela which killed still greater, though precisely unknown, numbers. For the people left to rebuild their lives, climate change wasn't a theory anymore. At the time Al Gore had only just ended an eight-year term as US vice president, but his government had done little to reduce dependence on hydrocarbons, and all our societies were continuing to increase the rates of deforestation and air and water pollution (Brown 2000). With Gore spuriously defeated in the US election, the new administration set aside the country's international agreement to do something positive about carbon emissions, because their oil company sponsors worried they might lose profits (see 'Earth Summit preparations' on page 72). Meanwhile, extinctions of flora and fauna continued apace, with biologists estimating that half of all life on Earth was at threat from extinction, because of the actions of humankind (Brown 2000). Environmental pollution had already been shown to undermine our health: as you read this you have at least 500 more chemicals circulating in your body than someone living in the 1920s would have had, and these increase your risk of allergy, infection, infertility and cancer (Colborn *et al.* 1997). In the world's industrialised countries, high levels of unemployment, falling real wages and the increasing use of short-term contracts were creating a climate of stress and insecurity for many (e.g. myself, mother, father and some of my friends). The more extreme symptoms of this malaise could be found in growing violent crime rates around the world and increased levels of armed conflict within states (UNDP 1994).

Why didn't people do something sooner? The fact that 40% of all media were controlled by five transnational corporations might have had something to do with it

(Simms *et al.* 2000). It didn't often pay to talk like this: it wouldn't help sell stuff (Ainger 2001; Chomsky 1992).[1] Moreover, the political process in most countries was captured, to a greater or lesser degree, by corporate interests. By the early 1990s academics had started writing about 'the stateless corporation in which people, assets, and transactions move freely across international borders' (Snow *et al.* 1992: 8). Governments were subject to a discursive discipline, as all their domestic policies had to respond to the overriding imperative of appearing attractive to international corporations and the financial markets (Strange 1996). Those financial markets were shifting trillions of dollars around the world in currency speculation every day (Simms *et al.* 2000). Thus the global economy was shaping state monetary and fiscal policy (Andrews and Willett 1997) and imposing a logic on governments to cut corporate taxes and weaken, or not enforce, social or environmental laws (Madeley 1999; Newell and Paterson 1998; WWF 1999).

The sacred cow of international relations theory—national sovereignty—was now being put to slaughter by a range of commentators (Agnew 1994; Boyer and Drache 1996; Camilleri and Falk 1992; Cox 1997; Rosenau 1997). So, by 2001, mainstream non-fiction was speaking of life in a 'Captive State' (Monbiot 2001) after 'The Silent Takeover' (Hertz 2001) of society by corporations. Some months after the US presidency was handed to George W. Bush by partisan judges, former US Labor Secretary Robert Reich (2001) wrote in the *New York Times* that business was 'in complete control of the machinery of government. The House, the Senate and the White House are all run by business-friendly Republicans who are deeply indebted to American business for their electoral victories.' Questionable state regulation of the oil company Enron, and firms providing fraudulent accounting and auditing services, compounded this perspective (see 'Enron's new clothes' on page 106).

No wonder, then, that the politicians' rhetoric didn't match the reality. They talked of 'free trade' while their liberalising and privatising policies had produced a world where trade was managed by a few transnational corporations.[2] One-third of world trade occurred between factories and offices of such corporations (ILO 2000: 8). In consumer durables the top five controlled 70% of the world market. Microsoft had over 90% of the market for computer operating system software (Simms *et al.* 2000). These were massive centrally planned economies, soviet-style corporate states that dictated what would be 'needed' and how, by whom and for how much these things would be made. Although our socioeconomic lives were governed by these corporations, most people still thought they lived in a democracy—perhaps because many of us were beginning to forget what democracy really meant.

'This is what democracy looks like' read a banner at the anti-WTO (World Trade Organisation) protest in Seattle in November 1999. Unfortunately, most protesters started talking about globalisation more than democracy. Journalists helped confuse everyone by suggesting 'globalisation' was a byword for free-market capitalism (Friedman 1999), or corporate takeover (Pilger 2001) and that campaigners were therefore 'anti-globalisation'. Globalisation had merely meant the stretching of social relations across time and space facilitated by technological advance (Giddens 1990). Most academics had referred to it in terms of the reducing cost of communication and transport, for some people and groups, which meant their activities could be coordinated around world (Held *et al.* 1999). It just so happened that, first and foremost, those people and groups were capitalists and corporations, who were actively globalising Western consumer culture. The globalisation of resistance, of alternatives, of solidarity, of community, of consciousness, and therefore respect and appreciation of diversity, was only getting started (Keck and Sikkink 1998).

Important issues nestling within the ambiguity of the term 'globalisation' were the nature and regulation of global capitalism, the spread of consumerism and, although not often talked about at the time, patriarchy. The environmental degradation and social dislocation we faced was a direct result of the policy paradigm that dominated political discourse in most of the world's nations. There were two pillars upholding this policy paradigm. The first pillar was the idea that increasing the production, consumption and amount of money changing hands in an economy was intrinsically good for society. This was sometimes called consumerism. The second pillar was the notion that international trade helped in this expansion and that it could best be advanced by deregulating economic activity. This was sometimes called neoliberalism. Both personal experience and academic research suggested that these pillars were made of sand and that we needed to reassess what really benefited people—yet most business, the media and politicians were largely carrying on regardless.[3] As David Korten, noted:

> The continued quest for economic growth as the organizing principle of public policy is accelerating the breakdown of the ecosystem's regenerative capacities and the social fabric that sustains human community; at the same time, it is intensifying the competition for resources between rich and poor—a competition that the poor invariably lose (1995: 11).

The growth imperative was a natural by-product of a system where money was lent into society with interest attached—hence the economy must expand. This growth imperative was increased by the flotation of companies on stock markets around the world so that directors had to strive to outperform each other in generating profits, or generating the appearance that they would generate future profits. This form of shareholder capitalism, dubbed 'savage capitalism' by Zapatista rebels, or 'hypercapitalism' in my last book, was spiralling out of control, becoming disconnected from the people living in its midst. This disconnection heightened the negative social and environmental consequences of the growth paradigm, as former Reagan adviser Jeff Gates noted:

> Lacking a reliable human-based signaling system for identifying investments that have damaging, even transgeneric effects, today's capitalism—indifferent, remote and numbers driven—continues to direct resources into projects that endanger our planetary resources (1998: xxv).

As mentioned above, the checks and balances on the growth paradigm that might have come from government were withering away. Instead, we had a global monarchy of money, where capital was bestowed with the divine right to govern our lives: 'Thy Kingdom Company, Thy Will be Done, on Earth as it is in Seven Eleven'. You didn't really count as a human being unless you were a human buying; or at least that is how it seemed for many HIV/AIDS sufferers. It took a huge campaign to stop pharmaceutical corporations from blocking attempts at providing medicinal drugs to people too poor to afford their patented products. New-born babies were contracting HIV from their mothers because of the 'rights' of some transnational corporations, which held 97% of patents worldwide, a situation that I covered in one of the first reviews (see 'Patients pending?' on page 61).

Many of the people I met in Europe and the US did not have much personal experience of these problems, but felt in some way responsible for suffering within a global community. What also drove them was a concern with the way all aspects of economic, political, social and cultural life were becoming sanitised, packaged and sold. As if we had to consume life, not live it. Why have local live music when you can play a CD? Why make friends when you can watch *Friends* on TV? We were possessed by possessions, belonging to belongings.

Different aspects of these problems, probable causes and personal emotions were held by people who were acting in the events described in the following pages. We will return to discuss the extent to which their efforts have been useful towards the end of this introduction, but first the dynamics of how this context inspired actions and institutions on corporate responsibility require some unpacking.

Driving forces for corporate responsibility

Most of the drive for corporate responsibility over the past centuries has come from workers and their organisations, rather than management, owners or consumers. It is widely understood that worker unrest with factory owners and other capitalists in most Northern countries at the start of the 20th century led to the establishment and legal protection of trade unions and a democratic political force for workers. This was an incorporation of worker demands that served to head off the revolutions against capitalism that had occurred in other countries. Critics of capitalism argued for the development of a 'producer politics' where workers unite in order to control capitalists' access to labour. The social democracies that emerged from this period embodied the notion that capitalism worked best if there was a counterbalancing force to capitalists through strong government and trade unions: capitalists needed the workers while workers, it was argued, needed the capitalists.

This social democratic system led to, or coincided with, a huge expansion of many economies during the 20th century. As described above, this balance has been upset due to processes of globalisation. Changes in working life have also led to a decline in producer politics. People are changing jobs more quickly than before. Family members no longer do what their parents did. Personal identity is not determined so much by one's work but increasingly by how one spends ones money and spare time. Thus the most recent political issues of our time are leading to different outcomes. A decade ago the British NGO New Economics Foundation was already reporting 'a dramatic increase . . . in international collective action through consumption' (Zadek *et al.* 1998: 8). In industrialised countries during the 1990s, concern about environmental and social issues led not only to workers uniting to demand better corporate performance, but to consumers uniting to do so. Whereas the establishment of trade unions and political parties incorporated the workers' movement, the establishment of NGOs has incorporated a 'consumer movement'. Although consumer movements date back to 1787 when Thomas Clarkson launched the first major boycott of companies over the British slave trade (Hochschild 2005), the scale and diversity of consumer action today is a phenomenon of late modernity.

Whereas producer politics gained its power through controlling access to labour, consumer politics gains its power through controlling access to customers. The events chronicled in this volume show that NGOs were mobilising consumer politics to change the behaviour of corporations in a number of ways. Corporate boycotts and direct-action protests are the confrontational outcomes of consumer politics, in contrast to the strikes and lock-outs of producer politics. Business–NGO partnerships are the coop-erative tools of consumer politics, in contrast to the business–union deals of producer politics. The development of global framework agreements between international cor-porates and global trade union federations can also be regarded as the result of new forms of consumer politics by trade unions, where unions in consumer markets increase the pressure on companies affecting union members in producing countries (see 'Industrial relations goes global' on page 71). Shareholder activism can be regarded as a form of consumer politics, if we view the drive for this as coming from consumers of financial and investment products; as such it has been theorised as a new form of social movement (Davis and McAdam 2000; Davis and Thompson 1994).

The key role of external pressure to drive increased attention to social and environ-mental performance from management is something I have witnessed and analysed, along with many other researchers (Murphy and Bendell 1997; Broad and Cavanagh 1999; Bendell 2000, 2004; Waddell 2005). This volume includes many instances of civil-society pressure on companies (see 'Stakeholder dialogue' in the 'Topics' section of the thematic index). Others have emphasised this external-pressure view of what was happening with contemporary consumer politics, and described an emerging 'cor-porate accountability movement' (Broad and Cavanagh 1999; Bendell 2004). Many of these commentators, as well as people in civil society, stress a philosophical difference between those who are trying to make companies more responsible, and those who are pressuring for them to be held more accountable (Hamann *et al.* 2003). However, in many cases managers of companies play a decisive role in driving forward corpo-rate change, and accept the need for new ways for themselves, their competitors and suppliers to be held to account by a wider group of stakeholders.

In 1999 I conceptualised the process of civil-society pressure as 'civil regulation', or the quasi-regulation of business by civil society (Murphy and Bendell 1999). This placed emphasis on the role of stakeholders having more influence over economic activity, but also recognised that people within firms could act as individual members of civil society, in facilitating or producing change in corporate practice. These perspec-tives on where the drivers for corporate responsibility are coming from is important for our understanding of the phenomena discussed in this book. For, if we believe that the drivers for change are entirely external to the corporation, this can lead to a view that non-statutory corporate responsibility practices are a professional response to social movements, not a movement in themselves. It is an important question, as it concerns whether this field is a defensive or a transformative one, whether we are a bunch of people with interesting jobs, or are actually doing something that signifi-cantly addresses the scale of global challenges today.

In the period chronicled in this volume there was widespread evidence of business executives taking a lead in transforming their organisations, and advocating for wider social change. The commercial arguments for such individuals to drive change that do not directly rely on campaigning pressure include:

▶ Stronger financial performance through operational efficiency gains, such as eco-efficiency

▶ Enhanced employee relations, thereby improving recruitment, motivation, retention, customer service, learning and innovation, and productivity

▶ Connections with voluntary associations and networks that generate new market intelligence and enable access to new markets

▶ Sustained resource base for raw materials, and healthy and secure environment for consumers and staff

Some entrepreneurs began to see business as having a key role in solving social and environmental challenges in scalable and financially sustainable ways (see 'Social enterprise' in the 'Topics' section of the thematic index). Many business leaders spoke of being part of a social movement, such as Hannah Jones, cited earlier. As Sandra Waddock (2008) illustrates in her book profiling corporate responsibility leaders, it was their personal commitment to find creative ways to promote public goals that motivated their work. Some observers, however, may question whether such individuals are the norm, and whether the majority of people working on corporate responsibility are, in fact, reactive. Some observers may question whether such individuals are the norm, and whether the majority of people working on corporate responsibility are in fact reactive. That is a valid concern, and so we need to look at the way mainstream strategies on corporate responsibility have evolved over the years, to judge how proactive business is and could become.

Evolving corporate responsibility

Various models of strategic approaches to corporate responsibility have been proposed, many of which appear to be useful for academics seeking to model complexity, but not so obvious for practitioners or policy-makers seeking to analyse levels of commercially feasible commitment from companies, or to influence company performance (Hockerts and Dyllick 2002). One model that was developed by a practitioner, Dr Simon Zadek, is most relevant for our purposes here in understanding how corporate responsibility strategies are evolving—and therefore where they are likely to take us.

Zadek (2004) demonstrates his model with the example of the sportswear and apparel corporation Nike. He argues that companies move through a phase of ignoring and denying, to one of reputation management, which sees stakeholder matters in terms of costs and risks. Then companies move to a third stage, where engaging with stakeholders on social and environmental issues is regarded as a mechanism for innovating the business models of the future. A fourth stage involves executives recognising the limits to voluntary action, and realising that engagement with other organisations, including governments and competitors, to influence the business environment, and so raise CR performance, is more financially viable. This model suggests that innovation, inter-organisational relations and business communications functions become more important as CR develops. The model reflects the evolution of corporate strategies described in this volume, and is adapted in Figure 1.

The key trends in corporate responsibility that can be identified from the events and views chronicled in this volume are:

Figure 1 THE CORPORATE RESPONSIBILITY PYRAMID

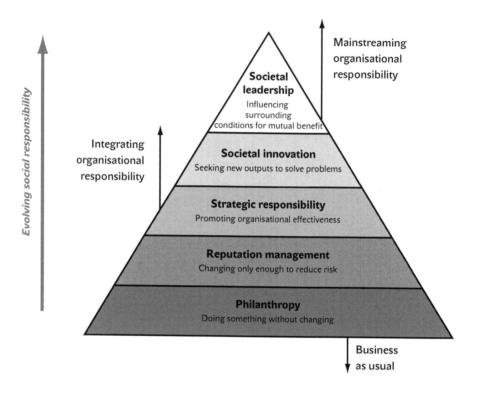

▶ **Standardising.** As more people and organisations work in this field, so the need to compare and benchmark performance increases, and new codes and qualifications emerge (see Functions → 'Accounting, auditing or verification', and also Topics → 'Sustainability reporting', in the thematic index)

▶ **Mainstreaming.** As the limits of individual corporate action in delivering commercial returns and addressing the scale of societal challenges become apparent, so more executives are looking at how to encourage broader changes in society to allow them to invest more in social and environmental excellence (see Topics → 'Political involvement' and Functions → 'Communications' in the thematic index)

▶ **Integrating.** As the commercial and legal relevance of performance on social, environmental and governance issues grows, so does the need to integrate this into the various organisational functions, such as marketing, design, human resources and so on (see the 'Functions' section in the thematic index)

▶ **Levelling.** As economic, political and cultural power shifts from the West to the rest of the world, so the CR strategies and performance of Southern corporations becomes more important, not only in the global South, but even in the West, and more CR initiatives emerge from non Western countries with their own values and emphasis (see Topics → 'Social development' in the thematic index)

▶ **Enterprising.** As the limits of existing business models and corporate forms in delivering solutions to societal problems appear, as well as the limits of tradition philanthropy and advocacy, so more companies seek to profit from provision of innovative market-based solutions to societal problems (see Topics → 'Social enterprise' and 'Clean technology' in the thematic index)

▶ **Yoyoing.** As the underlying drivers for corporate responsibility increase, so more societal challenges are translated into matters of corporate responsibility and opportunity, and so various issues yoyo to the top of the corporate agenda and suggest a redefinition of the challenge as one of sustainability, ethics, rights, accountability, governance, innovation, efficiency and so on. In light of such yoyoing, the 'responsibility' framework remains useful (see the 'Topics' section in the thematic index for a list of the variety of issues for business)

If you benefit from mnemonics, the initial letters make this a 'smiley'—':-)'—of emerging corporate responsibility trends. The mainstreaming and enterprising trends, which parallel the emergence of societal leadership and social innovation strategies from companies, show how executives have been learning through their engagement with corporate responsibility and that there is an endogenous desire from within the corporation to achieve greater social change. Although this resonates with the concept of a social movement, the trends towards standardising and integrating point more towards a process of professionalisation. Therefore, before progressing with a discussion of corporate responsibility activity as a social movement, it is important to examine how professionalisation relates to social movement.

Professional responsibilities

The term 'profession' refers to an occupation that involves training, qualifications and membership of a professional or regulatory body. Professions involve the application of specialised knowledge of a subject to clientele. In the period chronicled in this volume, a range of new standards and qualifications were launched or in development (see, for instance, 'Professionalisation: a new approach required' on page 279 and 'ISO wants consistency' on page 83). Professionalisation is the process of people coming together to establish, improve and ultimately protect a profession. On the positive side, this enables people to develop expertise and maintain standards of practice through peer review. It enables a reassurance for consumers of professional services that the provider is of a certain standard, with particular training, qualifications and experience.

One sociologist concludes that 'professions strike a bargain with society in which they exchange competence and integrity against the trust of client and community, relative freedom from lay supervision and interference, protection against competition as well as substantial remuneration and higher social status' (Rueschemeyer 1983). This suggests that professionalisation also poses some drawbacks for wider society.

Problems arise from protectionist 'occupational closure', whereby professionals seek to restrict supply of a service, to increase prices and wages. The process of standardisation may also reduce creativity and innovation in a professional practice. Professions also tend to resist government and public oversight, by claiming technical expertise. Thus they often translate socially contested knowledge into technical expertise, and remove it from debate in the public domain. Consequently, George Bernard Shaw (in 1906) even claimed 'all professions are conspiracies against the laity'. The way social auditing developed over the years reviewed in this volume illustrates some of the problems involved in the field of corporate responsibility (see Topics → 'Labour practices' and Functions → 'Purchasing or supply' in the thematic index).

Thus professionalisation of corporate responsibility practice raises questions about the accountability and responsibility of the practitioners themselves. Who should CR standards development and review be accountable to? CR practitioners or their intended beneficiaries? Should their intended beneficiaries not only be their clients but those affected by their clients' activities, such as employees, communities and the wider public? If so, what opportunities for meaningful participation in professional standards development can those constituencies really have, given they are so diverse and widely dispersed? The accountability of CR professionals will be a difficult challenge, as the field continues to develop. Conceptualising the profession as a movement would permit greater attention to the accountability of practitioners to the supposed ultimate beneficiaries of improvements to their clients' practices—something we return to below.

This raises the issue of professional purpose. In the 1990s many people entering the CR field as managers, consultants or investment analysts were doing so after a vocational career working on a particular social or environmental issue in an NGO. As the field has grown, many people today are attracted to work on CR for more generic reasons such as having an interesting job in business that does some good, rather than being passionate about working to solve a particular public issue.

The diversity of personal purpose found in CR was documented by Ruth Aguilera *et al.* (2007). They found one personal motivation is 'instrumental', focusing on what to do to deliver for the individual involved and their department or company. Another motivation they identified is 'relational', focusing on what will create harmony within a particular group with which the individual identifies, such as a department, senior management, or participants in certain fora. The other motivation is a 'moral' one, where the individual is pursuing a more public-oriented goal through their CR work. Although Aguilera *et al.* (2007) do not explore how these different motivations may affect the nature of CR and the outcomes for either firm or society, there are two areas where we can deduce an impact.

The first area comes to light from research on the role of values in influencing behaviour around sustainable development issues. If a person's values are largely 'extrinsic', focused on their own security and status in society, so their approach to a social or environmental issue will be mostly instrumental and relational. Research demonstrates that when they change their behaviour on an environmental issue due to such motivations, the environmental benefit will be short-lived. For instance, if you insulate your house for financial not environmental reasons, you save on the amount of heating fuel required, and can enjoy a hotter house for the same money, or keep it at the same temperature and fly somewhere with the savings. This 'rebound effect' means there is no net environmental gain from such behaviour. Organisations, such as companies, are amalgamations of these personal decisions. One example is the Derby City Council in the UK, which justified the expense of a large plasma screen in the city centre on the grounds that they had saved a lot of money on an energy-efficiency drive elsewhere (Crompton 2008). In the business world, this pattern recurs when a company champions the eco-efficiencies in their operations and thus justifies the expansion of those operations, whether or not they are *eco-effective*—meeting human needs in a sustainable way.

From this analysis, Tom Crompton (2008) asserts the importance of cultivating 'intrinsic values' that are focused on connection and compassion, and therefore not solely approaching organisational sustainability issues in an instrumental way. This does not mean that the CR practitioners should profess only moral motives, but that there needs to be an integration of instrumental, relational and moral motives, so that CR transformations can create individual and organisational benefits while contributing to deeper changes that benefit society. If professionalisation squeezes out the role of values through a focus on skill sets and knowledge, so CR will have a limited impact on social change.

This analysis does not mean that we should focus exclusively, or rely, on the values of CR practitioners and business people. Many politicians, civil servants and corporate leaders present an artificial divide between those who believe in the role of values in business and those who believe in regulation. They do so for instrumental reasons, seeking to justify government non-intervention in markets, or relational ones, seeking favour with elites who ostensibly benefit from such non-intervention (see Topics → 'Political involvement' and Sectors → 'Government or intergovernmental agencies' in the thematic index).

This brings us to the second area where purpose is important: inquiry. For a profession to be a smart one, it needs to inquire into the efficacy and importance of its work. The problem with professionalisation is that it implies a culture of behaviour that is practical and convivial in serving client interests. Actors in the CR space are engaging elites, many of whom have attained their wealth, status and self-esteem working in industries that require total transformation. Consequently, many conferences in the CR field leave the difficult questions unanswered, because they leave the difficult questions unasked. Those who do raise awkward questions about the basic business models of certain companies can be regarded as awkward themselves, for not being practical or convivial (which is seen as not being 'professional'). It can be more difficult for such people to win business from clients, or employment within companies, when those are not interested in a truly challenging agenda, and thus find it more difficult to become a leading CR professional. Consequently, the professionalisation of CR can create a conservative consensus that avoids some of the most fundamental issues.

Those fundamental issues became more acute during the five years reviewed in this volume. Carbon emissions, deforestation and natural resource consumption all spiralled, along with international and national inequality. Progress on the Millennium Development Goals was slow, with the 2005 target for gender equality in primary education missed that year. Climate change was proceeding at a pace beyond many scientists' original predictions. Thus Wayne Visser and I wrote in the review of 2004 that CR was 'at a critical juncture'. We asked:

[Is corporate social responsibility (CSR)] actually a red herring? Is it a distraction from the more fundamental transformation (perhaps revolution even) of the capitalist business model which is needed? And, as CSR becomes an established professional practice, will it take as given that its purpose is to benefit those who employ its professionals, rather than a primary goal of transforming the world? (see pages 216-17)

We called on CR practitioners to ask themselves, 'Is this enough?' and, if the answer was no, then to reflect on why they were doing their job; and, if it was to create social change, then to explore new ways of supporting broader change. We were asking people to consider themselves as part of a new movement, not just a new profession.

Social movements and business organisations

Although most ideas have had the word 'movement' appended to them at some time or other in the media, the study of 'social movements' is a well-established academic area. Social movements of national determination and worker emancipation have been described and analysed extensively, with theorists often focusing on the causal mobilising factors for such movements. Some argue that movements stem from adversity and disadvantage (Aberle 1966) or, conversely, from people's ability to access resources to pursue their self-interests (Heberle 1949). In 1980 Alberto Melucci coined the term 'New Social Movements' in recognition that the leading movements since the 1960s seem to be mobilised around issues of lifestyle and beliefs rather than material matters, and where activists regard participation in movements as success in itself rather than functional in producing some systemic revolution. Consequently, the study of the gay, women's and civil rights movements led to theories that focus on the role of identity and culture in collective action (Castells 1997; Finger 1992).[4]

The literature on social movements focuses on four areas that determine a group's capacity to act, including its interests, the social infrastructure, mobilisation processes, and political opportunity structures. A group's interests are determined by the gains and losses resulting from its interaction with other groups; 'social infrastructure' describes the degree of common identity and social ties linking the individuals or organisations that affect the group's ability to act on its interests; mobilisation is the process by which a group acquires control over resources needed for collective action; and 'political opportunity structure' concerns the power relationships in the political environment and the space for activism (McAdam 1982).

You may already begin to see the relevance of this area of scholarship for strategic planning by CR practitioners and their organisations: we could pay attention to how interests, social infrastructures, mobilisation and political opportunities can be optimised to achieve greater positive social and environmental outcomes (examined below in the section on 'Practical implications' on page 37). Therefore, not only do I agree with John Campbell that 'research on the determinants of corporate social responsibility would benefit from incorporating insights from the social movements literature' (2007: 957), but contend that the practice and future of CR could benefit if a social movements lens is applied. However, to my knowledge little scholarship has focused on the CR field in this way; notable exceptions include Meyerson and Scully 1995, Amanda Ball 2007, and Bendell and Ellersiek forthcoming).

This oversight within existing social movement scholarship is not surprising owing to a lack of detailed attention to values and to how movements can work within 'elite' or 'authority' organisations and classes rather than on them, from outside. This limitation is a result of methodological bias, rather than intellectual coherence. As with much social science, the study of social movements is tentative in its investigation of values and emotions. One leader of the 1960s protest movement, Gregory Calvert, suggested that academic study often missed the emotion and spirit of political action:

> Once a great people's movement has become a thing of the past, it is easy to forget or dismiss the spirit which gave it life and provided the inspiration that moved its participants to acts of faith and courage. Like a corpse seen as a 'dead thing,' a political movement can be dissected by historians, sociologists, or political theorists without ever discovering what made it live and breathe, what gave it hope and daring (Calvert 1991: 58).

Similarly, some suggest the counter-globalisation movement is about politics and economics (Hardt and Negri 2001; Hertz 2001). The poem I featured at the start of this book was intended to illustrate that people do not take to the streets because of abstract economic or political theories—we act because of our emotions and everyday experiences. Whereas values and belief systems are important in shaping this, much analysis of social action tends to consider the economic or cultural mechanics of social movements. This bias occurs because to develop an insight into the values and emotions at play in a group, rather than the discourses involved, you must experience them yourself, which poses a challenge to the objectivist basis of much social science (Reason and Bradbury 2002).

The second limitation is the focus of mainstream social movements theorists on observable episodes of contestation with elites or authorities. That focus is so ingrained in the field that most definitions of social movements include concepts of contestation with elites (Tarrow 1994; Tilly 2004). One reason is that most academics first learn about movements through media representations of them, and thus focus on attention-grabbing events, such as protests. What the protesters do the other 363 days of the year might be researched, but does not hold the same place in the construction of a concept of what the movement actually is. Defining a social phenomenon on the basis of 1 out of 364 days, or 0.27% of that phenomenon's existence, is incoherent. We should remember that the phenomenon here is the person—the social movement *par-ticipant*—not the 'social movement' which is just a term we invent to help describe why, how, and with what, they interact. That reminds us that intellectualising can blind us to reality as much as opening our eyes to it, as it replaces an experience with a label for that experience. As the iconic social activist Martin Luther King said, we make mistakes when we 'thingify people'. The dominant view of academia on social movements is therefore a 'spectacled view', the starting point of which are spectacles of contestation, viewed in terms of what concepts and methods are favoured at the time in their own profession: viewed, either metaphorically or in reality, from a library window.

One laudable intention for social movements theorists focusing on visible contestation with elites is that they are seeking to study the political power of ordinary people (Tilly 2004). That intention is not often expressed in print, due to mainstream academe's aspiration to be bias-free, rather than honestly and critically subjective (Reason and Bradbury 2002). What we must recognise is that 'ordinary people' may act with moral and relational motivations, or in the interest of a collective they share an identity or interest with, within the private sector. Economic life is a space for political and social struggle and expression. If we are interested in how society changes, then restricting our view to moments of contestation between groups and elites is not comprehensive. We should not identify whether a social phenomenon is a movement on the basis of whether it exhibits repertoires of visible contestation. As a distant, objectifying, and often value-free, approach, mainstream social movements theory can be better described as anti-social movement theory. A new approach is required that recognises and explores the role of values, daily actions and non-visible contestations and other efforts within powerful organisations. This approach would respond to the fact that people can participate in movements while at work, not just afterwards. It would recognise how they could participate in a movement from within elite organisations, rather than such organisations being simply the object of movement pressure. For instance, movement adherents might employ a 'businesslike repertoire' to articulate their views, including discussion of why a particular movement goal is commercially relevant (Scully and Creed 2005).

The new approach would recognise the moral purpose of many business people, who, when at work, 'desire to be involved not only with initiatives seen as directly affecting themselves or groups they identify with but also with causes they feel are fundamentally just and relevant to the establishment of a moral community' (Aguilera et al. 2007: 850). It would recognise that their moral motives, which relate to various social movement values, may at times supersede their instrumental and relational motives in corporations (Folger et al. 2005). It would recognise the central importance of everyday experiences of organisational behaviour and policy in constituting life as it is experienced, challenged and ultimately changed by most people today (Zald et al. 2005). It would recognise that 'because organizational life is subject to greater authority and fewer rights than the political and civic domain, the activism there may be particularly revealing about how to change powerful structures, even when the subversions seem small' (Scully and Creed 2005: 329). Finally, it would also respond more effectively to the changing mechanisms of social control, and thus social struggle, as highlighted by Marshall McLuhan (1970):

> The next revolution—World War III—will be waged inside your head. It will be a guerrilla information war fought not in the sky or on the streets, not in the forests or even around the scarce resources of the earth, but in newspapers and magazines, on the radio, TV and in 'cyberspace' . . . It will be a dirty, no-holds-barred propaganda war of competing worldviews and alternative visions of the future.

Social movements theories have already been used to explain dynamics inside business organisations, but not from a movement perspective. Some of the earliest attempts to use social movements concepts in understanding organisational processes explored the sociology of professions, and showed the political processes involved in the development of professional practice in pathology (Bucher 1962) and planning (Ross 1976). Zald and Berger (1978) provided an early attempt to demonstrate the utility of metaphors, concepts and theories from social movement theories to inform research on organisational studies. A limitation of that work is its focus on collective action generated by internal issues in the organisation, rather than public issues that are the focus of social movements (Zald et al. 2005). Meyer and Zucker (1989) also used social movements theories to explore matters of organisational efficiency, suggesting that poorly performing firms may not always be closed down, and this may be because of political efforts by organised alliances among groups—whether inside or outside the firm—that benefit in different ways from maintaining the firm; these include managers and other employees, as well as dependent organisations. Social movements theories were also employed to explain how a new field of organisations can emerge—a 'social movement industry' (McCarthy and Zald 1977: 1,219).

In response to a growing recognition of the impact of globalisation on both movements and organisations, there was some progress towards a new approach to social movements research during the five years chronicled in this volume. In particular, social movement theorists and organisational theorists started talking to each other. This is useful for business scholars because of the changing nature of industry within late capitalism, where matters of identity, meaning and voluntary connections become more important. The main focus of this emerging conversation has been to use social movements theories to investigate normal management issues, as was done previously, or to use organisation theories to look at the growth of social movements (as traditionally understood as external to business), or to attempt harmonisation of the terminologies of the different theories (McAdam and Scott 2005).

Some have been critical of the growing use of social movements theories to understand organisations for instrumental non-movement ends, and call for more work that regards organisations as sites where the aims of social movements can be pursued through 'workplace activism' (Creed and Scully 2000; Scully and Creed 2005; Ball 2007). A key concept to emerge from this focus on workplace activism is the idea of a 'tempered radical'—the 'individuals who identify with and are committed to their own organizations, and are also committed to a cause, community or ideology that is fundamentally different from, and possibly at odds with the dominant culture' (Meyerson and Scully 1995: 586). As an 'outsider within', the tempered radical 'can access . . . the knowledge and insight of the insider with the critical attitude of the outsider . . .' (1995: 589). Such people employ a range of subtle and overt tactics both inside and outside the organisation to help effect change (Meyerson 2001). With this in mind, developments in fields such as accounting can be understood as processes of social action and change (Ball 2007).

These developments in social movements analysis are helpful as they then naturally turn to questions of how a participant deals with the tensions between movement and organisational imperatives, and the challenge of co-optation. There can be tension between 'asserting claims related to movement goals . . . [and] . . . the desire to get ahead . . .' (Zald et al. 2005: 274). Meyerson and Scully (1995: 596) suggest that 'small wins may distract people from a more fundamental issue, provide a premature sense of completion, or steer a change effort off course'. Although welcome, this scholarship largely focuses on how social movements can enter corporations, rather than how movements can emerge from corporations or be about the corporation itself.

Some analysts have recognised that the corporation, its governance and ownership are sparks for activism (Davis and McAdam 2000) and that specific corporations can be a way for activists to identify interests, create identities and mobilise symbolic resources (Starr 2000; Bendell 2004). However, it is time to consider business organisations as a category of experience that is the centrepiece of a new social movement, that not only works on, through and within business, but even emerges out of it. The workplace used to be a key focus for social movements—for instance, the labour movement—and it could now return to a central, yet permeable, role in our understanding of social change. That is because today the boundary between organisations and their environment is 'more or less permeable; they are linked through the identifications and affiliations of actors, the normative and ideological commitments that actors within the organization share with those outside, and a variety of boundary-spanning organizations, processes and actors . . .' (Zald *et al.* 2005: 255).

This review of the recent scholarship on how social movements theories can be applied to the contemporary corporation, and its management, suggests we are on the cusp of a paradigm shift in both social movements theory and organisational theory, which would mean a return to treating business organisations as venues and sources of social movement, rather than just a target for social movements. A more 'open social movements' theory is emerging, which will hopefully be much more relevant to corporate responsibility practitioners, among others.

Key to this approach will be attempts to reclaim the processes of defining movements. To suggest something is 'a movement' is a political activity itself, suggesting that certain people and events are linked by a set of beliefs or experiences, and that they are moving toward a common goal. So by what criteria should we choose a term for the movement described in this book? At the time of writing there are many terms in play, in the English language, including 'corporate social responsibility', 'corporate citizenship', 'corporate accountability', 'corporate sustainability', 'sustainable business', 'social enterprise', 'sustainable enterprise', 'responsible enterprise', and 'responsible business'. People debate which term is most accurate or progressive. Some think the key criterion here is which term is most often used (in practice or academe); others prefer a term broad enough to encompass many activities and bring more people together; and still others seek a term that frames issues in ways that stress certain concerns while downplaying others. For some there is also an interest in being the originator of a concept, or owning the relevant domain names.

As described at the beginning, the term 'corporate responsibility movement' is one that is widely used by people describing themselves and practitioners like them. It is because of this already wide use and recognition of the term that I have chosen the terms 'corporate' and 'responsibility' for this book. In the last few pages you have become more acquainted with the term 'movement', and how indeed we could call this corporate responsibility domain a movement, despite some likely protestations from academics who prefer their movements defined by . . . protestations. In the next few pages let us look more closely at what 'corporate' and 'responsibility' can mean. That additional explanation is important, because in outlining 'a corporate responsibility movement' one contributes to the identification of that movement, and possibly even to its own self-identity.

What is 'corporate'?

'Corporate' is an adjective most often used to describe something related to a large business organisation—'the corporation'. In common usage it refers to the private corporation, which is a legal entity formed to carry out enterprise and distribute profits. As a legally defined organisation, the corporation does not have to be large or small, although the term is often understood as describing a large organisation. A closer look at this legal entity, and its history, is necessary given that the 'corporate' forms a focal point of the movement we are discussing. For that task we can review the development of commercial corporations in the United Kingdom over a period of 400 years, as it indicates the type of legal developments that occurred in most other countries.

The development of the British corporation can be seen as occurring in three waves (Bennett 1999). The first wave was when the financial demands of colonial expansion grew, so not-for-profit corporations were created to assist in carrying out trade with the colonies. Royal Charters were awarded in the 1600s and early 1700s to carry out the business in colonies. These were 'chartered corporations', some of which started, illegally, trading for a profit, the first being the East India Company. At this time, shares in some corporations began to be traded on a black stock-market. Over time, the Crown awarded charters explicitly for making profits, and corporations grew to such an extent that the East India Company was said to rule India. By 1720 the government became concerned with this situation as well as the levels of fraudulent activity. In response, it nationalised many of the chartered corporations and passed an act banning speculative buying and selling of shares, so that they could only be sold to persons genuinely taking over a role in running the corporation or partnership (Robins 2005).

A second wave of development came with the creation of corporations by Acts of Parliament to build canals, waterworks and later railways from the end of the 1700s onward. An Act of Parliament would authorise the creation of a corporation for a specific and narrow purpose and allow it to bring and defend legal actions in its own name (so protecting the financiers from personal responsibility should the corporation fail). The general view at the time was that corporations should be created only for very specific purposes and all other business activity remain in non-corporate forms where liability was not limited. Adam Smith commented in 1776 that the only trades that justified incorporation were banking, insurance, canal building and waterworks. He believed it was contrary to the public interest for any other businesses or trades to be incorporated and that all should be run as partnerships (Bennett 1999).

The third wave of development occurred in the mid-1800s after the Bubble Act (which prohibited the development of joint-stock companies without a Royal Charter or Act of Parliament) was repealed, allowing shares to be traded freely, and the Joint Stock Companies Act of 1844 was passed, allowing corporations to be created by a simple act of registration, so that they could conduct any business activity they decided on. This 'registered corporation' became the modern form, whose limited-liability status was increased by government in subsequent years. The aim was wide-scale liberalisation of the market—often called laissez-faire capitalism. This was part of a wider battle between the new merchant class and traditional landowners. In the 100 years that followed, they increasingly ignored the controls imposed on them by the courts, particularly judgements on whether the corporation was conducting business in keeping with its charter. Eventually, in 1966, the court abandoned any attempt at control of what commercial corporations could do. In 1989, the Companies Act enshrined the principle that a corporation could decide what business to conduct (Bennett 1999). It could be argued that in the 1990s a fourth wave of development began, with the enshrining of corporate property rights over national governments at the global level, through the emergence of bilateral and multilateral trade agreements such as the General Agreement on Trade in Services (GATS) (Bendell 2004).

However, before proceeding, we might reflect on how 'corporate' does not have to imply a private business. The term first appeared in English in 1398, as meaning 'united in one body', derived from the from Latin *corporatus*. As such, 'corporate responsibility' could refer to the responsibility of peoples when organised into collectives, whether large or small, for profit or not. It could suggest the way responsibility could be achieved, through being 'corporate' in terms of seeking unity with others. This notion of the corporate has slipped from our language, but may be of use in future discussion of the corporate responsibility movement.

What is 'responsibility'?

'Responsible' alludes to the words 'response' and 'able', and its origins in Latin include a sense of obligation, so it is not merely the quality of being able to respond to something or someone, but of already responding, or being committed to respond. In dictionaries the noun is described as 'a duty, obligation, or burden' or 'moral, legal, or mental accountability', thus adding to the sense that one's responsibility is not one's choice, but is a quality ascribed to you by others. However, in much corporate responsibility practice and discourse the concept is understood as voluntary choice of business people to be responsible. Many official definitions as well as academic definitions stress its voluntary nature. A distinction is also made by critics, who argue for more mandatory corporate accountability. These debates may arise because of the difference between a noun and an adjective. The term 'responsible corporation' uses the adjective form and thus describes a corporation that is being responsible. The term 'corporate responsibility' uses the noun form and describes a set of responsibilities (duties or obligations) that exist for corporations whether or not a particular corporation chooses to recognise and accept them. Corporate responsibility is the field of society's expectations of corporations. Someone can choose to manage a responsible corporation, but corporate responsibility is, as grammatical fact, the realm of responsibility of corporations, as co-defined by any society that uses the language. If I say to someone 'please be responsible', that is a request; but if I say 'it's your responsibility', that is a truth claim (albeit contestable, like most truth claims).

An Internet search will find that the term 'corporate social responsibility' is used about twice as often as 'corporate responsibility'. Its popularity is partly due to the popularity of TLAs—three-letter acronyms—in general. I chose to drop 'social' in the name for this movement for two reasons. The first is because its existence as an acronym, 'CSR', has led to the 'thingification' of the grammatical fact of corporate responsibility into a package of ideas and activities that a corporation can choose not to do. However, corporate responsibility exists as a matter of public interest, whether an individual business person seeks to manage a responsible corporation or not. The second reason for using the shortened term is that people have different understandings of whether 'social' includes environmental or economic issues, and thus the additional word actually adds greater confusion, not clarity.

The extent that the term engages environmental issues is something I will pick up on in a moment, but first I should explain the reason for not using the word 'accountability'. Although I have written extensively on these topics using the concept of accountability, I have come to realise the term 'responsibility' is more appropriate to a broader audience of practitioners, while also allowing for the same sense of duty and obligation that a 'held to account' understanding of accountability implies. In addition, many practitioners have come to understand that it is important to mainstream social and environmental performance across an economy in order to achieve either public or business benefits, and that mandatory mechanisms are required for that. The highest form of responsibility is to seek greater accountability for oneself and others in a similar situation (see 'Accountability is responsibility' on page 176).

As mentioned above, dropping 'social' makes it possible to clear up any confusion that this agenda does in fact include environmental issues. However, some practitioners prefer to use 'sustainable' or 'sustainability' as the framework for their work. This, they argue, includes the various social, environmental and economic dimensions of business. Indeed, the concept of 'sustainable development' has been understood by the international community since the 1987 Brundtland Report and the 1992 Earth Summit, as concerning social and economic development. However, for three reasons I do not believe that sustainability, nor even 'sustainable development', will allow a comprehensive framing for business people and researchers, going forward.

Firstly, despite its growing popularity, 'sustainability' is specialist jargon. Therefore, people who are new to these issues think sustainability and sustainable development concern the environment alone. I was reminded of this confusion when a Deputy Commissioner of the European Commission commented, after a presentation I gave at INSEAD about one aspect of business and sustainable development, that we should not only focus on the environment but instead talk about sustainable *human* development.

Secondly, the way corporate responsibility issues are making headway in the financial sector, a key area for the future, is under the rubric of existing legal fiduciary responsibilities: the UN Principles for Responsible Investment being a leading example. 'Sustainability' is regarded by many practitioners in finance as a moral evocation and they prefer focusing on issues of fiduciary responsibility, and how various societal issues relate to that, including environmental ones. Hence, 'responsibility' is their preferred term at this point.

My third reason concerns principle. We should recognise that 'sustainability' is a term that is championed most often by people who come from an environmental background. This is part of a well-intentioned attempt to reframe environmentalism as relevant to a broader range of people. Jonathan Porritt (2005: 38) has argued for environmentalism to reposition itself 'within a more progressive and radical frame . . . that allows the inevitable (as in the need for change) to be made desirable' and advocates sustainable development, and sustainability as the shorthand for that framing (although it is debatable whether it is actually that catchy). In my research I have found that, when environmental specialists work on social issues under the rubric of sustainability or sustainable development, they can make significant mistakes in misunderstanding core concepts of democracy, human rights, gender and accountability (Bendell 2005). For instance, on numerous occasions sustainability consultants have praised the responsibility of a company because of its environmental efforts and ignored violations of the human right of freedom of association at work with the explanation that trade unions have not always helped to progress an environmental agenda (Elkington 2008). It is important to recognise that certain issues are important in their own right, such as the absence of child labour or sexual harassment in the workplace, whether or not they can be related to a concept of sustainability. Many people working on child labour, women's rights, corruption or conflict, for instance, do not describe or understand their work in terms of sustainability or sustainable development.

By not choosing the sustainability frame for describing the movement in this book, I am not suggesting that anything other than a full embrace of environmental challenges would be responsible. Environmental issues are a key part of what society defines as the field of corporate responsibility. The definition of that field is evolving, as more people become aware that more eco-efficiency and less pollution will not deliver a sustainable economy, so that products, services and markets need to be redesigned urgently to deliver human well-being within environmental limits while restoring biodiversity (McDonough and Braungart 2002). I am, after all, an environmentalist. Neither am I arguing that environmental consciousness does not have the capacity to effectively embrace human rights. Some environmentalists are so inclined, due to an awareness of the sanctity and beauty of all life, whether human or not, and an appreciation that the natural state is a creative one, where every life form expresses itself freely. Within that deep ecological perspective we can find an affinity with human rights, but this is not yet the mainstream approach in the sustainability field.

One of my co-writers in the volume, Wayne Visser, seeks a truce on this debate by suggesting the acronym CSR be understood in future as 'corporate sustainability and responsibility'. That should work well for some practitioners and commentators, especially given the amount of organisations that have 'CSR' in their name. However, it presents the same limitations of defining this field as a voluntary set of practices, rather than a set of expectations and obligations. In addition, at the time of writing it was not a widely used term. In the Lifeworth Annual Review of 2007 I suggested 'responsible enterprise' could be used more often as it emphasises both values and commerce (Bendell *et al.* 2008), but in this book we employ 'corporate responsibility' due to its widespread use at the time of writing.

Exploring the corporate responsibility movement

With the previous discussion of terminology in mind, we can return to the definition I offered at the beginning of this chapter:

> The corporate responsibility movement is a loosely organised but sustained effort by individuals both inside and outside the private sector, who seek to use or change specific corporate practices, whole corporations, or entire systems of corporate activity, in accordance with their personal commitment to public goals and the expectations of wider society.

Labelling a field of experience in this way helps us to make some sense of that field, to identify patterns and what is emerging. We can begin to ask questions that are typically asked of social movements, in ways that may help practitioners and policy-makers more effectively. For instance, sociologists identify several dimensions of social movement. Examining the corporate responsibility movement in relation to these dimensions raises questions of form: specifically the depth, direction, targets, provenance and range of changes sought.

One dimension of movements is the depth of change they seek—to reform or transform society. Reform movements are those dedicated to changing some norms, usually legal ones. An example is the movement supporting the right to abortion. Some reform movements may advocate a wider change in custom and moral norms, such as the condemnation of pornography. A radical movement, however, is explicitly seeking to change value systems and power relations. One example is the American civil rights movement, which demanded full equality under the law to all Americans, regardless of race. With this is mind, we can inquire whether the corporate responsibility movement will develop as a reform or radical movement. Could there be reformist and transformational factions to the movement? What might success look like for a reformist approach, and for a radical one? I return to this discussion below in 'Transforming the corporate system'.

Another dimension of movements is the direction of change they seek—to innovate or to conserve. Innovation movements want to enable particular technologies and associated norms and values. The open-source software movement is one example, whereby people are collaborating to share the benefits of computer software freely (see 'Rethinking intellectual property' on page 281). Conservative movements seek to preserve existing practices, norms and values. For example, the anti-automation Luddite movement aimed to fight specific technological changes during the 19th century. With this in mind, we can inquire whether the corporate responsibility movement is about innovating something new, or restoring something that is being lost. Could there be innovative and conservative factions to the movement? What might success look like for an innovative approach, and for a conservative one?

A third dimension of movements is the target of their change efforts—groups or individuals. Group-focused movements target specific organisations or groups, the systems that they shape. Political movements that seek change in government are an example of such movements. Individual-focused movements are more interested in changing the minds and behaviour of individuals. Most religious movements would fall under this category. With this in mind, we can inquire whether the corporate responsibility movement is focused more on changing individuals within corporations, or about changing corporations and the systems within which they operate. Most practitioners speak of changing a corporation, and some aim to change the systems they operate within. However, relatively little attention is paid to the rules that create and shape corporations, when compared to most corporate responsibility work, which often engages individuals to encourage them to choose to adopt or change specific corporate practices. If the aim is individual change, then should we be clearer about the type of changes sought, such as the extrinsic values described earlier? Or might CR practitioners actually be limiting themselves by speaking as if part of a corporate-focused movement when they are doing little about the factors that affect all such corporations?

Another dimension to movements is the provenance of change—whether old or new. Old social movements of the 19th century in Europe fought for specific social groups, such as the working class, peasants or Protestants. They were based on materialistic goals such as improving the standard of living or the political power of the working class. New social movements rose to prominence from the second half of the 20th century, particularly in industrialised countries, such as the feminist movement, civil rights movement, environmental movement, gay rights movement, and anti-nuclear movement. These are based around issues that go beyond, but are not separate from, materialistic concerns or economic class. With this in mind, we can inquire whether the corporate responsibility movement is a new incarnation of old social movements, focused on materialistic struggles, a combination of new social movements, or an altogether fresh movement that is a hybrid of material and contemporary ideological concerns. The importance of the corporation as both the focus of the movement and the source of many of its adherents, yet its attention to broad societal expectations, suggests the movement is a hybrid of old and new.

The last dimension of movements we will look at here is the range of movements. Global movements have global objectives. Movements such as the communist and anarchist movements, and the counter-globalisation movement, seek to change society at a global level. However, most social movements have a national or even local scope, such as protecting a specific natural area, or regulating traffic speeds through a town. Increasingly, movements act at multiple levels, making connections between the challenges faced and changes required at local, regional, national and international levels. With this in mind, we can inquire whether the corporate responsibility movement has a local, national or international identity or structure. How important is it to have an international form to achieve its ends? Can a common set of interests and intentions be identified across diverse economies, cultures and polities? This volume describes the growing recognition of corporate responsibility worldwide, and the globalisation of terminologies associated with voluntary corporate action on social and environmental performance. However, the reasons for this may be completely different from the motivations of practitioners (see Box 1).

In addition to gaining insights by considering the dimensions of social movements, we can consider the key factors behind movement creation. First among these factors are the common interests that can be found among movement participants. What, we could ask, are the common interests among people working in companies, banks, environmental or humanitarian charities when they engage in the corporate responsibility field? And how could these be pursued collectively? The most apparent common interest that cuts across this diversity is finance, and the system of money and investments. This is why it was one of the top themes that emerged during the five years reviewed (see Sectors → 'Banking, finance or insurance' in the thematic index).

Second is the degree of common identity and social ties linking the individuals or organisations that affect a movement's ability to act on its interests. We could therefore ask again how the individuals in those diverse organisational types share an identity, and how that identity is fed by social connections in the past, and present. Reading the same books? Having similar pasts? Similarly seeking meaning to life? Having met at conferences and discussed such questions in the pub afterwards? Being Facebook friends? It is not a topic I dealt with explicitly in the years chronicled in this volume, although it does arise obliquely, in a discussion of the underlying values and purpose of this work. For instance, in the sections 'The fourth bottom line' (page 116) and 'The living dead' (page 320) I raised, with Rupesh Shah and Shilpa Shah, respectively, the spiritual dimension to corporate responsibility practice.

Third is the process by which a movement accesses the resources needed for its activities. The main issue here is the livelihoods of the movement adherents, as they are often participating through their working hours. Their wages are paid by private corporations, government grants or large foundations, which are all dependent on the

> **Box 1** VIEWS ON COMMON MOTIVATIONS OF CORPORATE RESPONSIBILITY PRACTITIONERS
>
> The definition of corporate responsibility I provide in this book says little about what is happening in the hearts and minds of the people involved. I have spoken with many CR practitioners during the years chronicled in this volume, in about 30 countries, and here I paraphrase the different views I have heard about the underlying process or belief that motivates many CR practitioners.
>
> ▶ People are seeking greater happiness through meaningful work in the largest professional area today, which is business
>
> ▶ People have given up on political parties to effect change and are seeking to do good through their everyday engagement with existing powers
>
> ▶ People are inspired by part or all of the sustainable development agenda and see business an important way to deliver on that agenda
>
> ▶ People believe the corporation is really the creation of its stakeholders not its stockholders and seek to affect it that way
>
> ▶ People are smarter about how to deliver long-term and more secure returns to shareholders by recognising social and environmental risks and opportunities
>
> ▶ People are concerned about particular social or environmental issues and want to achieve a scale of impact without relying on slow bureaucracies to decide to donate money, so turn to enterprise
>
> ▶ People are concerned by a particular social or environmental issue but want a bigger salary or status than is available outside the private sector
>
> ▶ People are trying to transform commerce so it reconnects with and serves the common interest, knowing that the pursuit of self-interest in the market does not automatically produce the common good
>
> Some of these views are compatible, some contradictory, some suggesting different balances of intrinsic and extrinsic values. Such motivations would be worth exploring in greater detail.

state of the market economy. As the personal financial responsibilities of movement participants increase and market conditions worsen, might they may be less inclined to pursue movement goals with the same rigour? This focus on the financial aspect of movement adherents connects with concerns about conflict of interest within the CR consulting and broader accounting profession (see Sectors → 'Business services or consulting' in the thematic index) and possibly egotistical and unaccountable behaviour from some non-governmental organisations (see Sectors → 'Voluntary associations or unions' in the the thematic index).

The fourth factor in movement generation is the political space and opportunity for activism in a particular society. This includes the protections of civil rights, the existence of independent media, and an open political system. With privatisation and commercialisation of more public organisations and spaces, the CR movement could be regarded as people responding to a shrinking of political space by bringing their values more explicitly into the private sector. Nevertheless, it is still useful to examine what is required in that external environment to facilitate the CR movement. Key is the role of civil society and media in shaping awareness of regulators, investors, staff and consumers to identify the field of corporate responsibility, and therefore build the commercial logic for companies to voluntarily address their social and environmental performance. Consequently, this perspective suggests that the CR movement could work on directing civil society and media attention towards corporate responsibility. The development of CR within the media sector is therefore relevant (see 'Responsible news' on page 237 and 'Broader media responsibilities' on page 240).

As I see myself as a participant in the corporate responsibility movement, I decided to test the theory on myself. I challenged myself to identify at least one thing that has emerged *in* me and one thing that has emerged *from* me for the corporate responsibility movement over the past 13 years, that relate to the four aspects of movement generation described above. In terms of common interest, I have learned that my interest is not related to a specific profession, such as consulting or academia, but with people who believe in being entrepreneurial in any sector in order to make economic activity contribute to a better world. For others in the movement, my consulting and training has sought to connect people to that sense of their own interest. In terms of common identity and ties, I have now developed camaraderie with people in a variety of sectors who are pioneering ways of making significant changes in business practice, and benefit from extensive networks of professional colleagues, many of whom I consider friends. For others in the movement, I have helped facilitate connections through online networks and newsletters, and promoted awareness of a potential common identity through my writings. In terms of resource mobilisation, I have benefited from people in the movement commissioning me to work with them on projects, and I have created more resources for such work by helping to conceive new non-profit organisations working on corporate responsibility that now have incomes of over a million dollars. In terms of opportunity structures, I have now benefited from the efforts of others to help shift the mainstream corporate responsibility agenda onto a more transformative one, and, for others in the movement, I have helped shape discursive opportunities through successfully challenging some mainstream interpretations of concepts through my writings. I recommend trying this assessment on yourself, to see how you are relating, or could relate, to the corporate responsibility movement.

A traditional social movement framework would also encourage consideration of the campaigns, repertoires and public representations that are being used or could be developed by the movement (Tilly 2004). Campaigns, not in a marketing sense, are organised efforts making specific claims on target institutions. What are the campaigns of the corporate responsibility movement? Some companies have joined with NGOs to put pressure on other companies to act, such as The Body Shop campaigning against Shell in the 1990s. Joint actions by companies in the period chronicled here included pressure from companies on governments to provide a regulatory system to combat climate change (see 'Climate for change' on page 75). However, public campaigning from companies remained rare, and most campaigns were internal and out of sight, involving younger staff in large organisations collaborating on how to persuade their directors to commit to becoming a responsible corporation. More concerted external campaigns and also a sharing of the lessons of internal organisational campaigns could be helpful.

Repertoires are the forms of action that are used by a movement, such as coalitions, public meetings, processions, vigils, rallies, demonstrations, petitions and media activities. To this we can add the 'businesslike repertoire' (Scully and Creed 2005). But could the corporate responsibility movement learn from more traditional repertoires in order to raise awareness of a common agenda? Might we see a march of the responsible entrepreneurs, advancing on, say, the International Institute of Finance, calling for a progressive system of global finance? Many business people already join rallies on issues such as climate change, and there were discussions among CEOs about waving placards together at the Bali conference on climate change, to symbolise their call for greater government action. Displays of the worthiness, unity, numbers and commitments of movement participants has often been key (Tilly 2004). Again, corporate responsibility practitioners could learn from how other movements have sought to build those forms of public presentation of their movement.

Other questions that come to light from a movement perspective include whether a charismatic leader will emerge, as in the case of most historic movements, or whether as an open social movement it will not be required or permitted, given the ease of communications and organising with modern information technology. Finally, and perhaps most importantly, if we think about the issues in this volume as aspects of an emergent corporate responsibility movement, we must then consider what the ultimate goals of the movement are, and seek clarity on what is progressive action and what is co-optation.

The global justice movement is often described as having 'one no and many yeses', suggesting it is about resisting the global application of one form of capitalism, and allowing a myriad of alternatives to emerge (Kingsnorth 2003). That view allows unity in diversity, and is one application of a participatory democratic world-view. Yet it also papers over substantial differences in opinion and does not encourage clarity about a vision of economic governance. The corporate responsibility movement could also be said to be about 'many yeses', because it begins with the incorporation of diverse personal values and societal expectations into specific business practices, whole corporations or entire corporate systems. Those personal values often relate to improving the situation of people or other forms of life, and societal expectations are founded on a widely held view that economic life should be more supportive of other life. So there is a common 'yes', for economic activities to achieve public purposes. Meanwhile, people working on a specific corporate practice, or even a whole corporation, have learned that to sustain changes at those levels they need to address an entire system of corporate activity, which leads them to consider matters of governance and of finance. In consequence, I believe it is possible to identify an emergent overarching goal for all the corporate responsibility movement, which involves bringing concepts of democracy and economy together.

Remembering democracy

Before continuing, it is necessary to briefly discuss the 'D' word, because, unfortunately, the concept of democracy got a bit lost somewhere between Athens and Washington, despite the enthusiasm inspired by the election of charismatic leaders such as Barack Obama. *Demos* means people; *kratos* means power: people power, or people rule. That doesn't mean elections every three to five years to choose between—physical appearances and rhetoric aside—Tweedle Dum and Tweedle Dee. People around the world increasingly have elections. What they don't have is democracy.

Moreover, the notion of democracy has become wedded to government, rather than to a way of life. David Held (1997: 252) notes how 'students of democracy have examined and debated at length . . . within the boundaries of the nation-state' but 'they have not seriously questioned whether the nation-state can remain at the centre of democratic thought'. John Isbister (2001: xi) says that 'an ideal democracy would give a voice to everyone who is affected by a decision. The real democracies with which we are familiar cannot reach this standard.' For example, poor children are affected by welfare systems but have no vote. Women in the global South are affected by family planning funding decisions in the United States but have no vote in their elections.

A post-state analysis of the writings of Dahl (1964) suggests that in a democratically governed society a community of people should have meaningful participation in decisions and processes that affect them and they should not be systematically adversely affected by another group of people, without being able to rectify the situation. This is because democracy is an ideal system of governance and a set of organisational forms that support the collective pursuit of individual preferences. This would mean a situation where individuals and communities have the capacity to participate effectively in shaping the social limits that define what is possible for them, without impairing the ability of others to do this for themselves—an everyday democracy where all organisations enable participation. Democracy is also inherently a global concept, because it is an administrative response to the universal principle of people being able to pursue their individual living preferences in harmony with others.

This conception of democratic governance is based on a belief in the human right to self-determine one's life-world. A number of other human rights stem from this, once we recognise the material foundations of self-determination and self-actualisation: namely, the right to basic necessities of life, which includes a safe environment. David Korten (1995: 307) states that 'there are few rights more fundamental than the right of people to create caring, sustainable communities and to control their own resources, economies and means of livelihood'.

From this approach to human rights and democratic governance, organisations or persons that affect you and your community, especially when they affect the material foundations to your self-determination, must be able to be influenced by you and your community. In other words, they must be accountable. However, as explained earlier, economic globalisation has undermined national state systems for the democratic governance of the economy: corporations are no longer acceptably accountable to the citizens of a nation through the machinery of national government. Organisation theorist Henry Mintzberg (1989: 328) therefore asks us 'how can we call our society democratic when many of its most powerful institutions are closed to governance from the outside and are run as oligarchies from within?' If we believe in human rights and the spirit of democracy, then we should use that framework for understanding corporate responsibility and the type of corporate and financial system we desire.

Transforming the corporate system

In the five years chronicled in this volume, many business people moved up the strategic CR pyramid (Fig. 1), and embraced societal leadership as central to being a responsible corporation. Consequently, in our introduction to the review of 2005 we outlined an emerging philosophy of 'serving systemic transformations' from within the business community. In subsequent reviews, we explored what this meant in terms of methodologies for social change (Bendell *et al.* 2007) and the urgency and direction of that change (Bendell *et al.* 2008).

Some practitioners and commentators even began to explore what this systemic approach implies for capitalism as a whole, and framed the purpose of corporate responsibility in terms of applying democratic principles to economic activity. The editor of *Business Ethics* magazine, Marjorie Kelly, explained that democracy is, in the economic arena:

> about shaping the system forces that act on all corporations. It's about consciously crafting new democratic system structures, structures of voice, structures of decision making, structures of conflict resolution, structures of accountability. Eventually this will mean changes in law. But legal changes must be of a different sort than we've attempted thus far. Laws controlling corporations now amount to a patchwork of regulations about working conditions, pollution, or consumer well-being, focusing on outcomes rather than underlying mechanisms. Thus we've been like home-owners chopping down nuisance trees which continually spring back, because we have failed to eradicate the roots. (Kelly 2002).

She consequently called for more attention to the relationship of the financial system to corporate practice. She gave this description of that relationship in the US:

> New equity sales were a negative source of funding in 15 out of the 20 years from 1981 to 2000. In other words, when you look back over two decades, you can't find any net stockholder money going in—it's all going out. The net outflow since 1981 for new equity issues was negative $540 billion. Rather than capitalizing companies, the stock market has been de-capitalizing them. Stockholders for decades have been an immense cash drain on corporations. They are the deadest of dead wood. It's inaccurate even to speak of stockholders as investors for more truthfully they are extractors. When we buy stock, we are not contributing capital: we are buying the right to extract wealth (Kelly 2002).

According to figures from the federal reserve in the US, in 2005 about 1 dollar in every 100 trading on Wall Street was reaching companies, with the other 99 all speculatively invested (Porritt 2005: 182). In the 1990s economist David Korten provided a powerful summary of the situation:

> The problem is this: a predatory global financial system, driven by the single imperative of making ever more money for who already have lots of it, is rapidly depleting the real capital—the human, social, natural and even physical capital—upon which our wellbeing depends. Pathology enters the economic system when money, once convenient as a means of facilitating commerce, comes to define the life purpose of individuals and society. The truly troubling part is that so many of us have become willing accomplices to what is best described as a war of money against life. It starts, in part, from our failure to recognize that money is not wealth. In our confusion, we concen-

trate on the money to the neglect of those things that actually sustain a good life (Korten 1997).

A year later the former advisor to Ronald Reagan identified the inconsistency within the current system:

> Today's capitalism embodies a curious and dangerous inconsistency. It extols the necessity of private ownership. Yet, while the capital is there and so is the capitalism, what's missing are people who can rightly be called capitalists. The reason for this is poorly understood: contemporary capitalism is not designed to create capitalists, but to finance capital. Without political will those dramatically different goals will never be combined. A more participatory capitalism could gradually displace today's exclusive, detached and socially corrosive ownership patterns (Gates 1998).

The mind-set of many of our bankers was also corroded by this situation. The few investment bankers, traders and hedge fund managers that I met often had a soulless view of their work, regarding it as a game with little meaning or impact on anyone, except to fuel their astronomical bonuses and lifestyles. As they were smart and worked hard, so they scoffed at people who would try to do anything about making companies more responsible, including me. 'If you care and are smart, then get rich by playing the game and give some money away' was their view. It became clear by 2008 this attitude had led to reckless ingenuity in the financial derivatives markets. Bankers were no longer fulfilling their core functions of looking after deposits, backing productive activity and helping people and institutions manage their risks.

Despite its central importance in shaping what corporations can do about their social and environmental performance, the financial system was not a key focus for corporate responsibility practitioners throughout the 1990s. As James Paul and Jason Garred (2000: 1) realised, most attention was focused on manufacturing, leaving services, and particularly financial services, neglected. In the years chronicled in this volume the attention did turn to finance, but largely areas such as project finance, retailed socially responsible investment funds, and institutional shareholder engagement with companies on the downside risks of social and environmental poor performance. A closer look at the systems of finance was not on the agenda. A key reason was that 'C' word could not be debated in professional circles—i.e. capitalism. However, the emergent overarching goal for the corporate responsibility movement, if it is to transform the corporate system, will be found only through a new dialogue about capitalism. Writing in 2008, amid extreme financial volatility and a collapse in trust and respect for financial institutions and their operatives, it is not possible to talk about transforming the corporate system without exploring in detail what form of capitalism could deliver on the desire for more economic democracy that seems at the heart of much corporate responsibility practice.

Towards capital democracy

In any dialogue about capitalism it is important to understand it in the plural, as capitalisms. Richard Whitley (2000) has documented clearly that corporate law, labour markets and so on differ across the world, so there are very different forms of capitalism. The lesson here is that we are not possessed by capitalism, but can choose the form we want. In doing this we must clarify what is the basic essence of these different capitalisms. Wikipedia is a good source for common wisdom. Here is the 'crowd-sourced' definition for the big C:

> Capitalism is the economic system in which the means of production are owned by private persons, and operated for profit, and where investments, distribution, income, production and pricing of goods and services are predominantly determined through the operation of a free market (en.wikipedia.org, accessed 19 October 2008).

It has recently become popular in social science to regard anything as 'capital', with at least five forms of capital now discussed: natural, social, human, manufactured, and financial capital (Porritt 2005). When this occurs, it is important not to ignore the fact that something is 'capital' on account of a specific power relationship: 'capital' is anything physical or virtual that someone or group can control sufficiently in order to extract an income or benefit from. A forest can be conceived of as 'capital' when it is being controlled by someone or some group to extract an income or benefit from it. The forests that are not controlled by someone to generate a yield would not be accurately described as natural capital. Yes, such a forest's impact on the environment underpins other capital and economic activity, but if not controlled by someone or group for their own revenue or benefit then capital is the wrong word to describe its value or worth. Forest dwellers may be harvesting materials from the forest, and completely dependent on it for their lives, but neither they nor their adversaries in oil exploration, for instance, would consider that they 'control' the forest. Yes, the forest is valuable even though it is not 'capital', and that is partly the point I am making here: not everything valuable can be called capital.

With the financial turmoil in 2008, the 'ism' seemed to be falling off 'capital'. Semantically, capitalism should simply mean a belief in capital, and a system that creates and maintains capital. Therefore, capitalism should be understood as the belief that more and more resources should be managed by specific individuals or groups to generate incomes or yields: i.e. to be managed as capital. Therefore, to believe in capitalism is to believe that it is good to control bits of existence to extract revenues or yields from them, mostly through controlling how other people interact with that bit of existence. It is a belief in creating and using property.

The above definition from Wikipedia indicates that the 'ism' involves the private ownership of capital, and the management of it to extract a profit for those owners, rather than just a revenue or benefit. This aspect of capitalism is not definitive, as economies in different countries have different forms of ownership and profit-taking. Even in so-called free-market economies, the state owns large portions of capital, and includes regulations on who can own capital, particularly if it is a large firm giving rise to competition issues (Whitley 2000).

If we believe in democracy, then this process of how material or virtual phenomena are turned into capital, by whom, and how this directly affects people, should be examined more closely. This means looking at the process of private property creation and use. Financial capital is one expression of property rights. In a democratic society, property rights should exist only because people collectively decide to uphold them; they are not inalienable but are upheld by society as a matter of choice. Therefore, if society confers us the right of property, then we have obligations to that society (Fitzgerald 2001). Today, property rights have become so divorced from this democratic control that they are undermining other human rights. A reawakening to a basic principle is required: there can be no property rights without property duties, or obligations. From such a principle, it should not be left up to the powerful to decide if they are responsible or not, or if they are carrying out their obligations or not. Instead, the focus shifts to the governance of capital by those who are affected by it—a concept that I have dubbed 'capital accountability' (Bendell 2004).

In the five years covered in this volume, most work on finance and ethics focused on questions of responsibility, not accountability, rights or democracy. Action on finance and ethics was limited to minority shareholders causing trouble for companies (shareholder activism), increasing the security of one's returns via expanded risk management assessments and corporate engagement (responsible investment), ethical venture capital (in environmental technologies, for example) or seeking moral cleanliness in one's own investments (screening out certain sectors from investment portfolios). Little had been done on the accountability of the people who invested, their demands for returns, and the people who managed their investments.

The fact that most current work on responsible or sustainable finance is based on a voluntarist view of responsibility is problematic from a democratic perspective. When funding an activity, people should not only have a responsibility to know what is happening with their property but should also be accountable to those who are affected by it. An obligation should therefore exist for owners of capital to invest only in activities that are accountable to those affected by them. If owners do not carry out their obligations, they should lose the right to the specific property involved. In essence, this principle would mean investors ensuring that those who manage their money require that the activities they fund/own are accountable to those affected. Thus when banks lend or when fund managers buy stocks—that is, when an activity is financed—the companies involved must be accountable to the people affected by that activity. Mechanisms would then be needed to ensure that banks, fund managers and, in turn, individual absent owners of capital carried out their obligations to ensure companies followed these accountability guidelines (Bendell 2004). Clearly this would pose a challenge to the current financial markets, where the derivatives markets have multiple links in a chain before affecting people—the consequences of which in 2008 only illustrate the importance of restoring some accountability to the real economy. Another dimension to capital democracy would be ensuring that processes of the capitalisation of aspects of life are more open to public discussion and review: for instance, intellectual property claims over genetic code need to be matters of public debate and consultation.

Promoting capital accountability would also involve creating more 'present' ownership. Owners of property are often more accountable if they are present with that property. For example, an owner of a factory experiences a face-to-face form of accountability by seeing those affected by the activities of his or her property. Closing the distance between those who own property and those who are affected by it can also be promoted by increasing employee, customer, supplier and community ownership of that property. Jeff Gates (1998) therefore argued for more 'up-close ownership' so as 'to link a nation's people to their workplace, their community, their economy, their environment—and to each other' (1998: xxv). Sharing the risks associated with an economic activity is another way of increasing the involvement of owners.

Creating more present ownership is also part of a process of democratising capital ownership in general, and efforts from within both governments and large corporations to encourage a greater diversity of capital ownership across an economy should be supported. This takes us beyond capital accountability to a broader economic democratisation agenda. Capital democracy describes an economic system that moves towards the creation, allocation and management of capital according to the interests of everyone directly affected by that process, in order to support the self-actualisation of all. This principle would mean not only more effort to hold capital accountable and democratise ownership, as described above, but also democratising money, democratising trade, democratising employment and democratising taxation, as I will now outline.

A key area for democratisation is the money system. There are two main aspects to that challenge: currency speculation and the creation of money. Currency speculators on international financial markets have no accountability to the people affected by the volatility in the cost of borrowing, devaluations and so forth that they help accentuate. At a minimum, owning the property of money should confer duties to the society or societies that underpin that currency. The concept of capital democracy might suggest that all financial transactions be taxed, due to the transactor's obligation to the social infrastructure that provides the opportunity for their transaction. Such a measure could end short-term currency speculation. It would also create resources that could permit the reduction or abolition of other taxes, such as some income taxes.

The other aspect of democratising the money system concerns not the way money is traded but the way it is created. Money typically enters the economy as debt, as it is provided to private banks who then lend it out, with interest attached. Consequently, we have a system where the total amount of money in the world is not sufficient to pay the total debts of the world—and never will. We are a perpetually indebted planet. This is a form of social control, as the amount of economic activity must continue to grow, which necessitates resource consumption and commodification beyond the levels we might otherwise choose (Douthwaite 1993). Not only is it logically impossible and ecologically mad to create a system that demands perpetual growth, it is not democratic to take this decision out of the hands of people. Today people are asked to spend, spend, spend, and borrow, borrow, borrow, in order to keep the economic system from collapsing. Democracy requires choice, and that is no choice. In addition, this process of money creation means that the private banks are given the opportunity to grow their profits in ways that others cannot. You or I cannot go to a central bank and ask them to print us money. The private banks do this and loan it out at interest, thus making more money every time the state-owned central banks create more money. This process became more noticeable in 2008, due to a series of cash injections and then bailouts from central banks and governments.

What might more democratic alternatives involve? One source of ideas is the system of Islamic banking. Many Islamic institutions consider usury, and thus interest, to be wrong, due to principles in Shari'ah law. First, money should be only a medium of exchange, a way of defining the value of a thing; it has no value in itself, and therefore should not be allowed to give rise to more money. The human effort, initiative and risk involved in a productive venture are more important than the money used to finance it. Second, a lender must share the risk with the borrower—the potential profits or losses that arise out of the enterprise for which the money was lent. Third, transactions should be entered into honestly with the minimum of uncertainty, risk and speculation. Fourth, investments should not support practices or products that are incompatible with the core beliefs of Islam. As a result, the charging of interest, trading in futures, speculation on currencies and investment in products such as alcohol were not permissible for many Islamic financial firms. In practice, Islamic banks usually work by taking an equity stake in the enterprises they help finance (see 'Unsustainable world-views?' on page 144). The crash of 2008 stimulated more worldwide interest in Islamic banking, as it became apparent that a more accurate description of the economic system in most of the West was not capitalism but moneyism—a belief in money making money no matter what the connection to real, non-financial, capital in the economy.

The democratisation of markets and trade is also an important part of the capital democracy agenda. The way market access is regulated not just by governments but by large corporations that can drive down prices paid to producers is something that needs to be addressed. It underlies the lack of resources available to suppliers that translates into poor labour practices and environmental protections (see Functions → 'Purchasing or supply' in the thematic index). The democratisation of employment is also a central aspect of capital democracy, including who has access to employment, how their wages and conditions are set, and freedom from discrimination in those processes.

Democratising taxation is another key aspect of capital democracy. The underpinning of democracy is that we have a government, and the underpinning of a government's ability to govern is tax revenue. The democratic view is that we should all contribute to collective costs for collective needs, and the wealthier we are the more we should give. The current situation does not live up to that ideal, owing to extensive corporate welfare and regressive taxation where the poor and middle class often pay proportionally and sometimes even absolutely more than some companies and wealthy individuals. Therefore, taxation has become as much a regressive and illegitimate process as it is progressive and legitimate (Johnston 2007). Capital democracy requires restoring progressive and fair taxation, which in the context of a global economy necessitates greater international cooperation on, and harmonisation of, tax codes.

We don't just need to reform capitalism; we need to reformat it. I have chosen the term 'capital democracy' for this vision of economy, as it is about a form of capitalism and an application of democracy.[5] It calls for returning decisions about capital to the people affected by it. What might happen when those who are affected by capital can govern it more effectively? They might choose to support profit-taking and the existing ownership patterns, if they determined these to form a useful system—or they might not. The important thing is that it would be their choice, not imposed by outsiders autocratically supporting or abolishing property rights. Thus the true revolution in economic democracy is not about abolishing capitalism or extending capitalism, but about creating choices for people to transform, reform or remove corporations and capital in certain contexts. This democratisation of capitalism could be the ultimate goal of the corporate responsibility movement: the seeds of these ideas are already to be found in the existing analysis and practices of many people working on corporate responsibility today.

Practical implications

As corporate responsibility professionals, we need to engage with each other to discuss what it is we are for, and whether we can achieve it within existing 'political-economic opportunity structures' and how to collaborate within our organisational roles, and outside them, in order to drive needed changes in those opportunity structures. To begin with, we need to recognise the institution and system that we are working on—the corporation and a form of capitalism. Then we need to connect to develop ideas and plans for working on a transformative agenda. We also need to understand what personal qualities we need to cultivate and maintain in order to pursue a transformative agenda effectively. Therefore, when I teach corporate responsibility I ask my students to reflect on their personal motivations and future aims in this field (Box 2).

> **Box 2** QUESTIONS POSED TO STUDENTS AT THE END OF A CORPORATE RESPONSIBILITY COURSE
>
> ▶ Why am I interested in corporate responsibility?
> ▶ Do I see my role as part of a new movement? A new profession? Both? Or neither?
> ▶ What does my answer mean for managing my career?
> ▶ What does this mean for us, as classmates, now graduating this class?
> ▶ Does this exist already?

Initiatives that are attempting to bring together corporate responsibility practitioners to explore the future of this agenda, and how to have a broader impact, are important. Initiatives such as Corporation 20/20, the Network for Sustainable Financial Markets and the Global Finance Initiative need to be supported and developed, to be able to bring together more practitioners and begin coordinating efforts, where possible. Connector organisations in this space, such as Net Impact, OpenSRI, Just Means, Pioneers of Change, WiserEarth, and the new Lifeworth corporate responsibility portal, have an important role to play, as do publishers with extensive reach in this field, such as Greenleaf Publishing. It is clear there is plenty of space for more movement organisations to emerge and promote a movement ethos and effort from corporate responsibility practitioners. The areas that require further work are both highly technical, such as finance law, and highly political, requiring strong coalitions and constant attention to democratic accountability. Bridging the technical and the participatory will be a challenge for any organisation seeking to help drive broader change towards capital democracy.

In addition to mobilising people around the systemic challenge, we need to look at the personal leadership qualities that are required to navigate this change process authentically. Looking at the five years covered in this book, there was limited senior business leadership towards a transformation of the corporate system. Many people in senior management have gone through a process of technical specialisation in order to rise up in a large organisation, and thus have expertise on a content area, and a particular skill set. However, leading an organisation to success through a transforming social system requires an ability to see the multidimensional nature of social, political, economic and cultural systems. Today's corporate leaders are often like square pegs in global wholes. Facing a complex situation, their emotional memory can inspire a headmasterly form of 'leadership' which does little for open exploration of the issues faced. The limitations of these specialists-turned-bosses is why graduates of masters of business administration (MBAs) have been valued by many employers. Yet most MBA courses give you little insight into the diverse factors influencing corporations today and the type of leadership required (see 'Moral Bankruptcy Assured [MBA]' on page 121). As corporations become more involved in cross-sectoral processes that govern markets, so the potential for unaccountable self-interested decisions may grow, and a personal commitment to accountability and democracy from corporate leaders is important. Any professional competency framework for corporate responsibility must, therefore, include assessments of the open-mindedness and cross-cultural and political knowledge of individuals. The Globally Responsible Leadership Initiative (GRLI) is one project taking up that challenge.

The word 'profession' derives ultimately from the Latin *professio* ('public declaration'); via its accusative form (*professionem*), it entered medieval French and came to mean specifically the taking of vows upon entering a religious order. From medicine to stonemasonry, joining a profession usually involves individuals taking an oath that requires adherence to ethical standards, which include practitioner–client confidentiality, honesty, and striving to be an expert in one's profession, all in order to benefit the client. There is usually also a stipulation about upholding the good name of the profession. We need to decide whether we are a new purposeful profession, and, if so, then create the necessary professional bodies and informal networks to promote this. Could we innovate a new concept of professional identity, where the professional serves not only the client but a set of principles that speak directly to the need for a sustainable and just world? A professional oath could then clarify that commitment, calling on us to see our work in business as a vocation. The Thunderbird Business School oath comes close to this approach.

The existing networks and membership bodies in this field—including Account-Ability, the Association of Sustainability Practitioners, Business for Social Responsibility, CSR International, the European Academy of Business in Society, the Skoll Foundation, the Social Investment Forums, the UN Global Compact and UN Principles for Responsible Investment, the World Business Council for Sustainable Development (WBCSD) and the World Economic Forum—all have specific mandates and organisational interests and so provide nodes in the profession, but are not professional institutes covering the broad corporate responsibility field of practice. In future, some form of Professional Institute of Corporate Responsibility could help, although it could also hinder, if the professionalisation processes described earlier squeeze out the movement spirit from corporate responsibility.

A social movements perspective of corporate responsibility indicates that practitioners need to shift their perspective from an organisational one to a movement one, and then learn how to build support for that shift within their own organisations. This would lead to individuals and organisations exploring how they can play a successful role in a broader change agenda, as part of a broader network and movement. This is a particular challenge for the industry of corporate responsibility consultants and NGOs, who may compete for attention, rather than work out how to relate to each other more effectively.

Research implications

There are many research implications that arise from looking at corporate responsibility as a social movement, and I will briefly mention a few.

For researchers of social movements, my main message is to consider business organisations as categories of experience that a social movement could actually be about and emerge from, rather than being a locus for a movement to exert pressure on. Just as the old social movements had much to do with the experience in an early industrial workplace, so this is a movement about experience in the contemporary workplace.

In general, the movement lens suggests more research above and below the corporate could be useful—namely, the system around the corporation and the individual within. The mainstreaming agenda for corporate responsibility, for instance, means that inter-organisational relationships, including networks, alliances and partnerships, as well as processes of marketing, lobbying and advocacy, become increasingly important, as well as analysis of how changes in institutions and governance occurs and how organisations relate to this. Consequently, social movements theory, institutional theory and network theory become ever more relevant. However, I would warn here that they will only help serve understanding of complex social realities if we do not treat those realities as mere data for the demonstration of our research competence or for our need to publish in traditional academic journals. It is a difficult challenge to be both relevant to practice and get published, and is something I faced when attempting to fuse social movements and network theories to understand the effectiveness of policy advocacy on corporate responsibility by NGOs (Bendell and Ellersiek forthcoming).

Another area that could be looked at as part of a movement agenda is cognitive framing. In the review of 2006 we argued that some key cognitive frames about the role of business and financial institutions in society were shifting, in ways that would influence a wider range of practices. We illustrated the importance of a major shift in the frame of climate change, towards something current, economic, humanitarian and personally relevant. We suggested more work would be done on the framing of attitudes. Partly as a result of that study I developed a project that would address the cognitive frame we identified at the top of a pyramid of frames about progress—'luxury'. The aim was to encourage a shift in how 'luxury' is understood, so it would have to imply social and environmental excellence; consequently, more luxury brands might aspire to being responsible corporations and communicate that authentically across emerging markets, thereby encouraging consumer awareness of the positive and negative impacts of their consumption, and the desirability of being a responsible consumer. We produced a report on the corporate responsibility of the world's most famous luxury brands, which appeared in over 50 newspapers worldwide, leading to the creation of the Authentic Luxury Network (Bendell and Kleanthous 2007). This highlights how the choice of a research topics can be a social movement act.

More research on the individuals involved in this field is required. 'Surprisingly, employees as the unit of analysis have received scant attention in the CSR literature', notes Ruth Aguilera and her colleagues (Aguilera et al. 2007: 839). The importance of extrinsic motivations in shaping socially and environmentally meaningful corporate responsibility effort was described above. How such values arise and are sustained in a commercial workplace will become more important to understand.

Meanwhile, the growing number of entrepreneurs tackling societal challenges through commercial activities could have implications for research, as larger companies could benefit from understanding the psychology and approaches of social entrepreneurs to attempt to integrate their approaches into business innovation (Elkington *et al.* 2008). Modelling the psychology and methods of successful social entrepreneurs may be useful.

These are just some brief examples, as corporate responsibility is a field crossing many different organisational functions, public issues, policy processes and geographical regions. As this area develops further, academics in business schools will face the dilemma of whether to develop greater specialisation for their own career, within existing business functions, such as marketing, accounting or human resources, and focus on research projects that primarily attend to existing theoretical debates and demonstrate methodological competence, or to be more interdisciplinary, applied and rapid in their research, although with robust methods, in order to be relevant for practitioners and policy debates. An effective career path may require a balance, to develop a niche without losing perspective. To do this will require the development of an approach to literatures in multiple disciplines that can cut through the detail relating to the theoretical preoccupations of those different disciplines to identify what is relevant to a more interdisciplinary and applied approach. What will also be required for academics is a system for evaluating how well one is delivering on such an approach, and a system for disseminating results in ways that achieve 'impact' as evaluated by various institutions of accreditation, rating and funding.

The growing focus on discrete disciplines within academia owing to government research assessments and a consequent distance from practitioners' priorities does not help university researchers to achieve the balance between relevance and rigour that I'm advocating for here. Business school leaders should collaborate in lobbying for changes to ratings systems so that the siloing of academics is reduced and more purposeful, relevant and interdisciplinary work is supported, esteemed and rewarded. In the absence of a change in this framework, university and business school heads would still do well to consider what the future needs of society will be in five-to-ten years, and plan for those, as government regulators and funders will probably follow these trends, as well as employers.

Broader transformations

It is unclear whether a system of capital democracy would create an environmentally sustainable society. As capital democracy involves making more economic decisions accountable to those affected by them, then this process would promote environmental sustainability to the extent of people's awareness and commitment to that aim. Perhaps the democratic spirit of people would be cultivated through an experience of democratic institutions and practices, and the resultant more equitable sharing of resources, and hence concern for collective challenges such as environmental ones, would be addressed better than now. However, there are some limits to the framework:

the concept of intergenerational equity does not fit within a framework of democratic principles and rights. However, given current life-spans, the rights of children should require us to consider the potential impact of today's decisions on the situation in 80 years' time. Whether capital is managed with a longer time horizon would depend on the views in society.

A democracy and human rights framework does not protect either the welfare of non-human life, or its freedom from extinction. However, human concern for these matters would translate into their view of what aspects of the natural world should be capitalised and how that capital should be owned and managed. Therefore, the extent of concern for animal welfare and biodiversity would depend, once again, on levels of human awareness. There is no guarantee, either, that a more democratic economic system would calm consumerism sufficiently for the economy to exist within the bio-capacity of the Earth.

Capital democracy will not be the panacea, and to attain global well-being and restore the biosphere will require a democratisation of other aspects of life—involving an awakening of all to our connectedness, to each other and the planet we live on. My involvement in world summit protests, NGOs, business, the United Nations and academia has helped me realise that we would miss the point if we blame a particular economic or political system for everything, or propose another system as the total solution. Some systems are better than others, feed certain aspects of human character not others. But, ultimately, the outcome of any social or organisational system will depend on us. Over the five years I witnessed common characteristics in people and groups working in all the arenas I engaged. Everywhere there was compassion, humility and inquisitiveness. Yet everywhere there was also pride, fear, manipulation and ego. Everywhere, including in myself. For instance, as the old Left woke up to the global protests, they set up front groups that brought hierarchical we-know-what-you-really-want-and-how-to-win politics. Theirs was a politics of envy not personal liberation. This naturally led to splits and aggressive criticism from those who rejected instant political solutions freeze-dried in the 19th century, and the bickering reduced the ability to engage the public more broadly.

I concluded my first book, with David Murphy, which looked at cross-sectoral partnerships for corporate responsibility, with the following hope:

> Perhaps we are on the verge of something bigger. People are beginning to recognise their small part in the wider world. People are beginning to think of the implications of their actions and people are beginning to listen to each other. Indeed, people are beginning to consider the needs of a 'we society' and not just a 'me society'. If these changes help to break down some of the alienation and competition we feel in work, in the street, in academia, even in our personal lives, then we may just stumble across a new way forward and reinvent the future (Murphy and Bendell 1997: 245).

Over ten years on, I do see something bigger. The barriers are being shaken between everything—including business and society, research and action, science and spirituality, progress and traditional wisdom. One contributor to this volume, Jules Peck, believes that what is described in these pages is part of a broader citizen renaissance where people are turning back from the idea that they should be consumers of politics, culture and society, and instead act as citizens in all areas of life. In this light the corporate responsibility movement, and the emerging common agenda for capital democracy, can be seen as one dimension of a growing global democracy movement (Korten 2006).

I did not meet my personal car-park poet Rik again after that protest, and cannot find him on the Web, so perhaps he dropped off the grid, living in an eco-village some-where. His poem reminds me of the scale of the challenge we face—it is one of spirit. My hope today is that a spirit of democracy and global citizenship is carried into the spheres of belief, religion and spirituality to lead to a transformation of consciousness that will make any new political-economic systems we create function for the well-being of all life on Earth.

Conclusion

A new wave of citizen staff, citizen managers and citizen entrepreneurs constitute the greatest social movement in the world today. Its greatness lies in the simple fact that most people on this planet work in the private sector, and spend most waking hours involved in such work. The everyday expression of their values and hopes, for a com-mon purpose, in and through that work can no longer be overlooked. Their efforts may not be visible on the street, but the hidden daily struggles at work are more substan-tial than recreational displays of discontent. Given their engagement within often pow-erful institutions, such citizen staff and entrepreneurs struggle against the forces of sycophancy and narrow self-interest. It is an emotional struggle, waged within.

'For me, corporate social responsibility in my life, I don't think it has worked' noted Dame Anita Roddick (2006) in an interview the year before she passed away. Anita was a champion of the corporate responsibility movement and her progressive busi-ness academy sponsored the first Annual Review included in this volume. She criti-cised the way corporate responsibility concepts had been hijacked by a profession of consultants and, in her lifetime, had lost its way. But she still held hope for what busi-ness and business people could achieve. 'I think the corporate social responsibility movement has got to have a bit more courage,' she said. 'And I don't think anything will happen until we get the financial institutions to change.' It is an insight that is now widely shared among corporate responsibility practitioners, as we see the emer-gence of an agenda for capital democracy. To begin thinking as a movement is essen-tial, according to Anita: 'If we start listening to the real forerunners of the planet—the environmental movement, the social justice movement—to help shape our thinking, then something will change.' In this introduction I have sought to map out how and why we can view corporate responsibility as a movement, and then evolve our prac-tices for greater impact.

Marjorie Kelly (2002) believes that we have a historic opportunity. 'We can become a new founding generation, completing the design in the economic realm that our forefathers began in the political realm.' She hopes that people working in this field today can drive the change:

> Taking on the challenge of economic democracy is a tall order, but there are tall lead-ers in the CSR movement today; leaders at the peak of personal power, with time yet in their professional lives for another major challenge. I'm thinking, for example, of the

first generation of socially responsible entrepreneurs, the founding fathers and mothers of socially responsible mutual funds, the authors of books, the heads of non-profits, the creators of stakeholder theory. I'm thinking of all the people who have defined CSR and built it into the industry it is today. When this generation passes, their like may not be seen again.

What is most clear from the people and events discussed in this book is that there are people who have a job, and others who have a vocation. Which are you?

References

Aberle, D. (1966) *The Peyote Religion among Navaho* (New York: Wenner-Gren Foundation).

Agnew, J. (1994) 'The Territorial Trap: The Geographical Assumptions of International Relations Theory', *Review of International Political Economy* 1: 53-80.

Aguilera, R., D.E. Rupp, C.A. Williams and J. Ganapathi (2007) 'Putting the S Back in Corporate Social Responsibility: A Multilevel Theory of Social Change in Organizations', *Academy of Management Review* 32.3: 836-63.

Ainger, K. (2001) 'Empires of the Senseless', *New Internationalist* 333 (April 2001).

Andrews, D., and T. Willett (1997) 'Financial Interdependence and the State: International Monetary Relations at Century's End', *International Organization* 51: 479-511.

Annan, K. (2006) 'Sustain momentum of corporate responsibility movement, Secretary-General stresses in message to business management forum', United Nations Department of Public Information, News and Media Division, New York, 23 October 2006; www.un.org/News/Press/docs/2006/sgsm10693.doc.htm, accessed 20 January 2009.

Ball, A. (2007) 'Environmental Accounting as Workplace Activism', *Critical Perspectives on Accounting* 18.7 (November 2007): 759-78.

Bendell, J. (ed.) (2000) *Terms for Endearment: Business, NGOs and Sustainable Development* (Sheffield, UK: Greenleaf Publishing).

—— (2004) 'Barricades and Boardrooms: A Contemporary History of the Corporate Accountability Movement' (Programme Paper 13; Geneva: UNRISD).

—— (2005) 'In Whose Name? The Accountability of Corporate Social Responsibility', *Development in Practice* 15.3–4 (June 2005): 362-74.

—— and A. Ellersiek (forthcoming) 'Noble Networks?' (Programme Paper; Geneva: UNRISD).

—— and A. Kleanthous (2007) *Deeper Luxury: Quality and Style When the World Matters* (Godalming, UK: WWF-UK).

—— et al. (2007) *Tipping Frames* (Geneva: Lifeworth).

—— et al. (2008) *The Global Step Change* (Geneva: Lifeworth).

Bennett, D. (1999) 'The Creation and Development of English Commercial Corporations and the Abolition of Democratic Control over their Behaviour', Program on Corporations Law and Democracy; www.corporatewatch.org/pages/dan_corp.html, accessed March 2004.

Boyer, R., and D. Drache (eds.) (1996) *States against Markets: The Limits of Globalisation* (London: Routledge).

—— and J. Cavanagh (1999) 'The Corporate Accountability Movement: Lessons and Opportunities', *The Fletcher Forum of World Affairs* 23.2: 151-69.

Brown, L.R. (2000) *State of the World* (Washington, DC: Worldwatch Institute).

Bucher, R. (1962) 'Pathology: A Study of Social Movements within a Profession', *Social Problems* 10.1 (Summer 1962): 40-51.

Calvert, G.N. (1991) *Democracy from the Heart: Spiritual Values, Decentralism, and Democratic Idealism in the Movement of the 1960s* (Eugene, OR: Communitas Press).

Camilleri, J.A., and J. Falk (1992) *The End of Sovereignty? The Politics of a Shrinking and Fragmenting World* (Aldershot, UK: Edward Elgar).

Campbell, J.L. (2007) 'Why Would Corporations Behave in Socially Responsible Ways? An Institutional Theory of Corporate Social Responsibility', *Academy of Management Review* 32.3: 946-67.

Castells, M. (1997) *The Power of Identity* (Oxford, UK: Blackwell).

Chomsky, N. (1992) *Deterring Democracy* (London: Vintage).

—— and E. Hernan (1994) *Manufacturing Consent: The Political Economy of the Mass Media* (London: Vintage).

Christian Aid (1999) *Taking Stock. How Supermarkets Stack Up on Ethical Trading* (London: Christian Aid).

Colborn, T., D. Dumanoski and J. Peterson Myers (1997) *Our Stolen Future: Are we threatening our fertility, intelligence, and survival? A Scientific Detective Story* (London: Abacus).

Cox, R. (ed.) (1997) *The New Realism: Perspectives on Multilateralism and World Order* (London: Macmillan).

Creed, D., and M. Scully (2000) 'Songs of Ourselves: Employees' Deployment of Social Identity in Workplace Encounters', *Journal of Management Inquiry* 9.4: 391-412.

Crompton, T. (2008) *Weathercocks and Signposts* (Godalming, UK: WWF-UK).

Dahl, R.A. (1961) *Who Governs? Democracy and Power in an American City* (New Haven, CT: Yale University Press).

Davis, G.F., and S. McAdam (2000) 'Corporations, Classes, and Social Movements after Managerialism', in B.M. Staw and R.I. Sutton (eds.), *Research in Organizational Behaviour, Volume 22* (Greenwich, CT: JAI Press): 193-236.

—— and T.A. Thompson (1994) 'A Social Movement Perspective on Corporate Control', *Administrative Science Quarterly* 39: 141-73.

Dollar, D., and A. Kraay (2002). 'Growth is Good for the Poor', *Journal of Economic Growth* 7.3: 195-225.

Douthwaite, R. (1993) *The Growth Illusion: How Economic Growth Has Enriched the Few, Impoverished the Many and Endangered the Planet* (Tulsa, OK: Council Oak Publications).

The Economist (2005) 'The Good Company: A Survey of Corporate Social Responsibility', *The Economist*, 22 January 2005: 1-22.

Elkington, J. (2008) Interview on Corporate Watchdog Radio.

—— and M. Lee (2006) 'It's the Economics, Stupid: Has the corporate-responsibility movement lost sight of the big picture?', *Grist*, 9 May 2006; www.grist.org/biz/fd/2006/05/09/lee, accessed 20 January 2009.

——, P. Hartigan and K. Schwab (2008) *The Power of Unreasonable People: How Social Entrepreneurs Create Markets that Change the World* (Boston, MA: Harvard Business School Press).

Encyclopaedia Britannica (2003) 'Social Movement', *Encyclopaedia Britannica*; www.britannica.com/eb/article?eu=109128, accessed March 2004.

Finger, M. (ed.) (1992) *The Green Movement Worldwide* (Greenwich, CN: JAI Press).

Fitzgerald, V. (2001) 'Regulating Large International Firms' (Programme on Technology, Business and Society, Paper No. 5; Geneva: UNRISD).

Folger, R., R. Cropanzano, T.A. Timmerman, J.C. Howes and D. Mitchell (1996) 'Elaborating Procedural Fairness: Justice Becomes Both Simpler and More Complex', *Personality and Social Psychology Bulletin* 22: 435-47.

Friedman, T. (1999) *The Lexus and the Olive Tree* (New York: Farrar Straus & Giroux).

Gates, J.R. (1998) *The Ownership Solution: Toward a Shared Capitalism for the Twenty-first Century* (London: Allen Lane).

Giddens, A. (1990) *The Consequences of Modernity* (Cambridge, UK: Polity Press).

Hamann, R., N. Acutt and P. Kapelus (2003) 'Responsibility versus Accountability? Interpreting the World Summit on Sustainable Development for a Synthesis Model of Corporate Citizenship', *Journal of Corporate Citizenship* 9: 32-48.

Hardt, G., and A. Negri (2001) *Empire* (Cambridge, MA: Harvard University Press).

Heberle, R. (1949) 'The Sociology of Social Movements', *American Sociology Review* 14: 346-57.

Held, D. (1997) 'Democracy and Globalization', *Global Governance* 3.3: 251-67.

——, A. McGrew, D. Goldblatt and J. Perraton (1999) *Global Transformations: Politics, Economics and Culture* (Stanford, CA: Stanford University Press).

Hertz, N. (2001) *The Silent Takeover: Global Capitalism and the Death of Democracy* (London: Heinemann).

Hochschild, A. (2005) *Bury the Chains: The British Struggle to Abolish Slavery* (London: Pan Books).

Hockerts, K., and T. Dyllick (2002) 'Beyond the Business Case for Corporate Sustainability', *Business Strategy and the Environment* 11.2: 130-41.

ILO (International Labour Organisation) (2000) *Sustainable Agriculture in a Globalised Economy* (Geneva: International Labour Office; www.ilo.org/public/english/dialogue/sector/techmeet/ tmadoo/tmadr.htm, accessed 20 January 2009).

Isbister, J. (2001) *Capitalism and Justice: Envisioning Social and Economic Fairness* (Bloomfield, CT: Kumarian Press).

Jenkins, R. (2000) 'Corporate Codes of Conduct: Self-regulation in a Global Economy', paper presented at the UNRISD *Workshop on Promoting Corporate Responsibility in Developing Countries: The Poten - tial and Limits of Voluntary Initiatives*, Geneva, Switzerland, 23–24 October 2000.

Johnston, D.C. (2007) *Free Lunch: How the Wealthiest Americans Enrich Themselves at Government Expense (and Stick You with the Bill)* (Portfolio Hardcover).

Jones, H. (2007) 'Corporate Responsibility as Innovation Engine' (Podcast; Stanford Discussions, 3 April 2007; sic.conversationsnetwork.org/shows/detail3243.html, accessed 20 January 2009).

Keck, M.E., and K. Sikkink (1998) *Activists Beyond Borders: Advocacy Networks in International Politics* (Ithaca, NY: Cornell University Press).

Kelly, M. (2001) *The Divine Right of Capital* (San Francisco: Berrett-Koehler).

—— (2002) 'The Next Step for CSR: Economic Democracy', Business Ethics; www.commondreams. org/views02/0815-09.htm, accessed February 2009.

Kingsnorth, P. (2003) *One No, Many Yeses: A Journey to the Heart of the Global Resistance Movement* (London: Simon & Schuster).

Klein, N. (2000) *No Logo: Taking Aim at the Brand Bullies* (London: Flamingo).

Korten, D. (1995) *When Corporations Rule the World* (West Hartford, CT: Kumarian Press).

—— (1997) 'Money versus Wealth', *Yes! A Journal of Positive Futures* 2 (Summer 1997); www. yesmagazine.org/article.asp?ID=885, accessed February 2009.

—— (2006) *The Great Turning: From Empire to Earth Community* (San Francisco: Berrett-Kohler).

Madeley, J. (1999) *Big Business, Poor People* (London: Zed Books).

Martin, R. (2007) *The Opposable Mind: How Successful Leaders Win through Integrative Thinking* (Toronto: McGraw-Hill Ryerson).

Max-Neef, M. (1992) 'Development and Human Needs', in P. Ekins and M. Max-Neef (eds.), *Real-Life Economics: Understanding Wealth Creation* (London: Routledge).

McAdam, D. (1982) *Political Process and the Development of Black Insurgency 1930–1970* (Chicago: University of Chicago Press).

—— and W.R. Scott (2005) 'Organizations and Movements', in G.F. Davis, D. McAdam, W.R. Scott and M.N. Zald (eds.), *Social Movements and Organization Theory* (Cambridge, UK: Cambridge University Press): 4-40.

McCarthy, J.D., and M.N. Zald (1977) *The Trend of Social Movements in America: Professionalization and Resource Mobilization* (Morristown, NJ: General Learning Press).

McDonough, W., and M. Braungart (2002) *Cradle to Cradle: Remaking the Way We Make Things* (New York: North Point Press).

McLuhan, H.M. (1970) *Culture is Our Business* (New York: McGraw-Hill).

Meyer, M.W., and L.G. Zucker (1989) *Permanently Failing Organizations* (Newbury Park, CA: Sage).

Meyerson, D.E. (2001) 'Radical Change, the Quiet Way', *Harvard Business Review*, October 2001: 92-100.

—— and M. Scully (1995) 'Tempered Radicalism and the Politics of Ambivalence and Change', *Orga - nization Science* 6.5 (September–October 1995): 585-600.

Mintzberg, H. (1989) *Mintzberg on Management: Inside our Strange World of Organizations* (New York: Free Press).

Monbiot, G. (2001) *Captive State: The Corporate Takeover of Britain* (London: Pan Books).

Murphy, D.F., and J. Bendell (1997) *In the Company of Partners: Business, Environmental Groups and Sustainable Development Post-Rio* (Bristol, UK: Policy Press).

—— and J. Bendell (1999) 'Partners in Time? Business, NGOs and Sustainable Development' (Discussion Paper 109; Geneva: UNRISD).

Newell, P., and M. Paterson (1998) 'Climate for Business: Global Warming, the State and Capital', *Review of International Political Economy* 5.4 (Winter 1998): 679-703.

Paul, J., and J. Garred (2000) 'Making Corporations Accountable', Background Paper for the United Nations Financing for Development Process; Global Policy Forum, December 2000.

Pilger, J. (2001) 'The New Rulers of the World', ITV TV (London), July 2001.

Porritt, J. (2005) *Capitalism as if the World Matters* (London: Earthscan).

Reason, P., and H. Bradbury (eds.) (2001) *Handbook of Action Research* (London: Sage).

Reich, R.B. (2001) 'Editorial', *New York Times*, 18 March 2001.

—— (2007) *Supercapitalism: The Transformation of Business, Democracy, and Everyday Life* (New York: Knopf).

Robins, N. (2005) *The Corporation that Changed the World: How the East India Company Shaped the Modern Multinational* (London: Pluto Books).

Roddick, A. (2006) 'Anita Roddick: Corporate Social Responsibility?', Interview; www.globalissues. org/video/733/anitaroddick/csr, accessed 27 January 2009.

Rodrik, D. (2000) 'Comments on "Trade, Growth, and Poverty" by D. Dollar and A. Kraay'; www. eldis.org/go/home&id=28826&type=Document, accessed 20 January 2009.

Rosenau, J. (1997) *Along the Domestic–Foreign Frontier: Exploring Governance in a Turbulent World* (Cambridge Studies in International Relations; Cambridge, UK: Cambridge University Press).

Ross, R.J.S. (1976) 'The Impact of Social Movements on a Profession in Process Advocacy in Urban Planning', *Work and Occupations* 3.4: 429-54.

Rueschemeyer, D. (1983) 'Professional Autonomy and the Social Control of Expertise', in R. Dingwall and P. Lewis (eds.), *The Sociology of the Professions* (Hong Kong: Macmillan): 38-58.

Saddar, Z. (2000) *The Consumption of Kuala Lumpur* (London: Reaktion Books).

Scully, M.A., and W.E.D. Creed (2005) 'Subverting our Stories of Subversion', in G.F. Davis, D. McAdam, W.R. Scott and M.N. Zald (eds.), *Social Movements and Organization Theory* (Cambridge, UK: Cambridge University Press): 310-32.

Simms, A., T. Bigg and N. Robins (2000) *It's Democracy Stupid: The Trouble with the Global Economy— The United Nations' Lost Role and Democratic Reform of the IMF, World Bank and the World Trade Organization* (London: New Economics Foundation).

Snow, C.C., R.E. Miles and H.S. Coleman (1992) 'Managing 21st Century Network Organizations', *Organizational Dynamics* 21 (Winter 1992): 5-21.

Starr, A. (2000) *Naming the Enemy: Anti-corporate Movements Confront Globalization* (London: Zed Books).

Strange, S. (1996) *The Retreat of the State: The Diffusion of Power in the World Economy* (Cambridge, UK: Cambridge University Press).

Tarrow, S. (1994) *Power in Movement: Collective Action, Social Movements and Politics* (Cambridge, UK: Cambridge University Press).

Teach, E. (2005) 'Two Views of Virtue: The corporate social responsibility movement is picking up steam. Should you worry about it?', *CFO*, 15 December 2005; www.cfo.com/article.cfm/5193459, accessed 20 January 2009.

Tilly, C. (2004) *Social Movements, 1768–2004* (Boulder, CO: Paradigm Publishers).

UNDP (United Nations Development Programme) (1994) *Human Development Report* (New York: Oxford University Press).

Veltmeyer, H. (1997) 'New Social Movements in Latin America: The Dynamics of Class and Identity', *Journal of Peasant Studies* 25.1.

Waddell, S. (2005) *Societal Learning and Change* (Sheffield, UK: Greenleaf Publishing).

Webb, T. (2005) 'Ten Years on from 1995: Corporate Responsibility in Modern Times', *Ethical Corporation*, 20 December 2005; www.ethicalcorp.com/content.asp?ContentID=4028, accessed 20 January 2009.

White, A. (2007) Interview on Corporate Watchdog Radio, 20 September 2007.

Whitley, R. (2000) *Divergent Capitalisms: The Social Structuring and Change of Business Systems* (Oxford, UK: Oxford University Press).

Williams, C.A. (2004) 'Civil Society Initiatives and "Soft Law" in the Oil and Gas Industry', *New York University Journal of International Law and Politics* 36: 457-502.

World Monitors (2001) *eMonitors* 106 (14 February 2001).

WWF (1999) *Foreign Direct Investment and Environment: From Pollution Havens to Sustainable Development. Report from the OECD Conference* (Paris: WWF-UK).

Zadek, S. (2004) 'The Path to Corporate Responsibility', *Harvard Business Review*, 1 December 2004; harvardbusinessonline.hbsp.harvard.edu/b02/en/common/item_detail.jhtml?id=R0412J, accessed 22 January 2009.

——, S. Lingayah and D. Murphy (1998) *Purchasing Power: Civil Action for Sustainable Consumption* (London: New Economics Foundation).

Zald, M.N., and M.A. Berger (1978) 'Social Movements in Organizations: Coup d'Etat, Insurgency, and Mass Movements', *American Journal of Sociology* 83.4: 823-61.

——, C. Morrill and H. Roa (2005) 'The Impact of Social Movements on Organizations: Environment and Responses', in G.F. Davis, D. McAdam, W.R. Scott and M.N. Zald (eds.), *Social Movements and Organization Theory* (Cambridge, UK: Cambridge University Press): 253-79.

Index

To help you navigate through these reviews, a thematic index has been prepared (pages 367-87). This will enable you to explore the reviews on the basis of either industry sector (e.g. agriculture), organisational function (e.g. marketing) or corporate responsibility topic (e.g. labour). There is also a list of all people and organisations discussed.

2001

1Q2001

January–March

Jem Bendell

'Glocalising' corporate responsibility

We are beginning to see more efforts to both promote and document corporate responsibility in less industrialised and transitional countries, where the social and environmental impacts of business expansion through globalisation can be more dramatically felt, but where there is less known about the range of positive and negative experiences.

February saw the launch of the India Partnership Forum, a new initiative to enhance corporate responsibility in promoting human development. In New Delhi, the United Nations Development Programme (UNDP) Administrator, Mark Malloch Brown, and the Director-General of the Federation of Indian Industry signed an agreement establishing the forum. Emphasising that the corporate sector can complement and not replace the role of the government in social development, UNDP's chief said that, in today's world, a significant portion of the capital for social development—for infrastructure, new jobs, even basic education and healthcare—comes from the private sector. 'A vision of development that leaves out the private sector is a very partial vision', he said. Arun Shourie, Minister of State for Disinvestment, Statistics and Programme Implementation, said that, 'by linking the corporate with the community-based networks we will multiply the impact'. He stressed the need for stronger monitoring and implementation mechanisms in the area of social development work.

Meanwhile, ethical investment received a boost in Brazil, when Unibanco launched a socially responsible investment (SRI) research service for Brazilian equities. The fourth-largest private-sector bank in Brazil, with over a thousand branches, claimed it is the first to begin assessing the social and environmental profiles of companies in

MARK MALLOCH BROWN, UNDP
ADMINISTRATOR: EMPHASISED THE
ROLE OF THE PRIVATE SECTOR

that country. The bank will not rank companies, but provides investors with information on social and environmental performance in the form of SRI reports. It marked the launch of the new service by releasing SRI reports on two companies—steel-maker CST and food manufacturer Perdigao.

In their effort to 'glocalise' corporate citizenship the UN Global Compact's team in New York has been pushing toward their target of 1,000 signatory companies. Already 216 Brazilian companies have expressed support and agreed to work with a local business association to implement the principles in company operations.

The United Nations country team also held a workshop of over 40 Malaysian business leaders to provide the community with information regarding the implementation of the Global Compact in their country, while in India over 20 high-level Indian business leaders demonstrated their support of the Global Compact and the implementation of its principles.

However, it was 'back home' in the US where the UN were making slower progress. the *International Herald Tribune* noted that 'many of the big names of American business have remained aloof' to the UN initiative (25 January 2001). Thomas M.T. Niles, president of the US Council for International Business (CIB), an American affiliate of the International Chamber of Commerce (ICC), told the newspaper that the main cause of American corporate hesitation was that important details on how the programme will work are still undetermined: 'US companies want to be sure what it is they are being asked to do before endorsing the compact.' For Mr Niles, the problem for American companies is not the Compact's basic premise ('American companies fully support the fundamental principles which form the basis of the Global Compact'); instead, he suggests that US companies need reassurances that the agreement will remain as it was presented by UN Secretary-General Kofi Annan in July 2000. 'The heads of some of the UN agencies involved made statements at odds with what had been presented by the Secretary-General, particularly on external monitoring and verification. These points need to be clarified. Companies need to receive the same, consistent message from all the UN officials involved: a clear idea of what is expected of them should they choose to endorse the compact.'

The Compact's Mr Dubee told the *International Herald Tribune* that 'the compact was never meant to be fine print carved in stone for lawyers, but is a broad framework inspiring action in support of the nine principles'. He explained that companies are challenged to be as creative as possible and to use their entrepreneurial skills in developing innovative solutions to concrete problems and that 'this concept has been understood by business leaders around the world'.

The caution from CIB seems to stem from a concern with having their business activities subjected to a greater degree of scrutiny by various groups. Rather self-evidently, Mr Niles commented that 'Inevitably, their postings on the Global Compact Web site will be examined in microscopic detail.'

The UN Secretary-General's office has established an experimental Global Compact Learning Forum at Warwick University's Corporate Citizenship Unit which will focus on the organisational change and learning issues involved in company engagement with the Global Compact. They will report annually and hold the first of what it is hoped will become an annual event in October 2001.

Virtual corporate responsibility

The first few months of 2001 witnessed a growing convergence of the Internet and corporate responsibility communities. It was not so long ago that people were claiming that the invention of personal computers would lead to the paperless office. The growth of the Internet is rekindling visions of a technotopia, but this time with social as well as environmental considerations being taken on board.

A new book looking into this idea, *The Weightless Society*,[1] was selling well (in traditional *printed paper* format) when this journal went to print (that's right: *print*). Which is why it was surprising to read, in the February 2001 issue of Continental's in-flight magazine, BP's Regional President for Eastern USA, John Manzoni, reassuring us 'the e-craze is using much more electricity than anyone ever imagined. There's a huge demand for electricity, huge demand for new power stations and a huge demand for gas.' It seems that the implications of the new economy, for corporate responsibility and sustainable development require further investigation.

In January 2001, a new survey of 150 technology companies warned that dot.com entrepreneurs are wrong in thinking their businesses have no impact on the environment or society, or that they can be irresponsible because they are new. The report, *Dotcom Ethics: E-business and Sustainability*, includes case studies from Amazon.com and eBay, and forms part of a year-long inquiry into the social and environmental opportunities from e-commerce and the new economy. The inquiry is being steered by a group of companies, government departments and think-tanks, and coordinated by the UK-based environmental non-profit Forum for the Future.

The report argues that new economy companies are all innovators with the opportunity to change for the good the way that business works. Yet they are not realising potential benefits, such as the lesser environmental impact of Internet use. Although more than two in every three respondents think the environment important for their businesses—and almost all are personally committed to safeguarding it—just over half say they do not have enough time or expertise to do anything about it.

One e-business leader who seems to be taking the issue seriously, Jeff Bezos, is a contributor to the new book, *Digital Futures* (Earthscan, 2001) edited by James Wilsdon of Forum for the Future. On the other hand, Bezos's company, Amazon, is currently experiencing troubled relations with the Washington Alliance of Technology Workers union, since it started laying off 1,300 staff in January, adding to fears that the new economy may become a jobless rather than weightless society.

Although dot.com entrepreneurs may not be seizing the opportunities offered by the Internet to become good corporate citizens, the existence of the Internet is certainly making corporate transparency and accountability more important. It is the ability of the Internet to facilitate communication that is making it a key weapon on the social responsibility battleground. 'Critics of large corporations use web sites to mount attacks on them and call for boycotts and demonstrations, while companies have begun using their own sites to promote examples of positive corporate citizenship', reported the *Financial Times* (Pike, 25 January 2001).

One example is TXU-Europe which has produced a printed summary report of its stakeholder engagement process and put more in-depth information online for those with an interest in seeking out further information. As more companies become interested in this form of communication, so a number of companies are beginning to specialise in online sustainability reporting, such as C21, who worked with TXU, and the newly launched Global-Responsibility.com.

The Coalition for Environmentally Responsible Economies (Ceres) is also using the web as a means of increasing the transparency of companies who have signed up to the Ceres principles, and a complete listing of 1999 Ceres reports is now available on the 'Corporate Reports' section on their website.[2] The UN Global Compact also seeks to use the web as a key tool in supporting transparency of signatory companies' pursuance of their nine principles.

Meanwhile, there are a number of new online services being established within the field of corporate responsibility. In the US, SRI Worldgroup is striving to help social investors and promote corporate social responsibility through a variety of Internet-based services, including SocialFunds.com, the Corporate Social Research Center, and CSRwire.com.

SocialFunds.com provides over 2,000 pages of mutual fund and corporate information; the Corporate Social Research Center offers viewers social and environmental performance reports for more than 1,500 publicly traded companies; CSRwire.com is a niche newswire service devoted solely to corporate social responsibility press releases and a resource for concerned investors, consumers and media. Other initiatives include business-impact.org and worldcsr.com, which is a gateway to websites of business-led organisations on corporate responsibility.

In January 2001, a new company was launched which uses the media to bring consumers together with indigenous producers through the Internet.

Viatru offers web-based Visible Commerce documentaries of the villages where products originate, helping consumers understand the importance of a product's origins, including the people who make them. Yahoo! named Viatru's web documentary on a linen product its 'site of the day'. The documentary takes you to the artisans' village to see and hear directly from the people, learn about the process that created these linens, and see the positive impact the trade will have on this community.

Viatru founder Michelle Long says: 'We see trade as evolving, or perhaps returning to a more meaningful personal connection.'[3]

Another recent growth area is in the web-watching services that provide clients with an audit of Internet content on social and environmental issues involving their operations. These include eWatch, NetCurrents, Cyveillance, IBNet and Infonic Ltd.

Jay Sauerbrei, Head of Marketing at Infonic Ltd, says many of their clients 'are subject to public pressure groups regarding issues such as genetically modified foods, human rights and environmental concerns', and that they use Infonic because 'the actions and opinions of online communities are beginning to make a very, very serious impact on the fields of public relations, investor relations and corporate brand management'. Infonic is currently providing regular reports for BNFL, Daewoo Cars, Levi-Strauss, Diageo and Unilever. In a novel way of building corporate transparency, Diageo has hired them to put an 'unvarnished' summary of recent independent media coverage of the company up on their site every week.[4]

However, the existence of these web watchers has raised serious concerns within civil society. Head of Research at Infonic, Mark Bunting, recognises that most of the companies selling these services 'advocate control . . . [and] sell themselves on the ability that they give their clients to stop other people doing things'. He argues that Infonic has a different strategy, and that it recommends to its clients that successful adaptation means engagement, not control.

The obvious objection is that clients of these services are under no obligation to use the information to engage, but can use it to pre-empt or undermine campaigners' activities. Mark Bunting questions why campaigners 'might be worried that companies will find out about their concerns and activities, as this assumes that campaigners have more chance of success if the companies they target remain ignorant of their endeavours'. Yet the power of a campaign to affect corporate reputation only really kicks in when an issue moves out of the virtual world and onto our TV screens and into our newspapers. Before this happens, processes of knowledge creation, critical independent debate, and the marshalling of people, resources and evidence around an issue are crucial. If these processes are increasingly interrupted at an early stage by a company with a commercial interest in the issue, will the critical nature of civil society be forever undermined? In such a society how will we really know what is going on and be able to decide what is important for us and the planet?

A leaked report from Sony demonstrates this concern, as it advocates using Infonic's services as part of a coordinated strategy that could include intervening in the potential funding of a campaign by the Silicon Valley Toxics Coalition. Mark Bunting recognises this new reality is a challenge for NGOs and suggests campaigners have to acclimatise to the new transparency of the Net, just like corporations.

There is no absence of free-to-use, non-profit, non-corporate services supporting research and practice in corporate responsibility. In February 2001, the International Labour Office (ILO) launched an online database of Business and Social Initiatives, which includes comprehensive information on private-sector initiatives that address labour and social conditions in the workplace and in the communities where enterprises operate. The database features corporate policies and reports, codes of conduct, accreditation and certification criteria, labelling and other programmes. It allows users to undertake customised searches to retrieve information on specific companies and organisations, countries, regions, business sectors and labour and employment issues. The ILO is keen to point out that a listing does not constitute an endorsement.

All of these new web-based initiatives raise the issue of access to information technology. Half the people on this planet have not even received or made a telephone call, let alone used the Internet, and most of us do not speak English. The Internet is a great communication tool for the connected, but one solution does not fit all situations, and we need to consider how representatives of workers and communities from Nicaragua to Namibia are going to have a voice in these new processes governing corporate policy and practice.

The United Nations Information Technology Service (UNITeS) is attempting to bridge this digital divide. Managed by UN Volunteers, UNITeS mobilises information technology professionals to help developing countries harness the power of information and communication technology (ICT) for human development.

One leading supplier of hardware for the Internet, Cisco Systems, is joining the effort by teaming up with the UNDP, launching an Internet training programme in Benin for Internet administrators from eight francophone countries in Africa. The 'training of trainers' course is a new step by UNDP, Cisco Systems, UN volunteers and other partners to bring Cisco's Networking Academy Programme to half of the world's 48 least developed countries. Cisco is also establishing a new Internet training centre in Burkina Faso.

Questioning globalisation

The World Trade Organisation (WTO) was criticised for sheltering itself from protest and scrutiny when it announced its next top-level meetings will be in Qatar, a nation with a questionable human rights record and little freedom for public protest.[5]

Meanwhile, the growing notoriety of the protests against global economic institutions, such as the World Bank, the International Monetary Fund (IMF) and the WTO, has established the issue of globalisation and its governance on the international business agenda, as illustrated by the discussions at January 2001's World Economic Forum (WEF) in Davos, Switzerland. 'Stung into action not just by the threat of anti-capitalist demonstrations but by many of its own members from poorer countries, the World Economic Forum turned into an unprecedented public expression of guilty conscience from the planet's most exclusive gathering of political and business leaders', suggested the *Financial Times* (Hugh Carnegy, 30 January 2001). George Soros told the participants that globalisation 'creates a very uneven playing field. The centre is rich and the periphery is less rich and the centre also controls the system.' Soros took part in a satellite link-up with the World Social Forum, held simultaneously in Porto Alle-

GEORGE SOROS:
'THE CENTRE
CONTROLS THE
SYSTEM'

gre, Brazil, which drew some 10,000 participants mainly from civil-society organisations.

A participant at WEF, Kumi Naidoo, President of CIVICUS, suggested that 'ultimately we should be looking to a combined World Social and Economic Forum which has representation from civil society, government and business. A forum that recognises that social and economic issues cannot be separated any longer. 'A forum that creates the basis for dialogue, and courageous and thoughtful action, that begins to make a significant difference in the lives of ordinary people all over the world.'[6]

KUMI NAIDOO: 'SOCIAL AND
ECONOMIC ISSUES CANNOT BE
SEPARATED ANY LONGER'

Post-Seattle, those who have for years questioned the merits of economic growth and free trade are no longer ignored by players in the global marketplace, although they are still considered misguided. For example, on 24 January 2001, journalist Martin Wolf wrote an article in the *Financial Times* entitled 'Growth makes the poor richer'. In it, he suggested that those arguing for the reversal of the effects of globalisation to increase equality 'might be right—but only because it would be a move towards equality of destitution'. Head of the Institute of Development Studies (IDS) Globalisation Team, Raphael Kaplinsky, responded by pointing out that 'the "losers" are not confined to those who failed to participate in the global economy (as Mr Wolf implies) but are also drawn from those who have participated but have done so inappropriately'.

The debate is set to continue, as either side marshals its evidence to show that growth and/or free trade is good or bad for humanity and the planet. The question to ponder is how business might be able to engage, openly, in this debate? If economic growth and 'free' trade *are* creating economic insecurity and environmental degradation, what would be the role of a responsible corporation of the future? There is a need for some serious scenario-planning around this question which places a successful corporation in a future society of free and fair trade operating with only resource-neutral growth. Currently, initiatives such as the World Business Council for Sustainable Development (WBCSD) and Global Compact seem to support the pro-growth argument, but the issue does not look like it will go away, as April 2001's protests against the Organisation of American States (OAS) in Quebec City will once again demonstrate. Francis Fukuyama once wrote[7] that the triumph of capitalism and electoral democracy marked 'the end of history'. We may not know the outcome of these debates sparked by global protests, but one thing is certain: *history has restarted.* (See 'Anti-globalisation: now it's your business' on page 91.)

Soft law or hard ball?

As they grow in number and notoriety, so-called 'soft laws' or voluntary initiatives (often described as self-regulation or civil regulation) are being examined more closely to see what they are actually delivering.

For example, the Tellus Institute published a report which examines private-sector motivations to participate in voluntary programmes, outlines public-sector constraints on such programmes, and undertakes a qualitative evaluation of several initiatives.[8]

Although many applaud the energy surrounding voluntary initiatives, there is also discussion about an appropriate legal framework to ensure social and environmental standards are enforced in the global economy. Kofi Annan raised this issue at the Davos WEF when he asked delegates 'how do you explain, especially to our young people, why the global system of rules, at the dawn of the 21st century, is tougher in protecting intellectual property rights than in protecting fundamental human rights?'[9]

In January 2001, the Royal Institute of International Affairs (RIIA) in London published a new Briefing Paper, which adds to the discussion on whether there is a need for tougher regulation of multinational corporations.

Governing Multinationals: The Role of Foreign Direct Liability[10] outlines the implications of one way of enforcing corporate environmental, social and human rights standards across borders—the increasing trend for parent companies to be sued in

HALINA WARD: WARNS AGAINST
A WAVE OF LITIGATION

developed-country courts for the activities of their subsidiaries in developing countries. Although no company has yet lost such a case, the report warns 'foreign direct liability' cases are now becoming more common. 'A single successful foreign direct liability case would likely trigger a raft of risk management thinking not only among internal company managers, but also within the insurance industry, lenders and investors', warns author of the report, Halina Ward. Just one or two successful cases could lead to a wave of copycat litigation.

Current cases include a series of actions in the US against Shell (over operations in Nigeria), Total (over operations in Myanmar) and Rio Tinto (over operations in Papua New Guinea).

In the UK, Cape plc is being prosecuted over the effects of asbestos in its mining activities in South Africa. The UK House of Lords decided to allow cases such as this when the domestic court where the alleged offence took place cannot hear the case competently, or the victims cannot afford adequate legal representation.[11] Meanwhile, the British Law Commission has put forward proposals for 'a special offence of corporate killing, broadly corresponding to the proposed offence of killing by gross carelessness'.[12]

Although such legal developments could drive up the social performance of corporate practices across the board, for those companies on the receiving end of litigation it might not be easy to spot the 'win–win'. In February 2001, Shell took the issue all the way to the US Supreme Court. They want the court to reverse a landmark legal precedent, made over 20 years ago in the *Filartiga v. Pena-Irala* case when the Second Circuit Court of Appeals held that foreigners had standing under the Alien Tort Claims Act. Shell wants to avoid contesting *Wiwa v. Shell*, a suit brought by relatives of famed Nigerian writer Ken Saro-Wiwa and another Ogoni tribe member, who were executed by the Nigerian government after leading demonstrations against Shell's oil development in their tribal land. The deliberations of the Supreme Court will be watched closely by human rights groups.[13]

Interface's CEO Ray Anderson suggested at a conference in Houston that, in the future, if executives did what he had done before his conversion to corporate responsibility, they would go to jail. Similarly, in his book *Crimes against Humanity* (Penguin, 2000), Geoffrey Robertson QC argues for global human rights enforcement mechanisms to apply equally to corporations and executives, as it is being proposed that they should to governments, politicians, generals and armies. It seems that, no matter what the US Supreme Court decides, Shell's action may only delay the inevitable, as the global economy advances the debate about a concomitant global legislature.

GEOFFREY ROBERTSON:
WIDEN THE SCOPE OF
HUMAN RIGHTS ENFORCEMENT

No stop to sweatshops?

News of labour abuses continued to hit the headlines in the New Year. The *New York Times* reported on 6 February 2001 that a report by the US Department of Labor found that workers in an American factory in Samoa that supplies apparel for J.C. Penney, Sears and others 'were often beaten and were provided food so inadequate' that some were 'walking skeletons'. The plant of 300 workers, mostly Vietnamese women, belonged to Daewoosa, a Korean apparel manufacturer, before its closure in January 2001. The report stated that 'management admits that they withhold meals from employees as a form of punishment when workers complain about food', and that women employed in the factory accused managers of routinely entering their barracks to watch them shower and dress.[14]

International union coalitions also kept up the pressure on companies to take responsibility for practices in supplying factories. The International Textile, Garment and Leather Workers' Federation (ITGLWF) brings together 250 workers' organisations, representing ten million workers in 130 countries. Their secretariat in Brussels issued a press statement on 24 January 2001 accusing the Chicago-based clothing multinational, Fruit of the Loom, of 'behaving disgracefully' in its treatment of workers in three continents. Condemning the company's activities in the Americas, Europe and Africa, the ITGLWF is now demanding that the company immediately clean up its act and respect international labor standards.

In what appears to be a first action of its kind, the union is lodging a complaint with the ILO to seek a determination as to whether the company's behaviour in its factory in Morocco breaches the Organisation for Economic Cooperation and Development (OECD)'s revamped Guidelines for Multinational Enterprises. (This action was sparked by the dismissal of eight union leaders who had established a union branch at a factory in Rabat, Morocco.)

These continuing cases of labour rights abuses can only add impetus to the social auditing movement and sections of the financial community, who have begun responding to concerns about sweatshops. The head of New York City's US$49 billion pension funds, Alan Hevesi, planned a shareholder resolution offensive in the US Spring in an attempt to persuade 27 US companies to adopt and implement the SA8000 labour practices standard of Social Accountability International (SAI, formerly CEPAA). McDonald's, Starbucks, Wal-Mart, K-Mart, J.C. Penney and Home Depot are among companies facing resolutions on the subject at their annual general meetings.

This support for SA8000, rather than other codes, will be welcome news to the speakers at SAI's conference, who complained about the proliferation of labour codes of conduct. Criticism was led by Michael Goldstein, chairman of Toys 'R' Us and a member of SAI's advisory board.

He argued that, if more companies and organisations develop their own codes, then factories will require numerous inspections, which will be both costly and could lead to confusion and fatigue. Goldstein said the solution was for all parties to work together to agree a single, globally applicable code.

Reasons why SA8000 has not yet reached this position of *de facto* global code probably include the fact that it is not an open membership organisation so that stakeholders in social auditing have found it difficult to influence the process in an open democratic fashion. Another reason preventing more widespread support for the code is that it aims to treat accredited certifiers in the same way, thereby preventing SAI from accrediting, at a reduced charge, small local NGOs to perform inspections.

In January 2001, another social auditing initiative, the Fair Labor Association (FLA) accredited the non-profit Verité to carry out factory inspections for FLA member companies. Verité was subsequently selected by Nike to inspect the Mexico Kukdong factory, scene of a labour dispute over the past months. An FLA university affiliate board member, the Kukdong factory management, Reebok (also an FLA member) and the Worker Rights Consortium (WRC) were also consulted about the choice of Verité. 'Collectively, we have called upon Verité to conduct a thorough and objective audit of Kukdong's practices and report its findings, along with any necessary remediation plan, back to the FLA, factory management, Nike, Reebok, and the general public', read Nike's letter to University presidents.[15]

Verité differs from a number of other social auditing providers, as it is non-profit, seeks to use local auditors, and makes the findings of its audits public. However, social auditing is still a new and highly contested profession, and in February 2001 their first audit of the Kukdong factory was already being questioned by the United Students Against Sweatshops (USAS). USAS complained that, while Verité auditors were present, around 70 workers who attempted to return to work were required to sign their affiliation to a union they did not support, and were then turned away. Nike responded with the information that, under Mexican Law, and the current collective bargaining agreement between the management of Kukdong and the union, the workers must recognise that union in order to be rehired. However, also under Mexican law, workers have the right to seek an election and a new representative union, so they should not have been fired in the first place when they sought to do this. Therefore, the Kukdong case demonstrates both the highly technical and highly political nature of issues such as freedom of association and collective bargaining which social auditors need to deal with.

Recognising both the potential of codes and problems with their implementation and auditing, The ITGLWF announced in February 2001 that it will begin training thousands of garment workers in factories around the world on how to encourage companies to comply with their codes of conduct. The ITGLWF will fund a three-year project to train some 6,000 workers on code compliance.

Also taking action on their concerns about the credibility of labour inspection and social auditing, two labour inspectors, Fernanda Giannasi of Brazil and John Graversgaard of Denmark, launched the Global Labor Inspection Network (GLIN) and began seeking new members. They stated that the network will work to end corruption of labour inspectors; organise independent conferences on the role of labour inspection; support international campaigns on worker health and safety; and monitor multinational corporations.

International Year of Volunteers

2001 has been designated the International Year of Volunteers, and we are already seeing more companies placing volunteers in the community. One such initiative is being piloted by Elena Artal at PricewaterhouseCoopers (PwC). The organisation is working with the Prince of Wales Business Leaders' Forum in the UK to place staff in NGOs such as Save the Children and Ashoka. The participants will spend approximately two months working with the NGOs between June and August 2001. The funding has been found internally, as PwC is 'convinced of the importance of this kind of development for our people'.

Volunteering is not new, of course, and for the past 30 years the United Nations Volunteers (UNV) programme has been placing volunteers throughout the world—currently around 4,400 volunteers of 149 nationalities serving in 139 countries.

Now UNV has teamed up with the UK's New Academy of Business and launched a collaborative inquiry 'to explore current trends in business–community relations, corporate responsibility and volunteering in eight countries: Brazil, Ghana, India, Kazakhstan, Lebanon, Nigeria, the Philippines and South Africa'. Through action research they aim to promote new models of business–community relations and enhanced corporate responsibility practices at the local level in developing and transitional countries. An additional dimension of the project is going to be the active participation of volunteers as partnership facilitators between UNV, business and local communities.

Meanwhile UNV has teamed up with Kraft Foods. In February 2001, Kraft scientists arrived in Kingston, Jamaica, for a two-week volunteer assignment helping the Jamaican Food Technical Institute improve food processing. It is the first in a series of missions around the world in which Kraft employees will work under the United Nations International Short-Term Advisory Resources (UNISTAR) activities of UNV.

2Q2001

April–June

Jem Bendell

Patients pending?

The most high-profile corporate responsibility issue in the first half of 2001 was whether pharmaceutical companies were helping or hindering the treatment of millions of HIV/AIDS sufferers in the South by their pricing and patenting of drugs. Early in 2001 there were signs that this issue was set to explode, with a number of intergovernmental, business and civil groups calling for action. The British development NGO Oxfam launched a 'Cut the Cost' campaign and challenged the largest pharmaceutical company, GlaxoSmithKline, to address the issue of drug pricing responsibly.

Meanwhile, UN Secretary-General Kofi Annan repeatedly raised the issue of AIDS, and, at the World Economic Forum, the President of MTV, William Roedy, joined him in challenging the business community to become more involved in the fight against the HIV/AIDS pandemic. Roedy told *Newsweek* that 'business has been totally inadequate in its efforts'. He added that MTV, which can reach one billion people, could 'create passion among a complacent population'. *Time* magazine became involved, with a cover story on Africa's HIV/AIDS crisis. In their 'You Can Help' section, *Time* pointed readers toward Netaid.org, so they could donate money to AIDS projects. Joshua Cooper Ramo, *Time*'s world editor, said,

> millions of people will die of AIDS in Africa in the next 15 years if the world doesn't start to do something about it. In addition to covering the story, *Time* has renewed its partnership with Netaid.org to deliver solutions that readers can get involved in. It's part of our ongoing commitment to global civic journalism.[2]

On 7 February 2001 the *Boston Globe* reported that the Indian pharmaceutical company Cipla had 'stunned the pharmaceutical industry' when it agreed to dramatically cut the annual price to Médecins Sans Frontières (MSF) of a year's supply of an AIDS drug cocktail to $350. Before the Bombay-based company dropped the price of its generic three-drug anti-retroviral package, the lowest price offered by companies that hold drug patents was around $1,000, while the same AIDS cocktail in the West would cost $10,400. MSF challenged the five pharmaceutical companies involved in the UNAIDS Accelerating Access Initiative to match Cipla's offer, make their prices public, and streamline the implementation process so that drugs can be delivered faster to patients.[2]

MERCK PRESIDENT
RAYMOND GILMARTIN:
CUTTING THE COST OF
AIDS TREATMENT

One month later the global pharmaceutical company Merck announced that it would immediately cut the price of its HIV/AIDS treatments for patients in developing countries. Merck said that the new prices were the lowest ever for the developing world ($600 for Crixivan; $500 for Stocrin) and meant them forfeiting some profits on their sales. Merck President Raymond Gilmartin said their goal was 'to spur efforts to accelerate access to these life-saving medications in those developing countries where the HIV/AIDS epidemic has taken such a widespread and devastating toll'. World Health Organisation (WHO) representative Jon Liden welcomed Merck's move, and suggested it was partly in response to pressure from generic drug manufacturers (such as Cipla).

However, criticism continued, with the director for international health research at the Center for International Development at Harvard University, Amir Attaran, arguing that the lowest-priced annual treatments were still more than the GDP per capita of many countries. There was a need for more companies to be producing AIDS drugs. Thus, the focus shifted to patenting and the regulatory restrictions on the sale of copycat products. Former World Bank economist Joseph Stiglitz suggested that, by not taking action on patents, pharmaceutical executives were effectively saying, 'we don't care if people die; to us intellectual property rights are supreme'. Indian manufacturer Cipla threw the cat among the patents when it announced that it wanted the South African government to let it sell its generic version of eight HIV/AIDS treatments which were only permitted to be sold by the companies that held patents for them. The line had been drawn: patents or patients; profits or people? The question being asked was, 'Which side are you on?'

A fraught week passed when Bristol-Myers Squibb took a step across that line, announcing that it would no longer try to stop generic-drug makers from selling low-cost versions of one of its HIV drugs in Africa (the drug known as 'Zerit'). His company planned to make the drugs available under its existing ACCESS partnership programme with international agencies, including UNAIDS, the World Health Organisation, the World Bank, UNICEF and the UN Population Fund. John L. McGoldrick, executive vice president at Bristol-Myers, argued that the move was not about profits and patents. 'We seek no profits on AIDS drugs in Africa, and we will not let our patents be an obstacle.'

The move was welcomed, while some questioned why Bristol-Myers Squibb was going to the Pretoria High Court with 39 international pharmaceutical companies to challenge a South African law aimed at easing access to AIDS drugs. In its lawsuit, the Pharmaceutical Manufacturers Association of South Africa contended that the law unfairly invalidated patent protections by giving the health minister broad powers to produce—and import more cheaply—generic versions of drugs still under patent.

The fact that more than 4.5 million South Africans are currently infected with HIV, while five of the multinationals suing the government had global sales more than three times South Africa's national budget, was not lost on the world's media. 'It is indefensible for billion-dollar drug companies to take South Africa to court to stop it buying cheap essential medicines,' said Oxfam Policy Director Justin Forsyth. 'This court case demonstrates how powerful drug companies are bullying poor countries just so they can protect their patent rights on life-saving medicines.' It seemed to be a black-and-white story, in more ways than one.[3]

The criticism mounted and within weeks the pharmaceutical industry dramatically dropped its case against the government. Corporate responsibility had become a major concern for the industry, to the extent that the *Financial Times* suggested the companies were fighting a price war as they sought to outbid each other and generic manufacturers to supply cheap AIDS drugs to Africa. This price war reached a significant point when, in June 2001, Pfizer Inc. announced it would offer an antifungal medicine at *no charge* to HIV/AIDS patients in 50 least-developed countries where HIV/AIDS is most prevalent.

Cheaper drugs may help, but Dr Josef Decosas, director of the Southern Africa AIDS Training Program, warned that it would take a major coordinating effort to change the situation. 'Even if you make these drugs available for free, the systems to deliver them are not there . . . they can't even distribute treatments for tuberculosis, which cost $1 a month', he said. 'HIV in Africa is contracted and spread through a web of causations—economic, developmental, social—and when you start focusing on a single solution, like anti-retroviral, you fail.' As employers in Africa have existing administrative systems, it seems they could play a useful role.

In May 2001, companies began taking on this role, when the South African Chamber of Business backed a plan to make low-cost HIV/AIDS treatments widely available to company employees and families. The mining conglomerate Anglo American took the lead, saying that the estimated $4.5 million a year it will need to pay to treat its employees would be offset from savings due to fewer death benefits and less absenteeism.[4] The mining firm employs 160,000 workers in Africa and estimates 20% of them are infected with HIV. The company intends to treat employees and their spouses, which could exceed 50,000 people. The head of their medical programme, Brian Brink, said that purchasing anti-retroviral drugs 'isn't a cost that's going to kill the company, it's a cost that's going to protect the company'.

Recognising the complexity of the problem and the new opportunity for action, UN Secretary-General Kofi Annan called on the pharmaceutical companies to join governments and civil society in the fight against AIDS by participating in a Global AIDS and Health Fund. The aim is to finance prevention measures and health services for HIV/AIDS patients in poorer countries, an endeavour estimated to require $7–10 billion annually.

However, an alliance of NGOs at the annual meeting of the WHO expressed concern that the new fund could serve the interests of the pharmaceutical industry instead of the needs of poor countries. The groups involved in the alliance—Health Action Inter-

UN SECRETARY-GENERAL KOFI
ANNAN: CONTINUES TO
HIGHLIGHT THE AIDS ISSUE

national, Health Gap Coalition, Act Up–Paris and Oxfam UK—argued that commercial interests should have no place in governing the fund. As the companies have no track record in tackling the AIDS problem, this scepticism is to be expected. Proving to be a positive partner for change on the ground is the only counter to the scepticism.

The dispute over AIDS could be the first high-profile battle in the war for drugs. Some companies have realised that the issue of poor people's access to all drugs is 'in range'. Therefore, in a first step beyond AIDS drugs to other serious diseases, Swiss pharmaceutical company Novartis cut the price of a treatment for malaria—a disease estimated to kill around a million people each year. The company will sell Riamet to the WHO for $2 per treatment—about one-tenth of its price elsewhere, and around what the company states is cost price.

Also in range is the issue of regulating intellectual property in a global economy. The AIDS dispute illustrates the ethical dilemmas that can arise when knowledge and its application are held back from those most in need. This raises the question of whether corporate citizens should push for governments and the World Trade Organisation to formalise more rules on Trade Related Intellectual Property (TRIP), or whether they should lobby for the creation of more flexible rules. The current fervour for enforceable TRIP agreements looks certain to set corporations on a collision course with the poor, with civil society and, indeed, with our moral selves. A sustainable global trading system should support executives and investors in meeting their own moral bottom line. Otherwise, moral outrage could risk the very concept of patenting itself.

The increasing instances of companies deciding not to enforce their intellectual property rights for drugs in developing countries can be welcomed. However, this will mean pharmaceutical companies have even less of a commercial interest in such countries than they do at the moment. This is important as these companies finance the majority of research into drug treatments. Currently, only 10% of medicines in development are for diseases that afflict those in developing countries.[5]

GlaxoSmithKline (GSK) announced in June 2001 that it intended to tackle these difficult issues. It published *Facing the Challenge*, a report summarising the company's emerging contribution and commitment to improving the health and well-being of people living in the developing world.[6] Calling for greater collaboration, Jean-Pierre Garnier, GSK's CEO, said, 'If the health of the developing world is to improve, then all sectors of our global society—governments and international agencies, as well as the private sector—must work together in new kinds of partnership, backed by significant funding.' The company has established a Corporate Social Responsibility Committee, which is chaired by Sir Richard Sykes, non-executive chairman, GSK, to advise the board on issues of significance in the relationship between the company and society, and will keep the company's policy on healthcare in the developing world under review.

Just money?

Research published in May 2001 suggested that company performance on social and environmental issues was already holding greater sway on the decisions of investment analysts, although institutional investors still need some persuading. A report commissioned by the UK company-led group, Business in the Environment (BiE), showed that a third of analysts judge environmental factors to be 'quite or very important' when evaluating companies—a sizeable increase from 1994 when only a fifth claimed the same. The figures for social issues have increased by an even greater margin, from an eighth to a third of analysts seeing them as important over the same period.

However, the report, *Investing in the Future*, showed that only a fifth of investors identified environmental and social factors when asked to consider specifically non-financial indicators. Derek Higgs, chairman of BiE, thought, 'this survey shows that an appreciation of corporate environmental and social responsibility has grown in the City, and that the integration of economic, social and environmental strategies is valued'.[7]

DEREK HIGGS: BIE'S REPORT IS
ENCOURAGING

A new toolkit for pension fund trustees and fund managers was launched in May 2001, to provide advice on how to improve the impact of pension fund investment on people in the poorest countries in the world. Funded by the UK's National Lottery, *Just Pensions* sets out clearly how to design and implement a socially responsible investment (SRI) policy through positive engagement between pension funds and the companies they invest in. Checklists of sample questions for trustees and fund managers, and useful answers to questions about the legal implications of SRI, are included. Project coordinator Duncan Green said there has been a desperate need for 'clear guidance on best practice in areas such as labour standards, human rights and corruption'.

Just Pensions is the result of collaboration between pensions professionals and NGOs specialising in development issues. Managed by War on Want and Traidcraft Exchange, with an advisory group of experts from the investment world and NGOs, it is the latest example of the 'new frontier' of relations between business and NGOs outlined by Rob Lake and Jem Bendell in the book *Terms for Endearment*.[8] Formerly with the NGO Traidcraft Exchange but now working with the investment company Henderson, Rob Lake is one of many NGO staff who have been taking positions in the financial sector as SRI grows.

An established player in SRI, the Domini Social Equity Fund caused a stir when it sold all of its 1.2 million shares in the retailer Wal-Mart. Firm president Amy Domini said that Wal-Mart was removed primarily because the company has refused to implement a monitoring system for the overseas factories that supply its inventory. A report from Domini states that the firm, along with a coalition of investors from the Interfaith Center on Corporate Responsibility (ICCR), approached Wal-Mart's management about using a third-party monitoring system for its factories, and Wal-Mart finally rejected the idea.

FTSE, the UK-based stock market index firm, introduced four new indices that 'may help establish a global standard for socially responsible investments'. The four indices, named FTSE4Good, will consist of a tradable and a benchmark index for each of four geographical areas: the UK, Europe, the US and the rest of the world. The UK and European indices went live in June 2001. According to FTSE, FTSE4Good is grounded in the principles put forth by global conventions on business conduct. Examples of such conventions include the Coalition for Environmentally Responsible Economies (Ceres), the UN Global Compact and the Organisation for Economic Cooperation and Development (OECD) Guidelines for Multinational Enterprises.

'We want it to be a step towards encouraging companies to adopt socially responsible principles', said Mark Makepeace, FTSE Chief Executive, at a news conference. Makepeace also announced that licensing fees from the indices, estimated to be $1 million in the first year, would be donated to the United Nations Children's Fund (UNICEF). FTSE will evaluate a company's commitment to social responsibility by examining performance in three areas: minimising damage to the environment, supporting and protecting human rights, and fostering good relations with a full range of stakeholders.[9]

For a number of years groups concerned about corporate responsibility issues have tabled motions at annual general meetings that call on the company to explain or abandon existing policy. One such case came when Friends of the Earth took its campaign against the Ilusu Dam in Turkey to the boardroom by purchasing US$43,000-worth of shares in the construction company Balfour Beatty in order to submit a resolution challenging the company's board to show that they care about their reputation and about their environmental and social performance.[10] Resolutions such as this rarely pass, and often campaigners regard 10% of shareholders voting in favour as a success. Yet these tactics seems to be having an increasing effect, behind the scenes.

SocialFunds.com reported that many companies have been responding to shareholder resolutions on social and environmental issues, even before they reached AGMs. In 2001, shareholder resolutions concerning equal opportunities and other employment issues have been particularly successful. These included resolutions on the disclosure of employment data, sexual orientation-based discrimination policy, glass ceilings, workplace violence, and policies concerning employees with disabilities.

For example, Walden Asset Management filed a resolution with American International Group (AIG), an insurance and financial services company, on policies to eliminate bias based on sexual orientation. The resolution was withdrawn when AIG agreed to adopt and implement a written equal employment opportunity policy barring discrimination on the basis of sexual orientation.[11] A resolution regarding glass ceilings was filed with Newell Rubbermaid, by Calvert Asset Management, but was withdrawn because 'Newell has committed to promoting women and minorities from within, and is now considering publishing a diversity report that would illustrate all of the company's programs', explained Nikki Daruwala, a Senior Social Research Analyst at Calvert.[12]

Calvert was also in the news for its work with the World Resources Institute (WRI). Referring to the WRI report, *Coming Clean: Corporate Disclosure of Financially Significant Environmental Risks*, they called on the US Securities and Exchange Commission (SEC) to strengthen its enforcement of rules intended to protect investors. Currently, the SEC's guidelines and rules require companies to report not only information about current conditions affecting the firm, but also any known risks and uncertainties that are likely to have future significant financial effects. 'Few companies do a good job of reporting on environmental liabilities and risks. Our research shows that companies with significantly different environmental performance and risks are often indistinguishable from each other when evaluated by their annual reports. This lack of transparency could pose a heightened risk for investors', said Dr Julie Fox Gorte, Calvert's senior environmental and technology analyst[13] (see 'Money fashions change' on page 97).

Reporting rights

One notable success for shareholder activism was when the board of the Canadian oil company Talisman agreed to commission a social report on its activities in the Sudan. The East African country is caught in a civil war, and there has been criticism of government attacks on the south of the country, which Christian Aid argues is motivated by their desire to control the oil reserves there. A variety of human rights groups have criticised the oil companies Talisman, TotalFinaElf, OMV, Lundin and BP (via PetroChina) for aiding the government's military effort through their direct or indirect involvement in oil exploitation in Sudan.[14]

In 2001, Talisman published its social report on Sudan to mixed reaction. Using an approach pioneered by The Body Shop *Values Report* in 1995, Talisman published comments from a range of stakeholders, both positive and critical. The comments were chosen by consultants from PricewaterhouseCoopers (PwC) as reflecting the views of stakeholders. For example, on the key issue of whether Talisman should pull out of the Sudan, two opposing views were presented. A Church leader, from the capital Khartoum, was quoted as saying: 'we the churches actually feel that the oil exploration should be suspended until peace is achieved'. As counterweight, the director of a Nairobi-based international NGO operating in Southern Sudan was quoted as saying: 'If you pressure Talisman to leave Sudan then will the remaining actors take any action to address these critical issues? At least Talisman have taken notice and responded.'

Representing stakeholder views in this way is an interesting device, although it raises the issue of the legitimacy of the quoted stakeholders, in terms of their own accountability and independence from commercial interests. In the specific example quoted above, the level and nature of community embeddedness and responsiveness of a Church group and an international NGO would be different. Presenting opposing views in this way gives the impression that there is a legitimate debate, so it is not a neutral device. More information on the stakeholders is required.

Talisman's report chronicled some important social development work. However, in May 2001, Amnesty International (AI) released a statement criticising the report for 'underplaying the serious violations being perpetrated' and thereby 'not accurately reflecting the overall human rights situation'. They pointed to confirmation that, in spite of Talisman's advocacy against the use of oil infrastructure for offensive military purposes, there were four instances of non-defensive usage of the airstrip at Talisman's operations in Heglig, in 2000. An independently funded investigation in April by journalist John Ryle and the international human rights lawyer Georgette Gagnon concluded that military usage had been 'considerably higher'—and that it continues. The investigation determined that at least two of the governments' helicopter gunships are based at Talisman oil facilities in Heglig. 'Defecting soldiers from the Government of Sudan army base in Heglig and civilian victims of gunship attacks testified to investigators that gunships have flown regular sorties from Heglig to attack civilian settlements', they report.

The key issue for many critics is whether the companies should continue operating in the country when the revenues the government obtains from oil operations are funding their war effort. Talisman respond that 'the expenditure by a sovereign government of its revenues is an issue that the company has limited ability to address', and cite some examples of their advocacy efforts to encourage the government not to use oil revenues for military purposes. However, groups such as Christian Aid and AI argue that all oil companies should freeze their Sudanese operations now, as they believe this will make the government listen to calls for peace. As the companies involved have yet to respond in this way, the NGOs have called for more action by governments where the multinational corporations are headquartered, in order to make them act on human rights.

In June 2001, US House of Representatives passed the Sudan Peace Act [H.R. 2052]. The Act requires companies wishing to raise capital in the US for operations in Sudan to enhance their reporting requirements, specifically to disclose their relationship to violations of human rights in Sudan. Africa Subcommittee Chairman Ed Royce explained: 'This report will be a valuable tool in alerting American investors to the nature of their potential investment. This should serve as a deterrent to foreign companies raising money on US markets for oil development activities in Sudan' (see 'Anti-globalisation: now it's your business' on page 91).

In May 2001 Premier Oil also published a social report on its operations in Burma (Myanmar). This is a country under a military regime where, according to The Burma Campaign (UK), eight million people, including children, are used as forced labour each year, with the threat of torture, murder and rape, and where one million others have been forcibly displaced from their homes.[15]

The leader of the elected government, Nobel Peace Laureate Aung San Suu Kyi, under house arrest for years, had asked Premier and other companies to leave the country, in order to cut funding to the military dictatorship. Her call was backed by the UK government, where this relatively small oil company is headquartered. In a similar fashion to Talisman, the company downplays this issue, with their manager of corporate responsibility Richard Jones arguing that 'it's not our company's role to question the money going to the government or what use it makes of it'. Instead, the report, researched and written by the consultancy EQ Management, and reviewed by Warwick Business School's Corporate Citizenship Unit, focuses on the impact of the company on communities living near the oil pipeline—who were consulted by researchers hired by the company. Warwick's review argues that the repressive environment 'unavoidably compromises the ability of Premier Oil's community stakeholders to be fully expressive' (see 'International perspectives at Warwick' on page 85).

The business case for social reporting stems from its place within a process of building positive stakeholder relations. By ruling out the key issue of funding dictatorships on the one hand, and attempting dialogue with threatened communities on the other, this report might not facilitate this goal. Instead, the report has brought renewed attacks on the company, in the mainstream media such as the *Financial Times*. Premier's efforts do not appear to satisfy the principles of inclusivity and relevance, nor uninhibited stakeholder dialogue, set out in the Institute of Social and Ethical Account-Ability's (ISEA), AA1000 standard.[16] However, the media attention attracted by these contentious reports should concern the wider social auditing and reporting community, as it risks the reputation of the emergent profession. Professional bodies such as ISEA will need to show leadership in communicating what is and what is not acceptable in this field, and rapidly implement procedures for accreditation, peer review and complaints.

Unfortunately, Sudan and Burma are not unusual as countries where profits are being used to fund conflict (directly or via tax). In May 2001, Global Witness announced that investigations have found that profits from the Liberian timber trade have been financing the conflict in Sierra Leone, and called for an embargo (China and France are the top importers of Liberian timber).[17] This follows the controversy surrounding the diamond trade with Sierra Leone, and the campaign by Amnesty International for the industry leaders Hoge Raad voor Diamant of Antwerp and the De Beers group to take effective measures to develop a tamper-proof system to prevent 'conflict diamonds' from entering the international market.

The seriousness of these issues makes it important that the UN Global Compact has prioritised work on business in conflict zones. In addition, UN Secretary-General Kofi Annan has asked Undersecretary General for Africa Ibrahim Gambari to work with oil firms to push the peace process forward in another war-torn country, Angola. 'What we are saying [to them] is be an ally in the peace process', Gambari said in a Reuters interview. He said oil companies operating in Angola could contribute to peace efforts because they have 'leverage on the government', adding that 'the government will listen to them'.

Governments have also been encouraging oil companies to take a lead on these issues, although not through regulation, as the NGOs Christian Aid and Amnesty International have been calling for. One initiative involved seven leading oil and mining companies signing a voluntary code of conduct on human rights issued jointly by the UK Foreign Office and the US State Department. The principles, which seek to curb abuses at facilities in developing countries, require companies to observe the UN Declaration on Human Rights, to recognise the importance of business support for human rights, and to be open about their actions and experiences.

The new code was the product of 18 months of discussions between the companies, NGOs and the two governments, making it the first instance of the three sectors agreeing a code for ethical corporate conduct. The seven include US oil companies Texaco, Chevron and Conoco, and BP Amoco and Shell from the UK. ExxonMobil, the largest oil producer, has yet to endorse the principles. Mining groups Rio Tinto and Freeport-McMoRan have also endorsed the principles. Amnesty International welcomed the development, but said only mandatory codes would ensure compliance. It added that 'companies need to recognise that guidelines like this are only credible if they are enforceable'. However, John Bray, a consultant at security specialists Control Risks Group, said NGOs could be expected to enforce the code. 'If companies publicly subscribe to these principles, then they can be held accountable', he said.[18]

State-of-the-art reporting?

To those who have been observing the move towards social and environmental reporting during the early years of the 21st century, the name of Novo Nordisk will be familiar. This Danish company has taken a lead on corporate social responsibility practice and reporting. Now de-merged into Novozymes and Novo Nordisk under the overall Novo Group, the company has released its year 2000 report, *Values in a Global Con - text*.[19] Novo Group's approach to its social responsibilities begins with its Charter that 'company activities, practices and deliverables are perceived to be economically viable, environmentally sound and socially fair'.

There were two types of assurance given for the report. First, there was assurance by Deloitte & Touche that the quantitative statements are correct. Second, there was a type of 'civil assurance' for the relevance, completeness of the report and the process behind its production, given by Simon Zadek, chair of ISEA. Key points of contention could relate to Novo's biotechnology work, its use of animal experimentation, and its position as a pharmaceutical company (see above).

However, when reading the report these issues seem buried. Although the company consulted with stakeholders, it is difficult to see who was contacted, how they were contacted, who refused to participate and what the range of views on controversial subjects was. Although the company refers to the concept of accountability throughout the report, one could argue that the accountability of those who give assurance could be open to some question.

While Novo Group might be satisfying the few experts in the emerging field of social reporting, this report does not appear to satisfy the dual objectives of risk management and innovation through dialogue. Could an investor be sure that Novo Group is well placed to reduce the risk to its reputation by satisfying stakeholders, or well placed to innovate products and processes by having positive relations with these stakeholders? It is not certain from this report. As social and sustainability reporting continues to evolve, what is not included in such reports is likely to be a source of growing debate.

Although a number of criticisms can be made of Talisman's and Novo's reports, the fact that they have reported on social issues is a major step forward—a step that the

vast majority of companies have not yet taken. The UK-based Industrial Society estimated in their report, *Corporate Nirvana: Is the Future Socially Responsible?*, that only
4% of FTSE 350 companies report on their social performance.

The need to mainstream social and environmental reporting highlights the importance of the Global Reporting Initiative (GRI). As the earlier news about pharmaceuticals and AIDS, oil companies and conflict illustrates, many corporate responsibility
issues are highly contentious. Therefore, reporting protocols need to be developed in
a way that satisfies a wide range of stakeholder views. The GRI's multi-sectoral approach
has been hailed as key to its progress. In Nairobi, Kenya, at the opening session of the
Governing Council of the United Nations Environment Programme (UNEP), UNEP
Executive Director Klaus Töpfer told national representatives, including ministers and
senior government officials from more than 150 countries, that the United Nations'
relationship with Ceres and the rapid progress of the GRI should be viewed as leading
examples of how successful partnerships with civil society can create international
change[20] (see 'Reporting developments' on page 94).

UNEP EXECUTIVE DIRECTOR
KLAUS TÖPFER: GRI SETS AN EXAMPLE FOR
BUSINESS–CIVIL SOCIETY PARTNERSHIP

How might governments support voluntary corporate responsibility initiatives? A
first step is to specify them in their contracts with companies. GRI reported what it
believed to be the first specification of its Guidelines in a legal contract. Wisconsin
Electric (a private US utility) and the Wisconsin Department of Natural Resources (a
government agency) signed an Environmental Cooperative Agreement which, among
other things, requires Wisconsin Electric to prepare an annual environmental performance report in accordance with GRI's Sustainability Reporting Guidelines. As part of
the agreement, Wisconsin Electric must demonstrate measurable improvements on a
variety of criteria, and in return will benefit from more flexible regulation.[21]

Industrial relations goes global

The history of industrial relations has, in many parts of the world, been characterised
by confrontation. In the last couple of years, however, the possibility of a new era of
collaborative global industrial relations has come into view. New framework agreements are being signed by multinationals and international federations of trade
unions. These agreements allow unions to deal with corporations at a global level on
the basis of common principles, including fundamental workers' rights that are incor-

porated in the core conventions of the International Labour Organisation. Among the international union organisations that have reached such agreements are the International Union of Food, Agricultural, Hotel, Restaurant, Catering, Tobacco and Allied Workers' Associations (IUF), Union Network International (UNI), and the International Federation of Building and Wood Workers (IFBWW).

One of the earliest agreements was signed between the oil company Statoil and the International Federation of Chemical, Energy, Mine and General Workers' Unions (ICEM) This was renegotiated in 2001 to incorporate principles contained in the UN Global Compact. Statoil operates in 23 countries worldwide, and employs about 16,000 people. The pact with ICEM 'makes good business sense', said Geir Westgaard, a Statoil vice president. Complying with and furthering the Global Compact in cooperation with trade unions 'is part of securing our "licence" to operate internationally', he said. 'If you are in business in challenging areas of the world, you absolutely want and need to act ethically, sustainably and socially responsibly.' Reflecting on the huge challenge of integrating values and principles into everyday business practice across the globe, he noted that 'the unions as well as the NGOs are globe-spanning knowledge-based organisations . . . They give us early warning of problems we should be aware of, and allow us to take early action to mitigate risks.'

Jim Baker, director of the Department of Multinational Enterprises Organising and Recruitment at the International Confederation of Trade Unions (ICFTU), noted that, 'in a little over a year, we have gone from two framework agreements between international trade secretariats and multinational companies to nine'. Suggesting that this is the beginning of a new collaborative era of global industrial relations, Mr Baker said that, 'just a few years ago, only a few corporations would have been willing to seriously discuss anything with unions at the international level'.

Earth Summit preparations

In April 2001 the chairman of Shell, Sir Mark Moody-Stuart, launched a new initiative aimed at rallying the collective forces of world business in the lead-up to 2002's Earth Summit, which is taking place in Johannesburg ten years after the first summit in Rio de Janeiro.[22] At a press conference in the United Nations, Sir Mark unveiled 'Business Action for Sustainable Development' (BASD)—a new initiative he said would provide a focal point for business preparations. He said that 'many of us in business believe

CHAIRMAN OF
SHELL, MARK
MOODY-STUART:
UNVEILED
'BUSINESS
ACTION FOR
SUSTAINABLE
DEVELOPMENT'

we have come a long way since [the First Earth Summit in] Rio. We want to now take a seat at the table, listen to what other members of society have to say and discover what role we have to play in the development and delivery of a sustainable future.'

The BASD is a joint initiative of the International Chamber of Commerce (ICC) and the World Business Council for Sustainable Development (WBCSD), which was established for the first Earth Summit by Stephan Schmidheiny.

WBCSD FOUNDER
STEPHAN
SCHMIDHEINY

Not everyone welcomed this news; there were those concerned that companies with interests in fossil fuels might undermine the process. The NGO CorpWatch warned that the BASD would be scrutinised and monitored by NGOs concerned with corporate influence at the UN. 'These are the same discredited companies that attempted to greenwash themselves at the first Earth Summit in Rio, and have been slowing environmental progress ever since', said Kenny Bruno, UN Project Coordinator for CorpWatch. Sir Mark recognised that there would be some scepticism, and suggested that, 'by acknowledging that a future built on sustainable development is very much in the interests of business, people will realise that there's an element of self-interest and hopefully a lot of the suspicion will flow away.'

With the Kyoto agreement now in hot water following the Bush administration's decision to refuse ratification, climate change will be a primary concern for the Earth Summit. The fact that the business contribution will be headed by an oil executive won't help convince critics that business will support the action needed. 'It is especially ironic that a Shell executive is taking this role, because through its actions Shell became a symbol of environmental destruction and complicity in human rights violations in the 1990s', said Victoria Corpuz, Executive Director of Tebtebba Foundation, an indigenous organisation based in the Philippines. Kenny Bruno said: 'If they want us to believe they have become part of the solution, they will have to prove it.'[23]

While Shell's leadership on social and environmental issues raises questions, another company's lack of leadership has placed it on the hit-list of groups concerned about climate change. Seen as a major funder and influencer of the Bush presidency, Exxon is being blamed for the US administration's refusal to ratify Kyoto. While George Bush witnessed protests from climate activists across Europe in June 2001, the groups Greenpeace, Friends of the Earth and People & Planet jointly launched a boycott of Esso (the consumer brand of Exxon in Europe). Will the impact of StopEsso.com make companies aware of their wider responsibilities before making political donations in the future?

3Q2001

July–September

Jem Bendell

Compact news

The Global Compact, a UN programme intended to help businesses become better corporate citizens, celebrated its first anniversary on 26 July with more than 300 corporate partners, up from 44 at its launch. New UN Assistant Secretary-General Michael Doyle outlined the idea is to use the Global Compact website as the foundation for a learning network where companies can share best practices on CSR. 'It's going to be a genuine learning exchange', he said. Earlier in the month his predecessor, John Ruggie, explained to Warwick University, UK's 4th Annual Corporate Citizenship Conference the plans for the Global Compact Learning Forum, to be based at the university. Professor Ruggie explained that the Compact 'has explicitly adopted a learning approach to inducing corporate change, as opposed to a regulatory approach'. More of his thoughts are summarised under 'International perspectives at Warwick' on page 85.

After the anniversary, it became clear that some environmental and human rights groups were disappointed that the Global Compact would not be doing more than acting as a learning forum. 'Viewing the program solely as a learning experience represents a wasted opportunity in assuring corporate responsibility,' said Arvind Ganesan, the director of business and human rights programmes for Human Rights Watch. 'The progress we expected on moving beyond just a learning forum hasn't occurred yet.'

While the analysed process of reviewing case studies submitted by signatory companies will be by Warwick University's Corporate Citizenship Unit and staff at MIT, some NGOs have produced their own analyses of the conduct of those companies. The website CorpWatch offered a series of case studies, starting with a study of Aventis, the biotech firm whose StarLink genetically modified corn was found to have strayed into the food supply. CorpWatch argued that this meant Aventis violated the Global Compact's precautionary principle, which implies that no products should be marketed if effects on health and the environment are unknown. More case studies are promised in the coming months.[1]

In addition to its learning role, the Global Compact is also proving to be a mechanism for involving corporations in intergovernmental conferences on social and environmental issues. For example, in August 2001 United Nations Secretary-General Kofi Annan and United Nations High Commissioner for Human Rights Mary Robinson

hosted a panel at the World Conference Against Racism to discuss the impact of racism and discrimination in the workplace. The dialogue sought to draw attention to private-sector initiatives that promote equality and inclusion in and out of the workplace. Participants included representatives of Volvo Car Corporation, the International Confederation of Free Trade Unions, Eskom (South Africa), Satyam Computer Services (India), the United Nations Environment Programme and the International Labour Organisation.[2] Kofi Annan was 'encouraged by the commitment of Compact participants who have agreed to throw their considerable weight behind the cause of diversity and non-discrimination'.

One company that had come under fire on racism and diversity issues announced a $7.8 billion minorities programme. Toyota Motor Corporation was attacked in the US by Rev. Jesse Jackson following an advertisement that was accused of being racially offensive. The funds will add new minority-run dealerships each year and increase spending on minority advertising, job training and community support. The announcement puts flesh on the deal reached between the company and Jackson earlier in the year to avoid a threatened boycott against the car-maker.

Climate for change

In the heat of July 2001 in Germany, delegates managed to agree to proceed with the climate-cooling Kyoto Protocol, without the world's biggest polluter, the United States. As the ink was drying, the protocol was already creating heated debate within the business community, especially in large organisations where parent companies and subsidiaries had opposing views. For example, Swedish auto-maker Volvo publicly supported Kyoto while its parent company in the US, Ford, did not. Coca-Cola, like Ford, belongs to the US Council for International Business, which opposed Kyoto. But Coca-Cola's subsidiary in Spain endorsed the treaty. Pedro Antonio Garcia, from the Spanish subsidiary, said, 'You cannot operate if you are against the Kyoto Protocol in a European context. It's the price of entry.'

In the US, Executive Vice President of the National Association of Manufacturers (NAM), Michael Baroody, wrote to George W. Bush, 'thanking' him for his opposition to the agreement. 'On behalf of 14,000 member companies of the NAM—and the 18 million people who make things in America—thank you for your opposition to the Kyoto Protocol on the grounds that it exempts 80 percent of the world and will cause serious harm to the United States.'[3] Baroody made selective use of statistics. He calculates 80% based on population, not total carbon emissions, 25% of which are produced by just 4% of the world's population living in the United States.

When President Bush dismissed the Kyoto climate change treaty as 'fatally flawed', he meant to spare companies such as the members of NAM from paying to control pollution. But, now that about 180 countries have pushed ahead without the US, some American businesses with overseas operations are left wondering if they've missed out on a commercial opportunity. This is because that, under the treaty, companies that reduce their own emissions of greenhouse gases can sell credits to other companies whose emissions are growing. Although criticised by many environmentalists as letting big business off the hook, this new system means that money will be made from reducing carbon emissions.[4]

No wonder, then, that a new initiative established to help companies express their support for the Kyoto Protocol had generated significant support. Signatory companies of Emission55.com 'call on the governments of the world to ensure the entry into force no later than 2002 of the Kyoto Protocol. This will require ratification of the Protocol by at least 55 countries responsible for 55% of the carbon dioxide (CO_2) emissions from industrialised countries.' A diverse range of companies have already signed, including Otto Versand, Ricoh and the Credit Suisse Group.[5]

Meanwhile, the world's largest oil group, ExxonMobil, which trades as Esso in many European countries, was beginning to show signs of concern over the StopEsso.com campaign. ExxonMobil is considered a big influence on the Bush administration because, critics say, it helped bankroll the Bush presidential race to the White House. The StopEsso.com campaign widened to include Germany, Norway and New Zealand as well as Britain, where it started. While ExxonMobil representative Lauren Kerr stated that the company did not expect a significant impact, a spokesman for Esso UK told the *Guardian* newspaper that they were 'concerned about the boycott'. The newspaper reported that the company was planning a public relations strategy to try to 'win back customers'.[6] Their strategists might want to look at a new survey that found some 80% of adults take corporate responsibility into account when making purchasing decisions, and 70% do so when making investment decisions.[7] As The Body Shop began daubing 'StopEsso' straplines on company trucks, corporate lines were also being drawn.

The problem, of course, is that different people have different social and environmental concerns. In its September 2001 issue, the US-based *Sierra* magazine assessed the environmentalists' best choices for green gasoline companies. The article ranked oil and gas companies not just on the climate change issue, but on a range of human rights and environmental commitments and practices. The key issue for *Sierra* was some companies' plans to drill in the Arctic National Wildlife Refuge, leading to BP, Chevron, Phillips Petroleum and, yes, ExxonMobil, being named the 'Dirty Four'.[8] Corporate beauty, it seems, is in the eye of the beholder.

Humane resources

It's one thing to focus on consumer and investor concerns; but perhaps equally important is how company staff feel and react to their employer's position and performance on social and environmental issues. *Business Ethics* magazine reported that companies making job offers to prospective employees might find themselves faced with questions about the firm's environmental commitments. A growing number of employees—nearly 100,000—have signed up to the activist website Ecopledge.com, making a commitment to reject job offers at corporations that 'fail to take specific, positive environmental actions identified by Ecopledge.com researchers'. Among the steps identified are stopping the sale of polluting products, increasing recycling, and ending controversial developments. Companies targeted by Ecopledge include Boise Cascade, BP Amoco, Coca-Cola, Citigroup, DaimlerChrysler, Dell, Disney, Nestlé, PricewaterhouseCoopers, Sprint and Staples.

Further reinforcement of this trend came with publication of the third annual POLLARA survey for the Women's Executive Network which showed that the most important factor attracting women executives to an employer is the organisation's ethical conduct. The organisation, Canada's largest public opinion and marketing research forum, found that women placed ethics ahead of other factors such as the quality of the organisation's leadership, the quality of its products and services, its overall reputation, and remuneration.

So it seems that many professionals do need a purpose for the paycheque. For example, Nick Wright of UBS Warburg, the investment banking division of UBS, told the Warwick Corporate Citizenship Conference that 50% of all applicants asked about corporate responsibility during their interviews. And a survey of 255 UK employees by the Industrial Society found that more than half claimed to have chosen the company they work for because they 'believe in what it does and what it stands for'. Study author Stephanie Draper, head of corporate social responsibility at the society, said a tight UK employment market is putting pressure on companies to become 'employers of choice'. (Despite fears of a recession in the US, the labour market in the West remains tight, especially for highly skilled individuals.) The findings 'challenge prevailing recruitment and retention strategies which centre on pay and benefits,' she added. 'Other priorities such as ethics and reputation are now playing a more important role.' It is therefore no surprise that Lifeworth.com reported high uptake in its new *CSRJobs Bulletin*, which lists job opportunities in the corporate responsibility field. It reached over 1,000 subscribers within a month of launching its service.[9]

SRI 'R' Us

Socially responsible investment (SRI) research bodies from 12 countries joined forces to provide data on companies' social and environmental performance for institutional investors. The Sustainable Investment Research International (SiRi) group explained that it will offer standardised profiles of the largest 500 global companies as well as SRI consultancy services. SiRi will have a combined total of 100 researchers to draw from, who will focus on environmental performance, employment practices, customer relations, community involvement, governance standards and supply chains. The group spent the previous year standardising the research practices of its members, who will pool their research on companies in the FTSE Eurotop 300 index, Standard & Poor's 100 in the US, and 100 Canadian and Japanese corporations. Each member will continue to research its respective national markets. The partners are: Kinder Lydenberg Domini from the USA, AReSE (France), CentreInfo (Switzerland), Caring Company (Sweden), Scoris (Germany), Triodos Bank (Netherlands), Michael Janzi Associates (Canada), Avanzi (Italy), ECodes (Spain), Stock at Stake (Belgium), the Sustainable Investment Research Institute (Australia) and the Pensions Investment Research Centre (UK). The plan is that they will be joined by a Japanese partner.[10]

Indications that interest in SRI is growing in Japan came when the first Japanese bank signed up to a United Nations statement on sustainable development. By signing the UN Environment Programme (UNEP)'s 'Statement by Financial Institutions on the Environment and Sustainable Development', the Development Bank of Japan (DBJ) committed itself to a 'precautionary approach' to environmental management. The statement, set up in 1992, also requires the state-owned bank to recognise that 'sustainable development depends upon a positive interaction between economic growth and environmental protection'. Most of the 171 financial institutions that have signed to date are European, so UNEP hopes that DBJ's lead will increase the number of Asian signatories. Deputy governor of DBJ, Takashi Matsukawa, said the bank would help UNEP to get other financial institutions in Asia involved.[11]

Efforts such as this, aimed at increasing the profile of SRI in the South are important. Given the limited experience and capacity the South has in this field, it is understandable yet regrettable that no Southern groups are involved in the SiRi initiative at this stage. Although the key financial centres are in the North, most quoted companies have extensive operations in the South, where their positive and negative impacts need to be researched, analysed and prioritised by independent and informed local people. As investors' interest in information that is credible to a broad range of local and global stakeholders grows, so this may become a more serious issue (see 'Money fashions change' on page 97).

Branding criticism

Echoing concerns from leaders in the private sector that NGOs are sometimes too quick to condemn companies that begin working on corporate responsibility, a representative of Amnesty International (AI) called on NGOs to give the benefit of the doubt when companies make public statements about their aspirations on human rights. Writing in the third *Visions of Ethical Business*, edited by Warwick Business School's Malcolm McIntosh, AI's business group manager Peter Frankental argued that 'when a company associates itself with values of any kind it is often making a statement of how it wishes to be perceived, rather than of what it actually does'. This, he explained, 'creates a gap between aspirations and reality . . . which causes many NGOs to dismiss aspirational statements as a public relations exercise'. He warned that, if NGOs reject a company's aspirational statements, they risk 'throwing the baby out with the bath water', as before a company can integrate social values into its operations it must develop the aspiration to do so. Considering the importance of corporate reputation and branding, Frankental suggested that 'a company that ties its flag to the mast of human rights is offering a hostage to fortune. If it fails to deliver on its stated commitments, its credibility will be at stake.'[12]

This issue arose at a seminar on corporate power and globalisation hosted by Respect Europe. Delegates from NGOs and corporations discussed how NGOs are often dependent on the media for communicating their message, and that this can affect the way they talk about companies. To be heard, NGOs must brand themselves and their criticisms as much as companies brand themselves and their products or services. Hypocrisy is a better story than mere malpractice, so NGOs and activists may find it easier to attract media attention if they focus on those companies that say they are addressing the issues.[13] This reveals the complexity involved with communicating corporate responsibility policies, and the importance of developing understanding with NGOs.

The politics of partnership

In July, August and September of 2001, a spate of publications appeared that analysed the proliferation of corporate codes of conduct. In a new book from the Carnegie Endowment for International Peace, Virginia Haufler explores codes of conduct across three different policy arenas: environment, labour and information privacy.[14] She identifies the common driving forces for, challenges to and questions from the increasing application of voluntary codes of conduct. In the magazine *Foreign Policy*, an article described an emerging 'NGO–industrial complex' constituted by businesses and NGOs working together on ethical codes of conduct and certification.[15] 'While certification will never replace the state, it is quickly becoming a powerful tool for promoting worker rights and protecting the environment in an era of free trade', argue Gary Gereffi, Ronie Garcia-Johnson and Erika Sasser.

The UN Research Institute for Social Development (UNRISD) previously theorised these relationships as forms of 'civil regulation'—the quasi-regulation of business by civil society.[16] It followed up this work with a new report welcoming developments in corporate codes of conduct and certification, but warning of the 'danger that codes may be seen as something more than they really are'. Report author Rhys Jenkins cautions that they 'can be used to deflect criticism and reduce the demand for external regulation. They can also undermine the position of trade unions in the workplace.' He argues 'how vitally important it now is to develop strategies to ensure that codes are complementary to government legislation and provide space for workers to organise'.[17] A new report funded by the Aspen Institute's Nonprofit Sector Research Fund suggests that NGO involvement in codes of conduct and certification can be challenging and lead to conflict within civil society. The report chronicles both the difficulties and successes faced by Rainforest Alliance in certifying Chiquita Brands International plantations with its Eco-OK scheme.

Collaborative relations between the private sector, governments and NGOs is the subject of a new report from the World Bank's Business Partners for Development (BPD) project. *Endearing Myths, Enduring Truths* draws on partnership examples in natural resources, water and sanitation, road safety and youth development, to argue that tri-sector partnerships 'benefit the long-term interests of the business sector while meeting the social objectives of civil society and the state by helping to create stable social and financial environments'.[18] The World Bank's BPD is one of a number of organisations promoting the concept of inter-sectoral partnership. In the UK, the International Business Leaders Forum (IBLF) launched the 'Partnership Brokers' website, which is

DANISH PRIME MINISTER POUL NYRUP RASMUSSEN:
EUROPE IS IN A UNIQUE POSITION TO MOVE FORWARD
IN IMPLEMENTING PUBLIC–PRIVATE PARTNERSHIPS

intended to act as a resource for partnership-building. In the US, new specialist agencies have appeared in this field. The Copenhagen Centre is also actively promoting the idea of inter-sectoral partnership.

At the end of June 2001, 400 people from all sectors gathered in Copenhagen to hear Danish Prime Minister Poul Nyrup Rasmussen's speech on 'Partnerships and Social Responsibility in the New Economy'. Mr Rasmussen said that Europe and the European Union is in a 'unique position to take a major step forward in implementing and mainstreaming corporate social responsibility and public–private partnerships'.[19]

These groups advocate that at local, national and international levels partnership-building has emerged as the approach most likely to bring about truly sustainable development. They argue that bridge-building between the public sector, the private sector and civil society is effectively promoting social cohesion, environmental stability and equitable economic growth. Proponents point to projects such as Togo's first Cisco Networking Academy, opened at the University of Lomi in August 2001. That project is part of a global effort by the United Nations Development Programme (UNDP) and Cisco, the leading supplier of computer network routing equipment, to set up Networking Academies in 29 of the world's 49 least-developed countries by the end of 2001. There are now more than 70 innovative international public–private partnerships, according to an inventory by the Geneva-based Initiative on Public–Private Partnerships.

Although many would welcome such initiatives for IT development, not everyone working on corporate responsibility shares the view that public–private partnerships are *always* desirable. Some are concerned that public–private partnerships can mask the commercialisation of sectors that had hitherto been the preserve of the public sector, such as water, health and education. Julian Liu of the Center for Economic and Social Rights argued in a letter to the *New York Times* that

> international financial institutions and multinational corporations are pushing privatization plans that transform water from a common resource available to all into a commodity for purchase. The result: low-income communities around the world are forced to seek water from polluted and untreated sources, leading to needless deaths from waterborne diseases. For these reasons, international human rights law recognizes the right to water as an essential component of the rights to life and health. Government and business should also recognize that the right to safe drinking water must neither be bought nor sold.

The World Health Organisation (WHO) has also realised the sensitivity around this issue, dedicating the August 2001 edition of its *Bulletin* to the question of public–private partnerships for drugs and vaccines.[20] WHO argued that 'partnerships between the public sector and private enterprise can bring wide benefit in terms of improved health, but there must be safeguards to make sure that their prime focus is healthier populations rather than richer companies'. Overcoming just three of the world's biggest killers—tuberculosis, malaria and HIV/AIDS—requires action by both governments and the private sector, according to the *Bulletin* editor-in-chief Richard Feachem. 'Either alone will be insufficient', Feachem warned. Public–private partnerships can increase the chances that the biotechnology revolution will benefit not only the rich but also poorer populations, he said, so long as the respective energies and expertise of both sectors are efficiently harnessed to attain their common objectives.

Writing from his experience as chief scientific officer of the Medicines for Malaria Venture, Robert Ridley urged commentators to focus less on the differences between public and private bodies and more on the opportunities that partnerships can offer. The aim, he says, is not 'bargaining to obtain maximum advantage to one side or the other' but 'commitment to a common goal through the joint provision of complementary resources and expertise, and the joint sharing of the risks involved'.

Possible pitfalls in WHO's interaction with industry were highlighted by Yale University's Kent Buse and WHO's Amalin Waxman. For example, could WHO's advocacy functions become subject to commercial pressures, and could the organisation's traditional concern for the poorest and least commercially 'attractive' populations be influenced by partners with necessarily different concerns? To ensure that WHO's involvement in partnerships reflects its constitutional commitment to equity and public accountability, the authors propose, among other things, that WHO's relations with the private sector be based on clear benchmarks of 'good partnership practice'.

The concern raised in the earlier section 'Patients pending?' (page 61) was where the necessary investment into research for the development of drugs and vaccines for the poorer countries of the world would come from, especially when pharmaceutical companies were slashing their drugs to cost price, due to corporate responsibility considerations. The answer suggested in the *WHO Bulletin* is a combination of factors that provide both 'push' and 'pull'. ' "Push" factors include public investment in the basic research required and tax credits to participating companies. "Pull" factors include offering to extend the validity of patents on products and a prior commitment by the public sector to purchase finished products that meet agreed specifications.'

Will EU require it?

The relationship of corporate responsibility to regulation was the focus of an interview with the European Commission official in charge of the development of European policy on corporate responsibility, Dominique Be. He was reported in the September 2001 issue of *Ethical Performance* as saying he wants corporate responsibility to develop on a voluntary basis because this encourages innovation and genuine enthusiasm for the concept. Be drafted the European Commission green paper which defined corporate social responsibility as 'a concept whereby companies integrate social and environ-

DOMINIQUE BE: WANTS
CORPORATE CITIZENSHIP
TO DEVELOP ON A
VOLUNTARY BASIS

mental concerns in their business operations and in their interaction with their stake-holders on a voluntary basis'. Therefore the EU would not consider legislating to compel companies to adopt corporate responsibility strategies.[21]

The green paper is a discussion document, and the Commission's thinking is at an early stage. The underlying theme of the green paper is that social responsibility is in everyone's interest, but will be meaningless without rigour and transparency. So companies need to produce reports with sufficiently uniform information to allow comparisons. Also, users of such reports need the assurance of external input and verification to be able to rely on the information presented. Similarly, consumers who want to buy products that have been produced responsibly need a simple, authoritative labelling system. And investors who want to back responsible companies need clear criteria that can be consistently applied. The paper stresses the importance of transparency and dialogue, with the need for developing multi-stakeholder consensus on the way forward.

Consensus might not be easy, as some would argue that the threat of litigation is a key motivating factor for voluntary initiatives. Professor Ralph Steinhardt from George Washington University Law School maintains that 'the prospect of litigation may have accelerated the use of voluntary, marketplace initiatives pertaining to corporate citizenship in human rights'.[22] As the coordinator of the Voluntary Codes Forum, Kernaghan Webb, suggests, 'there is often a legal element to voluntary initiatives, and a legal framework within which such programs operate'.

Thus, the political implications of concepts such as 'public–private partnership' and 'corporate responsibility' as well as the role of legislation began to be discussed on listservs during this period.[23] These discussions suggest that most professionals agree that the growth in corporate responsibility is a *result* of deregulation and privatisation. Some go further and argue that corporate responsibility is an *answer* to deregulation and privatisation, while others question whether it is enough to solve the problems that arise. Some go further still and suggest that corporate responsibility is a *justifica-tion* for more deregulation and privatisation, while others argue the importance of good regulation and key public services being provided as a right and not for profit. There is no consensus among professionals working in this area, although some seem to assume so.

ISO wants consistency

While the european commission was stressing the need for greater consistency in corporate responsibility terminology and practice, across the Atlantic, the US Ethical Officer Association (EOA) was asking the International Organisation for Standardisation (ISO) to consider developing a solution. The EOA represents 400 mainly US-based multinationals, including companies such as GM, Microsoft and Philip Morris. Following in the wake of ISO 9000 (the quality standard) and ISO 14000 (the environmental management standard), proposals are now being drawn up to create a new ISO standard for ethical business conduct. Termed a 'Business Conduct Management Standard' (BCMS) by the EOA, it would focus on management processes rather than ethical outcomes. It would aim to specify the internal structures, processes and resources that would be required to enable a company to be consistent in the implementation of its principles of ethical conduct. One of the arguments used in favour of the proposed standard is that the authority of a verifiable ISO standard would help companies to fend off the competing demands generated by a plethora of codes and guidelines.[24]

Some groups working in corporate responsibility may raise questions about the benefit of this proposal. ISO 14001 has been criticised for giving the semblance of environmental quality and consistency when it allows companies to set their own environmental standards and priorities (apart from requiring legal compliance). Therefore, an ethical ISO standard could disguise very different ethical performance among certified or registered companies. This is a concern, given the current state of corporate ethical codes that often ignore key issues such as freedom of association and collective bargaining. In addition, some may be concerned that, as ISO standards are suited to large companies who can document complex management systems, so the widespread adoption of BCMS might marginalise already-disadvantaged producers and independently run SMEs (small to medium-sized enterprises).

The EOA's suggestion that the BCMS could be based on a company's self-declaration of commitment and performance may concern many NGOs who have for a number of years advocated the importance of independent verification. Commercial auditing firms, whose ISO 14001 auditing services have proved lucrative in the past five years, may echo their concerns. However, these auditing firms and NGOs may disagree on the appropriate form of independent verification, given the high costs of commercial audits and their current limited expertise on labour rights issues.

In addition, those local NGOs already involved in monitoring factories' codes of conduct may question the legitimacy of ISO, given that its membership is restricted to national standards organisations and that it has developed a methodology for auditor accreditation that is more suited to commercial auditing companies. For example, the Independent Monitoring Working Group (IMWG) has developed a form of ethical standards monitoring that is predicated on a different methodology to ISO, by involving local NGOs as ongoing monitors, advisors and arbitrators of disputes. In September 2001, the IMWG released a report on the history and development of independent factory-monitoring initiatives in El Salvador, Guatemala and Honduras.[25] The initiative started in 1995 when labour problems at the Mandarin International factory in El Salvador became widely reported. Most apparel companies doing business at the factory stopped sourcing their brand-name products from the facility. However, Gap Inc.

agreed to stay and explore the creation of an independent factory-monitoring programme in El Salvador. They also agreed to work with the Business for Social Responsibility Education Fund (BSREF), the Interfaith Center on Corporate Responsibility
(ICCR) and, later, the Center for Reflection, Education and Action (CREA) towards that
goal; and hence the Independent Monitoring Working Group (IMWG) was formed.

In the report, IMWG argues that it has demonstrated that companies and NGOs from
Central America and the US can join forces to enhance efforts to respect workers'
rights. 'During this five-year collaboration, we have learned a great deal about how different perspectives can enrich efforts to create fair, harmonious and productive working conditions', said Rev. David M. Schilling of the ICCR. In El Salvador, the IMWG
engaged four local organisations that formed the original Independent Monitoring
Group of El Salvador, or GMIES. The primary objective of monitoring was to promote
harmonious and productive working conditions through verifying factory compliance
with national labour laws, international conventions and Gap Inc.'s own 'Codes of Ven-
dor Conduct'. The report emphasises the importance of attending to the rights of workers in global supply chains, and providing workers with a new channel through which
to raise concerns about their treatment and the conditions under which they work.
Therefore, they contend that independent monitoring works best when it is joined with
effective internal factory systems that allow workers to express their concerns without
fear of retaliation. They also argue that an independent monitoring process should
provide for a third party to act as intermediary or negotiator, when problems or concerns arise.

This is interesting news for other players in the labour standards monitoring field,
such as Social Accountability International (SAI). It shares a similar methodological
approach to ISO, accrediting international firms to carry out inspections, and doesn't
put the same emphasis as IMWG on continual monitoring, dialogue and mediation at
the local level. More information on its approach is contained in the book *SA8000: The
Definitive Guide to the New Social Standard,* which features case studies of companies
using the standards.[26] In July 2001, SAI teamed up with the International Textile, Garment and Leather Workers' Federation (ITGLWF) to conduct a workshop in the Philippines. The programme builds on the ITGLWF's network of study circles: factory-based
groups that have proven to be very effective for worker education and organising. Over
the course of three days, 32 study circle leaders worked with the materials, geared
towards promoting worker awareness about globalisation and human rights in the
workplace and fostering worker participation in codes of conduct.

With the question of retailer responsibility for the social and environmental practices along their supply chain now firmly established on the corporate responsibility
agenda, a report from Egypt started some retailers thinking 'How low can you go?'.
Down the supply chain, that is. Human Rights Watch (HRW) issued a report showing
that Egyptian children working in cotton-farming cooperatives worked long hours,
were routinely beaten by foremen, and were inadequately protected against pesticides
and heat exposure. The child labourers, most between the ages of seven and twelve
(the country's legal minimum age for seasonal agricultural work), earned an average
of three Egyptian pounds (about one US dollar) each day. 'The way children are treated
in the cotton fields is deplorable', said Lois Whitman, executive director of the Children's Rights division of HRW. Although retailers might already have thought they were
bending over backwards to deal with social and environmental issues involved in the

manufacture and assembly of their products, it seems there are issues of concern right at the base of the supply chain. Perhaps it is not feasible for retailers to go any lower down the supply chain? Perhaps this is a question of suppliers and governments needing greater capacity to deal with these issues?[27]

International perspectives at Warwick

In July 2001, the UK University of Warwick's Corporate Citizenship Unit (CCU) held its 4th annual conference. Delegates from industry, government, civil-society organisations and academia flew in from around the globe to discuss the latest news, views and research of people working in collaboration with the CCU.

During the opening plenary, former Assistant Secretary-General Professor John Ruggie shared his thoughts on, and hopes for, the UN Global Compact. Professor Ruggie explained that the Compact would be using its website as a way of showcasing corporate experiences in implementing the nine principles, and facilitating the review of corporate submissions by civil society. He explained that it was a practical and pragmatic decision to focus on encouraging and facilitating changes in corporate practice, as the UN did not have a mandate to directly regulate companies. Therefore, he identified the Learning Forum as the heart of the change mechanism envisaged by the UN Secretary-General's office. Ruggie noted that there are differing opinions on the efficacy of a learning approach in creating positive change, but stressed that the Global Compact was only part of the solution to the problems posed by economic globalisation. He noted a number of the challenges that they will face in future. 'There are some things that a learning model by itself cannot achieve. The Compact's recognition and promotion of a company's "good practices" provides no guarantee that the same company does not engage in "bad" ones elsewhere', he warned. In addition, Ruggie noted the possibility that some companies would seek to join in order to deflect criticism—including that coming from other agencies in the UN system.

In a packed workshop on 'Shared Values and the Global Compact', Dr Malcolm McIntosh expressed the aim to start 'a global conversation' on the role of the corporation. He reported mushrooming interest in the Compact from around the world, because of 'the moral authority of the UN', which gave the principles 'a certain prove-

MALCOLM McINTOSH: AIMS TO START 'A
GLOBAL CONVERSATION' ON THE ROLE
OF THE CORPORATION

nance'. McIntosh explained that the first submissions from corporations were being analysed by members of the Learning Forum and would be posted along with comments from reviewers and selected NGOs over the coming months. He explored the key issues that they would consider when assessing the submissions, noting the complexity of the area and how they would themselves be learning how corporations can operationalise the Compact's principles.[28]

During the second plenary featuring presentations on experiences in South Africa, Burma and Vietnam, Gavin Anderson of the Development Resources Centre in South Africa stressed that the development challenges faced by his country were so great that individual companies would need to work together to drive positive change. He suggested that corporate responsibility should not be seen as the activity of individual companies but as a collective process. He called for an active 'corporate citizenry' to work together on social and environmental challenges.

Jerry Sternin, of Save the Children USA, excited delegates with his experiences of working in Burma and Vietnam. He introduced delegates to the idea of 'positive deviance'. He asserted that in communities throughout the world there are a few 'deviant' individuals whose uncommon behaviours or practices enable them to 'outperform or find better solutions to pervasive problems than their neighbours with whom they share the common resource base'. He showed that you could find appropriate solutions to development challenges by identifying the problem and identifying how some 'positive deviants' manage to cope better, and then devising an intervention that allows that deviance to be copied by others. This was essentially a development studies lecture, which was of interest to delegates for two reasons. First, companies are increasingly involved in development work in Southern countries and are hungry for the experiences and ideas of the governmental and voluntary development communities. But they were also interested for a quite different reason: Sternin was describing how to provoke positive behaviour—something that delegates are aiming to do, not so much in the South, but in the boardrooms of corporations. Sternin's theory suggests that more research could be conducted on the positive deviants who are champions of corporate responsibility in the business world. If we can identify what made them take a lead and how, then it might be possible to replicate their positive deviance across the private sector.

Delegates also heard the perspectives of people working on aspects of corporate responsibility in Latin America. Marcello Paladino, of Austral University in Argentina, argued that 'Latin America needs new leaders' and those socially aware business leaders should take on responsibility for the state of Latin society. He stressed that 'enterprises are related to social transformation' and that the values embodied in ethical business are the values that could help their society progress. Emphasising this political dimension to business, he suggested that 'management is a political discipline, as it [business] can't be understood outside the community. Enterprises without the community do not exist.'

Another workshop focused on the 'Challenges for Development Professionals Working with Business Partners in Zones of Conflict'. In his presentation entitled 'Securing a Licence to Operate in Zones of Conflict', the Vice President for Social Responsibility at the Norwegian oil company Statoil, Geir Westgaard, dealt with the difficult issue of oil companies operating in places such as Burma and the Sudan. He argued that oil companies should not be expected to try to influence the way oil revenues are spent in war-torn areas where they operate. 'There are real limits as to how far beyond the factory gate a corporation can move without jeopardising its licence to operate,' he said. 'Even though the role of the corporate sector has increased significantly with globalisation, business has to be careful about demands that fall outside the scope of legitimate action by a commercial entity.'

As discussed in 'Reporting rights' on page 67, some NGOs have called on oil companies such as Talisman to freeze its operations in war-torn countries, where oil revenues not only fund the purchase of arms but are considered to be a key reason why governments wage war against separatist groups. However, Westgaard suggested it was 'highly questionable' whether international oil companies should be telling host governments how to spend their oil revenues—and warned that such moves could easily transform corporate social responsibility into political interference.

Westgaard's depiction of economic activity (oil production) as non-political and political activity (civil war) as non-economic was questioned by some during discussions, especially as there appeared to be an economic motive for the Sudanese government waging civil war. Interestingly, Westgaard's analysis seemed somewhat contrary to the presentation from Richard Jones of Premier Oil, who emphasised how corporate constructive engagement with regimes such as the Burmese military dictatorship could help catalyse change and protect human rights. Jones chronicled Premier's initiatives such as training Burmese security personnel on human rights principles and law, and also intimated that its high-level advocacy efforts might help develop the government's thinking. Perhaps with more dialogue the various opinions on these issues might begin to converge. For example, while Westgaard was reluctant to unilaterally place conditionalities on its investment, he suggested that 'if and when we do . . . it will be as part of a broader effort that involves the international community. The conditionality should then be imposed by legitimate international bodies such as the United Nations . . . with the oil companies cast more in a supporting role.'

After examining the feedback from delegates, the CCU outlined their plans to make the 5th annual conference an opportunity for more dialogue and debate on the issues raised, including different and perhaps more critical stakeholder perspectives.

4Q2001

October–December

Jem Bendell

Post 9/11

The terrorist attacks in the United States on 11 September 2001, and their aftermath, had a significant impact on many political, economic and social aspects of life during the last quarter of 2001. Not surprisingly, activities within the area we call 'corporate citizenship' or corporate responsibility were also affected, with the full implications of these terrible events only beginning to be understood as the New Year dawned.

During the immediate aftermath of the attacks, concern about the US economy deepened and a range of major companies announced they were laying off workers. Boeing, the world's largest aviation company, cut 30,000 jobs, with their CEO, Phil Condit, saying that September 11th and the aftermath was 'a horrible situation . . . the job cuts go right hand in hand with that'. However, the BBC noted that Boeing would be buoyed by military and space technology spending, while in October 2001 the company unveiled a $1.6 billion deal to supply China with 30 jetliners.[1] Thus November 2001's *Reputation Impact* reported the 'skepticism that corporations are using the impact of September 11 as an excuse' for strategic corporate restructuring.[2] South Africa's *Busi - ness Week* said 'it should be remembered that the mark of true business leadership is to succeed in bad times as well as good, and lumping all the blame on Bin Laden . . . is simply ridiculous'.[3]

Some corporations contributed to this criticism of mass redundancies, with General Motors launching a 'Keep America Rolling' campaign and noting that 'the best way we can respond to these acts of terrorism on our soil is to . . . keep our employees working'. Despite the economic downturn, many companies gave generously to disaster appeals. Millions of dollars of support for victims and their families was pledged by corporations across America, with retail outlets also helping customers to make donations. ShopRite stores collected more than $500,000 from customers who chose to have a $2 or $5 donation tacked onto their grocery bills, the money being split between the Red Cross and the Salvation Army. Businesses in Europe also responded, some donating several million dollars, among them DaimlerChrysler ($10 million) and Deutsche Bank ($4 million). In-kind donations were also made, with Novartis offering its entire supply of Apligraf, a skin replacement used to treat burn victims. US *Business Week* applauded the response of some business leaders, saying that 'the past few weeks have shown us a corporate leader means much more than just managing the bottom line'.

Pharmaceutical companies were not among those receiving this glowing praise. As the anthrax scare swept America, so Bayer, the maker of an antibiotic that fights the disease, had its ethics—and its patriotism—questioned. The Canadian government threatened to ignore Bayer's patent on Cipro and buy 1 million tablets of a generic version from another company. The US Secretary of Health and Human Services, Tommy Thompson, took similar action stating that Bayer 'are going to either meet our price— or else we're going to go to Congress and ask for some support to go in and do some other business'. Not surprisingly, Bayer caved in and agreed to sell the US and Canada cheaper Cipro at the knockdown price of 95 cents a pill—rather than the original $4.50.

Bayer, who had initially threatened to sue the Canadian government for breach of patent, was one of the 39 corporations that, earlier in the year, took South Africa to court when the country said it would use emergency legislation to purchase cheaper generic drugs to treat people with AIDS (see 'Patients pending?' on page 61). Clearly, all death is sad, and avoidable death is wrong. In 2000 four people died of anthrax in the US, while an estimated 2.4 million people died of HIV-related causes in Africa.[4] Mallen Baker argued in *Business Respect*[5] that although 'the pharmaceutical companies have the right to profit by their research and development into solutions which genuinely enhance human well-being . . . as things currently stand, patents are licensed monopoly'. He insisted that 'there is now a fundamental challenge to the industry to establish the framework of fair protection for innovation that is widely seen to be free from abuse'. The challenge is great as prices usually drop about 25% once competition from generics has been introduced, so that companies take a short-term hit on their bottom line.

However, with the whole basis of their business continuing to be questioned, will the drug companies club together to take the necessary action to generate legitimate practices in this area? Not yet, it seems. In the run-up to the World Trade Organisation (WTO) meeting in Qatar, a group of less-industrialised countries asked the organisation to reinterpret rules in order to give governments the right to access affordable medicines. Their initiative was blocked by Switzerland, Japan and, undaunted by events at the time, Canada and the US. So, instead, the WTO passed an agreement ensuring that less-industrialised countries must introduce intellectual property laws that uphold multinationals' patents (97% of all patents are held by multinationals). The WTO may have put people and corporations on a collision course.

Wider implications

The President of the International Chamber of Commerce, Richard McCormick, suggested that 'the collapse of the World Trade Center needn't foreshadow darker days' and that 'business people must recognize the social importance of what we do'. This illustrates how, as time passed, people began to reflect on what the wider implications of September 11th might be. Not so much *how* did it happen, but *why* and what could be done to prevent further atrocities from happening in the future. The mainstream

ICC PRESIDENT RICHARD McCORMICK:
SEPTEMBER 11TH NEEDN'T
FORESHADOW DARKER DAYS

media tended to focus on the 'war on terrorism' and the recession. Most coverage of business and economics was limited to discussing issues such as whether the 'war on terrorism' justified fast-tracking trade negotiations, or whether it had become a 'patriotic duty' to go and shop.

However, some industry leaders were heard to suggest that one lesson from September 11th should be a focus on the long-term economic and environmental health of the whole world.[6] In conferences such as those of Business for Social for Responsibility (BSR) in Seattle, and Social Accountability International (SAI) in Amsterdam, similar reflection was taking place. During the plenary at SAI's conference the director of the International Business Leaders' Forum (IBLF), Robert Davies, said that international business has 'a critically important role to play' in managing the effects of conflict and terrorism and that 'business could contribute to tackling the conditions of alienation and destitution in which fanaticism flourishes'. He called on business people to think more critically about what economic and financial globalisation is, or is not, delivering for the world's people and argued that the 'trickle-down' effect is not working.

IBLF DIRECTOR ROBERT DAVIES:
BUSINESS HAS A CRITICAL ROLE TO
PLAY IN MANAGING THE EFFECTS OF
TERRORISM

Some hoped that the latest round of WTO negotiations, 'The Doha Development Round', would rise to the challenge of managing economic and financial globalisation in ways more supportive of sustainable development. However, the talks attracted renewed criticism, with Barry Coates, Director of the World Development Movement, arguing that rich countries had 'exploited the vulnerability of poor countries in order to force their agenda on them'. This was reflected by Richard Bernal, one of Jamaica's official delegates, who during the conference said 'we are made to feel that we are holding up the rescue of the global economy if we don't agree to a new trade round here'.

Coates criticised the neoliberal agenda of the WTO, suggesting that 'little has changed' for the world's poorest countries, as 'their exports are blocked, their businesses are wiped out by foreign multinationals and their farmers are driven off their land by subsidised exports from the rich countries'. The location of the meeting meant that there were no protests like in Seattle two years previously. Although not well covered by the mainstream media, there were reports of thousands of people protesting in hundreds of different cities, including Bangkok, New Delhi, Seoul, Ljubliana and Tehran, all to coincide with the WTO conference.[7] In the first *Global Civil Society Year - book*, published by the London School of Economics,[8] the editors asserted that 'global capitalism must either learn to seriously engage with these protests and join in the attempt to civilise globalisation, or prepare for more massive and more violent protests ahead'.

Anti-globalisation: now it's your business

Reference to such protests as a reason for corporate citizenship is not new—and continues. In November, the *San Francisco Chronicle*[9] mentioned protests as a reason for renewed interest in corporate social responsibility, while the first issue of *Ethical Cor - poration*[10] magazine featured pictures of riots at the G8 summit in Genoa on its cover and asked corporate readers whether they would like to see such activities outside their own headquarters (the vast majority of demonstrators were, of course, peaceful). Many commentators suggested that this 'anti-capitalist' backlash meant companies should take individual action to demonstrate their responsibility and protect their reputations. This view has been promoted by consultancies who have sought to help companies with stakeholder engagement and social reporting initiatives. However, corporate responsibility initiatives by individual corporations may not provide a panacea. It can certainly be argued that the challenges are more systemic.

For example, two key issues for activists have been 'third-world' debt and international currency speculation. The austerity policies imposed on indebted countries to ensure they pay interests on their debts has led to 19,000 children dying from preventable causes every day, according to Christian Aid.[11] This has created a backlash against the World Bank and International Monetary Fund (IMF) who were responsible for imposing these policies, and the rich-country governments who supported and benefited from the process. The debt crisis has also weakened economic, social and political stability in indebted countries and undermined the reputation of global capitalism generally.

It is impossible to see how an individual corporation's responsibility policy or social report would help tackle this issue, or indeed the related problem of international currency speculation. With $1.5 trillion switching hands (or rather computer screens) every single day,[12] the French activist group ATTAC (Association for the Taxation of Financial Transactions for the Aid of Citizens), along with War on Want in the UK and other NGO, trade union and campaigning groups, has called for a tax on this speculation in order to stabilise the world economy, to lessen the pressure on governments to seek favour from the financial markets, and to generate a source of revenue for poverty

SIMON ZADEK: CALLS FOR CHANGES
IN THE CORPORATE TAX REGIME TO
FAVOUR RESPONSIBLE COMPANIES

alleviation and sustainable development. This so-called Tobin tax (named after the Nobel prize-winning economist James Tobin, who first proposed such a tax in the 1970s) has been estimated at being worth over $250 billion a year. Its proponents argue that the G7, UN or OECD should now take the lead in its establishment in the nine developed countries where 84% of foreign exchange transactions take place.

The idea that collective, not individual, action is required by corporations to help shape the regulatory structure in ways that support corporate responsibility has begun to be discussed in some circles. The Foreign Policy Centre published a pamphlet by Simon Zadek which called on governments, business and civil society to work together to 'shift the terms of competition to ensure that social and environmental objectives are addressed through the market'. One of his key proposals is for changes in the corporate tax regime to favour responsible companies. He also calls for more effort on consumer education and the establishment of credible social labelling schemes.

In October 2001, the Belgian Chamber of Representatives took its own initiative in this area, announcing a social labelling scheme for products from less-industrialised countries. An independent body will test companies applying for the label on their social rights performance. A similar scheme is being considered in France, and some are arguing that the social label will eventually grow to become EU-wide, although the experience with EU's Eco-label for environmentally preferable products is not that encouraging.

Although most of Zadek's recommendations are directed at government, he makes the case for companies to embrace a new generation of corporate responsibility thinking. He argues that corporate responsibility 'will remain distrusted and inadequate' unless government creates the conditions under which it can be more effective for both business and society. Zadek's main focus is on incentivising and rewarding rewarding corporate responsibility. Whether this would be enough to tackle either the trademark trouble faced by transnational corporations, or the systemic problems posed by economic globalisation, is uncertain.

The experience of Nike illustrates the paradox of power at the heart of corporate responsibility initiatives. In September 2001 it published its first corporate responsibility report.[13] CEO Phil Knight said that readers would not only 'see a few accomplishments' but also 'more than a few challenges'. The report illustrates how Nike has pursued one of the more progressive policies of a branded clothing company the period reviewed by this volume; yet despite this investment of time and money it remains a key target for brand-bashing activists. Although many activists focus on specific concerns such as pay and conditions in supplier factories, companies such as Nike are seen as celebrity symbols of the global economy. There is concern about the power of such corporations in shaping people's lives, from workers to consumers. Therefore the more it tackles the specific issues its critics raise or supports community initiatives, the more its problematic position of power is both consolidated and contested. Consequently, resistance to Nike might not be assuaged and its social responsibility work might prove to be of limited financial value if it is undercut by competitors without such a symbolic profile. Therefore, although there are interesting developments within the financial community, discussed below, the concern remains that the lack of global regulatory mechanisms will leave responsible corporations vulnerable to being undercut by more ruthless competitors. Recent developments in the case of Talisman are instructive.

The Canadian Oil company decided to sell its Sudanese assets after US legislators threatened sanctions that could cost the company its US stock exchange listing, the concern being how the Sudanese government was using the oil revenues and installations to wage a religious civil war. Selling its assets was not what campaign groups such as Christian Aid were seeking from Talisman; rather, they wanted it to freeze its operations and seek to work with other oil companies to ensure a common approach (see 'Reporting rights' on page 67).

It was not surprising, then, when Canada's *Financial Post* reported on 23 November 2001 that Asian, Saudi, Japanese, Swedish, Austrian and Sudanese (with foreign capital) companies were considering buying Talisman's assets. Thus the effect on the situation in Sudan could be negligible, even negative, while this precedent also means that other US listed companies will not be able to compete on level terms with companies from other parts of the world. A lose–lose for business and society. It is difficult to see how issues such as these can be tackled without effective intergovernmental action. For Nike and for Talisman, the solution may lie in more credible and legitimate mechanisms for democratic global governance.

These cases suggest that protesters' concerns about a lack of such effective and legitimate mechanisms to check transnational corporations may also become a strategic business concern. You don't always value something until it's gone, and, after decades of deregulation, we see that business actually needs regulation. Combined with the issues of 'third-world' debt and currency speculation, there is an emerging business case for so-called 'anti-capitalism' or 'anti-globalisation'. Zadek's paper does acknowledge that the carrot approach to corporate responsibility may not be sufficient, and that various sticks 'to hold global institutions—including multinational business organisations—globally to account' should be considered by government. Thus a new level of analysis for corporate responsibility may emerge, which focuses on where and in what ways a corporation lobbies for or against intergovernmental cooperation to promote sustainable development. Perhaps it is *this* that should be discussed in social responsibility reports?

Reporting developments

According a review of the largest 100 companies listed in *Fortune* magazine's August 2000 Global 500,[14] over half are now engaging in some form of social and environmental reporting. Despite the efforts of initiatives such as the Global Reporting Initiative (GRI), there is a wide variety of reporting styles, with little agreement on what constitutes relevant information. Mallen Baker noted[15] that, whereas 'a financial analyst looking at the annual report will know where to find the essential information, and how to interpret it', social responsibility reporting 'is so often a mish-mash of narrative and figures, replete with photos of happy smiling children but with no solid data set that communicates in real terms what is the health of that organisation'.

In December 2001, his organisation, the UK-based Business in the Community, launched a new online 'CSR reporting channel' with the aim of providing a common framework of indicators to report against. Over the coming two years a group of 20 companies will test the framework.[16]

The reporting framework being developed by GRI received a significant vote of confidence when in November 2001 the UN's Global Compact office announced that it had formed a new cooperative framework. In the future, company submissions made under the aegis of the GRI could also be considered as submissions fulfilling the participation requirements of the Global Compact. Georg Kell, Executive Head of the United Nations Global Compact Office, explained that the two approaches are mutu-

GEORG KELL: THE
GLOBAL COMPACT AND
THE GRI ARE
CONSISTENT

ally consistent. 'The Global Compact promotes responsible corporate citizenship through learning and action on the basis of nine universal principles, whereas the Global Reporting Initiative promotes transparency and accountability through reporting,' he wrote. 'Companies may wish to use their involvement in the GRI as an example of their commitment to the Global Compact.'

It was a busy period for the Global Compact, which was the subject of events in various countries including Latvia, Spain, Russia, UK, Philippines and Brazil. The Employers' Confederation of the Philippines (ECOP), in cooperation with the Philippines Chamber of Commerce and Industry (PCCI), with the support of the International Labour Organisation (ILO), held a meeting on the UN initiative that was attended by about 25–30 CEOs.

Meanwhile, some of Russia's top business leaders met with Louise Fréchette, the UN First Deputy Secretary-General, to discuss corporate responsibility. The meeting, organised by the Union of Industrialists and Entrepreneurs, was the first UN Global

LOUISE FRÉCHETTE, UN FIRST DEPUTY
SECRETARY-GENERAL: PRESIDED OVER THE
FIRST GLOBAL COMPACT MEETING
TO TAKE PLACE IN RUSSIA

Compact meeting to take place in Russia. At the meeting Interros became the fourth Russian company to sign up.

Meanwhile, in New York, the second-largest Russian oil company, Yukos, with approximately 100,000 employees, signed a partnership framework agreement with UNOPS, the UN system's major provider of project management services. In so doing the company also formally joined the Global Compact.[17] The agreement aims at establishing the conditions for cooperation between Yukos and interested UN system organisations in the Russian Federation and adjacent countries in a variety of areas. Yukos said it would like to work with UNOPS and other UN agencies, in such areas as social investment in post-conflict societies; environmental clean-up and management; educational and cultural exchange in support of peace or stabilisation processes; bridging the digital divide; small and medium-sized enterprise development and assistance; and healthcare.

Is it just business?

The global spread of corporate responsibility initiatives would not please one former OECD economist, who considers it a 'misguided virtue'. On 15 November 2001, *The Economist* ran an article called 'The Curse of the Ethical Executive', which summarised the views of David Henderson's new paper for the Institute of Economic Affairs.[18] It wrote:

> It is more than 200 years since Adam Smith observed that people enjoy their daily bread thanks not to the benevolence of their baker, but to his selfish pursuit of profit. In that observation and its implications lies the case for market capitalism. In their economic lives, people behave as though they had no regard for the public good. Yet the outcome, through the operation of the invisible hand, serves the public good better than any social planner could ever do.[19]

Henderson argues that the fad for corporate social responsibility is doing real harm, as it 'poisons public opinion' against market capitalism by undermining the belief that people's pursuit of financial self-interest is socially beneficial, and by loading costs onto production that then reduce profit, which in turn reduces tax revenues for governments. He argues that corporate responsibility proponents' 'capitulation to anti-profit ideology, their pandering to anti-capitalists and their preference for "enlightened coop-eration" over ruthless competition' is legitimising the arguments of such critics when they should be tackled head-on. The appropriate response to corporate responsibility should be 'not to laugh at it or tolerate it, but to recognise it for the danger it is and oppose it'.

In an argument reminiscent of Milton Friedman's, over 40 years ago,[20] Henderson posits that, 'when it comes to business ethics, it is worth remembering that managers do not, as a rule, own the companies they are directing'. Friedman suggested that spending money on social responsibility initiatives was literally stealing from own-ers—the shareholders. However, the legal responsibility of managers is not so much to increase profits as it is to do what the owners want. In recent years this has been to maximise shareholder value, something that is not affected by profits so much as *the market for shares*, which is a product of a number of factors, including corporate repu-tation. Furthermore, Friedman and Henderson make the assumption that owners would be solely interested in maximising shareholder value. Instead, with the growth of SRI, trillions of dollars' worth of company shares are now owned by people who have other motives, including the future health of the planet and its people.

Interestingly, Henderson argues against corporations adopting global standards on social and environmental performance. 'In a profoundly non-uniform world, uniform standards are a bad idea, especially for the poorest countries, which may be unable to support them economically.' This is an argument often heard by exporters from less-industrialised countries, but hardly ever from the people who work in the plantations and factories making those exports. Can we really tell them that freedom from sexual harassment, the right to join a trade union or to work in a safe and healthy environ-ment are luxuries their country is not 'developed' enough to afford?

In today's global capitalist system, Adam Smith's baker raises more questions than it answers. What if people want to buy organic bread? What if they want to buy from a baker who runs his own place? Aren't these market preferences? What if one baker buys out most of the other bakeries, increases prices, and moves his operations to a tax-free enterprise zone? Aren't his customers also citizens who can think about what kind of society they want and then take action, as 'citizen consumers'?

What if the bakery is owned by shareholders who don't want the baker to maximise profits by externalising all social and environmental costs because they are interested in their children's future?

Adam Smith had in mind a much more up-close capitalism than the one we have today, a capitalism where owners, workers and consumers were neighbours and inter-acted on a social as well as economic basis.

Perhaps corporate responsibility might be reflecting the fact that with global com-munications we are able to reconnect owners, workers and consumers, and bring cap-italism back closer to home? What David Henderson's does tell us is that there is a growing diversity of views on corporate responsibility thinking and practice as it enters the mainstream, and that we would do well to consider the political and philosophical assumptions behind our own thinking on the matter. Some emerging perspectives are categorised in Box 3 on page 221.

Money fashions change

The impact of corporate citizenship issues within the financial community continued to rise in the last quarter of 2001, illustrated by reports on shareholder activism and the size and number of socially responsible investments (SRIs). The year 2000 saw more shareholder social activism, according to research by the Investor Responsibility Research Centre, with 158 social issues proposals going up for proxy vote. Support for social policy resolutions grew, rising 1% to 8.6%. The number of proposals receiving more than 10% support also grew significantly, with almost 28% crossing this threshold (10% is the level needed to achieve continued resubmission of a proposal). Many of the issues responsible for the current rise in shareholder interest have been around for some years, slowly gaining support. Global labour standards, genetically modified organisms and sexual discrimination were among the hot topics in 2001.

The US's Social Investment Forum, published its 2001 *Trends Report*, which showed how assets held within a socially screened portfolio grew at over 1.5 times the rate of similar non-screened managed funds. Between 1999 and 2001, SRI funds grew by more than a third to top the $2 trillion level for the first time ever. This 36% growth rate contrasts with the 22% rise for all investment assets under professional management in the US. However, the value of individual investments fell across the board.

Steve Schueth, spokesperson for the Forum, argued that in a bearish market the fact that social investing has grown considerably over the past two years is remarkable. 'This speaks volumes about the staying power of this industry and about the commitment of socially conscious investors to the dual objectives of making money and making a difference', he said. The Forum is a national non-profit membership association of over 500 social investment practitioners and institutions, dedicated to promoting the concept, practice and growth of socially and environmentally responsible investing.

A similar initiative was launched in the European Union by the Belgian Presidency's Conference on Corporate Social Responsibility in Brussels. The European Sustainable and Responsible Investment Forum (Eurosif) is supported by the European Commission, various non-governmental organisations, investment institutions, and five European SRI Forums. The Forum reflects the growing interest of European governments in SRI, with the UK, Australia, Belgium, Germany, France and Sweden all having introduced some form of SRI legislation.

The performance of SRI funds was the subject of research for a number of academics. Drs Pontus Cerin and Peter Dobers of the Swedish Royal Institute of Technology analysed the performance of the Dow Jones Sustainability Group Index (DJSGI) in comparison with the Dow Jones Global Index (DJGI). According to the study, evidence continues to support the claims of others that the DJSGI outperforms DJGI, with a regional exception in Europe, where the DJSGI has slightly underperformed the DJGI. However, rather than assuming that the effective management of social and environmental risks and opportunities was the determinant variable, Cerin and Dobers looked at other factors and found that the market capitalisation value of corporations in the DJSGI is two and a half times larger than the corresponding average for the DJGI. This, coupled with a technology bias in the SRI index, was argued to contribute to the better performance of the DJSGI in 1993 and 1999.[21] It will be interesting to examine the performance of the FTSE4Good and DJSGI over 2001.

Although research into determinant variables for SRI versus non-SRI performance is interesting, what such work overlooks is the importance of fashion in investor behaviour and therefore portfolio performance. In his book *The Crisis of Global Capitalism*,[22] George Soros argues that perfect knowledge of markets and companies is impossible and that investor behaviour is determined by fashion. Thus, he argues, what is important *in financial terms* is not so much what is valid in any objective sense but what is believed to be true. Therefore he was happy to invest in 'fertile fallacies'—stocks inflated by a common wisdom within the financial community that he didn't necessarily agree with. Having questioned whether social responsibility might actually add costs to business, one investor asked on the ethical investment web-board of Interactive Investor, 'is the bottom line that these things are just fashionable funds?'[23] The fact is that the 'bottom line' of share value is investors' perception of value drivers and of other investors' perceptions of such. Therefore, if SRI is a changing fashion, then it might just set up a virtuous circle of investor confidence in corporate responsibility. A changing fashion can fashion change. Professor Michael Hopkins of MHCi pondered whether, once recessionary fears dissipate, SRI could be the 'next dot.com boom'. To avoid it going the way of the once-fertile fallacy of dot.comism, corporate responsibility leaders would need to reshape market regulations in ways that rewarded good corporate performance and punished bad.

Then, perhaps, more mainstream investors would come on board and SRI evolve from its position of being a possible fertile fallacy to being a positive fertile fantasy. As Professor Hopkins writes:

> September 11th has spurred interest in social development. None of us in that field welcome the fact that vile acts have given impetus to concerns about social development. Nevertheless, the acceleration of interest in social development both through the nation state, and through corporations, are likely to herald a boom in social investment. Fashion means profits not only on the catwalk but also on the boardwalk!

2002

Foreword

Paul Gibbons
Managing Director, Future Considerations[1]

Dear Reader

A recent trip to Blackwell's stunned me. I stepped back from the shelves in order to get an overall perspective on the ideas and conversations that business people will pay money to read. On this occasion, about 30% of the titles were related to corporate ethics, or governance, or sustainability, or CSR, or partnerships, or business's role in economic development. Good news!

But adding a time dimension to this view of the bookshelf would reveal periods where Re-engineering, or Total Quality, or E-transformation would have dominated the shelves. So are we seeing a paradigm shift—the beginning of a change in corporate consciousness—or a fad? How can we tilt it toward one or the other of these extremes? One of the things that research reveals about management fads is that their conceptual claims far exceed their delivered results. TQM (Total Quality Management) had huge successes (arguably changing the entire corporate culture of Japan in the '50s and '60s). It was rigorously researched by hundreds or academic followers, and was a conceptually rigorous blend of the hard and soft aspects of organisations—the technical and the human.

It was a very robust discourse—yet where is it today? What I believe to be true about management fads is that any truly radical and worthwhile idea will be much easier to conceptualise than it is to implement. That includes (especially) corporate responsibility. This produces an 'implementation gap' with gurus and pundits making big promises and organisations on the ground under-delivering. Disillusionment sets in and publishers, writers, consultants and managers are looking for 'the next thing'.

Why does this under-delivery and disillusionment happen? Because change is hard.

Policy is orders of magnitude easier to develop than it is to implement. Cynics who attended Johannesburg bemoaned an 'implementation gap'. While their cynicism is not welcome, we need to get better at helping organisations make material their noble policies, be those the Global Compact, or an internal code of conduct, or an environmental management system. My observation of the 'new paradigm' world is that change skills are very thin on the ground. We are better at advice and recommendation. But, as my grandmother used to say, 'that and sixpence will get you on the bus'.

If change is hard, culture change is even harder. TQM and BPR (Business Process Reengineering) both required significant cultural changes in organisations to deliver their results. In accord with the paradigm of the time, the results they promised were entirely financial. Yet, even with the imperative of financial results driving the change, many of these programmes were abandoned without results. In the worlds of 'corporate citizenship', 'business ethics' or 'corporate social responsibility', we are often play-ing for non-financial results and the financial imperative can be less clear. Yet for our work to succeed we will require a cultural change every bit as great as that demanded by TQM and BPR. From Future Considerations' perspective, as experts on leadership and culture change, this is the very rabbit that we are going to have to pull out of the hat. My 'exam questions' for you to ponder while reading this Annual Review are:

▶ What internal changes will need to take place in your organisation to manifest the external changes you wish to see?

▶ What are the change implications of the policies you espouse? How will these be addressed? What are the behaviour changes that will drive the change?

▶ How will the culture changes required be achieved in your organisation?

▶ What kinds of leaders do you need and from where will you get them?

▶ Is your organisation ready to engage in value-based and moral conversation that lie at the heart of corporate citizenship?

▶ Do you have the tools to engage in dialogue across widely divergent world-views and seemingly opposite stakeholder objectives?

While we don't claim to have easy answers to these questions, we want to engage with others in finding the answers. So please enjoy this Annual Review, which has been a privilege to support

Introduction

From review to preview

Jem Bendell and Tim Concannon

2002 was the year in which stories about corporate responsibility escaped from environment and society newspaper columns and landed squarely on the front pages. CEOs went from heroes to zeros, as corporate governance debacles spread from Enron and WorldCom to other US companies and then to other parts of the world. In Europe, where people had said 'this will never happen here', share values of Vivendi and Marconi collapsed under the same accusations of false accounting, misguided 'visionary' leadership and creative mismanagement as their American cousins. The implications of these scandals were discussed in the World Reviews of the *Journal of Corporate Cit - izenship* (see 'Enron's new clothes' on page 106 and 'Greed Inc. or Greed Ltd?' on page 118).

The new interest in corporate responsibility was limited to a set of old issues. Honesty and legality, rather than broader notions of managerial responsibility, were considered. This was illustrated by George Bush, who, as Mallen Baker noted, 'discovered corporate responsibility post-Enron, and oversaw the creation of legislation in the US to require higher standards of corporate governance, whilst missing many of the essential messages businesses have already embraced within the corporate social responsibility movement'.

It was too soon to say whether the broader agenda would be supported from the fall-out of these corporate scandals, but some suggested it might open the door to a new corporate culture (see 'Moral Bankruptcy Assured [MBA]' on page 121). The US government responded to pressure for new legislation to address accountancy oversight and corporate governance.

Elsewhere, the pressure for new legislation was somewhat different, focusing on the wider responsibilities of corporations. The European Commission produced its thinking on the topic, signalling that it had accepted the argument that corporate responsibility to society, rather than just shareholders, needed to be based on voluntary action (see 'Consulting caution' on page 140).

However, France brought forward legislation to require social and environmental reporting. Australia changed its pension laws, so trustees would have to disclose their social and environmental considerations. In the UK, campaigners drafted a bill for compulsory reporting, although the government did not move on the matter (see 'Compulsory reporting' on page 130). These initiatives indicated a change in mood among some professionals involved in corporate responsibility—and a reconsideration of the role of government in promoting it. Some corporate leaders began calling on government to do more to create incentives for sustainable enterprise. They were joined by a number of NGOs and think-tanks, who called for governments to move beyond market fundamentalism and become involved in creating a framework for sustainable business (see 'Neo-regulation?' on page 155).

This debate was fuelled by a growing unease with limited evidence of a financial case for companies behaving responsibly. In 2002, so-called sin stocks, such as tobacco and alcohol, grew, while many indexes of more responsible companies slumped. The reality was that political changes continued to shape the business environment. War talk and military spending in the US boosted related stocks there, while the election of the Greens in Germany boosted environmental stocks there. Thus 2002 reminded many of how political and social factors affect business priorities and performance—including activist campaigns and government regulation, two issues that feature prominently in this Annual Review (see 'Sin stocks rock?' on page 132).

Debates about the role of government were compounded by the World Summit on Sustainable Development. Ten years on from the historic Rio summit, which created global agreements on climate change and biodiversity, the WSSD was held in Johannesburg. What surprised many in the international community was how voluntary agreements between business, government and civil society displaced binding agreements as the main show.

Over 200 of these 'Type 2' voluntary agreements were announced: many of them rebranded existing initiatives, marking the establishment of partnership as a key concept on the international policy agenda (see 'Johannesburgled?' on page 127). This resulted in a backlash, and as time passed it appeared that WSSD marked a key staging post in a new movement for corporate accountability. NGOs from around the world began called for an international convention to guarantee greater corporate accountability, to the consternation of some business leaders, not others (see 'Convention-al warfare' on page 136). This gave greater importance to the ongoing negotiations at the United Nations High Commission of Human Rights (UNHCHR) on drafting 'Human Rights Principles and Responsibilities for Transnational Corporations and Other Business Enterprises' (see 'A future treaty?' on page 138).

The progress of this in 2003, and business reaction, will be key. One aspect of the campaign proposals for a new treaty was a mechanism for more judicial procedures against corporate malpractice. This was in light of the inability of courts in some 'developing' countries to deliver substantive justice for victims of corporate misdemeanours. For example, although Nicaraguan workers, who were poisoned by a pesticide, won a verdict against US companies, there was little chance of them receiving the damages payments from companies with no assets in Nicaragua (see 'Locating justice' on page 151). That substantive justice may be located only in the countries where sued corporations have assets, made the Alien Tort Claims Act (ATCA) in the US particularly important, and a number of cases progressed during 2002 (see 'Litigation nation' on page 141).

Given the importance of ATCA, the International Chamber of Commerce began a lobbying campaign to have it reformed (see 'Locating justice' on page 151). The ICC had also lobbied against the UNHCHR process, described above. Regressive lobbying from certain trade associations created rumbles within the community of corporate responsibility professionals and campaigners.

These rumbles were set to explode in 2003, as NGOs geared up to place the political activities of corporations and their associations firmly on the top of the agenda of corporate responsibility (see 'The political bottom line' on page 153).

It also appeared that 2003 would witness a broader scaling-up of the corporate responsibility debate from the micro level of individual corporate practice to the macro level of the corporate sector's role in international development. In 2002 tensions remained over the role of bilateral and multilateral trade agreements in helping or hindering sustainable development. Southern Hemisphere countries continued to decry Northern protectionism—especially over issues such as the United States' vetoing of a deal on drug patents, which directly responded to pressure from corporations (see 'The political bottom line' on page 153). The new director of the World Trade Organisation's call for a code of conduct for corporate lobbying of trade delegations was therefore likely to be discussed once again in 2003 (see 'Sustainable positions?' on page 129).

The development charity Oxfam focused on unfair trading, which it suggested was perpetuated by large corporations for their own interests. They launched a report about the crisis in coffee prices, calling for all stakeholders to support moves to make the trade more beneficial for poor producers in the 'developing' world. If the coffee campaign progresses in 2003, we could see the beginning of wider engagement between the corporations and questions about the structure of trading relations in the global economy (see 'Stinker drinkers' on page 133).

2002 saw the United Nations increasing its engagement with the corporate sector. This occurred under the framework of the UN Global Compact, but also through direct partnerships between certain UN agencies and companies. These new partnerships grew both praise and scorn, and 2003 looked certain to witness more of a debate about the way the UN should or should not engage with corporations (see 'Too close for comfort?' on page 122 and 'A McFudge?' on page 135). Certain elements of the UN were not restrained in criticising certain corporate practices.

A UN report on mining in the Democratic Republic of Congo (DRC) accused corporations of exploiting the African country's mineral wealth in tandem with criminals. The UN said the companies involved had breached the OECD's code on multinational enterprises, although the OECD replied that it would have to decide this matter, and would look into it only if its official complaints process was called upon. Consequently, 2003 looked set to bear witness to the effectiveness, or not, of voluntary measures such as the OECD code, and the willingness of international bodies such as the UN to redress the costs of corporate malpractice (see 'Rumbles from the jungle' on page 147).

The emergent profession of 'social auditing' continued to grow in 2002, but with it did criticism of its practice and potential. Reports suggested that commercial auditors and business-led initiatives were not delivering real change for workers around the world.

The solution, some suggested, would come from involving the intended beneficiaries more closely in the agenda setting and delivery of ethical trading initiatives (see 'UnWRAPping monitoring' on page 149). The criticism of social auditing paralleled a growing concern that people from certain sectors of society had limited access to the emergent practice of corporate responsibility. For example, principles of sustainable finance developed by a British NGO were considered by the United Nations Environment Programme (UNEP) as applicable globally, even though they did not integrate lessons from the rapidly expanding Islamic finance sector (see 'Unsustainable worldviews?' on page 144).

The need to pluralise cultural perspectives on corporate responsibility is a challenge for all involved, including the authors of this review. We have sought to offer a review of trends in the global operating environment of business. Nevertheless, we do this from a Western vantage point, even if seeking to draw on non-Western cultures. It is something that we will continue to work on in future quarterly World Reviews of the *Journal of Corporate Citizenship*.

1Q2002

January–March

Jem Bendell and Rupesh Shah

Enron's new clothes

A few months into 2002 and the broader implications of the collapse of Enron for the accountancy and professional service industries were becoming apparent. The role of Andersen, Enron's auditors up until the time of the energy company's bankruptcy, fostered a renewed debate about the conflicts of interest that could exist in the world of transnational commerce. Some companies, including Ford, ended their auditing contracts with Andersen while others, including Unilever, announced that they would no longer give consulting work to those firms they used as auditors. This was a response to the accusation that, as both an auditor of and a consultant to Enron, Andersen might have had a considerable financial interest in maintaining the façade of a viable energy company.

Noticing this threat to their business, other members of the 'big five' accounting firms sought to alter their governance and corporate structures appropriately. PricewaterhouseCoopers (PwC) spun off its consulting arm and Deloitte Touche Tohmatsu (D&T) announced the separation of Deloitte Consulting from its main business. James Copeland, chief executive officer of Deloitte Touche Tohmatsu, said they 'came to this decision very reluctantly. I believe that, for our firm at least, the independence issue related to providing both auditing and consulting services is one of perception only.'

However, *The Economist* magazine, in exploring these troubles, concluded that 'accounting will always be as much art as science'.[1] Moreover, Harvey Pitt, the chair-

JAMES COPELAND, DELOITTE TOUCHE
TOHMATSU CEO: THE INDEPENDENCE ISSUE
IS ONE OF PERCEPTION ONLY

person of the Securities and Exchange Commission in the USA stated that 'there is no true number in accounting'. The implication of this is that the social and economic context within which auditors work influences the financial 'reality' they uncover and report. One question this raises is how the existence of a financial relationship between the auditor and auditee affects the audit—a question that applies not only to financial matters but also to the social and environmental performance of a company. Some therefore question whether the growing reliance on social and environmental certification by commercial audit firms is advisable. Assistant Professor of Law at Osgoode Hall Law School in Toronto, Stepan Wood, notes:

> The Enron scandal and the questions about the accountants' complicity illustrate in a stark way the importance of Garrett Hardin's question, *qui custodiet ipsos custodes*—who will watch the watchers?

When verification and certification of compliance with environmental and social standards are entrusted to private professionals who depend for their revenue on the clients they are monitoring, who treat information about their clients' performance as strictly confidential and who have close working relationships with their clients, there are huge risks of 'regulatory capture'.

The issue of conflict of interest raised more questions about the role of the values and integrity of auditors and how the interplay of an auditor's own sense of accountability to client, employer, society and self might affect the quality of the auditor's work. This is a major challenge for a profession that has traditionally prided itself in seeing the process of accountancy as mechanistic and value-free.

In this context, a report from the International Business Leaders' Forum (IBLF) on the corporate responsibility of major professional services companies published in January 2002 was particularly timely.[2] Many of the companies reviewed, including KPMG, PwC and D&T, provide consultancy services on aspects of corporate citizenship, and so this was a chance to consider how they practise what they preach. The study found that professional services companies, the so-called 'guardians of market capitalism', could do more both to change their own practices and to leverage their significant experience in institution building, building human capital and strengthening local business systems to contribute to sustainable development.

While the accounting and auditing community was awakening to the importance of personal values, elements of the corporate citizenship community continued to professionalise service provision in traditional ways that reduced the focus on values. The 2001 review in this volume reported on the emergence of a group of practitioners, researchers and academics who have begun to relate their activities directly to a shared field known as corporate citizenship or corporate social responsibility and warned that the increasing notoriety of this profession would bring greater scrutiny from critics and sceptics. If and when legitimacy of professionals working in this area is challenged, what would be more important: personal and organisational purpose and experience, or certification to one of the new professional institutes in this area? And what form of organisation would be a more credible partner for a corporation: a professional services company or a non-profit organisation with a history of campaigning on related issues? It seems the practice of corporate citizenship could necessitate a redefinition of 'professionalism'.

By talking of the 'art' of accounting, *The Economist* gave voice to the socially con-

CHAIRMAN OF KPMG LLP,
STEPHEN G. BUTLER: TIME TO
MOVE THE AUDITING MODEL
INTO THE INFORMATION AGE

structed nature of accounting figures. In doing this, the magazine inadvertently put its finger on the pulse of an academic vein of work that has for sometime been rejecting the notion of pure objectivity and the existence of a single, scientifically rational truth. This is particularly important for the growing field of accounting for intangible assets, such as corporate reputation and social capital. Some accounting executives argued that, post-Enron, we need a completely new approach. The chairman of KPMG LLP, Stephen G. Butler, said that his company had 'for several years' urged the modernisation of the current systems of investor information. 'It's finally time to move the auditing model of the industrial age into the information age. Specifically we can no longer ignore the intangible assets of knowledge based companies', he said. This was not news to people who have been working on initiatives such as SIGMA, which is an initiative looking at methodologies for quantifying the social and environmental assets of a company. However, the challenge is that intangible assets such as corporate reputation are in the eye of the stakeholder, so the traditional approach of a company documenting its assets and inviting an audit of that documentation may not be appropriate. A new form of accounting will need to look outside as well inside the company. When these new forms of accounting develop, we will need to remember that there will be no one true reality to measure, and that some values may not even be quantifiable.

There is a danger here that we will be creating assets that can be seen only by those clever enough to measure them. The emperor's new clothes might prove no more 'real' than Enron's old ones. We are really asking the question 'what is wealth?'. It is a strange world where so much money tracks 'confidence' in securities and currencies, creating or dissipating that confidence as it moves, while billions live in money-poor economies. Will any of these debates about current accounting practices make any difference to sustainable development and social justice? Well, just maybe, if we reflect on how these debates provide lessons beyond individual company accounts. *The Economist*'s analysis of accounting practices inadvertently forms a fundamental critique of national accounting systems, which we have increasingly used to measure 'wealth' and human progress over the last 50 years. Gross national product (GNP) measures only the gross amount of money changing hands in an economy, and not the social and environmental quality of that economy and the society it operates within. GNP measures the noise of an economy but can not tell whether this is in tune with society and the environment.

Be reasonable

Public relations (PR) firms were in the spotlight in the new year, following the ejection of Lord Peter Melchett from the board of Greenpeace International after his move to Burson-Marsteller, the major PR firm. This sparked debates in newspapers and magazines about whether activists could and should work with industry to seek change. In February 2002 a *Newsweek* article entitled 'Pinstripe Protestors' reported that a 'cultural revolution is underway as protesters in pinstripes figure out how to work the capitalist system'.[3] They quoted a Greenpeace director in Germany, Fouad Hamdan, saying that he 'finally realized it's all about money'. Treating this as 'news', these reports ignored the fact that this 'revolution' has been under way for ten years with organisations such as WWF-UK having worked with the timber trade on sustainable forestry initiatives since the early 1990s.[4] For most, the debate has moved on, and now focuses on what can and can't be achieved through working with business, and how collaboration need not and should not preclude conflict or efforts at regulatory reform.[5]

In a sense, the key issue is not the existence of these collaborations but how they are presented to a wider audience, and whether they are marketed as something more than they are. The issue of responsible marketing and advertising hit the headlines in January 2002. In China, Pabst, the beer company behind the Pabst Blue Ribbon brand, announced the withdrawal of adverts that appeared in Tibet celebrating the 50th anniversary of the 'peaceful liberation of Tibet'. The company had been hit by protests as pictures of the adverts circulated around the Internet. The president and CEO Brian Kovalchuk posted a letter on the company website that confirmed the withdrawal but did not give the apology demanded by some of the campaigners.[6]

The *Jakarta Post* in Indonesia reported[7] that, after a wave of criticism from politicians and educators, the cigarette manufacturer HM Sampoerna pulled a series of its cartoon advertisements, which featured animated characters, including ants, roosters, snails and a dancing squid. The company denied it had targeted children with the promotion, but agreed that the series should be withdrawn to 'prevent misinterpretation' although it added that cartoons were in line with its other adverts, which were 'creative and modern'.

It seems that it is quite possible for people around the world to hold different understandings of creativity and modernity. One institution of creative endeavour, the University of Nottingham, UK, decided in 2001 to accept £3.8 million in sponsorship from British American Tobacco (BAT) for the establishment of a corporate citizenship research centre. In response, the team of cancer research scientists at the university elected to move elsewhere and the editor of the *British Medical Journal* resigned his post at the university. Conversely, in January 2002, faculty members at the Harvard School of Public Health, USA, voted not to accept research funding from tobacco manufacturers and their subsidiaries. The vote puts current practice into official policy and is consistent with Harvard University's 13-year-old policy of not holding stock in tobacco companies.

The tobacco industry has been under further criticism from the World Health Organisation (WHO), which accused tobacco companies of using 'dirty tricks' to undermine efforts to set up an international treaty aimed at cutting the number of deaths from smoking. WHO estimates[8] that four million people die from smoking-related ailments every year and in March 2002 they resumed negotiating a global treaty with measures that could include worldwide legal curbs on tobacco advertising, marketing and subsidies. The tobacco industry is said to favour self-regulation via the adoption of voluntary codes for marketing standards. According to BAT, the voluntary standard would represent a ' "raising of the bar" and establish a benchmark for the industry world wide'.[9]

In the January/February 2002 edition of *New Internationalist* magazine, Bob Burton and Andy Rowell quoted from a (leaked) memorandum of a Wall Street tobacco analyst at Credit Suisse.[10] The memo said the tobacco industry's development of a voluntary marketing code is 'to improve the tobacco industry's image' and that 'by proactively setting new international standards the multinationals could be trying to counter a number of proposals that the WHO has been working on to curb the amount of cigarettes that are consumed on an international basis'. This case seems to add weight to the argument that companies often adopt voluntary codes when there is the threat of new legislation. This suggests that a company's adoption of voluntary codes should not necessarily be regarded as indicative of corporate citizenship, but that we should consider these in relation to a company's stance on national and international regulation and the range of their lobbying activities.

The moves by Harvard and the work of the WHO suggest that tobacco is part of a group of sunset industries where ethical legitimacy has disappeared. No matter how many organic or fairly traded cigarettes they might eventually produce, some may think it easier for a packet of Camels to pass through the eye of a needle than for a tobacco company to be socially responsible. However, this is not a view shared by FTSE4Good. In January 2002 this British index of 'ethical' stocks was reported[11] to be set to lift its ban on companies making tobacco, allowing them to join the listing by the end of the year. The index committee suggesting that it would admit tobacco companies if they were improving their records on issues such as public health, the environment and human rights. A spokesperson for FTSE4Good said: 'if you are trying, then you are worth investing in'. But what might constitute 'trying'? The Parliamentary Undersecretary of State at the UK's Department of Health, Lord Hunt, said that 'the most appropriate social criterion on which to judge BAT's performance would be its success in moving, in partnership with its employees and suppliers, away from tobacco towards less harmful forms of economic activity'.

FTSE4Good expressed the same attitude towards arms and nuclear firms. Corporate citizenship is now even on the radar screens of some in the defence industry. The United States General Accounting Office released a report on how its military shops,

CLARE SHORT: UK SECRETARY FOR
INTERNATIONAL DEVELOPMENT:
CALL FOR A RESPONSIBLE ARMS INDUSTRY

which sell items such as army clothing, could 'better assure that their goods are not made by child or forced labor'. And in March 2002, at a development policy forum in the UK, the Secretary for International Development, Clare Short, suggested that an arms industry that acted responsibly would be vital in providing governments such as Thabo Mbeki's in South Africa with the potential to take on peace-keeping roles across Africa. The value of ensuring that military equipment and clothing is not manufactured by child labour would be seen in the lived experience of children who are no longer employed inhumanely. However, can the production of weapons of destruction for profit ever be an activity worthy of association with the aspirational concepts of sustainability, social responsibility or citizenship?

Whose realities?

The idea that, whoever you are, you can learn to do better seems like an intriguing starting point for changing society; but many have balked at such an all-encompassing interpretation of responsible and ethical behaviour. The diversity of opinions of what constitutes responsible practice seems open to a plurality of interpretations. A report on corporate responsibility research and education in the *Financial Times* in the UK seemed to agree, recognising that the interpretation of CSR varies from one business college to another and from country to country.[12] However, the paper suggests that some good, early research would clarify *the true* meaning of corporate social responsibility.

Such a view that suggests the possibility of discovering a singular truth about CSR seems to be defied by the way language and knowledge is used in a diverse world of shifting expectations, perceptions and motivations. For instance, in responding to a report criticising his company, Willie Tan, president of Tan Holdings Corporation of Saipan, retorted that the 'report was wrong when it used the term "sweatshop" to refer to our clean, air-conditioned facilities'.

Similar language games were being played at the Winter Olympics. In February 2002, following a protest by the American Anti-Slavery Group and the Free Burma Coalition that parts of the 2002 Winter Olympic Torchbearer uniforms were made in Burma, the media relations department of the Salt Lake Organising Committee riposted that the 'torch relay clothes were *not* made in Burma. They were manufactured in Myanmar.'

We might laugh off the second quote with a knowing smile. We might also regard some of the postmodern play with language as slightly off-the-wall. However, there are some significant issues regarding the way that destructive power relations are perpetuated through our ways of systemically and often unknowingly privileging certain discourses, types of knowledge and certain 'expert' voices over others.

In a London workshop organised by the New Academy of Business in March, there was a deliberate attempt to shake up the sometimes-cosy world of corporate citizenship debate and practice in Europe with some vibrantly real voices from the global South. Claudia Blanco and Lesbia Guerero from Nicaragua were funded to visit the UK and spent two weeks speaking their own truths about the realities facing them in their daily struggle of working in plantations and factories. This was one of the first times that a workshop of CSR professionals was confronted with people from the farms and factory floors that form the backdrop to corporate citizenship practice. Claudia and Lesbia repeatedly brought proceedings and rather distant discussions about procedures for monitoring and reporting back to the very real problems of poor workplace practices for their lives as working mothers. The workshop was part of a piece of research exploring codes of conduct, which takes a specifically gender-based perspective on issues of corporate responsibility.[13]

Women have been particularly active in moving forward corporate practices elsewhere. Following an international activist campaign coordinated by Burma Campaign UK, the UK's leading lingerie brand Triumph eventually 'reneged' on its commitment to Burmese production and announced plans to withdraw its facilities from Rangoon. Its response to the consumer boycott was to note that the public debate in Europe on the political situation in Burma is one 'that has become increasingly emotional and that has led to planning uncertainties which Triumph can no longer accept'.

Meanwhile, in February 2002, Dita Sari, the prominent labour rights and social justice advocate from Indonesia, announced that she had reconsidered an earlier decision to accept a Reebok Human Rights Award. Ms Sari said:

> On the one hand, this is a kind of recognition of the struggle and the hard work that we have done for years. But on the other hand, we are very conscious of the condition of the Reebok workers from the third world countries. As a trade union, we strongly put a lot of pressure to achieve what every worker deserves: higher wages, better working conditions and a brighter future for their children. The low pay and exploitation of the workers of Indonesia, Mexico and Vietnam are the main reasons why we will not accept this award.

Another woman made international news in March 2002 as she was imprisoned for her views on the Indian legal system. The prize-winning author Arundhati Roy is also known for her stand against 'the collaboration between western corporations and the Indian ruling establishment', the Narmada Dam and the effect of globalisation on India.[14] In an article on the flowering of feminism across the global South, Madeleine Bunting argued that Roy's 'feminism is not about imitating masculine models of achievement or competition, nor about sexual power; it is not about glass ceiling or stilettos. Her feminism is about articulating a voice and a sensibility which is authentically feminine and offers no deference to a largely male-determined status quo.' She noted that 'Roy is not a one off; she is standing on the shoulders of thousands of grassroots woman activists.'[15]

In the West, women are already playing key roles in communities of corporate citizenship practice, as illustrated by the hundreds of members of the CSR Chicks network in London. Despite this, the relevance of feminism to the practice of corporate citizenship has not been widely recognised. This is a pity, as feminist insights into corporate power could prove valuable for thinking and practice on corporate citizenship.

Working world

Separately, the Indonesian Children's Welfare Foundation (YKAI), in cooperation with the Ministries of Manpower and Transmigration, and the state Ministry for Women's

Empowerment, launched a national campaign aimed at raising public awareness of the rights of the country's 1.3 million housemaids, of whom over 300,000 are between the ages of 10 and 18. Part of the campaign is to call for households employing house-maids to provide better conditions and allow them one day's rest each week.[16] In Aus-tralia approximately 4,000 home care workers in New South Wales refused to wear uniforms made in sweatshops. In a campaign coordinated by the Textile, Clothing and Footwear Union of Australia, the home care workers gained support for an interna-tional anti-sweatshop campaign with an agreement that all their uniforms would now carry the Fair Wear label. Meanwhile, Social Accountability International (SAI) pub-lished the first revised version of the SA8000 standard which included the addition of home workers to the standard.

Also in January 2002, a report by Human Rights Watch claimed that domestic women workers in Guatemala face persistent sex discrimination and abuse. Domes-tic workers, many of whom come from that country's historically oppressed indige-nous communities, do not have the legal right to be paid the minimum wage, nor do national labour laws provide adequate protection for domestic workers who are under the age of 18. The report by Human Rights Watch also identified serious discrimina-tion in the growing number of maquilas of Guatemala's textile industry—another female-dominated industry sector. In the maquilas, in order to get a job in a factory, women must often reveal whether they are pregnant, either through questions on job applications, in interviews or through physical examinations. The US-based clothing manufacturers and retailers that have contracts with discriminatory maquilas include Target, The Limited, Wal-Mart, GEAR for Sports, Liz Claiborne and Lee Jeans. All of these have codes of conduct or terms of engagement that prohibit discrimination.

In another action the International Textile, Garment and Leather Workers' Federa-tion (ITGLWF) wrote a letter to World Trade Organisation (WTO) general secretary Mike Moore aimed at getting protection for workers in an ongoing labour conflict at two Korean garment plants in Guatemala, regarding the attempts to organise workplace unions under the umbrella of the union federation FESTRA. ITGLWF general secretary

ITGLWF GENERAL SECRETARY NEIL KEARNEY: A CLEAR NEED FOR A SOCIAL DIMENSION TO TRADE

Neil Kearney said the violations of the right to organise demonstrate a clear need for 'a social dimension to trade' and the need to hold the government of Guatemala to account. Kearney has also sought to affect the conditions for factory workers in Sri

Lanka's free-trade zones. Again, it is foreign-owned factories that have come under fire as the ITGLWF cites anti-union practices, such as employing baton-wielding security guards to intimidate union members, telling new workers not to join the union, firing or transferring workers who protest unfair conditions, claiming that unions are 'illegal' in the free-trade zones, threatening to hand union activists over to the police for their legitimate activities, and refusing to attend meetings called by the labour force. Kearney wrote to President Chandrika Bandaranaike Kumaranatunga and to Minister of Labour Mahinda Samaraweera suggesting that if action was not taken the international union would submit a complaint to the International Labour Organisation. The ITGLWF also wrote to two Korean-owned companies, Dulon Zippers and Cosmos Macky, urging them to ensure the disputes are resolved.[17]

The same month, the International Confederation of Free Trade Unions[18] produced a report condemning the 'miserable' situation faced by working people in Malawi, and challenged the government to meet its obligations to protect its citizens. The report states that 'more than twenty per cent of the workforce on commercial plantations, especially tobacco plantations, are children. Much child labour on these commercial plantations is hidden because the tenant farming system encourages the whole family to work.' Although the tobacco industry is the central element of Malawi's trade strategy, the report claimed 'its workers face severe poverty and poor working conditions'.

Already developed?

Despite the ongoing difficulties across the global South for workers seeking to secure their rights, work on improving corporate responsibility has been moving on apace. The Chilean Benchmarking Group has been created to identify, study and promote good practices of corporate community involvement initiatives in Chile. An initial report by the group suggests that, 'despite the success of corporate citizenship programs in the US and Europe, it must not be assumed that external models can be imported for direct application to Chile, nor to any other developing country'.[19] Meanwhile, New Africa Capital has developed an 'empowerment index' to measure progress in the areas of employment equity, corporate social involvement, skills development and control. The tool, which aims to measure actual results that have been achieved within companies rather than aspirations or goals, was created by an in-house team with the participation of various stakeholders and is currently being piloted within the group.

In Asia, TERI, the Tata Energy Research Institute, organised the Delhi Sustainable Development Summit as advance preparation for the World Summit on Sustainable Development later in 2002 in Johannesburg, South Africa.[20] Also in preparation for the summit, the Centre for Social Markets is establishing an initiative to get local enterprises from the South to take part in a 'Southern Business Challenge'. One of the initial aims of the challenge is to provide a business voice at the summit in Johannesburg other than large, Western multinationals.

In Manila, a partnership between the Philippine Business for Social Progress (PBSP) Centre for Corporate Citizenship and the British Council organised a lecture for small and medium-sized enterprises exploring the possibility of CSR as an alternative model for global competitiveness. This was in preparation for 'CSR Week' in the Philippines, which was scheduled for July 2002. The week-long event, to be led in 2002 by PBSP, the Asian Institute of Management and the League of Corporate Foundations, was an initiative of former President Estrada. The week will include a one-day workshop in Manila coordinated by the United Nations Volunteers (UNV) programme and the New Academy of Business. The workshop is part of an action research project, Enhancing Business–Community Relations, which the New Academy is currently coordinating with UNV in seven Southern countries: India, South Africa, Brazil, the Philippines, Lebanon, Ghana and Nigeria. The programme is developing practices for corporate responsibility in these regions and includes a series of national workshops between April and September 2002 in each of the countries.[21]

In Lebanon UNDP (United Nations Development Programme)/UNV, Schtroumpf, FTML-Cellis, Tetra Pak and Coca-Cola Middle East are jointly launching a new project to increase awareness of corporate social responsibility and environmental protection. The partnership will seek to promote Schtroumpf's second 'Go Green' contest between March and July 2002, targeting close to 20,000 students in major universities of Lebanon. Another exercise in awareness-raising of corporate responsibility is due to take place in Ghana in March 2002, where another UNV project is aiming to sensitise and build the capacity of local youth groups, community and opinion leaders to demand corporate accountability.

Initiatives tackling corporate reporting have also been moving ahead in the South. In Taiwan, ten member companies of the World Business Council for Sustainable Development–Taiwan (Republic of China) completed environmental reports based on the Global Reporting Initiative (GRI) Guidelines. The reports have been compiled into a single document: *Sustainable Care: Roadmap to the Green Century*, written in Chinese.

South African Finance Minister, Trevor Manuel, welcomed a study on socially responsible investment (SRI), suggesting that SRI has an important role to play in the country's investment landscape. In response to the lost decades of development (the 1980s and '90s), African heads of state have been developing a project to engender a renaissance in the continent's fortunes under the name of New Partnership for Africa's Development. With the first annual African Corporate Citizenship Convention in April 2002 in Johannesburg and the second World Summit on Sustainable Development later in the year, it may be in the context of African rejuvenation that the CSR community will be most challenged to demonstrate its usefulness and validity. This New Partnership initiative has emphasised the potential role of foreign direct investment in the process of helping Africa to play a more equal role in the global economic game. Africans are in need of vital goods and services through strengthened local cycles of economic activity. However, one of the last things that they probably need is a new colonial force of consultants, advisers and practitioners ready to offer 'help' that reinforces existing power and knowledge structures, extracts money from the local economies and draws down the stock of common environmental, cultural and social good.

Can the CSR community shape innovations such as SRI to contribute to a form of people-centred, environmentally sustainable development rather than merely to replicate the problems of externally driven neoliberal economic volatility?

The fourth bottom line

Perhaps the various world-views across Asia, Africa and South America have unique contributions to make in reframing the contribution of business to society. We might also take insights from the values of various woman activists in those regions, such as Arundhati, Claudia, Lesbia and Dita. This is because, for over the past 400 years, Western patriarchal societies—through their businesses, governments, families and other groupings—have attempted to separate the individual self from wider communities (both human and ecological) within which it is embedded. They have placed primary value on the individual part in the system, a system that is perceived as dead and mechanical. In contrast, many societies in Asia and Africa in particular have retained a way of understanding the world that is based on the primary value of relationship and the radically interconnected and organically alive nature of reality. As Nicholas Florio, country chairman, Caltex Philippines, Inc., indicates in the following statement, an understanding of the contribution of business within society in a more holistic way requires a different way of conceptualising and speaking about the world:

> How does one separate the heart from the soul? How does one differentiate the body from the spirit? How can a business thrive if it cannot acknowledge that there are certain social voids and inequities that have to be filled?

As well as reminding us that the vastly generalised reference to countries of the South as still 'developing' or 'emerging' needs to be dropped, the statement also registers the growing interest in the place of spirituality in business. In January 2002, the International Business and Consciousness Conference was held in Santa Fe, New Mexico, USA.[22] In April 2002, the Dalai Lama was scheduled to speak at a conference on 'Spirit in Business: Ethics, Mindfulness and the Bottom Line'.[23] The conference's medium-term goal was to launch a series of dialogues on 'Business as an Agent of World Benefit' and the long-term objective of launching the Spirit in Business World Institute. The conference will take place in New York, where in 2001 the place of religion and spirituality in the world was brought into sharp focus.

Some will have major concerns with attempts to unite spirituality and for-profit business. They could cite the track record of corporations successfully tapping into previously free expressions of community, love and creativity and selling them back to society for a profit. One worry is that spirituality will be similarly repackaged and sold back to us in neat, easily consumed packages. Another critical story is that, if spirituality becomes another management principle—a fourth bottom line—its contribution will be evaluated in terms of the common denominators of financial performance and economic growth, and CSR professionals will seek to calculate the 'spiritual capital' in an organisation. Spiritual awareness can (should) lead to a non-competitive outlook and a disinterest in material possessions—something that would not be 'productive' in a capitalist and consumerist context. Most spiritual traditions suggest that spirituality cannot be measured, cannot be divided, and should never be used for self-centred ends, such as the generation of profit. That would be a perversion of spirituality. Is it not time to recognise those ways of knowing and feeling that cannot not be reduced to a mathematical output; and to respect their non-quantifiable contribution to the health of humanity? Perhaps the new accountancy will be embarking on an impossibly intangible task.

Another story may be told about spirituality and business: that it is impossible to separate spirituality and other human values from entrepreneurial activity; and our attempts to do otherwise have failed. By pretending that we can leave our values in the business reception room we have merely been concealing a reality that human values are always at play in all decisions. The more disturbing conclusion from this is that, by espousing a value-free system of decision-making, business people have been hiding the way in which structures that serve their purposes are reinforced. Isn't it about time we were more mindful of our economic lives? Then we might just find that the fourth bottom line is the only bottom line we need.

2Q2002

April–June

Jem Bendell

Greed Inc. or Greed Ltd?

'The wickedness of Wall Street.' No, not a slogan from an anti-corporate campaign, but the title of a cover-page story in that well-known radical magazine, *The Economist*. And it was not unusual, as *BusinessWeek*, *Fortune* and other mainstream business magazines lamented a crisis of confidence at the heart of Corporate America. Goldman Sachs CEO Hank Paulson was reported as saying that, in his lifetime, 'American business has never been under such scrutiny, and to be blunt, much of it deserved.'

Let us review the evidence. Enron eclipsed after it was found to have cooked the books. Andersen atomised as it was found guilty of shredding records about those Enron recipes. K-Mart KO'ed and under investigation for similarly creative accounting. Dynegy in denial over debt cover-ups. Former telecom superpowers WorldCom, Qwest and Global Crossing humbled as all are investigated. Adelphia and Tyco wobbling as their CEOs resign under suspicions of malpractice or incompetence.[1]

While *BusinessWeek* pointed the finger at the managers of these companies, *The Economist* preferred to blame 'arrogant investment bankers' who 'exploited their supposedly independent analysts to peddle dubious shares to gullible investors'. *Fortune* magazine thought that, taken together, phoney revenues, wildly high executive pay, interest-conflicted investment analysts, and boards of directors asleep at the helm were symptoms of something deeper. 'This isn't just a few bad apples we're talking about here. This, my friends, is a systemic breakdown. Nearly every known check on corporate behavior—moral, regulatory, you name it—fell by the wayside, replaced by the stupendous greed that marked the end of the bubble. And that has created a crisis of investor confidence the likes of which hasn't been seen since—well, since the Great Depression.'[2]

According to a Pew Forum survey, now Americans think more highly of Washington politicians than they do of business executives.[3] 'Yes, it is that bad', said *Fortune*. 'Rarely have business and its leaders been held in such low esteem', said *Business Week*. Clearly, investing, like all aspects of commerce, requires a degree of trust. Without the trust that directors and auditors aren't fiddling the figures, that analysts are playing it fair and reported numbers reflect reality so that investors aren't being conned—capital markets will grind to a halt. Chairman of the Securities and Exchange Commission (SEC), Harvey L. Pitt, said 'It would be hard to overstate the need to remedy the loss of

SEC CHAIRMAN, HARVEY L. PITT:
WE NEED TO RESTORE PUBLIC
CONFIDENCE

confidence . . . Restoring public confidence is the No. 1 goal on our agenda.' *Fortune* agreed, saying that 'real reform is once again needed to restore confidence in the system'.

The big investors have woken up to this need for reform. Pension and mutual funds have nearly US$8 trillion riding on the US stock market, 65% of its value, up from 51% in 1990. Therefore they both have a stake in the general health of the stock market rather than individual firms and a voice that cannot be ignored. Chris Davis, who oversees US$35 billion at New York investment firm Davis Selected Advisors began putting together a group who together manage US$500 billion–1 trillion, or nearly 10% of the stock market. This group is targeting companies in the Standard & Poor's 500-stock index on corporate governance and executive compensation issues. *BusinessWeek* reports that 'Labor unions are taking up the cause, too, using their vast pension funds as a big stick to beat up errant management.' They report that 'sometimes the threat of a vote does the trick. The AFL–CIO withdrew shareholder resolutions it filed after Goldman Sachs, Merrill and J.P. Morgan Chase all agreed to break the links between compensating research analysts for the investment-banking business they help generate.' The magazine reported that these pressures were helping to create reforms in the New York Stock Exchange (NYSE) and Nasdaq who were now 'falling over themselves to prove that they offer superior protection to long term investors'.[4]

What kinds of reform would do the job? The NYSE set out new corporate governance requirements for companies whose shares it trades, to take effect from August 2002. The proposed requirements included that a majority of a company's board of directors must be independent (i.e. they must not have a material relationship with the company, nor worked for their company or auditor in the past five years) and that a shareholder vote will be necessary for all stock option plans.

Meanwhile the SEC, which was itself established after the last crisis in confidence at the time of the Great Depression, published a range of new measures to reform oversight and improve accountability of auditors of public companies. The proposed rules established the framework for a Public Accountability Board—a system of 'private-sector' (but not 'self-') regulation that would not be under the control of the accounting profession.[5] Other new rules proposed included a requirement that CEOs personally certify the accuracy of financial statements put out by their companies. As these measures were announced, President George W. Bush said that 'there's been a lot of talk about corporate responsibility here in America, and there needs to be'.[6]

Thus it was shareholder concerns, rather than those of other stakeholders, that mainstreamed corporate responsibility mid-2002. It was self-interest rather than social and environmental solidarity that led mainstream corporate America to talk of the responsibilities of professionals in business and commerce. While corporate citizenship academics, consultants and managers were busy attending to their sweatshop codes, recycling projects and stakeholder dialogues, someone else's version of corporate responsibility exploded onto the front pages.

As much of the pressure for reform is coming from self-interested shareholders, so some of the reforms may actually undermine some of those aspects of corporate responsibility that people have been working on for a while. For example, the rule changes on stock option plans may not only help curtail wild 'fat cat' payments but also innovative approaches to encouraging employee commitment to and participation in a business through employee share ownership plans (ESOPs).[7]

For example, in the UK 75,000 staff of the supermarket Tesco received £38 million-worth of shares, which had been held in trust for three years. Tesco staff can choose to keep their shares or cash them in.[8] Another example is the proposal from Nasdaq that directors whose charities receive large donations from their companies should be thrown off audit committees, something that could undermine corporate philanthropy. Therefore, the time must be right for those who have been working on wider corporate responsibility issues to stand up and be heard to explain the broader corporate responsibility agenda that recognises shareholders among a web of other stakeholders and acknowledges that pension owners may have concerns other than maximising dividends and share price.

The time is right for this kind of leadership, which must address values as well as regulatory reforms if it is to succeed. Former Federal Reserve Board Chairman Paul A. Volcker told *BusinessWeek* he believes that the real problem is one of values in corporate America. 'Corporate responsibility is mainly a matter of attitudes and the attitudes got corrupted by the mentality in the markets in the 1990s. We went from "greed is good" being said as a joke to people thinking that "greed is good" was a fundamental fact.'[9]

The magazine wished 'If Only CEO Meant Chief Ethical Officer' and argued that the very same personal attributes that propelled people to the top were those that led to abuse, and made them ill equipped to lead business out of its current confidence crisis.[10] They suggest that 'this year's CEO scandals could even end up changing what companies look for in a CEO as they attempt to restore investor confidence . . . For instance, stakeholders are likely to become increasingly skeptical of highly aggressive CEOs.' The magazine cites Michael Hoffman, executive director of the Bentley College Center for Business Ethics, as suggesting that a new type of 'servant leader' will be required—one who looks out more for employees, customers and the company rather than for him or herself. 'I think boards of directors and search firms need to begin looking for people with a tremendous amount of integrity,' Hoffman said. 'If you can't trust a business and you can't trust a person running it, you're probably not going to invest in it.' Already NGOs have appointed former corporate CEOs to run their affairs. Could we witness a time when former directors of NGOs take the helm of major multinationals?

Moral Bankruptcy Assured (MBA)

If business is seeking a new type of leader, then mainstream business education is failing to address this crucial need. In April 2002 an article in the *Financial Times* reported on a survey conducted by the Aspen Institute, which studied MBA students' attitudes to business and society.[11] The report surveyed MBA students from 13 business schools at three points in time: before they started their programme, halfway through and, most recently, on graduation.

Ben & Jerry's, The Body Shop, Hewlett-Packard and Johnson & Johnson are four of the companies that graduating MBA students would most like to work for—but most of them end up in traditional MBA job sectors such as management consulting and investment banking. The *Financial Times* reported that 'what is abundantly clear is that students' sense of social responsibility decreases as they go through their MBA programme', lending weight to the joke that MBA stands for 'Moral Bankruptcy Assured'. For example, as they begin their degree, more than 40% say that one of the primary responsibilities of a company is to produce useful, high-quality goods and services; but by the end of the programme just over 30% think this is valuable.

Students are not altogether happy with what they are being offered. The report shows that MBA students are unsure how social responsibility contributes to business success but most would like to learn more about it. Unfortunately, these sorts of course are rarely available at business school. Judith Samuelson, executive director of the Aspen Institute, says students are very clear that they want issues of social responsibility to be part of the core MBA programme.

By assessing only MBA courses, the report does not mention the work of the New Academy of Business, established in 1996 by Anita Roddick after she became dismayed at the state of education in business schools. Run jointly with the Bath School of Management, its MSc in Responsibility and Business Practice has been oversubscribed and boasts alumni that include Lise Kingo, now Senior Vice President, Stakeholder Relations, Novo A/S, and Paul Dickinson, a co-founder of the Social Venture Network and of sustainability-oriented start-ups such as Eye Network.[12] New Academy's Dr Rupesh Shah notes that 'not only do we have people coming from major players like PwC, Accenture, Rio Tinto, Volvo and Allied Domecq, but also people who aren't seeking to change old businesses—people who are setting up new ones that do business differently'.[13]

The *Financial Times* also notes the worrying implications for business. 'One of the most disturbing findings of the report is that although business schools are supposed to train leaders who can raise complex issues within the companies in which they work, most MBA graduates say that if their values conflict with those of the company in which they work, they will simply look for another job.' Or, in *Fast Company* parlance: ' "Big" and "powerful" may describe an MBA's ideal employer today, but "bad" is not sexy anymore.' The magazine asserts that 'the prospect of losing top MBA talent can strike terror into the heart of any red-blooded CEO, even in lean times'.[14]

Given the macho metaphors in much business reportage, it is interesting that the Aspen study found differences between male and female MBA students' perspectives on potential employers. When defining a well-run company, women put emphasis on stable employers that adhere to a strong mission, produce high-quality goods and services, and operate according to a strong code of ethics. Men, on the other hand, put more emphasis on offering high financial returns to shareholders. Women report that, if the values of the company they work for conflict with their own, they are likely to find it more stressful than men. They are, though, more likely to opt out and find another job than to raise the issue. Although no empirical data is available to confirm this, it does seem that there are more female than male professionals working on CSR portfolios in Europe and North America.

The research is heavily biased to North America, where 11 of the 13 international business schools participating in the Aspen study are located: Columbia, Yale, Darden School, Carnegie Mellon, Haas School at UC Berkeley, Kellogg School at Northwestern University, Mendoza College at the University of Notre Dame, Wharton School at Pennsylvania (all US) and the Ivey School at the University of Western Ontario and Schulich School at York (both Canada). The London Business School and IMC in Budapest were also included. In Europe there was significant movement in this field, culminating in the launch of the European Academy on CSR, in July 2002. The academy aims to integrate CSR into the mainstream of European business education, helping deans and professors at business schools and universities promote new teaching models.[15]

Too close for comfort?

In June the UN published a book on its growing number of partnerships with business, to tackle a range challenges in the pursuit of broad UN goals.[16] *Building Partner -ships* provides an overview of the evolving relationship between the UN and the private sector, ranging from traditional procurement and consultative arrangements, which have been in place since the founding of the UN in 1945, to the new types of innovative partnership that have emerged.

BUILDING PARTNERSHIPS AUTHOR
JANE NELSON: REVIEWING THE
EVOLVING RELATIONSHIP BETWEEN
THE UN AND THE PRIVATE SECTOR

With more than 150 examples of UN–business partnerships, the book, authored by Jane Nelson of the International Business Leaders' Forum (IBLF), showcases a range of partnerships on issues such as enterprise development and access to education, health, water, energy, information technology and capital, to conflict prevention and support for human rights and governance. These partnerships include the Information and Communications Technology (ICT) Task Force which works to harness information and communications technology for development.[17] It also includes the Global

Alliance for Vaccines and Immunisation (GAVI), which includes pharmaceutical companies in efforts to provide immunisation services to ensure that all children, however poor, have equal access to vaccines.[18] Expressions of concern about this particular relationship, and debates within the World Health Organisation (WHO) about the pros and cons of working with pharmaceutical companies were reported in previous Annual Reviews.

For some in the UN system, business is becoming too close for comfort. Peter Utting of the UN Research Institute for Social Development (UNRISD) believes that 'various UN institutions appear to be paying insufficient attention to certain risks associated with partnerships, including conflicts of interest, self-censorship, the poor choice of partners and the tarnishing of the UN's reputation'.

Whereas UN Secretary-General Kofi Annan is pleased to claim that 'the doors of the United Nations are open as never before to the dynamic constellation of nonstate actors', Peter Utting cautions that, 'if institutions such as governments or UN agencies are to serve the public interest, they must keep a certain distance from the private sector'. As the Director of the UN Children's Fund (UNICEF) Carol Bellamy previously expressed, an organisation such as the United Nations is driven by a set of ethical principles while business and industry are driven by the profit motive. She warned that 'it is dangerous to assume that the goals of the private sector are somehow synonymous with those of the United Nations, because they most emphatically are not'. Therefore Utting believes that 'tensions and conflicts of interest are likely to arise when private interests exert undue influence over the decision-making processes of public-interest organisations'.[19] He recommends that UN agencies make an effort to assess the track record of particular companies before entering into partnerships, as UNICEF has tried to do, and to periodically review performance. 'Consultations with civil society organisations could play a role in these processes', Utting says.

Another possibility, he suggests, is a central UN repository of information about the behaviour of corporations, which agencies and others could consult before entering into partnerships, such as the UN Centre on Transnational Corporations, which existed prior to 1992 when it was abolished partly due to pressure from certain member governments.

One of the initiatives profiled in the UN book, the Global Compact, is not currently able to fulfil a watchdog role, as it relies on companies reporting on their practices, and as efforts are focused on learning about best (and improving) practice rather than monitoring and shaming poor practice.

In its current form the Compact appears attractive to industry around the globe. In May 2002, the Global Compact was officially launched in Japan. More than 120 people from 73 Japanese companies attended the event. Yuzaburo Mogi, the Chief Executive Officer of Kikkoman, discussed the process that led Kikkoman to engage in the Global Compact, while Mr Yoshiharu Fukuhara, Honorary Chairman of Shiseido, highlighted the importance of responsible business practices in the context of globalisation.

In Manila that month, the Employers' Confederation of the Philippines (ECOP) held its National conference, at which 146 companies pledged their support for the Global Compact by presenting letters of commitment addressed to the UN Secretary-General. Speaking at the conference, senior officer of the Global Compact, Fred Dubee, suggested that participating organisations set clear goals with associated strategies and time-frames for implementation. Also speaking there, the President of the Philippines, Gloria Macapagal Arroyo, said that ECOP's support of the Global Compact complements her own government's programmes to combat poverty and bring about social reform.

Whether the Global Compact will be a catalyst for business support for the role of government in providing public services and effectively regulating the market is yet to be seen. This will be key for critics who fear that voluntary initiatives in general and partnerships in particular support a broader agenda that aims to further weaken the regulatory role of the state.

Not enough, says UNEP

In early June 2002, the United Nations Environment Programme (UNEP) marked 30 years of its engagement with the private sector. It did so with a meeting in Bali, Indonesia, where the Fourth Preparatory Committee Meeting for the World Summit on Sustainable Development (WSSD) was taking place. Addressing 100 senior government officials, tourism and other business-sector executives, Jacqueline Aloisi de Larderel, UNEP's Assistant Executive Director, outlined the findings of 22 industry-sector reports prepared by UNEP, in partnership with 29 industry associations, to assess progress by business towards sustainable development since the Rio Earth Summit, ten years ago.[20] The sectors studied included accounting, advertising, chemicals, construction, engineering, food and drink, information and communications technology, oil and gas, and tourism.

Mrs Aloisi de Larderel said that 'the reports found a growing gap between the efforts of business and industry to reduce their impact on the environment and the worsening state of the planet'. She continued that 'this gap is due to the fact that in most industry sectors only a small number of companies are actively integrating social and environmental factors into business decisions, and because improvements are being overtaken by economic growth and increasing consumption of goods and services, which rely on natural resources and systems'. The implication was that governments and intergovernmental agencies would need to play a stronger role in regulating the market for sustainable development.

That a collaboration between a UN agency and business could lead to a critical assessment of business contribution to sustainable development may, at first, surprise those who are concerned with corporate influence at the UN. However, looking at the sectoral reports themselves, they do not actually make the arguments that UNEP suggests in the press release.[21] Instead, most reports profile the industries' perceptions of the key social and environmental issues they face, present a range of positive examples of companies addressing those issues, and encourage more voluntary efforts from industry, such as codes, certifications and reporting.

On closer reading, the reports represent a view of sustainable development that can be accommodated within a deregulating, export-led economic growth paradigm. This concerned one commentator on the report, Professor Rob Gray, director of the Centre for Social and Environmental Accounting Research at the University of Glasgow, who wrote:

> I would have liked to have seen more recognition that there are conflicts between good business practice and social, environmental and sustainability issues. If the new agenda can be driven entirely by what makes good business sense then the only reason we have not made more progress is because business people are stupid or otherwise distracted. This is not an entirely plausible explanation. There are issues of a social, environmental and sustainability nature for which no business case can exist—I would like us all to recognise this more often and more explicitly.

The issue of climate change is illustrative. The report on tourism sidesteps issues of pollution in transportation, referring to the separate report on aviation and including a footnote praising the aviation industry.[22] That aviation report, written by the Air Transport Action Group (ATAG) does not deal effectively with the key issue for aviation: the growth in air transport and associated emissions of greenhouse gases.[23] Although the report notes that the Intergovernmental Panel on Climate Change (IPCC) estimated in 1999 that the sector is responsible for 3.5% of human-induced climate change, it uses largely irrelevant statistics to downplay the relative impact of air transport. Why compare the carbon emissions of a person flying 6,000 miles in a full aircraft and someone driving that distance alone in a car; by train, bus or boat would be more realistic. In any case, the main options presented as ways of addressing carbon emissions are technological, by improving efficiency and reducing emissions, and operational, by looking at how aircraft are handled. The possibility of offsetting carbon emissions through carbon sequestration is mentioned, but only voluntary action is recommended. There are no critical voices in this report, which might have highlighted the need to end the tax-exempt status of airline fuel, and bring the sector directly under the national requirements of the Kyoto Protocol.

The report argues that the role of aviation in supporting developing countries means that we need to consider trade-offs between social, environmental and economic aspects of sustainable development. Some would question whether air transport is so essential to the sustainable development of poorer countries. For example, Xavier Font of Leeds Metropolitan University, UK, who compiled a CD-ROM of research reports to support UNEP's work, notes that many studies show that over 60% of the money spent by tourists in developing countries actually 'leaks' back to other, usually developed, countries. Even so, the principle of trading off social, economic and environmental aspects of sustainable development is not absolute, but relative to certain limits. If climate change is becoming global enemy number one, and air transportation the largest-growing contributor to this, then stopping the growth of air transport and mapping out development strategies based on other forms of mobility must be on the agenda.

However, the report was written by an organisation committed to growing air transport. Hence ATAG's emphasis on 'partnership solutions . . . built on common goals, empathy, open feedback, flexibility, as well as the ability to compromise and to share rewards'[24] can be questioned, as they could not willingly agree to curtail the growth in air transport. Therefore, we may ask: 'Who is being uncompromising?' By lending its name to this report, UNEP may help exclude certain voices and entrench a growth imperative in aviation.

Here we see that terms such as 'partnership' and 'consensus' might serve both progressive and regressive ends, and context is key. The sectoral reports use these terms heavily, which is not unusual for the sustainable development and corporate citizenship literature today. So, as these terms are increasingly used, we must ask: is it because they are pertinent in the particular context or merely because they are 'trendy' or, worse, because they serve the interests of those who use them?

The sectoral reports were accompanied by an overview, *Ten Years after Rio: The UNEP Assessment*.[25] It is in this document that UNEP's Executive Director Klaus Töpfer warns that 'the downside of good examples . . . is that they may obscure the broader picture'. Nevertheless, the report is heavily focused on voluntary approaches to corporate responsibility, and its recommendations concerning these are more developed than those about other mechanisms and policies. The report identifies 'key gaps and stakeholder concerns' with various voluntary approaches. They argue:

▶ Few voluntary initiatives are directly linked with government policy and regulatory framework in a way that would complement the strengths and weaknesses of both.

▶ Many sectors still have not developed such codes of best practice to guide their members.

▶ Many often remain just good intentions, with little effective implementation, monitoring and verification programmes to ensure their effectiveness and credibility.

▶ No effective sanctions can be applied to those not adhering to the voluntary initiative. Even the best voluntary initiatives can be publicly harmed by 'free-riders'— companies that do not effectively apply the industry's voluntary standards.

▶ Many voluntary initiatives focus on the environmental aspects of sustainable development only.

The report did not list any similar 'key gaps and stakeholder concerns' for either its sections on multi-stakeholder dialogue or inter-sectoral partnerships, which illustrates how these concepts have risen to a level where they are seen as inherently good ideas.

UNEP suggests that there could be a mutually reinforcing relationship between voluntary and regulatory approaches. Therefore they call on business to adopt, effectively implement and monitor sector-wide voluntary initiatives that are '*in support of* and beyond regulatory requirements' and on governments to 'seek ways to integrate voluntary initiatives into their policy and regulatory framework'. The editors emphasise the role of governments in combining regulatory, economic and voluntary instruments, in spurring social and technological innovation, and in ensuring that laggard or negligent companies do not benefit at the expense of those investing in best practices. Therefore the report asks business to 'follow the examples of proactive companies and associations in shifting from reactive, obstructionist modes to more cooperative partnership approaches to meet global, national, regional and local environmental governance needs and sustainability goals'. However, it says very little about the role of business in lobbying government to avoid social and environmental regulation, or to negotiate those bilateral and multilateral trade and investment agreements that some argue are antithetical to sustainable development goals.[26]

The report suggests that work on the social dimension of sustainable development 'is still in its infancy', which is a view held by many environmental specialists who have only begun to work on social issues and know little of industrial relations and human rights. (The UN's International Labour Organisation and Commission on Human Rights have been around far longer than UNEP.) The lack of understanding of the social dimension to sustainable development is illustrated by a spartan section on human rights where, oddly, the voluntary workplace standard SA 8000 and the stakeholder management standard AA 1000 are both mentioned.

Johannesburgled?

The UNEP reports were prepared to help inform governments ahead of the WSSD. Before the opening of that summit, some participants in the preparatory meetings were already disillusioned with what it would achieve. Efforts were effectively beached in Bali, at the Fourth Preparatory Committee Meeting, according to the NGOs Consumers International, Danish 92 Group, Friends of the Earth, Greenpeace, Oxfam, the World Wide Fund for Nature, and ANPED, who released a joint statement that said: 'Hardly any country can leave Bali without embarrassment. The list of guilty parties is a long one, but it starts with the three who shamelessly hijacked the process in Bali: the United States, Australia and Canada. They are abandoning their responsibilities to their citizens and to poor people across the world.'[27]

Some saw the WSSD as an irrelevance from the start, as it was likely to have no mechanisms for implementation and leave those international institutions with a major impact on development, such as the World Trade Organisation (WTO), World Bank and International Monetary Fund (IMF), beyond the scope of any agreement reached. Nevertheless, the NGOs said they were 'appalled at the unwillingness of powerful countries to align international trade rules with sustainable development'. Interestingly, their press release was carried on the website of Business Action for Sustainable Development (BASD), which was coordinating the contributions of the World Business

WBCSD PRESIDENT BJÖRN STIGSON:
WE ARE TAKING ON RESPONSIBILITIES
THAT SOME GOVERNMENTS ARE NOT

Council for Sustainable Development (WBCSD) and International Chamber of Commerce (ICC) to the Johannesburg summit. So did these organisations share the same frustrations as NGOs? Yes and no. In June 2002, WBCSD president Björn Stigson told Reuters, 'I think we are taking a lot of responsibility dealing with these issues, and some governments aren't.'[28] He highlighted the intransigence of the US administration on issues such as the Kyoto agreement as not helping the international business environment. 'We see sustainable development as a real issue for society. Businesses cannot thrive and be successful in societies that fail', he said.

So what should governments have been doing at the WSSD to make societies succeed? There seemed to be some confusion. A range of NGOs and trade unions were pushing for a 'corporate accountability convention' to be agreed. Friends of the Earth described this as 'a legally-binding international treaty which requires international companies, wherever they operate, to adopt best practice in their operations and to be accountable for their environmental and social damage to citizens and communities'.[29] Yet the Vice Chair of BASD, Lord Holme, said previously that calls for such governmental action were a compromise with a 'fundamentalist minority' and should not be an outcome of the WSSD.[30]

In the run-up to Johannesburg the BASD and WBCSD websites did not have any detailed proposals for effective governmental and intergovernmental intervention to support a more sustainable and equitable functioning of the global market, and focused instead on company best practice.[31] One special report on sector-wide initiatives for the WSSD did note that 'sustainable development is too big for companies to handle individually, regardless of their size' and called for more cooperation between companies, but stopped short of saying this meant government needed to intervene.[32]

Calls for a corporate accountability convention were being taken more seriously in other circles. The Royal Institute for International Affairs (RIIA) asked the question: was *Corporate Accountability in Search of a Treaty?* in a briefing paper published in May 2002.[33] The paper summarises the cases of Thor Chemicals and Cape Asbestos Company, who were both prosecuted in the UK for transgressions in South Africa (and both resulted in out-of-court settlements), and explores how an international convention might affect these instances of 'foreign direct liability' (FDL) and, therefore, corporate social and environmental performance.

Report author Halina Ward ponders whether we should really be encouraging Western courts to take on more of these cases rather than tackling problems with the state of legal systems in some Southern countries. However, she suggests that, if FDL actions are supported by a convention, then MNCs might become advocates of better legal systems in developing countries, rather than undermining them. In this sense a convention might serve as both as a stopgap measure and as a catalyst.

The report does not explore the way FDL and a corporate accountability convention might act as a deterrent for future transgressions. As it seems not many businesses or their stakeholders are currently aware of FDL, perhaps a convention might add greatly to the profile of home-country prosecutions and add to the deterrent effect of such? More research on the matter is required.

Studying this area may become important as there is a trend for more FDL actions. This trend has prompted World Monitors to launch a quarterly report on case law developments in business and human rights.[34] The key issue in FDL cases is whether courts decide that it would not be possible for the plaintiffs to receive justice in the country where the abuses are alleged to have taken place—and they are increasingly deciding that they would not.

For example, in June 2002, a California State Court judge ruled that the lawsuit claiming oil company Unocal Corp. was complicit in human rights abuses committed by the Myanmar (Burma) military regime will go to trial in September 2002. A Federal Court action asserting similar claims against Unocal had been dismissed on summary judgement grounds in August 2000. The lawsuit was filed in 1996, and alleges that Unocal was partly responsible for human rights violations committed by the

Myanmar military junta during the construction of a pipeline, in which Unocal was a joint-venture partner with the Myanmar military government. The suit alleges that Unocal and its partners, including TotalFinaElf, were aware that forced labour was to be used before they agreed to build the pipeline. The plaintiffs' co-counsel, civil rights lawyer Paul Hoffman, said he hoped that 'this will serve as a message to Unocal and other firms that deal with regimes engaged in human rights violations that if you do business with the devil you can be held responsible for the devil's work.'[35]

Sustainable positions?

As the WSSD drew closer, it became apparent that those practices and ideas grouped together as 'corporate citizenship' and 'corporate social responsibility' were now at the epicentre of the tectonic debate about the relationship between business and the state, particularly in the context of international development. On the one hand, business leaders such as BP CEO John Browne emphasised the beneficial role of corporations in poor countries and argued that free trade would benefit them.[36] On the other hand, the UN Conference on Trade and Development (UNCTAD) released a report showing how many lower-income countries had increased their share of world trade without seeing a corresponding rise in income, which suggests 'free trade hurts the poor'.[37] Therefore, it is interesting to note that, according to one source at the negotiations in Bali, the WSSD secretariat rarely called on UN agencies to input their expertise into the process, which surprised and frustrated many delegates.

The issue of water, on the agenda at Johannesburg, was illustrative of the potential conflict between advocates and critics of economic globalisation. Some argued that water privatisation threatens the basic human right of access to affordable potable water and waste-water sanitation.[38] Others pointed to certain best practices that suggested market incentives would encourage greater efficiency in water delivery and waste-water sanitation methods.[39] Therefore, SocialFunds.com reported that 'solving the world's water problems may depend on properly regulated water privatization and corporate initiatives that introduce new technologies and reduce water consumption'. With reports on public–private partnerships to find sustainable solutions to water problems, and an awards programme to recognise corporate development of water and waste-water technologies that improve environmental performance, the WBCSD's 'Access to Water' Council Project supported the latter view.[40]

While Johannesburg drew the focus of debates, the ongoing negotiations at the World Trade Organisation (WTO) seemed to have much more of a bearing on the operating environment of companies involved in water services. Leaked documents showed the European Union was 'demanding full-scale privatisation of public monopolies across the world . . . Requests for the opening up of sensitive sectors of its trading partners' economies including water, energy, sewerage, telecoms, post and financial services', reported the *Guardian*.[41] The European Commission denied that its efforts to bring about trade liberalisation would hit state-run services in poor nations.[42]

Nevertheless, in Europe as in the United States, the role of corporate lobbying in shaping domestic and foreign trade policy was beginning to receive the spotlight. In June 2002, many observers were surprised when the WTO's Director General designate, Dr Supachai Panitchpakdi, was reported in the *Observer* to want 'to introduce

SUPACHAI PANITCHPAKDI:
WANTS TO CLAMP DOWN ON
LOBBYING BY MNCs

tough rules to clamp down on any lobbying by multinational companies that is aimed at influencing the world's trading system.'[43] In London Dr Panitchpakdi said he wanted a new code of conduct for multinational firms, 'which is something that I'm not getting support for from countries around the world, particularly some advanced countries'. An inside source at the WTO told us that they knew nothing of the proposals and cautioned that 'a director general cannot by himself alter the rules of the WTO; only a consensus of the WTO members can'. The newspaper suggested that the proposals 'will infuriate international businessmen' and said that corporations were already mounting a campaign against the initiative.

What might this mean for corporate citizenship? Would it be consistent for a company that is seeking to demonstrate good corporate citizenship to join a lobby against such proposals? Currently the corporate citizenship agenda, as illustrated by the range of issues covered by the Global Reporting Initiative (GRI), and echoed by debates at the burgeoning number of conferences, has little to say about corporate lobbying. Perhaps it would be consistent with a commitment to transparency for corporations to report on the nature and rationale of their governmental and intergovernmental lobbying activities?

Compulsory reporting

Reporting is one area where there was growing steam for regulatory reform to promote corporate citizenship. In June 2002, the European Parliament passed a resolution stating that companies should be required to supply information on the social and environmental impact of their operations. The resolution treats corporate social responsibility as a voluntary concept, but suggests to some that the creation of a comprehensive EU framework on corporate social responsibility, in line with similar legislation in Denmark, the Netherlands and France, is not far away.

In the UK, which some regard as ahead in debates on corporate responsibility, only 79 of the top 350 companies produced substantive reports on their environmental performance by the end of 2001. Craig Bennett of Friends of the Earth UK said: 'We need a new law to oblige companies to report on their environmental performance, to a common standard.' His organisation is part of the Corporate Responsibility (CORE) Coalition, which also involves the non-governmental organisations Amnesty International UK, CAFOD, the New Economics Foundation and Save the Children UK. The CORE Coalition is asking the UK government to require mandatory economic, environmental, financial and social reporting.

Perhaps it is from these types of initiative that new reporting frameworks will be proposed, which address the political dimensions of corporate activities—such as their lobbying, tax and industrial location strategies?

3Q2002

July–September

Jem Bendell and Désirée Abrahams

Sin stocks rock?

The 'business case', or financial rationale, for companies to be more responsible to our planet and its inhabitants has been essential for any proponent of corporate responsibility, be they consultant, activist, academic or manager. The business case is comprised of factors such as corporate reputation, staff morale, consumer confidence and government relations, among others.[1] It allows proponents of corporate responsibility to challenge the idea that a manager should not be concerned about responsibility but focus entirely on making money for their ultimate bosses—the shareholders; with a business case, this becomes a false distinction, as *good* business is good *business*.

In the Northern summer of 2002 the business case became a little frayed around the edges. In an article for the *Public Affairs Newsletter*, Alexander Evans of the Institute for Public Policy Research (IPPR) questioned why, if consumers are so green, sport utility vehicles have been the top-selling product line in the US. Moreover, he noted that, 'if green stock indices had outperformed their more traditional brethren, it was more because ethical funds tended to be overweight in technology stocks during the Long Boom of the 1990s than because of any fundamental competitive advantage attached to saintly behaviour'.[2]

While socially responsible investments have wobbled and fallen, the Texas-based research and investment agency Mutuals.com, which manages $240 million in assets, pointed out that 'unethical' stocks have remained strong. 'Look at any public information on [defence] stocks like Lockheed Martin or General Dynamics. You'll see that they outperformed the S&P 500 Index by wide margins over the past 15 years.'[3] Its 'Vice Fund' went on sale to the public in September 2002, advertising itself as a 'socially irresponsible fund' that would invest clients' assets in tobacco, gambling, liquor, in addition to defence. These industries 'will continue to experience significant capital appreciation during good and bad markets. We consider these industries to be nearly 'recession-proof'.[4] For example, alcoholic-beverage stocks gained 62.57% over the five years, compared with an 11.8% gain for the Standard & Poor's 500 share index.

In addition to the obvious choices, such as British American Tobacco, Boeing or Lockheed Martin, the fund managers have given themselves 'lots of flexibility' to find stocks with a natural affinity with their concept. For example, Vice Fund portfolio co-manager Dan Ahrens told the *Philadelphia Inquirer* that he might invest in Harley-

Davidson Inc. because its motorcycles could be associated with drinking. This 'Explicitly Socially Irresponsible Investment' (ESII) might be just a fad and niche, with the Vice Fund being a clever marketing idea to gain coverage through controversy. Hence Ahren's response to the possibility of pickets outside their Dallas office: 'We'd kinda like that', he said.

The existence of such funds is worth reflection. It suggests we need to analyse the context of the business case for corporate responsibility more closely. Researchers have been able to find evidence of companies making money from good or bad practices. Whether there is a business case or not depends on the company and the industry sector in question as well as the cultural, economic and political environment.

Political events in the Northern summer of 2002 reminded us how people shape the context of doing business, and in turn the business case for corporate responsibility. Defence stocks such as Lockheed Martin (+40%), Northrop Grumman (+25%) and General Dynamics (+4%) shot up because of the US government's increase in the military budget and the threat of war. Meanwhile, political developments in Germany in September 2002 had a major effect on the business case for environmental investments. Reuters noted that 'companies with an environmental edge saw their stocks gain after the Greens' success'. The wind power specialist Plambeck shot up 15% in Frankfurt, while the green energy firm Umweltkontor rose 3.3%.[5]

Perhaps once researchers remind themselves of the shifting political environment for business that turns social and environmental issues into market indicators, they will no longer look for a fixed reality to discover about *good* business being good *busi - ness*. Instead, the political and social factors that affect business priorities and performance will become more important—including activist campaigns and government regulation, two issues that featured prominently in the Northern summer of 2002.

Stinker drinkers

Are you a 'stinker' drinker? most probably, if you had a coffee this morning. According to the latest Oxfam report, *Mugged: Poverty in your Coffee Cup,* which discusses a crisis taking place in the coffee industry, the quality of our cappuccinos may not be up to scratch. A source from the International Coffee Organisation (ICO) confirmed that up to a fifth of ingredients in some coffee cups are 'not recognised as coffee'.[6] Apart from dust and other undesirables, the ICO have noted that unripe, over-ripe and fermented beans otherwise known as 'stinkers' owing to their 'unique' fragrance, have infiltrated the processing stage. Part of the reason for this has been the continual slide in prices paid to coffee farmers which makes good growing, processing and transportation practices increasingly difficult to sustain financially. Although already 3,900 people drink Nestlé's instant coffee every second, supply has been increasing far beyond demand.[7]

Although this is a serious problem for the coffee industry, it was an NGO that helped communicate this to consumers as part of a campaign for a more sustainable and economically beneficial international coffee trade. With their proposed 'Coffee Rescue Plan', Oxfam have advocated many changes to benefit Southern producers. The key developments being pushed are: the destruction of up to 5 million bags of coffee stocks (paid for by the major coffee brands); trading in only top-quality coffee beans that meet the ICO standards; and commitment by the four roaster companies (Kraft Foods, Nestlé, Procter & Gamble and Sara Lee) to make at least 2% of their volumes Fair Trade coffee.

'Fair Trade' is a specific term, referring to the standards of Fairtrade Labelling Organisations International (FLO) that have been established to bring products to market 'in a way that ensures the farmers receive a decent return'. With a strong emphasis on cooperative management, the Fair Trade standards require people in supply chains to work to transparent terms of trade and guarantee decent production conditions, at the same time as addressing some of the key obstacles that prevent poor farmers from accessing markets. These include measures such as partial pre-financing of orders to avoid small producer organisations falling into debt; payment of a premium for use by mutual agreement between producers; contractual commitments that allow farmers to make provision for long-term production planning; and the guarantee of social and environmental conditions that reflect International Labour Organisation (ILO) conventions on working conditions. Additional standards for environmental protection have been introduced progressively over recent years. Nearly 200 coffee cooperatives representing 675,000 farmers, more than 70 traders and around 350 coffee companies are already registered as Fair Trade.

Despite this key area of action, Oxfam recognises that 'a systemic, not a niche solution, is needed'. Hence, it says that the Rescue Plan should be a pilot for a longer-term 'Commodity Management Initiative', whereby governments would take measures to regulate supply and gain a higher percentage of revenues for those at the bottom of the supply (and value) chain.

In this respect, coffee-producing governments have already agreed to a plan that aims to reduce supply by improving the quality of coffee traded. However, history does not provide much confidence. Supply-management initiatives were pursued by governments from 'developing' countries before the 1980s with most falling apart under pressure from 'developed' countries and their corporations. The response of corporations to such proposals today, both publicly and privately, will be crucial to the success of such an initiative and therefore should be a key corporate citizenship issue.

By September 2002, Domini Social Investments came out in support of the initiative, commenting: 'These firms bear significant risk to their brand names as consumers become more educated about the true costs of their morning cup of coffee, and turn to higher-quality, more sustainably produced brands. Investors ignore the substantial ramifications of this global crisis at their own risk.'[8] Nevertheless the Coffee Rescue Plan did not receive extensive media coverage, with minimal governmental endorsement and a fairly insignificant amount of company acknowledgment.

Perhaps this is because Oxfam had not targeted a high-profile corporate brand in order to pressure it to support its proposals. The history of current leaders in the world of corporate citizenship, such as B&Q, GSK and Shell, points to the importance of such brand-bashing in driving public and corporate action.[9] Perhaps a greater focus on spilling the beans about the dust and dirt in our average cappuccino would have brought more of us out of our coffee-shop armchairs in uproar, and thus created more of a reaction from the business and governmental communities. Here we see the perennial problem facing any media-oriented campaign: how to translate an issue of economics and politics into something a consumer can understand, talk about and act on while having a 'cuppa'.

By focusing on coffee, a popular and highly branded consumer product, Oxfam was attempting to do just that. It could have picked any number of more 'boring' products to complain about problematic power relations in the international trading of agricultural commodities. The ILO reported that 'prices of agricultural commodities have been on an almost continuous decline since 1980, and since developing countries are heavily reliant on agricultural exports . . . falling commodity prices have contributed greatly to their difficulties . . . Annual losses in purchasing power due to deteriorating terms of trade are estimated to cost developing countries US$2.5 billion a year and mean that countries have to run faster merely to stand still.'[10]

Therefore, if the coffee campaign progresses, we could see the beginning of wider engagement between the corporations and questions about the structure of trading relations in the global economy.

A McFudge?

Consumer campaigns have a mixed record in delivering change. One only has to glance at the latest top ten of the 'World's Ten Most Valuable Brands' to see that, despite regular bad publicity on social and environmental issues, the reputation of many companies for offering what consumers will buy remains intact.[11] McDonald's comes in at eighth place, with a profit value of $26.4 billion. Despite the McLibel trial, endless critical reports about its nutritional value, environmental record, animal and worker rights violations and now, to add to the list, the decry from aid agencies regarding the introduction of the McAfrika burger in Norwegian outlets, McDonald's remains afloat on the rough seas of corporate reputation. Its latest partnership with the United Nations Children's Fund (UNICEF) indicates the buoyancy of its brand. Despite a public letter signed by 50 public health specialists to Carol Bellamy, Executive Director of UNICEF, outlining why the agency should not be allying itself with McDonald's, the McDonald's World Children's Day remained set to take place in November 2002.[12] This public–private partnership (PPP) was just one of the 200 Type II outcomes of the World Summit on Sustainable Development (WSSD). This new partnership will involve a UNICEF-fundraising pop concert to be held in China on 'McDonald's World Children's Day'. The Guardian newspaper noted that we would only participate in this by 'enjoying' a Big Mac as well.[13]

That partnerships between business and the UN have increased was discussed in the previous quarter, where certain concerns of UN staff and supporters were noted. In that review Carol Bellamy was quoted as reminding us that the values of the UN and private business were not synonymous.[14] In addition, in 1999 she cautioned UN agencies to use 'due diligence' when assessing the character of a potential 'partnership' company. 'Without due diligence, one runs the risk of becoming associated with companies whose past records suggest that they may not be the best partners', and went on to say, 'UNICEF attaches ethical strings to its supply contracts, favouring companies that pledge to avoid links with such activities as landmine production and exploitative child labour.'[15] Critics on Transnationale.org might ask whether Carol Bellamy knew McDonald's had breached two ILO conventions (1 and 138) six times since 1997.[16] Four of those incidences took place since 2000, importantly after Kofi Annan introduced the Global Compact which requests participating companies to adopt the ILO Declaration on Fundamental Principles and Rights at Work.[17] Convention 138 is part of that declaration.

Convention-al warfare?

The Johannesburg Summit's emphasis on corporate partnerships as opposed to governmental action on regulating the market, raising taxes and investing in sustainable development was a concern for some. Speaking of the huge police operation, activist author Naomi Klein said she thought the United Nations 'should see what a bad sign it is to need this level of security at a summit. It wasn't always the case, but is a result of the merger between the goals of the United Nations and the goals of the private sector.'[18]

NAOMI KLEIN: A BAD SIGN WHEN THE UN
NEEDS SUCH A HIGH LEVEL OF SECURITY

Photograph courtesy *The Herald*/Gordon Terris
© SMG Newspapers Ltd

Just before the conference started, the charity Christian Aid said that business was 'wielding its influence to water down plans for tighter regulation'. It released documents that suggested an early draft agenda called for a 'multilateral agreement' on rules to make business accountable, but this was soon diluted to 'a framework' and in the end only promised to 'promote' best practice. Some critics said it was proof that big business puts profit before the planet, while some business leaders said such rules would 'decrease investment' in the world's poorest areas.[19]

As reported in the previous quarter, Friends of the Earth (FoE) had been leading a campaign for the Summit to launch a process for negotiating a convention on corporate accountability. Its proposals would involve governments agreeing to make companies accountable to a range of other stakeholders, such as the communities in which they operate. 'At present', FoE said, 'directors of publicly traded corporations have a duty to account to shareholders and maximise financial returns'. By establishing directors' legal accountabilities to other stakeholders, FoE hoped it would be redefining the nature of commerce. Part of this would involve directors being personally liable for any failings. The NGO even suggested the new International Criminal Court could try directors and corporations for environmental, social and human rights crimes.

The distaste of some business leaders for such international regulatory developments was mentioned in the review of the previous quarter. In the days before the Summit, Lord Holme re-emphasised his concern with those who criticise voluntary

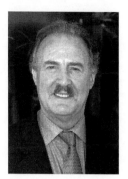

LORD HOLME: CRITICAL OF
CALLS FOR TIGHTER
REGULATION OF CORPORATIONS

initiatives as a distraction to the need for improved regulation of corporations: 'While some want to bind Gulliver hand and foot, so that he cannot move an inch, most want to ensure that he treads carefully—and that his giant footprint doesn't leave people squashed.'[20]

Nevertheless, FoE was joined by a range of other groups, including Christian Aid, who made this a central emphasis in their lobbying agenda and were far more successful than was generally expected. South Africa championed the issue during the negotiations and drew the support of the G77, European Union and others, whereas the United States was opposed to making any substantial requirements of companies. In the end the Political Declaration stated that governments 'agree that in pursuit of their legitimate activities . . . companies have a duty to contribute to the evolution of equitable and sustainable communities. We agree that there is a need for private-sector corporations to enforce corporate accountability. This should take place within a transparent and stable regulatory environment.'

The plan of implementation included a variety of paragraphs stating governments' aims to encourage or promote better corporate practice in relation to sustainable development. What forms such encouragement could take were not specified. However, paragraph 45 of this official document opened the possibility for negotiating new international legal mechanisms on corporate accountability. '[We will] actively promote corporate responsibility and accountability, based on the Rio Principles', the document read, 'including the *full development and effective implementation of intergovernmental agreements and measures*, international initiative and public–private partnerships, and appropriate national regulations, and support continuous improvement in corporate practices in all countries' [emphasis added].[21]

This statement had originally read 'existing intergovernmental agreements'; however, the word 'existing' was dropped during negotiations. 'The removal of the word "existing" is important because it seems to signal that the international community is no longer satisfied with the voluntary approach to corporate accountability. If this is the case, there are clearly significant implications for business', noted Justin Alexander of investment management company Schroders. Aware of this, and after negotiations had concluded on this section, the US delegation tried to insert an interpretative note stating that this paragraph still referred only to existing agreements. This interpretative note was not allowed, given that the section had already been agreed, but, after the signing of the declaration and plan the following day, the US issued a press release stating that it considered the scope to be existing agreements. Therefore Business Action for Sustainable Development (BASD) said that paragraph 45 only 'refers to existing agreements and is not a call for a new international regime'.[22] However, despite BASD and the US government's own interpretations, the official implementation plan does not restrict itself to existing intergovernmental agreements.

The private sector was left flat-footed and increasingly divided on how to react to the new pressure for intergovernmental action. Commenting on the reaction of the business lobbyists, the *Daily Summit* website said, 'one gets the impression they're a little irritated that the issue won't quite die'.[23] Despite the statements on the BASD website, and earlier comments from Lord Holme, the chair of BASD, Sir Mark Moody-Stuart, told the *Daily Summit* he was not averse to an emphasis on the better regulation of corporations, and, though the main effort toward regulating corporations should be at the national level, he accepted 'there is a role for international agreements'. However, he continued, 'it's going to be a long battle putting these agreements together'. The *Daily Summit* noted that, whereas Sir Mark was fairly relaxed about the proposals adopted, other business leaders thought they opened up a 'Pandora's Box'.[24]

What would be the logical next step in enacting this new and significant commitment from governments? First would be to review how existing intergovernmental agreements relate to corporations, the degree of compliance and ways of monitoring that compliance. Second could be the development of new international agreements. One such agreement was already being negotiated at the United Nations in the months preceding the Johannesburg Summit.

A future treaty?

If you're an international policy wonk, then Item 4 of the provisional agenda, of the 54th session, of the Sub-Commission of the United Nations High Commission of Human Rights (UNHCHR), which looks at the 'Promotion and Protection of Human Rights', will mean something to you. You will know that the item refers to a sessional working group on the 'Working methods and activities of transnational corporations' which by June 2002 had drafted *Human Rights Principles and Responsibilities for Transnational Corporations and Other Business Enterprises*.[25] You might also know that this is one of the most important international policy initiatives on corporate accountability in recent years.

The Draft Principles were discussed at the United Nations in July 2002, with little fanfare. The discussions were lightly attended by governments who, we were told, would show up if and when the principles progressed further. However, even at that stage the discussions about the principles illustrated the differences in thinking among the business community on the need for global social and environmental rules for business.

The Draft Principles attempt to turn the Universal Declaration of Human Rights (UDHR) into something more directly related to business. They cover issues such as the rights of workers, the right of people to security, the need for companies to respect national sovereignty and local communities, and to observe obligations with regard to both consumer and environmental protection. In his capacity as Deputy Chair of the FTSE4Good Advisory Committee, Dr Craig Mackenzie wrote to Professor Weissbrodt, who helped draft the principles: 'Following meetings with various human rights experts it has become apparent that the Draft Universal Human Rights Guidelines for Companies is the most useful interpretation of what human rights mean for business available.' The International Business Leaders Forum (IBLF)—which works with dozens of transnational companies and has helped to publish documents on human rights and business, such as *Human Rights: Is it any of your business?* and *Business and Human Rights: A Geography of Corporate Risk*—also supported the UN initiative. It issued a statement saying it 'wholeheartedly welcome[s] the . . . Principles . . . which go further than any of the existing codes and guidelines in defining human rights responsibilities of the private sector'. Moreover, it asserted that 'The Draft Principles are the most authoritative and comprehensive set of guidelines to date which make the UDHR applicable to companies.'[26]

However, the self-professed 'most representative global business organisations'— the International Organisation of Employers (IOE) and the International Chamber of Commerce (ICC)—disagreed with FTSE4Good and the IBLF. 'The IOE and ICC are still firmly of the view that further development of binding Human Rights Principles does not constitute a positive contribution to the current growth of voluntary corporate social initiatives and should not proceed', they noted in a formal contribution to the sub-commission.[27] Part of their argument was that 'to be effective and relevant to a company's specific circumstances, business principles and responsibilities should be developed and implemented by the companies themselves'. This might be news to some of their members who are involved in the Global Compact, where the principles are set by the UN, and a range of other initiatives such as the Forest Stewardship Council, Social Accountability International and the Ethical Trading Initiative, where non-governmental organisations have taken the lead in setting standards.

Comparing the process to that behind the International Labour Organisation's Declaration on Fundamental Principles and Rights at Work and the OECD Guidelines for Multinational Enterprises, the ICC said it was concerned that the process was not as inclusive, so that the principles 'lack essential business input'. This contrasted with the IBLF statement that 'the inclusive, cross-sector consultation process . . . has ensured that as many representative voices as possible have been taken into account'.

Whereas the IBLF thought 'the Draft Principles are complementary to the UN Global Compact and could very usefully build upon the human rights components of that initiative', the ICC communication used the existence of the Global Compact to suggest that this process was unnecessary. Moreover, the ICC claimed it indicated 'confusion within the UN' which therefore 'weakens its credibility just at the time when it is trying, more than ever, to engage with the business community'. To presume that the UN might be concerned about being perceived as credible to the ICC is, of course, questionable. More concerning to the UN might be how some members of the Global Compact might use its existence to undermine other initiatives within the UN system.

Perhaps in the context of the ICC's intervention, the President of the Novartis Foundation, Klaus Leisinger, stated at the sub-commission that, 'with all due respect for others' opinions: Compliance with the Human Rights Principles and Responsibilities as those we have before us is not only feasible, it is also a question of leadership for triple bottom line entrepreneurial success. And leadership occurs never on the position of the lowest common denominator.'[28]

Therefore we might question Lord Holme's retort to criticism of the ICC by Tony

NOVARTIS PRESIDENT,
KLAUS LEISINGER: COMPLIANCE
WITH HUMAN RIGHTS PRINCIPLES
IS A QUESTION OF LEADERSHIP

Juniper of Friends of the Earth, where he said 'far from disagreeing with [the] . . . call for greater corporate accountability, the ICC . . . represents businesses that are, in general, strongly in favour of improved reporting and appropriate regulation.'[29] Once again it appears that business urgently needs to have more open dialogue and innovative thinking on global governance issues. Events in Europe at the time suggested that consultants in the corporate citizenship field were not yet prepared to help.

Consulting caution

Under the headline 'White Papers Ease Regulatory Fears' the newsletter *Ethical Per - formance* reported how 'prospects of imminent regulation on CSR in Europe have receded with the publication of the European Commission (EC)'s communication on the subject'.[30] In its White Paper on corporate responsibility, the EC steered clear of regulating for the provision of social and environmental information, stating a policy objective of encouraging companies to voluntarily include social and environmental information in annual reports. On socially responsible investment, the Commission invited its new stakeholder forum to agree by 2004 guiding principles on how pension and investment funds should disclose any social and environmental policies they may have. *Ethical Performance* said that this 'will be seen as a victory for business, which has generally campaigned against regulation'. A look at the official submissions to the EC reveals that most service providers in the corporate responsibility field lobbied for the EC to take a voluntary approach.[31]

This is strange, as previous issues of this World Review have highlighted a variety of reports and arguments suggesting a business case for improved regulation on corporate responsibility while the Northern summer of 2002 witnessed yet another publication that implies a new approach to regulation: *Corporate Responsibility and the Competitive Advantage of Nations*.[32] Meanwhile, the author of a popular book on this subject called *Good Business,* Steve Hilton, wrote in *Ethical Corporation* magazine that, 'by embracing the movement towards a more structured and universal approach to corporate responsibility, the tired mantra that "doing good is good for business" is more likely to become a commercial reality'.[33] One wonders whether the consultants commenting on the EC's original Green Paper had done some reading beforehand.

Moreover, we might question their strategic thinking, as regulation would boost the market for services related to corporate responsibility. Although this is already grow-

STEVE HILTON: IN FAVOUR OF
A MORE STRUCTURED AND
UNIVERSAL APPROACH TO CSR

ing, a new survey by Ernst & Young suggests that it is still only a niche market. It reported 'only 11 per cent [of companies] have made significant progress in implementing the strategy [CSR] in their organisation'.[34] As Andrew Grant, Ernst & Young's Environment and Sustainability Services Principal, commented, 'While companies recognise the value of an integrated CSR strategy, the majority are failing to maximise the associated business opportunities.'[35]

Mid-2002, some in industry were already frustrated with their laggard competitors, and supported levelling the regulatory playing field upwards. In London, financier George Soros helped launch 'Publish What You Pay', a campaign to make oil and mining companies report the sums they pay to the governments of 'developing' countries. Commenting on this, Hilton said that, although this 'proposal that could be interpreted as an anti-business measure', it is 'wholly deserving of corporate support'. Some oil corporations told us that they support this as it would allow them to behave in a responsible manner, without being penalised relative to 'less scrupulous' competitors.

Litigation nation

The United States is widely known as a litigious society—but one that foreigners can take advantage of? By its mid-summer of 2002, there were a dozen suits being filed against North American and European multinationals for past misdemeanours under the Alien Tort Claims Act (ATCA), a 213-year-old US law that allows non-US citizens to sue foreign and domestic individuals or companies in the United States for abuses committed abroad. In addition to these legal wranglings, the Northern summer of 2002 saw Ed Fagan re-emerge as public hero number one, this time fighting on behalf of black South Africans who were exploited during the apartheid regime, against his old adversaries UBS and CreditSuisseFirstBoston.[36]

The overturn by the Ninth Circuit Court of Appeals, which now allows the plaintiffs of the *Myanmar v. Unocal* case to bring it to court, was a significant departure from the 'pending' stage that most ATCA cases assumed. Speaking on behalf of his Myanmar clients, lawyer Richard Herz commented, 'The Ninth Circuit has affirmed that US corporations cannot violate international human rights with impunity.'[37]

With this latest agreement, similar cases may yet see their day in court. This development raises a number of questions, which compound those raised in the review of the previous quarter. For example, should it be left to a domestic law to monitor the actions of a corporation that has global reach? Should it lie within a county court judge or jury decision? What about the country where the 'wrong' took place? Should it be allowed to have a say in the outcome? These and similar questions were posed by Elliot Schrage in the September 2002 edition of *Ethical Corporation*. In his article he claimed that it is in the global North's best interest to help install good judicial systems within developing countries. He sees that, 'when foreign victims can find meaningful redress in their home countries, US judicial activism will smack of judicial imperialism. In theory and in practice, local courts should be able to identify problems earlier, resolve them faster and tailor solutions more appropriately to local conditions.'[38]

Ideally, then, courts in 'developing' countries should be able to bring multinational companies to court with a good chance of realising justice. However, while cases such as Bhopal exist which highlight the complexities of bringing foreign multinationals to legal courts in such countries, the legitimacy for using national laws from 'developed' countries may remain strong. Not only has the Indian government received pressure from Washington to reduce the charges placed on Mr Anderson, the former CEO of Union Carbide, who will face culpable homicide charges over the 1984 Bhopal gas disaster, but also the government is anxious not to scare foreign investors away.[39]

Embracing diversity

In July 2002 The Copenhagen Centre produced a report focusing on the issue of diversity and ethnic minority integration in the European workplace. The report, 'Ethnic Minority Employment through Partnership',[40] looked at four European countries (France, Germany, the Netherlands and the United Kingdom) and identified how new PPPs are helping employ greater numbers of ethnic minorities. By focusing on 16 case studies that provide evidence of each country's 'best practices', this report flags up the benefits gained by all stakeholders. It also highlights the multifarious initiatives that have come out of such partnerships. One example is HSBC's 'Removing Barriers: Building Bridges' project which has been working to address the local population's high unemployment numbers by providing training and recruitment to the unemployed. HSBC's UK head office is located in the London Borough of Tower Hamlets, one of the most deprived areas in the UK, which also contains a large Asian population. The report suggests that, so far, the project has been successful. Since its birth, over 60% of those who have attended the programme have secured employment, and two people have become HSBC employees.[41] This initiative has also been rewarded by the Windrush Achievement Awards who in June 2002 shortlisted the bank for the award, based on its positive and constructive work with ethnic minorities.[42] This is welcome news amid reports of growing xenophobia, racism and anti-Semitism.[43]

Apart from this report, and a previous one by Respect Europe,[44] diversity issues have been generally underplayed in corporate citizenship debates. Is it because it is an issue laden with personal politics that some companies find hard to grapple with? Or perhaps it is something to do with the lack of ethnic diversity among professionals working on corporate citizenship itself? Some non-white professionals working in this field have expressed to us their acute awareness of the lack of diversity among consultants, business, academia or non-governmental organisations working on corporate citizenship issues. Given that there have been few workshops or conferences dedicated solely to addressing the issue of diversity, it was important that this was a major part of the agenda for the East Asia Economic Summit, held in Malaysia in October 2002.

Perhaps, though, it will be members of non-white communities that will foist diversity more overtly onto the corporate citizenship agenda. For example, the months from June to August 2002 witnessed the charge against Ford Motor Credit Company of racial discrimination towards its Hispanic clients. A study suggested that Ford had been found issuing relatively higher loan rates to Hispanics.[45] Although Ford denied these allegations, the damage will take some time and effort to rectify.

4Q2002

October–December

Jem Bendell and Tim Concannon

Unsustainable world-views?

Although most discussion of socially responsible investment since the turn of the millennium focused on the practices of the companies invested in, attention has increasingly turned on the responsibility of investors themselves. The role of the financial community in US corporate scandals post-Enron has played a part in this attention shift. By Christmas it became clear that a number of financial institutions, including Citigroup, J.P. Morgan Chase and Merrill Lynch, may be sued for their role in the creation of Enron's off-the-books partnerships that helped conceal that company's debts. A judge in Houston ruled that the defendants could be construed as having sufficient participation in the preparation of false statements about Enron's finances to merit the suit, and suggested that there was evidence to support the contention that they acted with an intent to deceive. This served notice that one of the primary lines of defence—that the financial institutions and legal firms were actually engaging in the normal practices of their business—was not likely to succeed.

Another reason for a focus on investors was the continued growth in so-called ethical investment. For example, in Australia, this industry may be opened to greater scrutiny if a proposal by the corporate regulator, the Australian Securities and Investments Commission (ASIC), to issue guidelines on the disclosure of investment practices, comes to fruition. In December 2002, ASIC asked for comments on a discussion paper that suggested it should provide guidelines for financial institutions on how to disclose information on the role of social and environmental issues in decision-making.[1] Currently it is financial firms themselves that largely define practice in this area. The process of assessing, rating and recommending companies on social and environmental performance may have to become more transparent and credible. The scope, methodology and inclusiveness of research, as well as the skills, qualifications and independence of analysts, need to be addressed. In time, questions such as whether information obtained by ethical investment analysts from particular companies is proprietary and should be in the public domain cannot be avoided.

Indicating growing interest in the field, in November 2002, the sustainable management magazine *Green Futures* focused on financial issues. A main feature considered the London Sustainability Principles, developed by Forum for the Future and the

Corporation of London.[2] These are seven principles, based on economic prosperity, environmental protection and social development. In Johannesburg these were recognised by the UN's Environment Programme to apply to all financial centres and markets, and the Corporation of London began introducing other financial centres to the principles, beginning in Geneva and then New York. Champions of the principles, such as Dame Judith Mayhew, referred to them as 'global principles'.

DAME JUDITH MAYHEW: CHAMPION OF
THE LONDON SUSTAINABILITY PRINCIPLES

A closer look at the principles suggests there was much more work to be done for them to encompass all dimensions of sustainable development and become truly global. The principles on social development said nothing significant about human rights, unequal trading structures, corporate accountability, anti-competitive business practices, corruption or political lobbying. Reflecting the environmental bias of the process, the term 'social development' was even mentioned in inverted commas, despite its much longer history than the term 'sustainable development'. The methodology for developing the principles, using case studies of best practice and workshops of interested corporate responsibility professionals (mostly London-based), may explain why they do not deal with more systemic issues, nor views from different cultures.[3]

Even when considering environmental issues, some may question whether mere exhortation could help change the way financial markets work. Some point to the systemic restrictions on fund managers, and, in turn, the boards of companies they invest in, questioning if they are acting in society's best interest. In the *Green Futures* issue, Nick Robins of Henderson Global Investors asserted that

> today's financial markets are still institutionally programmed to deliver the short-term maximisation of financial returns alone. Not only does this mean that financial markets lag behind the steady integration of sustainability factors in the rest of economic life; it also means that the primary signals that companies receive are in tension with their longer-term purpose.[4]

Not only is short-term profit a potential problem but also the very nature of money in most capitalist economies. Since most of the money in circulation is created in the form of loans from banks, nearly all of it has to be paid back *plus some more*, thereby creating a growth imperative in the economy. This poses problems for a world of finite resources, and, if resource-neutral growth is possible, not only would it require major state intervention but would increasingly impel the commodification of free public goods to create new markets. This would compound the social concerns arising from the concentration of power in the hands of those that control access to financial capital.

Such concerns have occupied both theologians and other followers of Judaism, Christianity and Islam. Centuries ago, the dominant view in Judaism and Christianity emerged that charging interest is permissible. However, today many Islamic institutions still adhere to the idea that usury, and thus interest, is wrong. This is because of a number of key principles in *Shariah* law. First, money should only be a medium of exchange, a way of defining the value of a thing; it has no value in itself, and therefore should not be allowed to give rise to more money. The human effort, initiative and risk involved in a productive venture are more important than the money used to finance it. Second, a lender must share the risk with the borrower—the potential profits or losses—that arise out of the enterprise for which the money was lent. Third, transactions should be entered into honestly with the minimum of uncertainty, risk and speculation. Fourth, investments should not support practices or products that are incompatible with the core beliefs of Islam. As a result, the charging of interest, trading in futures, speculation on currencies, and investment in products such as alcohol, are not permissible for many Islamic financial firms. The principle that thereby emerges is that Islam encourages investments 'in order that the community may benefit'.[5] In practice Islamic banks usually work by taking an equity stake in the enterprises they help finance.

In November 2002, the 9th annual World Islamic Banking Conference took place in Bahrain. The Conference was be convened under the patronage of H.H. Shaikh Khalifa Bin Salman Al Khalifa, the Prime Minister of the Kingdom of Bahrain. That the conference attracted delegates from most of the major Islamic financial centres of the world, as well as international organisations such as the World Trade Organisation, indicates the growing importance of the sector. The Islamic banking sector is expanding at around 15% per year. There are now more than 200 Islamic financial institutions spread across the Middle East, with more in the Far East, controlling assets of around $200 billion. Major players, such as HSBC and Citibank, have opened Islamic operations. There is even a Dow Jones Islamic index.

Environmental economist David Boyle suggested it was time to take a new interest in no interest:

> It isn't clear yet whether charging interest is overwhelmingly bad in all circumstances. But the issue is surely due for much wider debate—as environmentalists ask themselves if there isn't a basic flaw at the heart of the money system that powers unsustainability. Because if there is, something is going to have to be done about it—and it may be that the Islamic scholars have at least part of an answer.[6]

The Islamic financial community was also beginning to explore the connections between their practices and sustainable development, as indicated by the University of Bahrain's plans to explore 'Sustainable Development and Islamic Finance in Muslim Countries' at their 5th International Conference on Islamic Economics and Finance in April 2003.[7]

Given doubts about the coherence of the London Principles, and the important progress being made with Islamic finance, it seems premature to consider the principles as legitimate global standards, or even aspirations.

Rumbles from the jungle

In October 2002, a United Nations report on mining in the Democratic Republic of Congo (DRC) packed a political punch, by accusing corporations of exploiting the African country's mineral wealth in tandem with criminals.[8] The report by a five-member panel accuses 29 companies, the Rwandan government and army, the Ugandan army, Congolese and Zimbabwean government officials and other named individuals of continuing to exploit the DRC's resources in questionable ways.

The Congo is rich in gold, diamonds, cobalt, copper and coltan, which is used in mobile phones. The report notes that trade in these resources has helped fuel the four-year civil war in which more than two million people have died.

Significantly, the report called for the UN Security Council to introduce specific sanctions against named individuals and companies it claimed were involved, including travel bans, freezing personal assets and barring enterprises and individuals from 'receiving funding or establishing partnerships or other commercial relations with international financial institutions', or IFIs, such as the World Bank and International Monetary Fund. It also listed 85 companies the panel considered to be in breach of the Organisation for Economic Cooperation and Development (OECD) Guidelines for Multinational Enterprises, the voluntary code supported by many governments and business associations as the most appropriate way to police transnational business.

The report called for a body to be established to monitor any further exploitation of the DRC's resources, which can report back to 'National Contact Points'—the first port of call for any complaint through the OECD Guidelines procedure—in the home countries of the companies on the list. The OECD code allows for both 'naming and shaming' of companies in breach of the principles, and a theoretical 'monitoring' by the host country of the businesses' compliance with the code.[9]

Among the 85 companies listed in the report are Africa's largest steel producer, Iscor Ltd, Germany's Bayer AG, four Belgian diamond firms and the Belgian Groupe George Forrest mining group, British-based De Beers, Anglo American and Barclays Bank, Chemie Pharmacie Holland and the Dutch-based ING Bank, Canada's First Quantum Minerals and the US mining firm Cabot.

By the turn of the year, most of these companies were refuting the allegations. Barclays—one of the two largest banking groups in sub-Saharan Africa—responded to the report with bemusement: 'We have not been given any details of why we are included and have asked the UN for an explanation', said a Barclays spokeswoman.[10] The Belgian Groupe George Forrest mining group also responded with a statement: 'the experts have intentionally committed very serious negligences, causing at an international level the devastation of the commercial reputation of the Forrest Group and endangering its economical survival'.[11]

Nevertheless, the allegations were taken seriously by some, and, in November 2002, investigators in Brussels searched the offices of the Belgian affiliate of Dutch bank ING, which the UN report accused of money laundering.[12] As well as beginning criminal investigations, the Belgian government launched a parliamentary inquiry into the role of Belgian businesses in the DRC.

If the Security Council adopts the recommendations of the report, it may establish a reporting regime under the authority of the UN, which would meet some of the demands from activists calling for binding rules to govern corporations, for example at the Earth Summit (see the review of the first quarter of 2002).

How the UN will relate to the OECD guidelines and associated complaints processes, through National Contact Points, will be carefully watched by those interested in the effectiveness of voluntary measures such as the OECD code, and the willingness of international bodies such as the UN to redress the costs of any corporate malpractice.

At a meeting in December 2002 of the OECD Committee on International Investment and Multinational Enterprises (CIME)—the body that oversees the Guidelines—members of the committee took the view that, unless complaints are formally filed with National Contact Points, they will not have any legitimate right to act in the matter. According to the UK-based group Rights and Accountability in Development (RAID)—which attended some of the discussions informally—CIME members 'took the line that the UN Panel had exceeded its power in reaching the conclusion that the companies listed in the report had breached the Guidelines'. Therefore, it is up to individual groups in each 'host' country of companies named in the report to begin formal complaints (those countries include the UK, Belgium, Netherlands, Germany, Finland, Canada and the US). That international organisations cannot raise complaints directly to the OECD, at the international level—and that the OECD cannot mobilise itself when reports of breaches to its Guidelines arise from a body with the authority of the UN—will disappoint many who hope the Guidelines will be more than words.

In order to make complaints through National Contact Points the groups will need to generate their own evidence. The UN report contains various omissions, going into considerable detail about the perceived wrongdoings of some companies (such as First Quantum) but offering very little by way of evidence about others (such as Anglo American). 'Nothing in this report was put in without being corroborated, being cross-examined, having documents, having testimonies to prove it,' Mahmoud Kassem, Chairman of the Panel told journalists at a UN briefing. 'We are not asking for punishment, we are asking [corporations]—questioning them—to change their policy. When they have business in areas of conflict such as the Great Lakes region, and in particular the DRC, they have to act with full transparency and to stick to the guidelines of the OECD.'[13]

Very few complaints have been raised in the three years since the reformed Guidelines have been in operation. According to RAID, the US National Contact Point has sat on all complaints while it 'assesses their admissibility'. The UK Contact Point has allowed a well-documented complaint against a leading mining company to gather dust for more than a year. In the view of RAID:

> NGOs are left in the dark about what stage their complaint has reached. Inevitably the lack of feedback strengthens the impression that the procedures are there to protect the interests of companies rather than to promote the welfare and rights of the workforce or the communities in which the companies operate. It adds grist to the mill of those who believe that multinational corporations have greater influence over the [OECD's complaints] proceedings than NGOs or trade unions and undermines the core principle of 'equality of arms', which is the hallmark of a bona fide complaints mechanism.[14]

The OECD is believed to have referred the matter back to the UN Security Council by letter, offering 'help and clarification'.

Blood diamonds

So-called 'blood diamonds', it has been argued, have been used to finance civil wars in countries such as Angola, the Democratic Republic of the Congo and Sierra Leone. In November 2002, 35 countries agreed new regulations to control the trade in diamonds from conflict zones. Signatories to the Kimberley Process—agreed in the Swiss city of Interlaken—will participate in a system that will aim to certify that:

▶ Conflict diamonds do not enter the legal trading system between the point of mining and first export from a producing country

▶ Diamonds are not tampered with between their despatch from a producing country and their first arrival in a country where they will be cut, polished or traded

▶ Countries that cut, polish and trade in rough diamonds have adequate controls and procedures to ensure that conflict diamonds cannot enter their trade

Campaigners said that the process is just a code of conduct, and not enough to stop armed groups profiting from the trade. For example, research by ActionAid showed that many in the diamond trade are unaware of the agreement to self-regulate, and also of a European directive on conflict diamonds that enforces self-regulation. In November 2002, Amboka Wameyo, ActionAid's Africa Policy Officer, said:

> The diamond industry is totally unprepared to implement [the code of conduct]. The World Diamond Council, the industry's trade body, has not made public, even to its own members, details of its self-regulation scheme. No attempts have been made to educate jewellers, yet they are the ones who have to prove to buyers that they are selling clean diamonds.

Campaigning organisations including ActionAid, Amnesty International, Global Witness and Oxfam issued a statement from the signing which said: 'NGOs are deeply concerned that there is still no system for regular, independent monitoring of all national diamond control systems. Without this, the overall process remains open to abuse.'[15]

UnWRAPping monitoring

Criticism of Western-based, business-led initiatives on worker welfare issues in the global South grew toward the end of 2002, although the trade press on corporate responsibility was silent on the issue. For example, in November 2002 in front of representatives from many companies and multi-stakeholder initiatives on ethical trade, at a Renmin University conference in China, a variety of NGOs criticised the current practice of auditing. Delegates heard stories of workers being trained in how to answer inspectors' questions and receiving bonuses if the factory performed well in a social audit.

Marina Prieto, a Director of the Central American Women's Network (CAWN) and member of the Ethical Trading Initiative, made similar criticisms in her articles during this quarter. In one article she criticised the factory code and monitoring system developed by the Worldwide Responsible Apparel Production (WRAP). Originally the initiative of the American Apparel Manufacturers' Association, WRAP has stated its

MARINA PRIETO:
CRITICAL OF AUDITING PRACTICES

dedication to 'the promotion and certification of lawful, humane and ethical manufacturing throughout the world'.[16] WRAP now covers over 700 companies responsible for 85% of clothing sales in the US. More than 615 factories from 56 countries have registered to earn the 'WRAP Good Factory Seal of Approval'.[17] Prieto wrote that 'many activists in Central America and elsewhere have pointed out serious flaws in the initiative's approach'. She raised various points of concern, such as a lack of independence on its board, weak standards on some labour issues (especially those of specific concern to women workers), no public disclosure of monitors' findings, and the use of pre-arranged audits, so that companies might 'clean up' in advance.

CAWN published these concerns as WRAP became operative in El Salvador, thereby directly competing with a local civil-society initiative headed by the non-profit Salvadoran Independent Monitoring Group (GMIES), which was established in 1996.[18] This was the first-ever civil-society programme to conduct external monitoring of labour conditions in the *Maquilas* and has since monitored factories supplying both Liz Claiborne and The Gap. Prieto argued that, in contrast to WRAP, this initiative: emphasises the importance of maintaining a regular presence at the factory, with regular visits and various channels for workers to contact the monitors; stresses the need for workers to get to know and trust the monitors, and to learn what their role is; and insists on the right to publish at least some of their monitoring reports. She concluded that:

> The WRAP system should not be allowed to become the standard in El Salvador and across Central America because it would lead to major labour rights violations being completely ignored. Confidential reports by private-sector monitors often fail to convey an accurate picture of conditions in the *Maquilas*, meaning that consumers in the North would be unable to discriminate between companies on ethical grounds. Workers and their organisations would lose the struggle to improve labour conditions. And, with factory owners even forced to pay for monitoring, US companies and consulting firms would be the only clear winners.

The director of GMIES, Carolina Quinteros, was therefore sceptical of the intent of WRAP and similar initiatives that are dominated by commercial interests in Northern countries:

Initiatives such as WRAP reflect the intention of the big corporations to appropriate a concept that was created from activist movements in favour of human and workers' rights. The struggle for a code of conduct that reflects the responsibility of companies towards their workers . . . and the demand for a monitoring process that contributes to improving workers' conditions have been transformed into a business discourse. This discourse is closer to corporate public relations than to real undertakings towards workers and consumers.

Criticisms coming from representatives in the global South are particularly important given that most often the intended beneficiaries of initiatives such as WRAP are workers and communities in such regions. By October 2002, of the 12 board members of WRAP, none was from the South (most appeared to be US citizens). Meanwhile, apart from one consultancy in El Salvador, Reducción de Riesgos, by August 2002 all the auditors accredited to inspect and award factories this seal were US accounting firms. It appeared that the only way Southern stakeholders could participate in WRAP was by endorsing its principles, rather than having a say in its work. By August 2002, 13 trade associations from the global South had done so. The involvement of other, non-commercial stakeholders appeared to be non-existent.

In December 2002, a paper on a similar topic was published by the New Academy of Business. Reporting on research conducted with women's groups and trade unions in Nicaragua, the authors criticised current approaches to codes of conduct and their monitoring, while presenting the ideas of women workers for how progress could be made. The paper's title captured the key message from workers in the global South: 'If You Want to Help Us Then Start Listening to Us'.[19] Given this critique, the extent of accountability of corporate citizenship initiatives to their intended beneficiaries becomes important. Rather than being the exception, WRAP may find itself among other initiatives having its accountability challenged.

Locating justice

One of the Nicaraguan women involved in the New Academy of Business research project, Claudia Blanco, was mentioned in the review of the first quarter of 2002. A mother of eight, she was sacked after decades of working on banana plantations, because of, she claimed, her trade union activities. In November 2002, she was diagnosed with cancer. Unfortunately, it seems she had become one of the (possibly tens of) thousands victims of a pesticide used on those plantations. In 1977, the Environmental Protection Agency of the United States prohibited the use of Nemagon (DBCP). Nevertheless, it continued being exported and used in the banana plantations of Central and South America, Africa and Asia for ten years. Besides being toxic to the environment, it has been claimed to cause hundreds of deaths and serious health problems including birth malformations, sterility, cancers, and sight problems.[20] Victorino Espinales, a leader of the workers affected by the pesticide, said, 'the companies never told us that this product was highly poisonous and dangerous, and now, thirty years later we are seeing the consequences'.

Following a new law passed by the Nicaraguan government to enable legal proceedings against multinationals that produced, distributed and used Nemagon/DBCP (Law

384), hundreds of workers began suing seven US-based companies—Dole, Shell, Castle & Cook, Chiquita Brands, Del Monte, Occidental Chemical Corporation, Dow Chemical Company—and two Israeli companies: Dead Sea Bromine and Bromine Compound Ltd.

Amid reports that the US government was pressuring Nicaragua to amend/suspend the new law, in October 2002 there was a 10,000-strong demonstration in Chinandega, in the banana-growing region. Then, in November 2002, about 2,500 farm workers walked the 85 miles from that city to Managua to protest the lack of progress in their lawsuit. The marchers went first to the US Embassy, presenting officials with a letter about alleged attempts of former US Ambassador Oliver Garza to undermine Law 384. Embassy official Michael Stevens said that the only interest of the US government was to establish an equal playing field between those who are suing and those being sued.

Then the protesters went to the house of deputies to encourage them not to overturn the law. In response, Roberto Gonzalez, chair of the Labour Committee, said, 'none of the 92 deputies have the remotest idea of changing even one comma of this law', and said that the affected banana workers 'are giving us a lesson of bravery and dignity'. The government also announced the formation of a high-level commission to support the workers' demands.

A couple of weeks later, on 11 December 2002, 580 workers affected by NemagonDBCP won a court verdict in Managua, with Dow Agro Sciences, Shell and Standard Fruit (Dole) ordered to pay $490 million in damages. There are more than 4,000 further plaintiffs who are pursuing similar action. The problem for them is that the companies involved do not have significant assets, if any, in Nicaragua. The newspapers in Nicaragua are therefore reporting that the 'battle' will have to move to the US.[21] The experience with such cases is mixed. One, started in 1991 by Honduran workers against Dole, eventually stalled, but the company then offered an out-of-court settlement.[22]

Given the amount of time these processes take, and the real human costs of waiting around, various NGOs were increasing their support for victims and also ratcheting up their campaigning for companies to respond positively and swiftly. For example, the Associacion Italia Nicaragua has launched a Campaign called 'No More Chemicals'.[23]

That substantive justice may only be located in the countries where sued corporations have assets, makes the Alien Tort Claims Act (ATCA) in the United States particularly important. Dating from 1789, this federal law promotes respect for basic human rights by holding government officials and corporations liable for wrongs committed against non-US citizens. The first ATCA human rights claims were brought against foreign government officials, although, more recently, victims have filed suit against corporations alleged to be complicit in abuses.

One example is *Doe v. Unocal*, where Burmese villagers sued the California-based energy giant for complicity in abuses committed by the Burmese military. In September of 2002, a federal appeals court held that the plaintiffs had presented evidence that Unocal knowingly provided substantial assistance to the military in its commission of forced labour, murder and rape, while the military secured the project and built project infrastructure. In a similar case, Nigerian plaintiffs sued ChevronTexaco for complicity in the Nigerian military's human rights abuses associated with oil production in the Niger Delta. This case, ongoing at the time of writing, is based on two incidents:

the shooting of protestors at ChevronTexaco's Parabe offshore platform by soldiers allegedly flown in by ChevronTexaco, and the destruction of two villages by soldiers allegedly in ChevronTexaco helicopters and boats.

Just as the potential of ATCA as a tool of corporate accountability is being realised, Earth Rights reported that anti-ATCA lobbying has begun. The National Foreign Trade Council (NFTC), a trade group of some of the largest multinational companies, is being supported by the International Chamber of Commerce (ICC), to lobby Congress to amend the law. USA-Engage, the lobby arm of NFTC, 'has established a working group to provide support for companies that have been sued [under ATCA] and to explore remedies to the abuse of the law'. Earth Rights stated: 'it is no coincidence that the NFTC includes many of the corporations who are being sued. The NFTC's effort to "curb abuses" of the law is in fact an attempt by its members to avoid civil liability for wrong-doing.'[24]

The NFTC's new campaign follows previous corporate lobbying against the ATCA. A suit filed by the International Labor Rights Fund (ILRF) on behalf of 11 anonymous plaintiffs against ExxonMobil in a US Federal Court was questioned by the US State Department, after possible lobbying by the company. The suit held that the company was liable for the alleged abuses in the Aceh region of Indonesia because it provided 'logistical and material' support to the military. Presumably having prior knowledge of the US State Department's reaction, ExxonMobil petitioned the presiding judge to solicit an opinion from the government about whether this suit would have an adverse effect on US foreign policy. The State Department argued that the Indonesian government would view the case as a referendum on the human rights record of the Indonesian armed forces, which would dissuade it from cooperating with the United States in counter-terrorism. According to Human Rights Watch and other groups, this raises questions about the Bush administration's commitment to corporate responsibility.[25] Meanwhile, new reports of human rights abuses in Indonesia, with possible corporate involvement, arose as 2002 drew to a close.[26]

As the Nicaragua case illustrated, the inability of courts in various countries of the global South to deliver substantive justice to victims of corporate malpractice makes ATCA and similar provisions for Foreign Direct Liability (FDL) in other Western countries of importance to the global application of international standards. The Exxon-Mobil case and the lobbying by NFTC and the ICC may add to the increasing criticism of corporate lobbying, and increased focus on the political responsibilities of companies aspiring to be corporate citizens.

The political bottom line

A new book argued that, as a whole, business is still the enemy of sustainable development, mainly due to the political lobbying done by, or at the behest of, corporations. *Battling Big Business* documents cases of where corporations 'attempt to control their "enemies"—and how groups and individuals can fight back'.[27] As 2002 drew to a close, more people questioned the value of some corporate lobbying. In the UK in November 2002, Friends of the Earth complained about lobbying by the Confederation of British Industry (CBI):

whilst accepting the need to tackle climate change, [it] has actively opposed attempts to use economic instruments to alter the price of carbon to reflect its environmental damage—primarily the climate change levy [CCL], and the fuel duty escalator. The CBI have been accused of only representing the interests of its heavy industry members in such lobbying and criticised for not balloting its members on opposition to the CCL.[28]

Then in December 2002 concerns were raised when the International Chamber of Commerce (ICC) began lobbying governments against the implementation of the 'precautionary approach' to environmental issues. 'In evaluating the potential environmental or health effects of new products, governments should guard against an excessively precautionary approach that may stifle trade, economic development and technological progress', said the ICC.[29] The statement was issued against the background of growing business concern at moves such as the European Union's restrictions on hormone-treated beef and the campaign against genetically modified food that has kept food aid out of famine-stricken regions of Africa. The ICC statement on 'Precaution, Science, Risk and Trade' said: 'The responsibility remains with governments to ensure that precautionary risk-management measures they take in circumstances of uncertainty involve scientifically substantiated threats to health or the environment.'[30]

Further questions were raised about corporate influence over US government policy when in December 2002 the *Guardian* reported that Vice President Dick Cheney personally intervened to block a global deal to provide cheap drugs to financially poor countries.[31] Faced with opposition from all the other 140 members of the World Trade Organisation (WTO), the US refused to relax global patent laws that presently place the price of drugs beyond reach of most 'developing' countries. While trade envoys said that the negotiations were likely to resume in 2003, failure to reach an agreement on cheap drugs could collapse the entire WTO Doha agreement, which covers everything from cutting farm subsidies to introducing more competition in service industries. The paper noted that America's drug industry lobbied the White House to impose the narrowest possible interpretation of the Doha declaration, thus restricting any deal only to drugs to treat HIV/AIDS, malaria, TB and a shortlist of other diseases unique to Africa

That some corporations' lobbying activities run counter to the spirit and letter of their espousals on social and environmental responsibility was an issue raised in 1999 by the JANUS project. This developed a toolkit to help companies and/or trade associations analyse the misalignment between their corporate citizenship and lobbying positions, look for risks and opportunities within this and thus realign. At the time there was limited interest from companies.[32] However, one person involved in that work, Jules Peck, told us that during 2002 leading companies were 'showing signs of discontent with trade associations that do not adequately represent their interests. For many pioneering companies, environmental regulation or economic instruments would reinforce their competitive position by pushing other companies to internalise more of their environmental costs.' Now at the World Wide Fund for Nature UK, Peck indicated that many NGOs will be engaging each other and the private sector on the question of responsible corporate lobbying.

One of those companies that was breaking ranks with the party line of many trade associations on government intervention for sustainable development was BP. Their

BP CEO JOHN BROWNE:
'WE NEED THE HELP OF GOVERNMENTS'

CEO John Browne said 'we need the help of governments to establish the appropriate framework of incentives to move toward climate stabilisation'.[33] Earlier in the year, its rival Shell said the UK government had not helped in making more renewables possible, by providing the necessary incentives and disincentives to shift consumption and production.[34] The Chairman of Shell UK, Clive Mather, stated in December 2002 at a meeting of the Institute for Public Policy Research (IPPR) that his biggest worry with corporate citizenship was that much was not possible due to the short-termism of financial analysts.

SHELL UK CHAIRMAN, CLIVE MATHER:
SHORT-TERMISM HINDERS
CORPORATE CITIZENSHIP

Neo-regulation?

Ella Joseph of the IPPR argued, 'We can't just leave it to business to be good'.[35] Other NGOs heavily engaged in corporate citizenship issues in the UK also called for more imagination about government intervention. In a Forum for the Future report published in November 2002, authors Jonathan Porritt and Roger Cowe concluded by suggesting that leading corporate citizens need to enter the debate on the role of government intervention for sustainable development.[36]

The way government could create a framework for corporate citizenship was the subject of a study by the International Institute for Environment and Development (IIED) for the World Bank. Published in November, it underscored the fact that actions taken by the public sector could positively support businesses' overall contributions to sustainable development. The study demonstrated a need to go beyond problematic voluntary–regulatory distinctions when considering corporate citizenship, and explore the dynamic relationship between voluntary approaches and regulation.

ELLA JOSEPH OF THE IPPR:
'WE CAN'T JUST LEAVE IT TO
BUSINESS TO BE GOOD'

The study suggested that the public sector currently encourages responsible business practices through one or more of four key roles—mandating, facilitating, partnering and endorsing. However, the report noted that 'developing'-country governments are often constrained in their ability to respond to increasing pressures for corporate citizenship-related legislation and enforcement. Weak institutions, lack of knowledge and understanding, lack of financial and human resources, and lack of capacity to maintain standards are some of the main impediments to stronger encouragement of corporate citizenship by the public sector in the global South.

That a new suite of government measures to support corporate citizenship and sustainable development may be required makes a report for the World Tourism Organisation on the implications of multilateral trade agreements particularly pertinent.[36] This suggested that governments could be negotiating away their future capacity to intervene in the market for sustainable development through the current round on the General Agreement on Trade in Services (GATS). The authors suggested that a variety of government measures aimed at promoting corporate citizenship could, in future, be challenged by some interpretations of the GATS. That the new round of trade liberalisation talks under GATS has been driven by corporate lobbying brings us back, once again, to questions about the congruence of corporate citizenship and corporate lobbying. The political bottom line of business is a complex one, but one thing is certain—it will have to be addressed by practitioners and researchers in this field.

2003

Introduction

Rupesh Shah and Jem Bendell

The 'elevator pitch' is a game that is played among budding entrepreneurs seeking to refine their business idea down to a few snappy sentences. The idea is to imagine that you, as an entrepreneur with a great business idea, have just walked into an elevator. The woman standing next to you is a venture capitalist and you have the time it takes to reach your floor to convince her of your business idea.

Writing the introduction to this review feels like a similarly constrained task. However, we think we can be clear about one thing: while we hope the ideas might make your eyes wander over the horizon, we doubt that your reading of this review will make you a millionaire.

In 2003, the four quarterly World Reviews in the *Journal of Corporate Citizenship*, which make up this Annual Review, have explored issues such as the responsibility of corporations for war and HIV/AIDS, the emerging case for exploring the lobbying influence of firms and the impact of tax-avoidance strategies of TNCs.

As well as asking lots of questions of big companies, we have also been trying to cast a net wider, by exploring connections of responsible business practices to academic fields of economics and development, management education, leadership and business ethics.

There has been analysis of the dance between deregulation and regulation for creating accountability and numerous stories about legal challenges to business—from the ethics-based litigation in South Africa to anti-competitive strategies, the definition of commercial speech to news from the International Criminal Court in The Hague.

We have also written variously about the UN—from an exploration of the work of the International Labour Organisation in supporting health and safety in micro-enterprises to the contribution of its trade and development arm, UNCTAD and differing opinions about the role of private-sector partnerships in the work of the UN. So, do these different events in the world of business in 2003 add up to a coherent story—one that could be pitched in the space of an elevator attention span?

From review to preview

Jem Bendell and Rupesh Shah

As well as writing a lot about the world out there, as a group of authors we have grappled with how to engage with each other and write informatively and creatively, to look beyond the merry-go-round of PR and press releases and find events, debates and people who add more depth and colour to our understanding of corporate responsibility and citizenship.

Looking back at our introduction to the Annual Review for 2002, included earlier in this volume, we concluded by arguing for the need for ourselves as authors as well as others to 'pluralise cultural perspectives on corporate responsibility'.

So, here's our pitch: we think that seeking out the meaning of business practices for marginalised people and communities is a critical task, but also one full of potential for personal transformation. If practices conducted in the name of CSR and corporate citizenship don't go 'bottom up' in terms of increasing the role of the marginalised, then they may go 'bottom up' in the other sense of that term—failure.

We won't presume to predict whether more professionals working in this arena will embrace this challenge in 2004—but we can predict it will remain a challenge, as we have realised ourselves how difficult this is.

1Q2003

January–March

Jem Bendell and Mark Young

Mind the implementation gap

While the professional corporate citizenship community has built up a fair amount of expertise in engaging external stakeholders—often because of the threat of reputational damage if this fails—engaging employees and managers in this work has previously received little press. There seemed to be a growing focus on addressing this 'implementation gap' in the first quarter of 2003.

In a survey of CEOs prepared for the World Economic Forum in Davos, many 'acknowledged that their companies are still at the "starting blocks" in terms of establishing key performance measures for corporate citizenship issues and integrating these into executive development and recruitment programmes, or into performance appraisals and incentive structures'. Through the survey, the CEOs offered some advice on what works. The 'internal communication of values and policies' received more 'votes' by the CEOs than any other option in the questionnaire. It was listed as being one of the three most important factors by 90% of respondents. This was followed by 'establishing key performance measures'. 'Building internal skills and capacity' was also ranked highly, after the key external activity of 'engaging in dialogue and partnership with external stakeholders'.[1]

The United Nations Global Compact also looked at implementation. Its Annual Learning Forum discussed 'the experiences and problems of integrating the nine principles into core business operations'.[2] Participants 'felt the need for more analytical case studies; the dissemination of best practices; and a professional guide to the principles'. One such tool will be the Global Compact Performance Model for sustainable development, developed by Claude Fussler of the World Business Council for Sustainable Development (WBCSD). 'The model is based on the "plan, do, check, act" model', a working group noted. 'It embraces the following elements: (1) vision, (2) leadership, (3) empowerment, (4) resources, (5) policies and strategies, (6) processes and innovation, (7) impact on society, environment and value chain, and (8) reporting.'[3]

Training courses also looked at the issue. For example, Deloitte & Touche included a session on 'Implementing CSR: Change Strategies and Clearing the Hurdles on the Way' in their March 2003 workshop with the New Academy of Business. Publications also offered some advice. The organisation CSR Europe launched *Exploring Business Dynamics: Mainstreaming CSR in a Company's Strategy, Management and Systems*. In it

CLAUDE FUSSLER OF THE WBCSD:
DEVELOPED THE GLOBAL COMPACT
PERFORMANCE MODEL

CSR leaders such as Johnson & Johnson and BP explain how they have managed to translate the concept of CSR into a daily business reality, using tools such as integrated management performance systems, the balanced scorecard, and new forms of staff training and recruitment. Companies show how they have managed to combine CSR issues with a strong performance culture: for instance, by making non-financial goals up to one-third of their performance appraisals and reward structures.[4]

One such company is the food giant Danone. In February 2003, it announced the continuation of its 'Danone Way', which aims to mainstream social and environmental responsibility across the whole company. Says Danone:

> The programme features an intranet site that asks each company to assess their own performance on the basis of 130 questions related to issues such as food safety, human resource policies, environmental impacts and relationships with suppliers. At each company, a management committee conducts this self-assessment with the assistance of working groups bringing together managers and other employees.

Danone has created a link between corporate citizenship performance and reward. 'Up to 40% of the bonuses paid to each company are based on the performance in the "Danone Way" exercise.'[5]

As the focus on implementation grows, so the professional field of organisational development (OD) is coming into view. OD, normally left to the devices of the human resources professionals,

> focuses on various aspects of organisational life, aspects that include culture, values, systems and behaviour. The goal of OD is to increase organisational effectiveness and

PAUL GIBBONS, DIRECTOR OF FUTURE
CONSIDERATIONS: 'YOU NEED TO WORK DEEPLY
WITH EMPLOYEES' VALUES AND ORGANISATIONAL
CULTURE, AND THAT TAKES LEADERSHIP'

organisational health, through planned interventions in the organisation's processes or operations. Most often, OD Services are requested when an organisation is undergoing a process of change.[6]

At the heart of OD are questions around leadership, organisational culture and change management. Paul Gibbons, director of Future Considerations, a consultancy specialising in organisational development for corporate citizenship, points out that 'you need to work deeply with employees' values and organisational culture, and that takes leadership'.[7]

Taking the lead

If it will take leadership, it will take the development of the right sort of leader. LEAD (Leadership for Environment and Development International) has become a pioneer in developing leaders for sustainability in the government, NGO and corporate sectors. Among LEAD's capacity-building services is its 18-month international training programme in Leadership for Sustainable Development. Alumni of the programme form a network, and, according to LEAD's Mark Smith, 'there are some 1,200 LEAD Fellows in 70 countries. They belong to the worlds of academia, business, governments, media and NGOs.'

Speaking at the Delhi Sustainable Development Summit in February 2003, LEAD's Julia Marton-Lefèvre addressed the issue of leadership and governance in government, multinationals and intergovernmental organisations. In her speech, she observed that 'It is not difficult to find examples of flawed governance in our countries and in our professions. It is more difficult to find examples of governance that works for sustainable development.'

She went on to describe the sort of leader it will take to address this.

> Sustainable development needs better institutions. Institutions, however, are made up of individuals. We need individuals who can think big; who are committed, hard-working; who behave in an ethical way; are willing to share; and who are never afraid to learn from others.[8]

In March 2003, LEAD was in the news for launching a programme in partnership with Globalegacy. Globalegacy runs development projects in deprived areas, as they say, 'mobilizing alliances of the world's most influential institutions to invest money, people and ideas, collectively over a ten-year period in these communities to create sustainable social and economic benefits'.[9] They suggest it has benefits for all concerned. On the one hand, corporates put their people into the programme, as part of their leadership development. A young manager goes through 'a 3- to 12-month leadership experience—known as the "Externship"—working full-time to help community entrepreneurs build new local businesses that are economically, socially and environmentally sustainable'.[10] LEAD provides its leadership training to the participants. On the other hand, Globalegacy, and the communities it serves, are intended to benefit from the people and their skills.

This wasn't the only example of leadership development being tied to community activity. More corporates appeared to be learning the benefits of this sort of leadership development, both for their overall quality of future leadership, and the shift of their organisational cultures to a more citizenship-friendly mind-set. Shell's 'Project Better World'[11] and PwC's 'Ulysses'[12] combine the traditionally separate areas of employee community involvement and corporate leadership development; and others are following.

Responsible leadership

One of the most eagerly awaited additions to the field of leadership development for sustainability and corporate citizenship was the launch of the Global Institute for Responsible Leadership (GIRL). The founders include Joseph Jaworski, author of *Synchronicity: The Inner Path of Leadership*[13] and Peter Senge, who brought the concepts of systems thinking and the learning organisation to the masses through *The Fifth Discipline*.[14] They have partnered with such behemoths as Unilever, Royal Dutch/Shell, the World Bank, the US National Park Service and Oxfam to form the Institute. 'The Global Institute', they say, 'is dedicated to engaging, enabling and supporting 21st-century leaders committed to taking responsibility for bringing about positive transformation within our world and addressing the critical issues of our time'.[15]

JOSEPH JAWORSKI: CO-FOUNDER
OF THE GLOBAL INSTITUTE FOR
RESPONSIBLE LEADERSHIP

The Institute goes on to say,

> The most pressing challenges leaders face today require innovative thinking and collaboration across traditional boundaries: departments, organisations, sectors, and cultures. Yet we are entrenched in rigid patterns of behavior that limit our ability to transcend these boundaries and work together to effect deep change. To bring about the level of transformation needed in our organizations and our world right now, we need a new way of learning and of leading—one not limited to reflecting the patterns of the past but one that tunes into the possibilities of the future.[16]

Some management executives reading this might be nodding at this point. They will have experienced the frustration of bringing a corporate citizenship strategy to life—really to life: in hearts, minds and actions. Managing this change is a key part of their jobs, and one for which they are often ill prepared. The management academe has begun to address this challenge, as illustrated by a book published in 2003. *Leading Change toward Sustainability: A Change-Management Guide for Business, Government and Civil Society* by Bob Doppelt of The University of Oregon attempts to answer the question 'what process is required to create change within organisations to move them

THE UNIVERSITY OF OREGON'S BOB
DOPPELT: OFFERING GUIDANCE IN
MANAGING CHANGE TOWARDS
SUSTAINABILITY

towards sustainability?'[17] Doppelt suggests focusing on a company's governance system and its leadership. 'When an organisation has an effective governance system and effective, forward-looking leadership, it is much more likely to be able to marshal the tremendous forces required to transform its culture and successfully adopt sustainability-based thinking, values and behaviours.'

Governance and leadership was something that Andy Law of St Luke's, the advertising agency, had something to say about in his book *Experiment at Work*.[18] The company he founded became famous as a successful cooperatively owned advertising agency with a social conscience. In March 2003, Law was forced to resign after trying to sack two managers who then put the matter to a vote of the co-owners. 'There's a paradox between strong leadership and working as a cooperative,' Law commented. 'I'd probably be a little more dictatorial if I did it again,' he said.[19] This raises questions about the concept of leadership that GIRL and the wider corporate citizenship community must deal with. Can we speak of leadership that is empowering of others, when all power is vested in the leader? Is the best indicator of such leadership when people don't need or want to be led anymore, as happened at St Luke's? In engaging with such questions we could reflect on the existing debates concerning the problematic concept of employee empowerment.[20] We might also reflect on the way the concept of leadership is used outside the business world. Speaking about the invasion of Iraq in March 2003, the Leader of the US Senate, Bill Frist, told BBC radio that we are in a new era that requires decisive leadership. That, to some, leadership implies overriding others' opinions to implement your own, illustrates what a difficult concept it is.

Corporate responsibility for war

Although most media during the first three months of 2003 were dominated by coverage of the possible, then actual, invasion of Iraq, hardly a peep on this issue came from the corporate citizenship or environmental management magazines, newsletters and websites. Should there have been more coverage? To some, this was a war about liberation and prevention of future terrorism. To others, this was a war serving corporate interests: it was 'Big Oil's War', or even 'Globalisation's War'.

Polls showed that, before the war and outside the United States, people didn't seem to believe the leaders of the US and Britain any more than they believed the dictator in Iraq. War might provoke not prevent terrorism, some said. If there was a moral case for war, many wondered why some governments were now concerned for the Iraqi people after having let more than half a million of them die because of the sanctions they imposed over the previous 12 years. Some commentators, and even diplomats, wondered whether the war was a result of a personal vendetta, or oil interests, or even about the US demonstrating to the world it would not tolerate countries that did not support its world-view. This last analysis was supported by leaked documents from the Pentagon demonstrating that the war was planned years previously as a means of 'stabilising' the US position as the only superpower.[21] Mikhail Gorbachev summed this up as the US wanting to turn the rest of the world into its province. Meanwhile, more radical commentators even suggested the motive was to provoke a perpetual state of unrest and terrorism to permit a new form of domestic and international political and economic order.

One's understanding of corporate responsibility for the war will therefore depend on why you believe it was started. Some activists decided to push the oil connection. In the UK the StopEsso campaign, supported by Greenpeace and Friends of the Earth, began protesting on petrol/gas stations. A Greenpeace spokesman said 'the action comes in response to Esso's ongoing campaign to keep the US hooked on oil, fuelling war and causing global warming'.[22] In addition to ExxonMobil's political donations to the Bush administration, they could point to the fact that almost all of that administration had a background in the oil industry. Condoleezza Rice had a tanker named after her. Vice President Dick Cheney used to run oil company Halliburton—and was still paid by them—a company that was in line for a slice of a $900 million (£560 million) contract from the US government to start rebuilding Iraq after the war.[23]

As the chorus of protests chanting 'not in my name' grew ever louder, along with them suggestions that companies were war-profiteering, the cautious comments from the world's major oil companies as they jostled for position in a post-war Iraq did not inspire confidence. The US oil companies said this was a matter for governments, not them. The British companies said all they wanted to ensure was a level playing field in a post-war Iraq. But, as the US-led military began levelling more than just playing fields, was this a sufficient response?

Without the clear authority of the United Nations, the paramount body of international law, created specifically to promote human rights, it was unclear whether the US-led invasion was lawful.[24] If some companies are not only respecting but championing human rights as never before, can they make a coherent case justifying increasing their profits from the post-war dispensation in circumstances where war and peace had come about by such a dubious political and legal process? This issue is even more pertinent for those companies that are members of the UN Global Compact, and, therefore, we must assume, supportive of the UN's mission. Once the war was under way, some members of the US administration suggested that the organisation had become irrelevant.[25] Is it consistent for companies that are members of the Compact to support politicians or policies that undermine the UN? We should note that the Universal Declaration of Human Rights calls on all 'organs of society' to promote, rather than merely not undermine, the enjoyment of such rights by all peoples. Even those companies involved in the human rights debate were still not ready to come out in support of the UN and international law. Might it be the right time for the policy dialogue at the Global Compact on 'The Role of Business in Zones of Conflict' to broaden its scope to consider conflicts involving Western states? (See 'Exorcising the curse of oil' on page 192 for more on the oil industry and conflict.)

One commentator expressed exasperation at the lack of connection being made between corporate responsibility issues and the political strife. Simon Zadek reflected that 'the "corporate responsibility" stream of debates' at the World Economic Forum in January 2003 'were largely divorced from those covering the current political situation. So, while there was some debate about the economic interests (notably oil) underlying the current situation, this remained largely separate from the specifics of company behaviour.'[26] He said, 'there was no serious discussion about difficult questions such as the role of the armaments industry and the question of who gets what contracts in Iraq once the "war is won" and under what conditions'. In addition, he found 'no sense whatsoever of any "systemic complicity" by business in furthering the conditions for conflict by being core to (and not challenging) an economic model that in many ways reinforced unequal development outcomes'.

One specific suggestion he made was for a code of conduct for any business (or partnership) seeking a public contract associated with a post-conflict rehabilitation programme, in Iraq or elsewhere. On a broader level, Zadek suggested that

> we have to move beyond what individual, enlightened companies choose to do. This must include the amplification of the corporate community's progressive role in changing the framework conditions, including difficult policy areas covering international trade and investment, public subsidies, intellectual property and competition policy.

This reflects the call for a radical corporate citizenship in the conclusion of *Terms for Endearment*,[27] where companies would support changing the rules of the game to make the global economy more just and sustainable—and peaceful. (See 'Accountability is responsibility' on page 176 for more on this approach to corporate citizenship.)

Taxing times for corporate citizenship

War in Iraq was not the only issue that led people to suggest that corporate social responsibility (CSR) and corporate citizenship were avoiding the most important issues about corporations' relations with society. In January 2003 the *Observer* newspaper lampooned the 'the burgeoning Corporate Social Responsibility (CSR) industry' for having 'comprehensively failed to make the fair and transparent payment of tax a core issue'. What was the problem? Not-so-legal tax dodging, and not-so-illegal transfer pricing. Deloitte & Touche estimated that Europe-wide tax dodging was worth almost £100 billion a year. Meanwhile, one academic study estimated that transfer pricing has been costing the US Treasury $53 billion, and well over $50 billion a year to countries in the global South.

Transfer pricing is the practice where one company reports that it sells products to another company in the same group at a higher or lower price to ensure the profits can be recorded in the company that faces lower tax rates. It is about moving money from one country to another to avoid tax. This practice is not without social consequences, given the poor state of national budgets in many Southern countries, and because governments have little option but to shift the tax burden onto labour, raising the costs of employment and reducing the take-home wages.

The *Observer* pointed out how difficult it is to obtain good information about the regional breakdown of corporate revenues and taxes:

> It is impossible to know each territory in which a transnational corporation (TNC) oper-
> ates, nor the amount of tax paid to each jurisdiction. And transfer pricing will flourish
> as long as there is no obligation to report the split between third-party and inter-group
> trading, despite the fact that 60 per cent of world trade takes place within these firms.[28]

Isn't supporting a government, if not dictatorial or corrupt, through paying them taxes a corporate citizenship issue? Citizens pay taxes, after all. Craig Mackenzie, head of investor responsibility at Insight Investment, the asset manager of HBOS, told the *Observer* that 'tax is not even on the periphery when it comes to responsible investing'. It seems that corporate citizenship, or CSR, has yet to escape the mentality of 'look at how much better I am—than the rest, and than I was before'. Could corporate citizenship mature from being about trying to look nicer and actually grapple with systemic problems of the global political economy? Perhaps only if we change what we consider 'looking nicer' means.

A report by the Association of Accountancy and Business Affairs (AABA) went some way in this direction. Richard Murphy, author of the report, questioned why financial reporting remains so narrow. 'What does big business have to hide? I can't think of a

RICHARD MURPHY: 'MORE OPENNESS
AND TRANSPARENCY WILL GO A LONG
WAY TO RESTORING INVESTOR
CONFIDENCE'

greater measure of corporate accountability than paying your dues. More openness and transparency will go a long way to restoring investor confidence.' Murphy claimed that reporting turnover and tax by territory would shine a spotlight on TNCs in a manner in which CSR does not. If companies would publish information on: (a) all territories in which they operate; (b) the turnover to third parties in and out of each territory; (c) sales to group companies made from each territory; (d) tax rates in each territory; (e) actual tax paid in each territory, then we would know exactly how much the companies are avoiding paying by transfer pricing. Perhaps this could be a new dimension to George Soros's 'Publish What You Pay' campaign?

The *Observer* suggests that the consultants working on corporate citizenship issues at the Big Four auditors will see AABA's proposals a little differently. 'For behind the brochures and the stakeholder rhetoric sits a pinstripe mafia of tax planners and transfer price specialists whose *raison d'être* is to maximise profits in an age of mobile capital.'

The *Observer* article was touching on a key issue thinly hidden behind corporate cit-izenship: corporate power. Does corporate citizenship imply private enterprise entrenching its power in the global economy, by increasing its freedom to be helpful to others only as and when it so desires? Is it inherently anti-state and, therefore, anti-democracy? Or can it evolve to something more democratic? The *Observer* was clear on this: 'big business should pay its dues and governments should spend the proceeds'.

The questions of corporate power and democracy raised here in the context of war in Iraq and tax avoidance, but which have existed for decades, have not been well dealt with by the management studies academe. The Academy of Management (AoM) intended to address this in the annual conference, in Seattle, with the core theme of 'Corporations and Democracy'. Whether the crucial issues would be discussed was to be seen. (See 'Beyond management?' on page 198 for a report on this conference.)

Abuse of power

As the first quarter of 2003 saw more fraud and anti-competitive business practice cases prosecuted, it seemed that the old issues of corporate malpractice were still con-temporary.

The legal fallout of accounting scandals continued. In February 2003 the Securities and Exchange Commission (SEC) filed civil fraud charges against eight current and former officers and employees of Qwest Communications International Inc., alleging that they inflated the company's revenues by approximately $144 million in 2000 and 2001 in order to meet earnings projections and revenue expectations.[29] The same month Merrill Lynch announced that it had agreed to pay a total of $80 million in dis-gorgement, penalties and interest to the SEC to resolve the investigation regarding two transactions between Merrill Lynch and Enron in 1999.[30] The National Association of Securities Dealers (NASD) also took action, censuring and fining J.P. Morgan Securi-ties, Inc. to pay $6 million for 'unlawful profit sharing activities that took place at Ham-brecht & Quist LLC prior to its acquisition in 2000'. NASD found that Hambrecht & Quist received millions of dollars in inflated commissions from more than 90 cus-tomers who sought and received allocations of 'hot' initial public offerings (IPOs) from the firm.[31]

The practices of pharmaceutical companies were also challenged during the first quarter. Two of the world's leading drug companies, GlaxoSmithKline (GSK) and Phar-macia, were sued by the State of New York in February 2003 for allegedly helping doc-tors overbill the state for medicines bought by doctors. According to the suit, that price, reported to the government, is often much higher than the price actually charged to doctors, who then bill the government at the higher reimbursement rate, allowing physicians to pocket the difference at taxpayers' expense.[32] GSK was also being inves-tigated in Italy for giving perks to Italian doctors allegedly in return for prescribing more of its drugs.[33] Meanwhile, Bristol-Myers Squibb agreed to a $670 million settle-ment to claims that it used illegal tactics to suppress generic competitors for its patented drugs and therefore to inflate its profits.[34] The *Economist* considered pharma-ceutical company marketing to be sufficiently concerning for a special report with Transparency International.[35]

Aid Agencies Inc.?

On 22 January 2003 in London, there was the first European CEO Forum on Development. This was a private business round-table to be convened by HRH The Prince of Wales and World Bank President James D. Wolfensohn. The purpose of the private, informal meeting of invited CEOs of European companies and international companies with a major presence in Europe, was 'to share thinking and address critical development issues where businesses can influence key economic and social issues affecting both business and society'.

WORLD BANK PRESIDENT
JAMES D. WOLFENSOHN:
CONVENED FIRST EUROPEAN
CEO FORUM ON DEVELOPMENT

The idea that multinational corporations could be regarded as development actors is something the UN Global Compact has embraced. Head of the Compact, Georg Kell, said they face a challenging agenda in attempting to increase business contributions to development.

> First, it must be able to facilitate greater 'development' contributions from the core activities of businesses in developing countries. Capacity building of the local workforce and diffusion of technical know-how would be examples of such contributions. Second, it must encourage businesses to improve the enabling macro frameworks in developing countries. Businesses could be encouraged to set good examples by resisting corruption and taking a stand on human rights and thus contribute to inducing positive public policy changes which in turn can improve the environment for doing business.[36]

A new study, undertaken jointly by Tanzanian academics and the British consultancy ERM, suggested that there is a business case for fighting poverty in the global South. They looked at how poverty impacts on five private firms: a tea company, a sack manufacturer, an aluminium sheet producer, a foreign-owned brewery (one of Tanzania's largest private-sector employers) and a not-for-profit crafts business. It suggested that chronic poverty in low-wage countries such as Tanzania is bad for business and of concern to businesspeople.[37] 'Businesses know too well that in order to prosper, customers' purchasing power must be improved. One way of doing this is by helping them to fight poverty,' said Tanzanian researcher Dr Benedict Mongula of the University of Dar es Salaam. Gastone Gaudence Kikuwi, the secretary-general of VIBINDO, an umbrella organisation of small traders, said corporate citizenship schemes would do very little to ease poverty in Tanzania because a large chunk of the population—over 75% in 2001, according to the Tanzanian Planning Commission—works in the informal sector. He suggested big companies provide loans, training and market access to people working in the informal sector.

There is undoubtedly a need for more research on the complexities of business act-ing in the cause of development. A half-century of experience and debate within the research and policy communities on international development needs to be drawn upon by practitioners and researchers of corporate citizenship. Most business leaders are on a steep learning curve when it comes to the theory, practice and historical expe-riences of international development and under-development. Before one can learn, one needs to recognise there is something to learn . . . and to be prepared to 'unlearn' what you already 'know'. Will business leaders turn to contested theories about devel-opment as they seem, at first glance, more compatible with corporate goals? Or will a more critical engagement be possible, where managers explore the concept of 'devel-opment' beyond the narrow Western world-view of ever-greater materialism and com-mercialism? (See 'Some economics please . . .' on page 188 for a discussion of the developmental dimensions to corporate citizenship.)

Just do it . . . out of court

One court case in California was causing some consternation in the corporate citizen-ship profession.[38] The California Supreme Court agreed in 2002 to hear a case against Nike brought by Marc Kasky under the state's unfair trade practice and false advertis-ing law. Kasky argued that Nike's explanations to concerned customers about labour practices in its supply chain were aimed to promote its sales and were, therefore, a form of 'commercial speech' which should therefore be subject to the state's unfair trade practice and false advertising law. He argued that the claims made by Nike were false and wanted a court to consider the case.

Nike argued that its pronouncements on the issue were not 'commercial speech' so they should be protected under First Amendment rights on free speech and therefore the court should throw out the case. It appealed to the Supreme Court, which in Jan-uary 2003 agreed to review the California decision to hear the case. This was an unusual move, given that the case had not even come to court, so suggested that the Court considered the issues to be of unusual importance.

This decision pleased the corporate citizenship community as they worried that other companies might follow Nike in suspending their corporate responsibility reporting in case of further legal action. A campaign ensued to try to persuade differ-ent stakeholders, including some NGOs and trade unions, to support Nike on this issue.

However, the reaction of the corporate citizenship community could suggest a lack of historical understanding about the legal development of 'the corporation', an absence of concern about power and communication, and a primary interest in pro-tecting their own industry of social reporting. If, as is likely given its judicial history and current political persuasion, the Supreme Court rules that the case cannot be heard and, therefore, that all corporate pronouncements of labour issues are afforded the same protection as personal free speech, then there will be no legal mechanism for preventing misleading statements being made by companies on these issues. Worse, such a decision will further extend the legal recognition and protection of corporations as 'legal persons' which is considered by many to be inappropriate given their partic-ular power.

The argument—that if the Kasky case were allowed to proceed it would scupper social reporting, at least in California—is misleading. Companies could choose to report statistics on their social performance, such as the existence of trade unions, the number of court cases pending, out-of-court settlements reached, external certifications obtained, and data on the distribution of pay and benefits throughout the supply chain. They could even combine this with reporting on tax payments, as described above. Then, if they wished, they could venture opinions about their performance, which readers would be more trusting of, knowing that these would be covered by laws on false advertising. Given that almost 70% of experts read fewer than five social and environmental reports a year, perhaps reducing these reports to key indicators could help managers, consumers and investors make quick and informed decisions.[39]

What the Kasky case really shows us is that we need to have reporting mandated and it needs to be guided by indicators agreed by governments. No one says financial reporting is advertising, as it is required and regulated by governments—albeit not to the standards we might want. Only mandating social and environmental reporting in this way will remove it from the realm of public relations and give it a standing similar to financial reporting. To reach such a situation will require some of that contentious stuff that our new era requires: *leadership*. (See 'Go west, then go nowhere' on page 195 for information on how this case was resolved.)

2Q2003

April–June

Jem Bendell and Wayne Visser

Where there's smoke . . .

There are few sectors more controversial than the tobacco industry, especially when it comes to matters of ethics. Critics even go so far as to say that 'socially responsible tobacco' is a contradiction in terms, while tobacco companies themselves claim that they can be good corporate citizens, despite the risks associated with their product.

British American Tobacco (BAT) is a typical example of the paradoxical nature of the debate. On the one hand, it was cited by *Multinational Monitor* as one of Ten Worst Corporations of 2002,[1] but it is simultaneously the first tobacco company to be listed on both the 2003 Dow Jones Sustainability World Index and 2003 Dow Jones STOXX Sustainability Index.[2] In April, its AGM was marred by activist protesters from the Burma Campaign UK[3] and Friends of the Earth[4] and the directors faced shareholder questions on the ethics of its joint-venture partnership with the dictatorial Myanmar government (formerly Burma). On the other hand, it was provided with an ACCA award in the UK and a KPMG award in South Africa for Social Reporting.[5] Chairman of BAT Martin Broughton admitted that 'CSR is a challenge in a business involving risky products', but argued that 'it would be self-defeating if CSR were to become an exclusive club, admitting only businesses judged "safe and pure" '.[6]

At least there is one thing that tobacco companies and their critics both agree on and that is the central issue of the health impacts of cigarettes. According to the World Health Organisation (WHO)'s 2002 publication, *The Tobacco Atlas*, smoking kills 4.9

BAT CHAIRMAN MARTIN BROUGHTON:
'IT WOULD BE SELF-DEFEATING IF CSR
WERE TO BECOME AN EXCLUSIVE CLUB'

million people every year and 'of everyone alive today, 500 million will eventually be killed by tobacco'.[7]

In the face of sustained pressure by various stakeholder groups over the past few decades, tobacco companies no longer deny the link between use of their products and certain diseases. Bizarrely, many have even adopted the self-abusing slogan that 'there is no such thing as a safe cigarette' and pride themselves on the advice they provide for those who are trying to quit the addictive habit.[8] Given the de facto admission of guilt in terms of the harmfulness of their product, the industry faces an enormous challenge to their sustainability as they are hit by wave upon wave of liability suits. As the legal activity of the past quarter shows, the proverbial jury is still out on this question of long-term survival of tobacco companies, with some court case decisions going in favour of the industry and others against.

For example, while an Illinois court ordered in March 2003 that Philip Morris USA pay US$10.1 billion to smokers who claimed they were misled into believing that Marlboro 'lights' were less harmful to their health (the so-called Price case), two similar decisions were decertified on appeal in May: the Engle class-action case in Miami involving a judgement of $145 billion and the Aspinall case in Massachusetts.[9] RJ Reynolds and Lorillard also turned the tables in April 2003 by suing the State of California for TV anti-smoking adverts that suggest that tobacco companies deliberately target children by selling near to schools.[10]

Even the government is getting in on the act. The US Department of Justice filed evidence in January and March in its case against cigarette makers (including Philip Morris, RJ Reynolds and British American Tobacco's Brown & Williamson), claiming US$289 billion. The court case, which is based on the allegations of misleading advertising, is due to begin in 2004 and aims to recover the healthcare costs paid by the Federal Government over cigarette-related illnesses costing an estimated US$20 billion per year.[11] Not all governments are taking such a tough stance, however, given the powerful political and economic forces at play.

In June 2003, the *Asia Times* cited the World Bank as saying that almost 80% of tobacco consumption worldwide occurs in Asia, with China's estimated 350 million regular smokers alone accounting for half of the global total. Furthermore, about 11% of all tax revenues in China, the Philippines and Turkey are derived from tobacco sales and 9% in Indonesia, while the governments of Australia, Pakistan and Russia capture 70% of the income from every cigarette that is sold. And, at an economic level, domestic tobacco industries employ an estimated 3–5 million people in Asia.[12]

Together, these facts point to the powerful incentives that still exist in support of the tobacco industry. Anti-tobacco lobby groups will be quick to point out that these numbers do not automatically imply a net economic gain. For example, in the same article referenced above, the *Asia Times* cited a World Bank study in India that found that productivity losses resulting from medical afflictions were almost twice as great as national earnings from the production, sale and taxation of tobacco products.[13] But then there is also the pro-tobacco argument that, with increasingly transparent disclosure about the health risks associated with smoking, restricting consumption is interfering with individuals' freedom of choice. Others would retort that an addictive product is not one that can be defended on the principle of freedom of choice.

Many questions remain unresolved, particularly for those engaged in debates about corporate citizenship. By what criteria might we judge the ethics of tobacco companies? On their social and environmental principles and policies, or the extent of their stakeholder engagement and social responsibility programmes? Perhaps the transparency of their product information and sustainability performance reporting? Or would this avoid the key issue of a harmful product, and the power of addiction? Business in the Community's Mallen Baker suggested that one of the most important

BUSINESS IN THE COMMUNITY'S MALLEN BAKER: THE POSITION TAKEN BY TOBACCO COMPANIES ON THE REGULATION OF THEIR ACTIVITIES WILL BE CRUCIAL

things would be the position taken by tobacco companies on the regulation of their activities.[14] For years, efforts have been under way to regulate tobacco advertising, for example, often thwarted by corporate lobbying.

A significant milestone came in May 2003 when the Framework Convention on Tobacco Control was adopted unanimously by the WHO's 192 member states. The Convention requires countries to impose restrictions on tobacco advertising, sponsorship and promotion, establish new labelling and clean indoor air controls and strengthen legislation to clamp down on tobacco smuggling.[15]

Interestingly for those who would consider companies to always be adverse to such intergovernmental regulation of their activities, some tobacco companies were actually supportive of the move. The concerns of Asian tobacco producers about the US and other Western tobacco companies using trade agreements to lower trade barriers was key to some Asian governments' supporting the Convention. This was because local companies did not believe they would be able to compete with well-marketed Western cigarette brands. Consequently, they looked at Thailand, where the introduction of tough advertising laws had restricted the ability of new brands to penetrate the Thai market, despite the country being ordered by the WTO to remove its trade barriers to foreign tobacco companies. The fact that different companies in different regions of the world can support regulatory initiatives should not be missed by advocates of corporate accountability. (See 'Cracks in a wall of silence' on page 194 for more on progressive corporate lobbying.)

From de-regulation to re-regulation

There were a number of other international regulatory developments in the first half of 2003. A legally binding protocol to the Aarhus Convention was agreed, which required that signatory states ensure companies report annually on their releases (into the environment) and transfers (to other companies) of certain pollutants.[16] This came on the back of a raft of national legislation requiring corporate disclosure of environmental information. In a review of laws related to corporate citizenship, Halina Ward found that 'mandatory legislation on various aspects of business transparency is emerging around the world'.[17]

Earlier in the year a coalition of US non-governmental organisations joined together to try to extend legislation on the transparency of US companies operating abroad. The International Right to Know (IRTK) Campaign includes the union federation AFL–CIO, Amnesty International USA, Earth Rights International, Global Exchange, Oxfam America and the Sierra Club. Their proposal aims to extend the Emergency Planning and Community Right to Know Act of 1986. The legislation established a US Toxics Release Inventory, which required companies in the US to register information on their use, storage and release of toxic substances. This had a beneficial impact in reducing emissions by US companies over subsequent years. However, the legislation applied only to activities in the US, an irony given that the legislation was in part a response to the Indian chemical factory disaster in Bhopal in 1984 which killed thousands. The 200 groups backing the IRTK campaign argued that the US should extend its right-to-know laws geographically to cover US activities abroad, and qualitatively, to also cover important non-environmental issues.

The IRTK campaign's first report presents a series of case studies of corporate malpractice. The McDonald's case study alleges the use of child labour in China to produce its Happy Meal toys, the Nike case study focuses on labour rights in Indonesia, and the Unocal case study discusses human rights abuses in Myanmar. However, the report also suggests some positive benefits of corporate disclosure—not only to communities. Arguments presented under subtitles such as 'Companies as good ambassadors', 'Faith in US companies', 'US leadership' and 'Support for US companies,' suggest that the IRTK would benefit business. That a business case can be made for legal innovations on corporate accountability is intriguing and requires further investigation.[18]

It would be wrong to think transparency legislation is a panacea. First, legislation such as that proposed by IRTK would not necessarily improve accountability and performance unless other activities were subsequent on the basis of the information. Although IRTK highlighted the case of Bhopal as a reason for their proposals, it is debatable whether such legislation would have had an effect on the management practices of Union Carbide that led to a catastrophic accident (not a regular emission). Perhaps the Bhopal community would have wanted the plant closed down if they knew what was stored there, but then this would have depended on many economic, political and legal factors. Extending the jurisdiction of courts abroad also raises some questions, which we discuss below.

Although often posed in opposition to voluntary corporate responsibility measures, regulation innovations may actually lead to their uptake. For example, in 2002 the Johannesburg Stock Exchange became the first in the world to recommend that publicly listed companies report to the standards developed by the Global Reporting Initiative. The recommendation took effect by virtue of the JSE's adoption of the code proposed in the *King Report on Corporate Governance for South Africa*.

Rather than campaigning for new laws, some NGOs focused on testing existing accountability mechanisms. At the end of April 2003, Friends of the Earth Netherlands (FoE-NL) and environmental organisations in seven other countries filed an official complaint with the OECD against the British oil company BP and other companies that were involved in the construction of an oil pipeline from Azerbaijan to Turkey. They argued that the companies were violating the OECD Guidelines for Multinational Enterprises, and demanded that construction activities be postponed until these guidelines have been met.[19] The groups were not especially hopeful of success, due to prior experience of the OECD guidelines, as discussed in the review of the fourth quarter of 2002. However, they decided to test it further, and also launched a booklet on how to use the OECD complaints system, so that others might do the same.[20] The Trade Union Advisory Committee (TUAC) also produced a handbook on using the guidelines.[21]

Accountability is responsibility

As predicted in previous reviews, the question of corporate lobbying began to enter the mainstream of corporate citizenship in the first half of 2003. One aspect of this was the increasing interest of citizens' groups on the matter. Friends of the Earth hit out at Shell's Phil Watts who, as the chair of the International Chamber of Commerce (ICC), was accused of 'anti-accountability lobbying'. This was after the ICC had launched a campaign against the Alien Tort Claims Act in the US, with the UK branch declaring this as a major plank of its lobbying operation in the UK.[22] Soon after, in report on the state of sustainability reporting, the first technical recommendation from the judges of the main accountancy body of the UK was that 'reports should disclose the lobbying positions an organisation takes on key public policy issues.'[23]

Such concerns are already covered to a limited degree in the OECD Guidelines for Multinational Enterprises. The fifth general policy principle says that such companies should 'refrain from seeking or accepting exemptions not contemplated in the statutory or regulatory framework related to environmental, health, safety, labour, taxation, financial incentives, or other issues'. This could be interpreted to mean much more than bribery, and include lobbying for various exemptions such as those provided in free-trade zones, and weak monitoring and enforcement of various laws. The eleventh general policy principle states that corporations should 'abstain from any improper involvement in local political activities'—the key issue being what might constitute 'improper'. On environmental issues, the Guidelines are clearer, with point 8 stating that corporations should 'contribute to the development of environmentally meaningful and economically efficient public policy, for example, by means of partnerships or initiatives that will enhance environmental awareness and protection'.[24]

As mentioned above, the ability of the OECD code to ensure responsibility and accountability is questioned. Therefore, other factors will be important for making the political activities of companies a mainstream part of corporate citizenship. Given the particular power of investors, the 2003 revised guidelines for ethical investment, developed by the Interfaith Center on Corporate Responsibility (ICCR), mark a significant development. The new guidelines incorporate criteria on political lobbying, such as 'The company has in place a system of review that aligns and integrates its corporate social responsibility principles in relation to its lobbying activities at all levels' and 'The company establishes participatory structures representative of all stakeholders to ensure compliance with its lobbying policy.' The criteria are not explicit about whether they cover the lobbying activities done on behalf of companies by their trade associations and other bodies of which they are members. Nevertheless, a member of the Ecumenical Committee on Corporate Responsibility (ECCR) told us that they had already used the guidelines in their discussions with a major pharmaceutical company.

Meanwhile, in March 2003, a coalition of European investment funds with $943 billion under management included recommendations on lobbying in their statement calling on pharmaceutical companies to take swift steps to ensure that poor countries have access to essential medicines. This call was coordinated by ISIS Asset Management and the Universities Superannuation Scheme, who were behind a similar initiative in 2001 to place pressure on oil companies doing business in Burma, and a current initiative to address global climate change. Specifically the statement suggested that companies use their influence with governments to address the public health crisis in the global South, and also be both transparent about, and assess the impact of, their public lobbying positions on national and international trade law relating to intellectual property. The suggestion was that major risk management issues are arising from the lobbying positions taken.[25]

The increasing focus on the political activities of corporations means that corporate citizenship might increasingly be seen as necessarily including support for governments and intergovernmental agencies to intervene in markets. Given the need for all companies to change if we are to promote sustainable development, voluntary corporate responsibility need not, perhaps by definition should not, be 'voluntarist' and promote deregulation. Indeed, we may increasingly consider that the highest form of responsibility is to work for accountability.

Sins of the fathers

Companies in developing countries are not immune from the wave of ethics-based litigation that is sweeping the globe. South Africa is a good case in point, where a number of multinationals have become targets of civil liability suits in the past few months, with the mining sector having been particularly hard hit. The cases fall into two broad categories: those seeking reparations for alleged malpractice and benefits accrued during the Apartheid era, and those with claims for retrospective health damages associated with industrial practices of the past.

The Apartheid cases are being driven by Edward Fagan, the US civil damages lawyer, who won a US$1.25 billion settlement from Swiss banks for Holocaust victims and a US$5 billion award to compensate slave labourers in Germany during World War II. As the case kicked off in New York in May 2003, Fagan, in collaboration with South African lawyer John Ngcebetsha, is reportedly seeking more than $100 billion in compensation on behalf of tens of thousands of Apartheid victims from 34 multinationals, including such household names as Barclays, Bayer, Citigroup, Credit Lyonnais, Credit Suisse, Deutsche Bank, DuPont, General Motors, IBM, Lilly and UBS.[26]

Also among these targeted companies are the South African global mining giants Anglo American and De Beers, involving a damages claim of up to US$6.1 billion. Ngcebetsha, in an interview with *Business Report*, said that these companies had been targeted because the Truth and Reconciliation Commission final report had singled them out in its chapter on business and reparations, together with the mining industry, as having engineered the pass laws and migrant labour systems to suit their business plans. He claims that Anglo American and De Beers 'treated their employees in a slave-like fashion' and that 'their profits were derived in violation of a universal principle of our law'. He concludes that 'to the extent that they were unjustly enriched, they should be held liable'.[27]

South African President Thabo Mbeki has condemned the litigation, arguing that the government 'considers it completely unacceptable that matters that are central to the future of our country should be adjudicated in foreign courts which bear no responsibility for the well-being of our country and the observance of the perspective contained in our constitution of the promotion of national reconciliation'. The government's stance, including its rejection of a one-off wealth tax that was recommended by the Truth and Reconciliation Commission, is by its own admission largely predicated on fears that the court cases will damage the investment climate and business confidence in the country.[28]

THABO MBEKI: CONDEMNING CIVIL
LIABILITY SUITS AGAINST SOUTH
AFRICAN COMPANIES

This was not unusual. Halina Ward reported that Papua New Guinea (PNG) enacted new legislation, initially triggered by litigation in Australia against the mining company BHP Billiton, a major PNG investor, which makes it a criminal offence for citizens of PNG to bring legal proceedings in a foreign court for compensation arising from mining or petroleum projects in that country. The Indonesian government also reacted badly to their nationals' seeking justice abroad. Regarding the ATCA case against Exxon-Mobil's support for military oppression in Indonesia, the government argued that it 'cannot accept the extraterritorial jurisdiction of a United States court over an allegation against an Indonesian government institution e.g. the Indonesian military, for operations taking place in Indonesia'. In the 1970s countries from the global South were particularly vocal in support of mechanisms for holding corporations accountable to their citizens, and backed a range of initiatives at the international level. Since then, however, these examples show that many governments are now more concerned with gaining foreign investment in the hope of generating revenue to service debts, and reach the goals established for them by international financial institutions—a strategy that is questioned by many development economists.

In the particular South African case, the companies have been denying that there is any justification for the legal claims. Their defence is argued on the basis of their historical contribution to the country and their current active role in promoting affirmative action, black economic empowerment and corporate social responsibility programmes, which they claim are more effective means to redress the inequities of the past. However the saga unfolds, one issue is clear: companies can no longer ignore the potentially damaging consequences of operating in countries ruled by oppressive political regimes. Being seen to have supported governments with poor track records of corruption and human rights abuse may very well come back to haunt companies with liabilities in the future.

The other category of cases that has been in the spotlight in South Africa over the past quarter is retrogressive health damage claims, chiefly relating to companies historically involved in asbestos mining. In April 2003, in the largest settlement to date of this nature in South Africa, mining company Gencor agreed to pay compensation of more than US$50 million to the victims and families of those that contracted asbestos-related diseases, while UK-based Cape plc agreed to settle similar claims for £7.5 million.[29] Fresh on the heels of these settlements, a US$7 billion class-action asbestosis case was filed in May 2003 against South African company Goldfields, which is listed in New York, by the same legal team instituting the apartheid claims (Fagan and Ngcebetsha).[30]

Echoing these developments in South Africa, an 'agreement in principle' was reached in April 2003 in the United States by an association of about a dozen large companies called The Asbestos Study Group, which includes General Electric and General Motors, to pay US asbestos victims as much as US$100 billion over 30 years in an attempt to end all asbestosis lawsuits. About 700,000 claims have been filed against US companies that used asbestos, including 200,000 since 2000, and asbestos lawsuits have reportedly forced some 70 companies into bankruptcy.[31] Even Swedish–Swiss engineering giant ABB is partly blaming asbestosis claims for its $45 million reported loss in the first quarter of 2003.[32]

There is no doubt that we have not seen the last of these 'sins of the fathers' types of liability cases. But the ethical dilemmas abound. Some may question whether it is fair for companies to be tried retrogressively, i.e. held accountable for the consequences of actions that were legal at the time but have since become unacceptable. Meanwhile, others may remind us of the potential impact on discouraging foreign direct investment. Then there is the problem that arises if a company being sued goes bankrupt: has justice been served for the claimants who may not receive any compensation as a result? Whatever the answers to these complex issues, business is going to need to tune its radar increasingly to the horizon of the future, if it is to avoid future liability.

The blue backlash?

The fact that some Southern governments are concerned about the possible impact of Western-based initiatives on corporate citizenship poses challenges for advocates. It makes it increasingly important that Southern companies and NGOs participate in campaigns on corporate accountability and any initiatives on corporate responsibility that may have an international implication.

Other events in June 2003 made it increasingly important that those who are working towards social or environmental goals consider their accountability to the intended beneficiaries of their work, before those with counter-agendas use the issue to undermine social change. On 11 June NGOWatch, an initiative of the American Enterprise Institute (AEI) and the Federalist Society for Law and Public Policy Studies, was launched to examine the growing political influence of the non-profit or non-govern-mental sector. The stated purpose of www.ngowatch.org is to 'bring clarity and account-ability to the burgeoning world of NGOs'. Looking at the NGOs to be examined by this project, it is noteworthy that many with a lot of influence in the current order, such as the International Chamber of Commerce and think-tanks such as the Heritage Foun-dation, do not appear. Perhaps because the AEI does not consider such groups, or them-selves, as NGOs? We might agree, but as they do not theorise on the nature and definition of civil society and its constituent organisations as justification for their choice, this AEI project appears more like, in the words of Naomi Klein, 'a McCarthyite blacklist, telling tales on any NGO that dares speak against Bush administration poli-cies or in support of international treaties opposed by the White House'. The initiative warns that 'the extraordinary growth of advocacy NGOs in liberal democracies has the potential to undermine the sovereignty of constitutional democracies'. One may won-der about the lack of reflexivity within AEI, given that it is also an NGO and backed by powerful corporations.[33]

In the same month, the business consultancy SustainAbility also produced a report on this topic. In it they argued that, 'despite being key advocates of corporate account-ability few NGOs have adopted the same rules as their business counterparts, main-taining it compromises their flexibility'.[34] We should point out that many do have the same legal rules, being registered companies, and additional rules, if they have tax-free status (the Charity Commission oversees charities in the UK, for example). More-over, some NGOs such as Friends of the Earth and World Development Movement are membership organisations, with elected boards. Then, of course, there is the question of whether NGOs *should* adopt 'the same rules as their business counterparts'. As the report notes, the question of accountability becomes more pertinent the more power-ful an institution becomes. One may wonder whether a comparison with business is therefore appropriate or merely rhetorical. We may also question whether the motiva-tion of an organisation (such as private gain or public purpose) affects the levels of accountability that we may wish to see from different actors in society. Companies seek to extract profit from their economic and social interactions, which is a different pur-pose to that of NGOs and suggests a different intensity of focus on accountability ques-tions. If NGOs were to adopt the 'same rules', would this imply those rules developed by industry, such as AA 1000? Might this be an added bureaucratic process that could 'professionalise' NGOs in ways that distance them from the constituents they are meant to represent?

The question of NGO accountability is one that has been with us for decades. Within development studies, various commentators have stressed the need for NGOs to be more accountable to those they aim to support, and various groups such as ActionAid have sought to empower their beneficiaries by putting representatives on their board. Many analysts have argued that the increasingly close relations with government and Western funders militates against this downwards accountability of NGOs to their ben-eficiaries.[35] In this light, SustainAbility's conclusions about increasing NGO account-ability on the one hand, and increasing their collaboration with business and adoption of market strategies on the other, could be questioned. Commenting on the report, Gavin Power, Public Affairs Director of the UN Global Compact, said, 'The trends illus-trate that many NGOs are moving beyond a culture of criticism to one of engagement with business and other partners in a search for solutions. While at times it may be

GAVIN POWER OF THE GLOBAL COMPACT:
TODAY'S SOCIAL AND ENVIRONMENTAL
PROBLEMS REQUIRE A CULTURE OF
ENGAGEMENT

difficult for NGOs to collaborate, the scale of today's social and environmental problems requires it.'

Others have argued that more partnerships with business will actually undermine accountability, in ways that can not be fixed by technical approaches. For example, Marina Ottaway suggests that such partnerships are helping create a dangerously undemocratic 'global corporatism'. She argues that, despite claims about the potential of intersectoral partnerships to

> introduce greater democracy in the realm of global governance, it is doubtful that close cooperation between essentially unrepresentative organizations—international organizations, unaccountable NGOs and large transnational corporations—will do much to ensure better protection for, and better representation of, the interests of populations affected by global policies.[36]

MARINA OTTAWAY: PARTNERSHIPS WITH
BUSINESS WILL UNDERMINE
ACCOUNTABILITY

To avoid becoming agents of a corporatist world, the editor of *Development in Practice* has called on NGOs to move to more participatory and 'people centred advocacy'. Being 'in the market for change' as SustainAbility suggests, might undermine this, as market priorities and sponsors' concerns begin to predominate.

The issue of NGO accountability, therefore, remains an important one. Director of SustainAbility, John Elkington, told us that their 'report is designed as a provocation, on the basis that, the sooner NGOs wake up and respond, the better able they will be to leverage change in new ways'. Jules Peck of WWF-UK agreed: 'in general terms I feel the NGO community can expect a shake-up, and we cannot be complacent about changing social and political realities'. However, it seems that, given the concerns mentioned above, this shake-up and awakening might not be in line with SustainAbility's predictions. As Peck explained:

we have to refocus on talking to 'the people' instead of the cosy policy circles of CEOs and civil servants. Why? Because companies and governments plan for the short term, aim to serve certain constituencies, so it's only when the wider public are made aware and empowered to change will they vote, produce and consume in a way that supports corporates and governments to act.

(See 'Differing accountabilities?' on page 205 for further discussion of NGO account-ability.)

Given their questionable provenance, these two summer initiatives on NGO account-ability created some heat within civil society. Commentating on them, author of *The Post-Corporate World*,[37] David Korten, told us that 'the effort by corporations to discredit the public whistle-blowers who are exercising their rights as organised bodies of citi-zens to draw attention to corporate attacks on democracy, the public interest and the integrity of the United Nations is an example of cynical corporate PR spin and unmit-igated hypocrisy'.

Given such concerns it was significant that United Nations Global Compact and United Nations Environment Programme (UNEP) lent their names to SustainAbility's report. Jules Peck, of WWF-UK, who were consulted about SustainAbility's work, told us that 'adding the UN's name to this work might anger those who think the Compact is about diffusing criticism of companies by NGOs'. Others considered that the Com-pact was reacting to criticism from its NGO advisory board members, who wrote to demand the Compact begin to ensure companies delivered on their commitments. Judith Richter told us: 'I am very concerned that the Global Compact has endorsed and thus legitimised a corporate study on how public-interest NGOs should behave.' Author of *Holding Corporations Accountable*,[38] Richter asserted that

> this study, from a corporate-funded business consultancy, tells NGOs to make explicit not only their sources of funding but also their strategies. It suggests that NGOs should stop what it calls 'confrontational' and 'anti-business' campaigns and embark on 'part-nership' engagements with big business aimed at finding 'market-based solutions' to current problems. If these recommendations were heeded, it would put corporations and their lobby associations in a better position to lobby for a cut in funding of corpo-rate watchdog groups and networks. Over the years, several NGOs and citizen networks have successfully built up public awareness and pressure on socially irresponsible cor-porations. The UN's support, via the Global Compact, for the simplistic analyses pre-sented in this study may damage efforts to hold corporations accountable to the world's citizens.

Such concerns about the UN's support for the report fuelled further criticism of the types of engagement the UN is developing with the private sector. Korten said that 'part-nership with global corporations—which by their nature represent the exclusive inter-ests of the wealthiest people on the planet—seriously undermines the UN's essential role and credibility as an intergovernmental body created to democratically serve and represent the interests of all the world's people'. It seems an issue that is set to grow, as the UN finds itself as an *inter*-governmental organisation in a world with two new *non*-governmental superpowers—global business and global civil society. (See 'Else-where in the UN' on page 190 for more discussion on the UN's relations with busi-ness.)

Pulling rank

As corporate social responsibility has gone mainstream, so attempts to rank and rate performance have proliferated. Indexes such as the Dow Jones Sustainability Index and the FTSE4Good are perhaps best known, but these tend to take a conservative and inclusive approach. Their strategy is to encourage best practice, rather than to name and shame, or judge and exclude. Two new indexes that were launched in the last quarter are America's 100 Best Corporate Citizens of 2003 and the UK's Corporate Responsibility Index. They reveal some interesting results.

Business Ethics magazine's 100 Best Corporate Citizens,[39] launched in its Spring issue, ranks companies according to service to seven stakeholder groups: stockholders, the community, minorities and women, employees, the environment, non-US stakeholders, and customers. Some familiar names appear in the top 10—Intel (3), Procter & Gamble (4), IBM (5) and Hewlett-Packard (6)—which somewhat reflects the dominance of service-sector companies in the list. Extractive industries such as mining, chemicals and energy are not entirely absent, but no big-brand multinationals appear.

One of the refreshing characteristics of the list is that, unlike most multinational-focused indexes, this one places companies of all sizes side by side, from IBM with 2001 revenues of US$85 billion to Green Mountain Roasters (ranked 8th) with sales of just $96 million. Another interesting finding was the large variance between the rankings of individual companies in each of the stakeholder service areas. For example, Eastman Kodak (ranked 22nd overall) tied first in the employees category and also scored well on minorities and women, but was one of the ten worst-performing companies (i.e. ranked between 90 and 100) in the stockholder and environmental categories. Similarly, Eli Lilly & Company (ranked 72nd overall) tied first in the employees category, but was ranked 100th in the customer category. This range in performance across different stakeholder groups may suggest that companies manage their relations with different stakeholders in very different ways.

Business in the Community's UK Corporate Responsibility Index 2002,[40] launched in March 2003, ranks 112 voluntary participant companies, including more than half of the FTSE 100, based on performance ratings for Corporate Strategy, Integration, Management Practices (for community, environment, marketplace and workplace), Impact Areas (for product safety, occupational health and safety, diversity in the workplace, community investment, supply chain, global warming, energy and transport, and biodiversity) and Assurance. The big-brand multinationals from extractive sectors feature much more strongly in this index, with companies such as BP, Dow Chemical Company, Rio Tinto and Shell International all ranking in the top quintile, alongside mega-manufacturers such as 3M and Unilever.

Although the voluntary and self-selective nature of the index may draw criticism (e.g. companies are only required to select three of five social impact areas), the findings are nevertheless instructive about where most progress appears to have been made. For example, in the management practice areas, environment is furthest advanced, followed by workplace, community and then marketplace; while in the social impact categories the order of scoring was product safety, occupational health and safety, diversity in the workplace, community investment and lastly supply chain.

As much as everyone enjoys comparative rankings, it is important to assess each index critically. Is the organisation that is running the index credible and what is its vested interests? For example, a new Australian rating index launched in March 2003 on corporate social responsibility, produced by a private company called RepuTex and backed by a former Liberal political leader, has drawn high-profile criticism and refusals to participate from top businesses, such as Caltex, who question the organisation's motives and tactics.[41] At the same time, entirely voluntary, self-disclosure indexes with weak verification mechanisms will struggle to convince sceptical stakeholders of their value, given companies' natural bias to portray themselves in the best possible light.

In sum, though, most of these measures were developed by business for business. Certain key issues are yet to penetrate the corporate citizenship reporting and ranking process. Reports still rarely produce basic information on independent performance indicators rather than management processes. On the question of transparency, most reports still fail to provide basic quantitative data on the following: political donations, memberships of trade associations, payments to lobby groups, pollution records, average wages paid to different types of employee (including supply chain), pending court cases, court rulings, out-of-court settlements, admonitions or investigations from intergovernmental bodies, recognised trade unions, collective bargaining agreements, and multi-enterprise codes endorsed and certifications received. With such information, companies might be able to be indexed on the basis of their actual impacts on society rather than the appearance of their management systems.

The measure of things

Of course, quantitative data is only one type of information, with the inherent problems that statistics do not often reveal the complexities and contexts of phenomena being analysed. Despite this, surveys remain a dominant research tool in the social sciences. Three surveys on corporate citizenship were launched in the quarter, which provide some useful data for discussion.

The first, the 'CEO Survey: Sustainability and Corporate Reputation', was conducted from the Cambridge Business School's Judge Institute of Management and surveyed 34% of the CEOs from the Global *Fortune* 500. The research was designed to forecast the impact of sustainability issues on the reputation of large multinational corporations across seven elements: emotional connections, environmental credibility, financial credibility, knowledge, leadership and vision, quality, and social credibility.

One of the interesting features of the survey was that CEOs were asked to rank the importance of various sustainability issues in each of three scenarios for the future: fortress world, market world and transformed world. These categories, like all used in surveys, were derived from a particular and contestable way of understanding the world. The first was seen as a return to protectionism, the second representing a continuing of the current neoliberal paradigm and the third describing a sustainability road of social, ecological and economic balance. The overall importance ranking of the seven reputation elements for the future was as follows: first, leadership and vision;

joint second, skills and knowledge, and quality; joint third, financial and social credibility; fourth, environmental credibility; and fifth, emotional connections.

It is perhaps not surprising that, in the transformed-world scenario, social and environmental credibility rank highest. More surprising is that financial credibility scores highest in the fortress world, and low in the market-world scenario. It is also noteworthy that European companies consistently assign higher significance to environmental, financial and social credibility than their North American counterparts, who favour leadership and vision, knowledge, and quality.

The second featured survey is a study of CSR website reporting in Asia, conducted by the International Centre for Corporate Social Responsibility at Nottingham University Business School.[42] The research analysed the websites of the top 50 companies in seven developing Asian countries and compared the results to Japan and the UK. The findings show that the highest prevalence of CSR web reporting occurs in India (72%), followed by South Korea (52%), Thailand (42%) and Singapore (38%), while Malaysia (32%), the Philippines (30%) and Indonesia (24%) lag behind.

The researchers distinguish three waves of CSR reporting that are reflected in their results. The first is disclosure on community involvement, on which an average of 59% of the companies in the seven countries reported, and includes such activities as supporting local economic development, arts and culture, education and training, sport, and environmental conservation. The second wave, with 39% reporting, is production processes and relates to the management of environmental, health and safety impacts, as well as human resources and ethics policies and programmes. The final wave, with only 18% disclosing information, is employee relations, including employee welfare and employee engagement.

Also of interest was that the only statistically significant explanatory variable that could be determined for the level of CSR reporting was that firms that operated internationally were more likely to disclose CSR performance. In contrast, none of the socioeconomic factors reviewed, such as national GDP, national sector profile, life expectancy and adult literacy, showed any correlation with levels of CSR disclosure. Perhaps companies with a global profile have to be seen to be doing more on CSR than perhaps their national counterparts. However, with all 'statistically significant' findings, a correlation does not necessarily imply a cause. Moreover, correlations can be produced by the definition of one's categories—especially as the current concept of CSR has been developed largely in the West, and so companies with more contact with the West may have more exposure to it. Sceptics might therefore remind us that reporting on CSR does not necessarily accurately reflect social and environmental impacts, or even actual CSR performance.

Finally, in a KPMG East Africa Business Ethics Survey, released in July 2003, nearly 100 companies were asked about their ethics policies and practices.[43] The findings show that more than 80% have a written statement of values and principles, but only around a third have provided employee training on its application in the organisation. Also, 60% have appointed a senior-level manager responsible for ethics initiatives, and approximately half have instituted a whistle-blowing mechanism. Given the poor reputation that Africa has for corruption, it is clear that business will need to improve the performance reflected in this survey if it is to demonstrate that it can operate credibly and ethically in developing countries. The Director of Sustainability Services for KPMG

SHIREEN NAIDOO, DIRECTOR OF
SUSTAINABILITY SERVICES FOR KPMG IN
SOUTH AFRICA: AFRICAN COMPANIES ARE
MOVING IN THE RIGHT DIRECTION

in South Africa, Shireen Naidoo, told us that the survey results could have a continent-wide significance, in the context of the New Partnership for Africa's Development (NEPAD):

> Central to NEPAD's voluntary African Peer Review Mechanism is the Declaration on Democracy, Political, Economic and Corporate Governance. The Declaration states that good economic and corporate governance, including transparency in financial management, are essential prerequisites for promoting economic growth and reducing poverty. Our survey suggests that at least companies are moving in the right direction to give substance to this Declaration.

3Q2003

July–September

Jem Bendell and Tim Concannon

Principles on the line

In the Northern summer of 2003, major banks and finance institutions made a significant step forwards in addressing the environmental and social costs of their investment decisions. The Equator Principles[1] are a set of voluntary benchmarks, committing banks to follow World Bank environmental and social guidelines when financing large infrastructure projects.

About a dozen large multinational banks based in Europe and Canada have adopted the Principles, which will require clients to carry out environmental assessments, enter into a dialogue with affected groups, and take steps to mitigate their impacts.

The Principles were adopted as a result of an alliance between activists and progressive investors. The response from NGOs to their adoption was a cautious welcome. 'Major US investment banks are beginning to respond to the pressure that groups . . . are putting on them to recognise their role and responsibility in advancing sustainability', said Michelle Chan-Fishell, Green Investments Campaigner for Friends of the Earth, USA.[2]

Friends of the Earth and other groups—including WWF and AIDEnvironment—were part of a hundred-strong international civil-society coalition who in January issued their own 'Collevecchio Declaration on Financial Institutions and Sustainability', setting far more stringent standards. In June 2003, the group was critical of the scope of the industry-specified guidelines: 'The Equator Principles recognises that financiers have a role in and responsibility for the social and environmental impacts of their transactions. Whether or not the Equator Principles represent a significant initiative or a

MICHELLE CHAN-FISHELL, FRIENDS OF THE
EARTH: US BANKS ARE RESPONDING TO PRESSURE

negligible one depends on banks' commitment to strengthen them and be transparent in their implementation of the Principles.'[3]

This move towards increased attention by financial institutions to the social and environmental consequences of investment was highlighted in August 2003, when UBS Investment Bank—part of the Swiss-owned financial services giant—signed up US-based Innovest Strategic Value Advisors to train 400 bankers, research analysts and legal advisers. Matthew Kiernan, Innovest's chief executive, said UBS's executives would follow a high-level training programme—a kind of 'MBA in SRI. You wouldn't normally expect investment banks to be doing this. It is born of a growing recognition that environmental issues can cost companies money or create it.'[4]

Also in August 2003, eight UK-based institutional investors—representing over £454 billion in funds under management—agreed to co-fund a pilot programme to 'deepen and learn from collaborative approaches to active share-ownership focused on material social and environmental risks'. 'Investors are increasingly taking a collaborative approach to communicating with companies to discuss their shared concerns or highlight a collective position on investment risk issues—such as the "Investor statement on pharmaceutical companies and the public health crisis in emerging markets" ', according to the UK Social Investment Forum, reporting the announcement.[5]

Would there be more examples in 2004 of investors 'going it alone' to press companies for change, like the bold move in the earlier months of 2003 by the UK's ISIS Asset Management and the Universities Superannuation Scheme (USS)? Both funds tried to use their leverage in a positive way to urge drug companies and governments to improve access to medicines for the poor.[6]

It remains to be seen whether the collective goodwill of 'niche' ethical SRI funds and finance institutions signed up to the Equator Principles would be enough to assuage activists' concerns about the growing power and influence of investors.

Some economics please . . .

The United Nations Conference on Trade and Development (UNCTAD) moved more strategically into the arena of corporate citizenship in September 2003, with the publication of its 2003 *World Investment Report*.[7] Previously, UNCTAD had analysed the state of play in its 1999 report, but refrained from making any major recommendations on the nature and promotion of corporate citizenship. In the 2003 report, UNCTAD made two key contributions. It suggested, first, that corporate citizenship explore the economic impact of companies, and, second, that international investment agreements might be one mechanism for promoting or ensuring improved corporate practices.

UNCTAD noted that most corporate citizenship initiatives address 'social and environmental issues, leaving economic development issues out of their scope. Indeed, there has been a notable lack of debate on issues pertaining directly to the economic development interests of developing countries.' They suggested that the dominance of issues such as human, environmental and labour rights could be the result of the interests of developed countries, as well as 'the emergence of influential civil society interest groups that challenge companies to engage in a dialogue on their policies and performances and the fact that globally agreed standards on these issues exist'. How-

ever, UNCTAD argued the limited attention given to the economic impacts of companies is curious for at least two reasons: first, because the main impact of companies is
economic (they are business entities); second, this impact has increased with the
expansion of foreign direct investment (FDI), particularly for developing countries. Difficulties arise as there is no single model for, or understanding of, successful development. Nor is there a single internationally agreed instrument from which one could
derive specific development obligations, although progress is being made in this
regard within the context of economic and social rights, at the UN's Commission on
Human Rights.

UNCTAD suggested that the term 'corporate citizenship' be distinguished from 'the
concept of "corporate social responsibility" in that it addresses economic aspects more
explicitly'. They argued that this economic dimension will mean we consider how corporate citizens 'pay greater attention to contributing to public revenues, creating and
upgrading linkages with local enterprises, creating employment opportunities, raising skill levels and transferring technology'. The question of corporate responsibility
and accountability for paying taxes was discussed in a previous review, and UNCTAD
stresses this point, with transnational corporations (TNCs) 'expected to abide by the
spirit of a country's tax law and to meet their tax obligations in good faith—and not
purposely shift revenues through abusive transfer pricing to deny the governments of
taxes on income originating in their territories'.

UNCTAD also stresses the importance of compliance with national laws, and playing a constructive role in public policy debates. For example, companies could 'seek
to influence home country governments to open their markets more for imports from
developing countries. They can help create a business-enabling environment by
actively participating in public–private fora on improving investment conditions in a
given country. And they can also serve on advisory panels to national governments and
regional bodies.' This alludes to the political bottom line of business, discussed in the
review of the fourth quarter of 2002. Given the track record of many companies' political influence over home and host countries, this is a major issue for one's understanding of corporate citizenship. Yet calls for positive engagement on political-economic
issues also raises complex questions around democratic accountability. UNCTAD's
1999 *World Investment Report* discussed concerns over the accountability of the trend-
setters in corporate responsibility initiatives, yet the proposals in the 2003 report might
lead to more concern in this regard.

The second strategic contribution from UNCTAD in the 2003 report was their assessment of how international investment agreements might contribute to enhancing
good corporate practices, a novel thought given that such treaties normally focus on
government conduct, not that of corporations. Among the approaches and instruments they considered were linking voluntary standards to investment agreements,
perhaps making them legally binding. For example, the Joint Declaration in the
Chile–EU Agreement reminds us that the TNCs of these countries 'of their recommendation to observe the OECD Guidelines for Multinational Enterprises, wherever they
operate'. The legal and practical importance of such text is questionable, however.

Another suggestion appears more interesting, particularly as a strategy for future
negotiations on bilateral, regional or even multilateral investment agreements. This is
that investment agreements establish obligations on corporations to abide by certain
standards if they wish to enjoy the rights accorded by that agreement. Such standards

could include compliance with domestic laws, perhaps even home-country laws or international standards. This could become particularly relevant in any dispute-settlement procedure, where a company would need to have been conducting its operations in full accordance with the law and other relevant standards if it were to seek any recompense by making a complaint against a country. Perhaps a country could even revoke the licence to operate of a foreign investor, if it was in breach of obligations as outlined in an investment agreement. On one hand this would go a small way towards addressing the concern that investment and trade agreements give corporations rights without concurrent duties, and accountability. On the other hand, objections could be brought that such governmental power over foreign investors would counter the drive towards equal treatment for domestic and foreign companies. In response, we might rekindle the debate about governments having the right to revoke the charters of domestic companies as well as those of foreign subsidiaries in their country. UNCTAD did not explore such issues, suggesting that, by inclusion in an investment agreement, any obligation on foreign companies 'would need to be applied in a manner consistent with the protection standards (such as non-discrimination, fair and equitable treatment) granted in the same agreement'.

In summary, UNCTAD notes that investment agreements should not be expected to set out comprehensive rules for business activities, or substitute specific international agreements or voluntary efforts. However, they are the instruments that focus on the investment process, which necessarily involves corporations. 'In a time when the societal implications of corporate actions are receiving more attention and scrutiny, good corporate citizenship—especially when it combines the interests of host countries and firms—deserves a careful examination in future international investment agreements'.

The lack of progress on the Doha Agenda at the World Trade Organisation (WTO) conference in Cancún in September 2003 meant that investment issues were prevented from being included in further negotiations. The developing countries had effectively argued that, without rich member states delivering on their promises from the previous ministerial conference, there was no reason for them to agree on new issues with questionable developmental benefits. Given the increasing use of previously agreed, as well as newly negotiated, bilateral treaties relating to investment, there remained an important need for a multilateral forum to address the implications for sustainable development and corporate responsibility. Whether member states of the United Nations would give UNCTAD such a mandate was still to be seen.

Elsewhere in the UN

In August 2003 another UN body concluded a key phase in its work on corporate accountability and human rights. The Sub-Commission for the Promotion and Protection of Human Rights adopted the UN 'Norms on the Responsibilities of Transnational Corporations and Other Business Enterprises with Regard to Human Rights'.[8] The Norms make clear a range of legal obligations for companies, based on existing international human rights, labour and environmental standards. A coalition of NGOs, including Amnesty International, Christian Aid and the Forum for Human Rights, said the Norms 'constitute an authoritative interpretation of the Universal Declaration of Human Rights of 1948. The Universal Declaration applies not only to states and individuals, but also to "organs of society", including businesses.'[9]

Section Paragraph H.16 of the agreement was of particular importance in suggesting that these Norms might take on a life outside of the filing cabinet:

> Transnational corporations and other businesses enterprises shall be subject to periodic monitoring and verification by United Nations, other international and national mechanisms already in existence or yet to be created, regarding application of the Norms. This monitoring shall be transparent and independent and take into account input from stakeholders (including non governmental organizations) and as a result of complaints of violations of these Norms.[10]

Other UN agencies, such as the International Labour Office, already have processes for hearing complaints about countries whose commitment to various conventions on social and environmental issues is challenged: processes that have proved to be of limited importance in influencing the practices of countries, or their corporations. The exact working of any complaints process will therefore be key. The Sub-Commission mandated further work on possible complaints mechanisms, but any action on establishing such mechanisms would be decided at the next Sub-Commission and the 61st session of the main Commission on Human Rights. Therefore, there remained the opportunity for opponents of the process to kill it, as well an opportunity for proponents to promote understanding of the Norms, and their potential role.

In the review of the third quarter of 2002, the divided reaction of the business community to these developments was chronicled—some supportive, some not. One year on and there was little evidence that significant learning on this issue had occurred. Thomas Niles, president of the US Council for International Business, attacked the Norms on the BBC's World Service radio. Part of his argument was the growth of voluntary initiatives such as the UN Global Compact. One of the main authors of the Norms, Professor David Weissbrodt, countered that 'there are about 75,000 transnational corporations. Only 1,000 of them have joined the Global Compact. So what about the other 74,000?'[11]

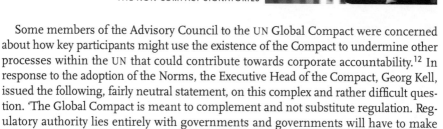

DAVID WEISSBRODT: NEED TO ADDRESS
THE NON-COMPACT SIGNATORIES

Some members of the Advisory Council to the UN Global Compact were concerned about how key participants might use the existence of the Compact to undermine other processes within the UN that could contribute towards corporate accountability.[12] In response to the adoption of the Norms, the Executive Head of the Compact, Georg Kell, issued the following, fairly neutral statement, on this complex and rather difficult question. 'The Global Compact is meant to complement and not substitute regulation. Regulatory authority lies entirely with governments and governments will have to make decisions on the Norms as adopted by the Sub-Commission of Human Rights. From the perspective of the Global Compact, we always welcome efforts that help to clarify complex human rights questions and that foster practical changes.'[13]

However, with no specific proposal for a binding agreement between governments, nor direct mechanisms of enforcement over corporations, the assumption that the Norms are 'regulatory' could be questioned. 'I wouldn't call these norms anything like "compulsory",' argued Weissbrodt, as 'they rely on existing law, and they apply those laws to companies . . . and then their "binding-ness" comes principally from the existing law, not just from the fact that we've restated it in one document that makes it easier for you to understand'.[14]

Kell's statement that the Sub-Commission's work is ultimately decided by governments is important, inasmuch as all the UN's work is so decided, including that of the Global Compact itself, via General Assembly authority over the Secretary-General. Given a context where some corporate participants in the Compact were lobbying to stop the progress of the Norms, some might ask whether the Compact office would take a similarly neutral view of any companies that worked with other UN agencies but lobbied their governments to curtail the Compact's activities? Such action would probably be considered counter to demonstrating support for the UN, something required of companies under the guidelines for partnerships.[15] Why should those guidelines not apply to companies in the Compact? Such difficult policy questions, and the associated accountability challenges that arise from increased UN–business collaboration were not explored by the Secretary-General's report on this topic to the General Assembly during September 2003.[16] However, the importance of this topic suggests it is one that will return.

Reporting on the human rights Norms, the *Guardian* argued that 'what is really necessary between now and March, when the full 53-nation UN human rights commission meets to consider the norms for approval, is evidence of a political will by world governments to hold businesses to account'.[17] Corporate lobbying would be key. Whether enough companies would embrace the form of 'radical corporate citizenship', described by the co-author of this review in the chapter 'Civil Regulation',[18] and support greater intergovernmental cooperation towards level playing fields for social and environmental performance, was still to be seen.

Exorcising the curse of oil

Even following the end of 'formal' hostilities in Iraq, the world's attention to oil-related issues remained largely fixed on the Middle East. However, oil politics in another part of the world were as important to questions of corporate citizenship—West Africa. Western military intervention, in the form of broad international coalitions acting under a UN umbrella—in Liberia and Sierra Leone—and social intervention on issues such as corruption and money laundering steadily increased. The role and influence of oil interests and oil companies was never far from discussions about these interventions. Whether companies could help the people of West Africa finally escape the plague of corruption and armed conflict that has arisen from the exploitation of their petroleum and other abundant natural resources was still to be seen.

In June 2003, the Publish What You Pay Coalition of NGOs—established to push for greater transparency in the extractive sector—was celebrating a considerable symbolic coup in getting Shell to disclose its political payments in Nigeria.[19] This and other events throughout the Northern summer underlined the growing importance of West African oil and natural resources to global markets and world politics. It also highlighted the growing dependency of this notoriously unstable, corrupt and poor region of Africa on the international oil industry.

Previously, in 2001, the Bush administration's controversial energy plan had specified West Africa as one key foreign source for petroleum, to end America's dependency on the Persian Gulf.[20] Vice President Cheney—who headed the energy task force and was himself the former director of the oil services giant Halliburton—refused to release a list of individuals consulted by the committee, a move that sparked a confrontation between the administration and the General Accounting Office. In June 2003, a senior CIA official, David Gordon, speaking at a meeting organised by the Corporate Council on Africa, predicted that African oil would be potentially more important to the US in a decade than oil from Russia or the Caucasus.[21]

In July 2003, when President Bush visited African states including Senegal, South Africa, Botswana, Uganda and Nigeria, the attendance of Colin Powell, Condoleezza Rice, and US business leaders, amply illustrated the growing importance of African natural resources to the White House.[22]

Within days of the visit, soldiers in the tiny island nation of São Tomé and Principe seized power, in a coup that appeared to be directly linked to a scramble for oil revenues.[23] São Tomé, which is often compared to Kuwait because billions of barrels of oil are said to lie offshore, will soon be tapped, fuelling tension over how to share it with its coastal neighbours, including Nigeria.

The Publish What You Pay coalition had highlighted Nigeria's disclosure of information about its dealing in the new São Tomé concession as an example of how Africa's most populous, oil-rich nation was cleaning up its act. Whatever the merits of efforts towards increased transparency in the West African oil sector being supported by the regions' politicians, it seemed to be a case of business as usual as far as the military were concerned.

Yet this civil-society initiative seemed to be faring better than the similar, UK-government-backed Extractives Industries Transparency Initiative (EITI),[24] which was being negotiated in June 2003. Earlier that year, a remark from Clare Short (Minister for International Development, until May 2003) seemed to demonstrate the apparent conflict within the Blair government on regulation of corporate power: 'We are not ruling out mandatory requirements,' Short said.[25]

Resistance to the scheme from the US and US oil companies was generally blamed for the UK's failure to come up with a mandatory system of disclosure, and for the UK's and France's seeming inability to argue for a tougher regime within the G8 at Evian. In addition, while it seemed that many in the oil industry wanted to open up to greater transparency on issues such as political payments, others wanted to pull off a sleight of hand by covering things up again, citing 'confidentiality' concerns.[26] Short had argued previously that 'Many oil companies would prefer something binding so that the best are protected from being undercut by the laggards.'[27] Those companies would need to act more forcefully to stop oil wealth fuelling corruption, war and further impoverishing the African continent.

Cracks in a wall of silence

In June 2003, what had seemed to be a wall of silence from big business on issues concerning regulation, started to show some cracks. At a European parliamentary hearing on transparency in the oil industry in June, BP announced that it preferred a voluntary approach but Shell said it could live with regulation provided it was even-handed and applied to all competitors.[28] Groups such as Christian Aid welcomed Shell's newfound enthusiasm for regulation[29] but felt that the patchy response from the sector as a whole showed the need for a global, binding approach, as was suggested by groups led by Friends of the Earth International at the World Summit on Sustainable Development (WSSD).

Also in June 2003, the UK-based NGO The Corner House produced a report alleging that the UK's Export Credits Guarantee Department allows corruption by British business to go unchecked.[30] The report called for international binding rules that place a legal responsibility on governments to take all reasonable steps—through preventative due diligence, and post-issue monitoring procedures—to ensure taxpayers' money doesn't underwrite corrupt business deals. This could include an incorporation of 'Publish What You Pay' (PWYP) principles on transparency into an international treaty. An example of how this might work might be provided by the G8-initiated Financial Action Task Force, which in 2002 threatened Nigeria and the Ukraine for failing to take adequate legislative measures to combat money laundering.[31]

Enthusiasm for a non-regulated approach to inducing better corporate social and environmental performance was dealt further blows during the Northern summer. The UK is seen as a leader in the corporate citizenship field, with a range of large corporations heavily involved in initiatives such as the Global Compact, a burgeoning industry of corporate responsibility consultants and specialist NGOs, and a growing socially responsible investment sector. However, the government of this 'leading' country revealed that only 40 companies had signed up to the 'Make a Corporate Commitment' scheme to publicly disclose environmental information.[32] Groups such as Friends of the Earth seized on this to argue that the UK's company law must make good social and environmental behaviour compulsory.

Meanwhile, the UK Company Law Review—which has been ongoing since John Major was Prime Minister—failed to find parliamentary time for yet another year. However, activists felt a glimmer of opportunity was offered to push a 'corporate accountability' agenda in the Department of Trade and Industry (DTI)'s proposal that—in line with the Turnbull Committee *et al.*'s recommendations—companies should consider 'intangible assets of the company'[33] (such as the value of the brand and 'reputation' as well as intellectual copyrights and patents; so, in theory, that could mean, for example, compulsory social and environmental reporting).

This will be done through an Operating and Financial Review (OFR).[34] An OFR Working Group on Materiality has been set up to figure out how this should work, pending the formation of a Standards Body to do it. However, activists criticised the DTI recommendations which leave it up to individual directors to decide what's material to their companies, thus providing no real prospect of an actual, uniform standard for reporting (similar to companies having to publish an environmental and/or social report to shareholders). In June 2003, AccountAbility released a report, 'Redefining Materiality: Practice and Public Policy for Effective Corporate Reporting', calling for a wider scope to material consideration and disclosure by companies. 'Labour standards, human rights and environmental issues rarely figure in investor-focused reporting', commented Simon Zadek, Chief Executive of AccountAbility and co-author of the report, 'yet in retrospect we see repeatedly how these issues impact on businesses' reputation, performance and profitability.'[35] It remained to be seen whether a standardless approach could give investors the uniform reporting they would need to assess 'reputational' risks adequately.

From the perspective of international development, a more regulated and thus uniform approach was also argued to be beneficial. A new United Nations Industrial Development Organisation (UNIDO) report questioned whether a purely unregulated approach to corporate citizenship was becoming a barrier to trade, locking Southern-domiciled small and medium-sized enterprises (SMEs) out of developing-world markets, supply chains and World Bank loan processes, by creating an unmanageable burden of reporting and verification.[36]

Go west, then go nowhere

The importance of the case being heard by the US Supreme Court, concerning Marc Kasky's suit against Nike, was discussed in detail in 'Just do it . . . out of court' on page 170. At the end of June 2003, the Court issued its judgement, effectively changing its mind that it was appropriate to hear the case at all. A sensible decision, some may consider, given that Nike was seeking that the Supreme Court stop a case from even being heard. The *New York Times* reported that the case 'became the focus of an intense debate, on the Internet, at the court and elsewhere, over the role of multinational corporations, the effects of globalization and the constitutional contours of commercial speech'.[37] Justice Stevens argued that issuing an opinion at this time would result in 'the premature adjudication of novel constitutional questions' that would 'apply with special force to this case', adding that 'this case presents novel First Amendment questions because the speech at issue represents a blending of commercial speech, non-commercial speech and debate on an issue of public importance'.[38] It seems that, when accepting to hear the case earlier in 2003, the Justices underestimated the complexities and political ramifications, and thus decided that California courts should work on this first, with the Supreme Court coming into play again if and when appeals are forthcoming. Within the published opinions from the court, Nike's attorneys found some hope, as 'a majority of the Court expressly rejected the central holding of the California Supreme Court that Nike's speech could be restricted as purely 'commercial'.[39] Yet neither did they find it to be purely non-commercial, and so the company's confidence could be questioned. Jeff Milchen and Jeffrey Kaplan argued that the result was probably due to Nike's over-ambitiousness in not only defending itself on this instance but in seeking a precedent that would give corporations more political power. 'Nike simply could have challenged Mr. Kasky's standing to sue, since he alleges no personal harm—a precedent that creates legitimate concerns about potential abuse of the law. Instead, Nike ventured beyond its direct interests to attempt a subversion of our Constitution.' The activists suggested that the ruling was, ironically, probably in the interests of Corporate America. 'If big business hopes to regain the dwindling trust of

Americans, demanding a right to lie is hardly the way to do it. So perhaps the US Supreme Court helped save corporate America from itself . . . by declining to rule on the Nike Corporation's claim of a constitutional right to lie.'[40] As argued above ('Just do it . . . out of court', page 170), the sooner a legal framework for social and environmental corporate communications is developed, at national and international levels, then the sooner such court cases will have legal benchmarks to work from, and society more credible information on which to act.

This story took a significant turn in September 2003 when Marc Kasky and Nike reached an out-of-court settlement. In the settlement, Nike agreed to make a $1.5 million payment to the Fair Labor Association (FLA).[41] This decision, like the case, proved controversial. Adele Simmons, the chairwoman of the board of the FLA, told the *New York Times* she applauded the deal: 'This money will be used, clearly, to contribute to our work on workers' rights.'[42] Kasky's attorney stated that 'this resolution benefits two key groups: factory workers and consumers worldwide. Given the FLA's collaboration across a wide spectrum of companies, universities and NGOs, it is an excellent vehicle for Nike to further develop its corporate responsibility efforts and allow interested consumers to measure the performance of Nike and other companies through public reporting.'[43]

ADELE SIMMONS OF THE FLA:
NIKE MONEY WILL GO TO WORKERS'
RIGHTS

However, others working on sweatshop issues were outraged, with some questioning the financial concerns of Kasky's lawyers, as the details of any payments to them were not disclosed. Moreover, some criticised the choice of the FLA. 'Nike and its corporate buddies basically run the FLA', said Andy Eisen, a student at Lake Forest College and a member of United Students Against Sweatshops (USAS). 'It's governed by and for the corporations that it's supposed to monitor.'[44] Students also attacked the FLA's operations as secretive and ineffective, saying that most important information is being kept from the public. They asked why Kasky would not have wanted the money to support a group more independent of corporate influence, such as the Worker Rights Consortium.[45]

Jeffrey Ballinger, executive director of Press for Change, one group that initiated the corporate campaign against Nike in the 1990s, argued that:

> if any money is going to come out of Nike to settle this kind of case, it should go to workers who were cheated by Nike. End of story. Nike has never been forced to pay for the cheating that has taken place at their contract factories—cheating that has been documented at their Indonesian factories for several years. Tens of thousands of workers being paid an illegal training wage. Nike admitted it in 1996.[46]

Stepping back, the settlement of this dispute reminds us how the norms and standards for private enterprise are themselves increasingly being privatised, as voluntary initiatives take a greater role. Countries and courts, North and South, seem unable to enforce on corporations those behaviours that have been determined by (at least superficially) democratic processes. Thus the power of corporations in shaping how these new private regulatory processes operate comprises an important research agenda for anyone interested in democracy. Looking one way or the other, either just at the law or just at voluntary processes, we can see only half the picture.

Future days in court?

Over the Northern summer, the prospect grew for 'corporate criminals' to one day appear in the dock.

Earlier in 2003 the Hague-based International Criminal Court (ICC) opened its doors and is now reviewing possible cases. The ICC's statute has a very strict remit covering accepted definitions of serious criminal acts. The general view of legal experts is that the criminal liability of corporations is not well established in international law.[47] A change to the ICC statute would be needed for the Court to put heads of companies on trial alongside heads of states and armies, when it comes up for review in 2008. However, this review will concentrate on whether the ICC has jurisdiction over contentious issues such as the illegal use of force, so activists in signatory countries to the ICC convention would have to lobby their governments hard—and soon—to get corporate accountability on the agenda.[48]

Despite all this—and in the present, febrile atmosphere of international relations— it appears that the Court won't necessarily be cowed into only prosecuting Washington and London's foes-of-the-moment, but might extend its remit to look at big business after all. The ICC statute just about allows this if it can be shown that an organisation clearly and materially abetted an act of mass killing, though this will obviously need to be tested in the Court at some point.

In July 2003, there were early signs that the ICC might bring prosecutions over the continuing genocide in the Congo. 'Companies who are doing illegal business and

LUIS MORENO OCAMPO, ICC'S CHIEF PROSECUTOR: LOOKING AT COMPANIES OPERATING ILLEGALLY IN THE CONGO

financing the crimes will know that we are following them', Luis Moreno Ocampo, the Court's chief prosecutor, told journalists at a press conference in the Hague.[49]

Also in 2003 a Belgian 'war crimes' law was amended to allow trials *in absentia*, and to authorise the Belgian courts to try cases that fall outside the jurisdiction of the ICC.

In June 2003, the US lobbied Belgium to drop the new law, including by threatening to suspend financial support for a new NATO building in Brussels.[50] However, according to a January 2003 *Guardian* article, there will be limits to the law's provenance with or without US pressure, indicating that—like the ICC, which will subject all cases to a pre-trial review to decide if they are admissible—it is likely to be a highly political legal instrument.[51]

Beyond management?

'As we gather in Seattle, the site of recent conflict and demonstrations concerning the global impact of institutions, the Academy of Management has the opportunity to both learn from and inform an on-going worldwide debate.'[52] So wrote Denise Rousseau and Andrea Rivero-Dabós in the programme for the 2003 Academy of Management conference, which took place in August 2003. With over 4,700 people participating on the conference programme, this is the largest management studies event in the world. The programme chairs invited members of the Academy to address the topic of 'democracy in a knowledge economy', explaining that 'the concept of democracy overlaps with a variety of contemporary organizational issues that warrant consideration by scholars, practitioners, and the general public'. They asserted that 'these issues reflect the particular expertise and interests of Academy members, including transparency, legitimacy, stakeholder interests, justice, power, competency, autonomy, control, and responsibility. We hope that 2003's theme stimulates productive theory development, research and debate on these and related topics.'

Did the Academy respond? Were these really issues really within the 'expertise and interests' of conference presenters? A database search of the thousands of papers and panel summaries provides an indication. There were three results for the search-term 'capitalism' and only one result for the terms 'anti-capitalism' and 'anti-globalisation' (in all spelling permutations). There were three results for the term 'lobbying', although one of these results included a paper that looked at the effectiveness of different corporate lobbying strategies, without even questioning the public policy implications or ethics: even more surprising given that the lobbying being analysed concerned accountancy regulation in the United States.[53] There was one result when searching for the term 'corporate power'. That session, which spoke to the heart of the conference theme, with presenters such as Marjorie Kelly and David Korten, bagged the 8:30 am slot and was attended by a mere 40 people.

Hundreds of delegates did cram into a room to see Henry Mintzberg speak on the topic of 'Getting Past Smith and Marx: Toward a Balanced Society', perhaps suggesting more about the pulling power of gurus in management studies than the topic of the session. Mintzberg presented his assertion that capitalism did not win the Cold War, but 'balance did'. In other words, a regulated and taxed capitalist market system was what served the West well, and the current neoliberal approach to capitalism and the management of market actors is becoming as unbalanced as Communism. This seemed to be a dramatic revelation to many attending, although not necessarily to those in the 'Critical Management Studies' division of the Academy, who have for some time been integrating political science into management research.

HENRY MINTZBERG:
CAPITALISM DID NOT WIN THE COLD WAR

Mintzberg then criticised management schools for being part of the problem. This led some members of the audience to ask what should be done to change the incentive structures within management academia, such as the publishing protocols for mainstream journals, in order to make it a friend not foe of social change. For example, the flagship *Academy of Management Journal* mainly publishes articles that use the mathematical to describe the obvious about the largely inconsequential. Even the *Academy of Management Review* has limited its contributors' interdisciplinarity and use of normative methodological approaches. Therefore, since the division 'Social Issues in Management' (SIM) was established in the 1970s with a progressive agenda, its members have had to conform somewhat to established protocols in order to be published and thus employed, leading to a body of research and teaching of only moderate impact, both intellectually and socially.

Mintzberg frustrated some with his suggestion of ignoring 'the academic publishing game'. 'That's alright for a Mintzberg to say, but for us?' retorted one young academic. He had, after all, chosen to speak at a management conference to people who bought his books, rather than a political science or sociology conference where his limited political theoretical analysis would not be treated with such respect. The burning issue that needed discussion at the time, and still does, is how to create progressive change in management academia, given the power of business in society and the role of education.

There were some signs of progress. Many of the sessions within the special-interest group Organisations and the Natural Environment (ONE)[54] were well attended, and 2003 was the first year that 'Critical Management Studies' (CMS) made it onto the conference programme as a special-interest group. A number of CMS panels did engage directly with issues such as workplace democracy and stakeholder relations with some interdisciplinary influence, and one discussing how advocacy should or should not play a role in management teaching and research.

Publishing will be part of the answer to increasing the contribution of management studies to progressive social change. Until the *Journal of Corporate Citizenship*, and others like it, create a truly interdisciplinary body of knowledge, and become better known in mainstream business schools and more highly regarded by government funders, then universities will not be able to employ and promote those who seek to make a positive contribution to contemporary management, through their academic research and teaching.

4Q2003

October–December

Jem Bendell and Rupesh Shah

Sex sells

In Pakistan the National Council for the Status of Women has called for a strengthening of the law in order to deal more effectively with sexual harassment at work.[1] The commission, which was set up in 2000, has recommended that the only way to address the current ineffectiveness of the law is to further explain sexual harassment at the workplace, with strict provisions in the law to curb the menace. The amendment they have proposed suggests that terms of up to six months in jail or a fine could be given for anyone who harasses women employees by uttering any word, making any sound or gesture or overture with sexual overtones. It also suggests placing responsibility for those in positions of immediate authority to take adequate preventative measures to avoid the occurrence of such incidents.

Women in another country have also been challenging current standards of acceptable behaviour. The group Concerned Women of America (CWFA)[2] have been involved in a campaign against department stores across the USA calling for companies to remove the fashion products of French Connection UK from their shelves. The campaign, echoed by various other lobbying groups in the USA, has been driven by a new product range and associated marketing material bearing the distinctive 'fcuk' branding. The CWFA accuses stores that stock the French Connection products of 'eagerly joining [fcuk] with the hopes of making millions by exploiting our children'.[3] Meanwhile, in Nicosia, Cyprus, the first campaign in the country by French Connection (with the strapline 'Christmas Shopping: FCUK It') has led to a number of citizens calling up the municipality with complaints. The owner of the local franchise, Soula Messiou, had to explain the campaign to mayor who apparently saw the funny side. She suggested that 'whenever we have FCUK t-shirts they sell faster than anything else'.[4]

Tom Reichart at the University of Alabama has launched *The Erotic History of Advertising*.[5] Reichart suggests that the fad of using sex in advertising is not recent, adding that Americans 'continue to respond to the lure of provocative marketing and, most important to business, they buy'. In the 1890s, advertisers would use erotic images, primarily of almost or partially nude women to sell products from cigarettes to soap. Subsequently, numerous brands have built their reputations on sex and sexuality. For example, in the 1940s Springs Cotton Mills ran an advertising campaign for their cotton sheets in the USA that became infamous. The campaign came to a head in 1949 with an advert showing a sleeping native American man sprawled out in an attitude of exhaustion in a hammock made of their company's Springmaid cotton sheets. The sheets at the time cost $1 and the strapline read: 'A buck well spent on Springmaid Sheet'.[6] Although briefly experimenting with the *risqué* style of advertising campaign again in the 1990s, the company that now owns the Springmaid brand—Springs Industries Inc.—has reverted to far softer forms of persuasion suggesting that after 50 years the company 'still stands for quality and value today'.[7] However, others still seek this form of enticement, because it sells well. Malaysian Airlines reported that passengers want airline hostesses who are 'young and pretty'. And, as we wandered around the shops in the UK and Switzerland in the run-up to Christmas, there is much evidence of the ongoing value of sex to sales. Items from the marginally sensuous bar of milk chocolate to the more mundane sticking plaster were using images of sexuality to boost profile and sales (if not our health).

Business responsibility for HIV/AIDS

Another more disturbing advert for sex and health is the HIV/AIDS pandemic. As World AIDS Day approached, media corporations such as the BBC put on special programmes about the disease. The role of corporations in either contributing to or alleviating the spread and impact of the disease was not often covered in the mass media. However, a number of initiatives and reports were announced at the time.

On World AIDS Day the World Economic Forum (WEF) reported that business was not yet playing a significant positive role in the fight against HIV/AIDS. It surveyed 8,000 corporate executives on their perceptions of the impacts of the disease on their business and the appropriateness of their response. Forty-seven per cent believed that HIV will have some impact on their business; this number is much lower in countries that to date have not been hard-hit by HIV. However, while many firms are concerned about current or future impacts of AIDS on their businesses and their communities, the study found that few have implemented measures to counter the threat. Fewer than 6% of responding companies had formally approved, written HIV policies, but over a third nevertheless believe their current policies and programmes are sufficient and effective. Thus WEF's Dr Kate Taylor argued that 'despite the ground-breaking efforts undertaken by leading companies, a great deal more needs to be done by the broader business community'.[8]

The United Nations published similar findings just two weeks earlier. The United Nations Research Institute for Social Development (UNRISD) not only looked at corporate perceptions of the problem but also the steps taken towards implementing policies and programmes to combat HIV/AIDS and how these compare with international standards. The study was coordinated by co-author of this review, Dr Jem Bendell.[9] The report documented a wide variation in specific HIV/AIDS prevention and mitigation components of corporate policies and programmes, and the extent of coverage provided to employees and their dependents. It explained that communities, suppliers and subcontractors are rarely covered by policies and programmes, even though most company respondents consider that HIV/AIDS—and the risks it poses to their workplaces and other business operations—must be tackled beyond the workplace. In addition, most companies do not consider how their normal operations and strategies affect poverty, and thus HIV/AIDS. This is despite the UN Declaration of Commitment on HIV/AIDS, which emphasised the importance of poverty and sustainable development on the spread and impact of HIV/AIDS. A book published at this time also suggested the importance of the political economy of HIV/AIDS.[10]

The report argued that not only is the corporate sector just beginning to wake up to the risks posed to business operations by HIV/AIDS but that it has still to awaken to its wider responsibilities, which arise from its influence over those conditions that encourage HIV/AIDS prevalence and undermine possibilities for mitigating its effects. That influence derives from some corporations' reliance on migrant labour, subcontracting, exerting downward pressure on production prices and wages, tax management and evasion, as well as negative influence over the international financial and trade institutions. It suggests that dialogue and action on the interface between business and HIV/AIDS has too often focused on the business response to HIV/AIDS, rather than HIV/AIDS's response to business.

The *Observer* newspaper highlighted this critical analysis when covering the report.[11] However, the report also mapped out a possible way to encourage wider engagement by large companies. As HIV/AIDS may pose significant risks to current and future corporate performance, so the financial community should increasingly be interested in whether the companies they invest in are attuned to that risk and manage it accordingly. Moreover, as this risk cannot be managed effectively by individual corporate action, it requires an economy-wide response. Therefore the UNRISD report makes the case for joint action from institutional investors such as pension funds, which could institutionalise more progressive corporate responses.

Although the financial community was still not responding as it might, some companies were beginning to address the risks to their business by becoming more involved in the communities in which they operate. Tata Steel was awarded a prize for 'action in the community' against HIV/AIDS, and explained that it was essential to promote awareness and treatment in the community if long-term risks to business are to be managed.[12] Six other companies—Anglo American, ChevronTexaco, Daimler-Chrysler, Eskom, Heineken and Lafarge—joined with them in announcing that they will use their facilities, employees and other infrastructure to expand workplace HIV/AIDS prevention and treatment programmes into communities where they operate.[13] Such initiatives are being promoted by groups such as the International Labour Office (ILO) and The Global Fund to Fight AIDS, Tuberculosis and Malaria as a practical response to situations where the state provision of services to communities is limited or non-existent and where some companies operating close to those communities already have HIV/AIDS programmes. Professor Richard Feachem, of The Global Fund, has expressed his hope that public–private partnership and co-investment in health services will be included in future proposals to the Fund. Therefore, we may increasingly see public and charitable funds being provided to corporations to run public health services.

For analysts of corporate citizenship and international development, this raises a number of issues. To what extent is the corporate provision of health services an appropriate response to the right to health? Is it sustainable when the business could leave, or its management change its approach to these issues, and curtail the programmes?

To what extent will such projects help promote and not undermine the development of public services, independent of the continued involvement of the corporation? As corporations may become recipients of funding from charitable and/or government sources, then how this money is dispersed will be keenly watched. Is it cost-effective? Are the supported programmes compliant with all laws and best practices such as those established by the ILO? Some of these concerns were already being raised. The conclusion from one workshop on this issue was that 'companies should not take on Government responsibilities but rather support Communities to be self-reliant'.[14]

Debates about corporate citizenship and HIV/AIDS parallel broader debates about the role of public–private partnerships in achieving social objectives. In November 2003, at the UNRISD conference on corporate responsibility, in summarising her forthcoming report, Ann Zammit highlighted growing concern about such partnerships regarding the way they can undermine alternative approaches to dealing with the systemic problems with the global economy that create maldevelopment. On the AIDS issue, the charity ActionAid has already accused pharmaceutical companies of using charitable donations of drugs as part of a strategy to undermine calls for curtailing patents and promoting domestic production capacities in developing countries.

A number of groups had been campaigning for an interpretation of the Trade Related Aspects of Intellectual Property Rights (TRIPS) Agreement, and accusing corporations of unhelpful lobbying: an issue covered in previous Annual Reviews (see 'Accountability is responsibility' on page 176). Responding to this campaign, Hank McKinnell, CEO of the major pharmaceutical company Pfizer wrote that he supported 'the efforts of the WTO to allow the poorest nations in the world to manufacture or import drugs needed to combat epidemics like HIV/AIDS at the lowest possible cost'.[15] However, the President of Oxfam America, Raymond Offenheiser, countered that

> Pfizer and other drug companies lobby heavily for provisions in the WTO patent rules and bilateral/ regional free trade agreements that block availability of generics, so that in the absence of competition they can have a monopoly market position and the resultant monopoly profits. In countries where resources devoted to healthcare are scarce, lack of competition and monopoly pricing by branded drug companies means that medicines are priced out of reach of the majority of patients. To help patients in poor countries, Pfizer should stop lobbying for policy outcomes that undermine their access to essential drugs.[16]

These exchanges were in the run-up to the Cancún Ministerial Conference of the World Trade Organisation (WTO) where a decision on TRIPS and access to medicines

HANK McKINNELL, PFIZER CEO:
SUPPORTS THE EFFORTS OF THE WTO

needed to be reached. One was reached, which was called 'historic' by WTO Director-General Supachai Panitchpakdi, who said it would allow 'poorer countries to make full use of the flexibilities in the WTO's intellectual property rules in order to deal with the diseases that ravage their people'.[17] However, there was resistance to the agreement by many poorer countries until the very end.

Campaigners argued that the agreement means that countries wanting to import cheap generics must jump through multiple hoops to prove they are in need, unable to afford patented drugs and incapable of producing the medicines domestically. Meanwhile, there is no guarantee that there will be a sufficient supply of drugs for them to buy, since the deal also puts up hurdles for countries wanting to export. 'A "gift" tightly bound in red tape', declared a coalition of NGOs, including Médecins Sans Frontières (MSF) and Third World Network.[18] A key concern was that, after 2005, it will become even more difficult for countries such as India to export generic copies of patented drugs. The 'deal was designed to offer comfort to the US and the Western pharmaceutical industry', said Ellen Hoen of MSF. 'Unfortunately, it offers little comfort for poor patients. Global patent rules will continue to drive up the price of medicines.'[19]

This debate again highlighted concerns about corporate involvement in the trade policies of governments. This concern extended into the area of the fight against HIV/AIDS, when the Senate approved the former CEO of drug company Eli Lilly, Randall Tobias, to head up the US response to HIV/AIDS. Campaigners pointed out that this company is a member of the industry group lobbying against a Canadian initiative to use the agreement reached at the WTO to begin exporting cheap drugs. 'Tobias's appointment is a bit like trusting the CEO of ExxonMobil to lead a government effort to promote solar power', wrote Naomi Klein.[20]

CORPORATE INVOLVEMENT IN
GOVERNMENT POLICY?
FORMER ELI LILLY CEO RANDALL TOBIAS

The dual questions of intellectual property and corporate lobbying were yet to feature in the discourse of those promoting corporate responses to the pandemic. For example, a November 2003 search of the website of the Global Business Coalition on HIV/AIDS for a discussion of TRIPS and the WTO process returned no relevant results. The issue is too important to be left off any serious assessment of corporate citizenship for much longer. If the concept of corporate citizenship is to mean anything, it must imply the obligations as well as rights embodied in the notion of citizenship. Property rights, including intellectual property, are upheld by political communities because they are functional to the societies that mandate those political communities. With rights come obligations to those who are affected by the exercising of that right and the society that upholds that right. Therefore, when property rights conflict with other rights, such as the right to life, or health, then we have a problem. More awareness of the political dimensions to the concept of corporate citizenship would therefore be useful if it is to be a serious concept for scholarship and a progressive one for society.

Differing accountabilities?

In October 2003, One World Trust's Global Accountability Project (GAP) hosted an international workshop in London to discuss best practices in organisations' relations with their external stakeholders. GAP aims to assess how open and receptive global organisations are to the internal demands of their members and the external demands of individuals and groups who are affected by the organisation's daily operations.[21] The workshop brought together a variety of international NGOs and companies, and some intergovernmental organisations. The British NGO seeks to develop indicators to measure the degree and quality of stakeholder engagement within the world's international organisations.

The workshop documented the participants' experiences and perspectives on approaches to and methods of stakeholder engagement. However, there was some disagreement with the starting premise of the organisers that stakeholder engagement was always 'good' and that you could usefully compare the practices of organisations with very different mandates and restrictions.

The conceptual framework for GAP's understanding of accountability divides accountability into eight management elements, ranging from member control of the organisation to complaints mechanisms. The intention is to compare the practices of transnational corporations (TNCs), intergovernmental organisations and international NGOs. One reason for this comparison is to attract media interest, by ranking organisations such as the WTO alongside well-known NGOs and large companies. Through this attention, the aim is to increase the debate about accountability, and therefore promote action.

This strategy worked earlier in the year, when GAP published its first report on 'member control'. The report gave the WTO a high score, and higher than a number of NGOs, for its mechanisms of accountability to members—a finding that generated press coverage. However, some questioned the results; by focusing on the accountability to members, the study ignored the accountability of those members themselves. At the WTO, the accountability of government delegations to the people in the countries they affect by their decisions remains a problem. Moreover, some delegations have used the WTO Secretariat more than others, and played a much stronger role in drafting agreements, which then structure the agendas of future negotiations. The same problem has also been seen in the context of the corporate sector. Although a company may be accountable to its shareholders, what then of the accountability of those shareholders' interests in profit-taking to the people affected by the corporation? In addition, defining companies' members as its shareholders, rather than its employees, could be challenged.

Some participants pointed out that trade unions were not present at the workshop on 'external stakeholder engagement'—and that most would regard themselves as internal not external stakeholders. However, as they were also not covered in the assessment on member control, some questioned whether One World Trust had effectively defined unions out of the process of assessing their employers' accountability. It was noted that unions have often expressed concerns at how the language of stakeholder participation is sometimes used to marginalise them.

The starting assertion of the organisers of the workshop was that engagement must be undertaken in a manner that links external stakeholders to the political processes

of decision-making; however, this became more problematic as the workshop progressed. Some participants noted that it would not always be beneficial for some international NGOs to be accountable to those they influence—such as the governments,
companies and international institutions they may criticise. Instead, the pressing issue
is the accountability of decisions and decision-making processes to the people whose
lives they influence. Decisions made by TNCs have much larger impacts on people's
lives than those made by NGOs. Stella Amadi, a participant from Rivers State College
in Nigeria, said after the workshop that the legal mechanisms for ensuring the accountability of such companies to the many people they can negatively affect is very weak,
and so comparing them with NGOs is not helpful.

A key theme that emerged in some of the summing-up was that, if all sectors of an
organisation are to be compared for their accountability, then the constituency that
demands that accountability needs to be more clearly defined. Principles of human
rights and democracy suggest that this constituency must be the people who are
affected by an organisation, not the people who can or do affect it. To investigate this
issue rigorously will require the assessment of the impacts of different organisational
sectors, and problems with the limits on decision-making within organisations that
are set by its institutional form (corporation, government or NGO).

Small is significant

The Millennium Development Goals (MDGs) are an initiative of Kofi Annan aimed at
reducing poverty and improving lives, which world leaders agreed on at the Millennium Summit in September 2000. The Secretary-General had already warned that the
world is falling short in meeting these objectives. Commenting in the UN's *Round Up*
newsletter, Roberto Bissio of Social Watch Uruguay said that 'in order to capture the
hearts and minds of the public . . . the MDGs still need to be translated from technical jargon into formulas that . . . can be readily understood by men and women in the
street'.[22]

One way of doing this is to translate it into the context of small-scale enterprise. In
November 2003, the Centre for Social Markets held its 3rd Annual Conference on Corporate Citizenship in Kolkata, India.[23] The focus of the two-day conference was on the
role of small and micro-enterprises in achieving sustainable development and helping
to deliver the Millennium Development Goals.[24] The positioning of the lofty aims of
the Millennium Development Goals alongside the world of small and micro-enterprises seems initially quite stark. However, the reality is that most businesses are small
or medium-sized enterprises (SMEs) and they employ the majority of the world's population.

In this context the work of the International Labour Organisation (a member of the
UN family) might be instructive. In the Northern autumn it began exploring the possibility of expanding its work on the social marketing of job quality in SMEs to Vietnam. Prior experience in Moradabad, India, and the Kumasi region of Accra, Ghana,
found that there are low-cost ways of improving basic health and safety in the workplace of micro-enterprises. Moradabad is a region known for its numerous brassware
artisans who work out of units in the family home. The introduction of colour-coded

trays was found to be an effective and cheap way to reduce workplace burns in the home units of the brassware artisans in Moradabad. The project was a joint initiative between ILO–SEED (part of the ILO's InFocus Programme on Boosting Employment through Small Enterprise Development) and New Academy of Business. Working with local trade associations and groups of workers, they have shown how these mechanisms can be marketed to the micro-enterprises by working with local culture and using local communications specialists. The media messages that were delivered during the social marketing campaign sought to convey the productivity and quality improvements that came from those small changes. This was something to which the men and women on the streets in Moradabad responded.

Another sector known for its modest means, but with great potential for supporting transformation, is the formal social enterprise sector. The sector has recently received some encouraging news from both sides of the Atlantic. Origo Inc. ran a series of events in San Francisco focusing on the key issues in creating a social enterprise, such as defining social impact, securing funding and 'being' a social entrepreneur.[25] In the US the sector is growing as reported in a Harvard Business School working paper by Jane Wei-Skillern and Beth Battle Anderson.[26] The paper explores the strategies for geographic expansion of non-profit organisations, reporting on a large-scale survey of non-profit leaders, who are currently engaged in or are seriously considering expanding their organisations by establishing branches and/or affiliates in new locations.

In the UK the sector is also making a bigger impact with a national newspaper reporting in a series of articles that small social enterprises are carving out a niche for themselves.[27] Meanwhile Co-operative News, the world's oldest cooperative newspaper, reported that the sector will become a 'force to be reckoned with' in the next 20 years due to its contribution to the economy and impact on social well-being.[28]

This trend is being spurred in Britain with government proposals to launch a new legal form of company called a 'Community Interest Company' (CIC). The Department of Trade and Industry has suggested that such enterprises, which will have to use their profits and assets for the benefit of the community and or wider public, will combine 'entrepreneurial spirit with a sense of social purpose'. The initiative has received support across a range of arenas. Fiona Mactaggart, the Minister for Racial Equality, Community Policy and Civil Renewal, stated:

> Community Interest Companies are an excellent example of how the Government can help communities help themselves. CICs offer a radically new way for organisations to pursue enterprise in the public interest, dedicating their profits to the public good, and creating real opportunities for people in areas where they are needed most.

The proposed legislation includes the suggestion that the CICs should produce annual reports on the actions they have taken to pursue their social and community objectives and to involve stakeholders in this process. This has parallels to the calls from civil society to hold corporations to account for their social and environmental performance and the way these have become attempts by large companies to regain trust in how they do business.

Some commentators might consider the formal creation of a new institutional form for social enterprise as an indictment against the current institutional creation of 'the corporation', which exists in a similar form in most capitalist economies today. If people in business require legal vehicles to facilitate the pursuit of the public interest

FIONA MACTAGGART, UK MINISTER FOR
RACIAL EQUALITY, COMMUNITY POLICY
AND CIVIL RENEWAL: CHAMPIONING CICs

'where it is needed most', what does this say about the state of the overall system and culture in which these companies operate? Some historical perspective on the history of the legal invention called 'the corporation', and how during its 400-year history its form and regulation changed so that it no longer had to act in the interests of 'the state' (or, previously, 'the empire') might help us reflect on the implications of this initiative. Roger Warren Evans, a barrister-at-law, explores this growth of the modern cult of artificial personality, in 'The Rise of the Abdroids'.[29] Equally important would be to look again at the role of 'limited liability' in shaping the practices of those in business. Such issues were discussed during a panel of a conference on corporate responsibility, organised by UNRISD, and the argument made that the 'DNA' of corporations—their legal ownership, liabilities, purpose and accountability—needed to be included in a broadened corporate citizenship agenda.[30]

ROGER WARREN EVANS: LOOKING AT THE
MODERN CULT OF 'ARTIFICIAL
PERSONALITY'

Business ethics evolves

The academic world of business ethics seems at last to be waking up to the challenges posed by major shifts and currents in the global business environment. Once the discipline seemed to be obsessed with long-dead philosophers, and typically engaged in an unending battle to 'prove' that certain business practices were either right or wrong according to whatever theory was the flavour of the day. There now appears to be a new generation of business ethics research, writing and teaching that has embraced a much broader agenda—one that corresponds more closely with the themes covered in these reviews.

This new generation was illustrated by a number of developments during 2003. In Budapest, at the end of the Northern summer, the main association for business ethics scholars in Europe, the European Business Ethics Network (EBEN), held its conference. This was titled 'Building Ethical Institutions for Business' and allowed 'the participants to reflect and debate on the role of institutions in the transformation of business toward a more human and ethical form'. Not here a focus on individual managers' ethical dilemmas and problems which has characterised much business ethics work in the past, but rather a discussion of 'stakeholder activism, global governance structures, corporate social responsibility, corporate governance, corporate citizenship, ethical investment, stakeholder society, Internet-enabled corporations, environmental regimes, human rights, future generations, and ethical institutions for corporate accountability'.[31]

Similarly, on perusing the pages of the *Journal of Business Ethics*, which is probably the most widely read source of scholarship on the subject, it became immediately clear to us that academics in business ethics are now beginning to frame their work in ways other than the ethical theories of Aristotle, Kant, Mill and the rest of the traditional business ethics canon. These big guns of philosophy still feature in the journal, but many writers also choose to go in different directions, and integrate their work within current debates about corporate citizenship, sustainability, globalisation or gender (to name just a few).

Another illustration of this trend was the publication of a textbook, *Business Ethics: A European Perspective*. The subtitle 'Managing Corporate Citizenship and Sustainability in the Age of Globalization', indicates that this is not a traditional business ethics tome.[32] The book still discusses ethical theories and ethical dilemmas, but it frames all this within the broader debates conjured up by the subtitle. Dirk Matten, one of the co-authors, told us that 'Most books on the market tend to relegate subjects like "ethics and international business" and "green business" to half a chapter each at the end of the book. We wanted to integrate globalisation and sustainability as central concepts throughout, right from page one to the end.'

That a business ethics textbook can combine discussion of ethical theories as diverse as rights, justice, feminist ethics, and postmodernism with analysis of developments in business relations with all the major stakeholder groups could mark a major step in the development of management education. 'We wanted the book to stay true to the traditions of the business ethics subject, but at the same time we felt it was necessary to rewrite the rules about what should be covered in a business ethics textbook. The existing books simply didn't cover all of what we saw business ethics teachers across Europe teaching to their students,' explained the other co-author, Andy Crane.

DIRK MATTEN (LEFT) AND ANDY CRANE AT
THE LAUNCH OF *BUSINESS ETHICS: A
EUROPEAN PERSPECTIVE*

The problem with business ethics has been that ethics came after business, both literally and conceptually. The context was nearly always assumed and managers asked to respond to a consequent dilemma. Today many managers and students of business are asking for something different—for ethics to be the starting point for their work. Consequently the 'business ethics' academe is evolving from treating managers as hostages to fortune toward helping them become masters of destiny.

Mastering minds and destinies

Despite advances in business ethics teaching, mainstream management education still requires a paradigm shift if it is to place values and their ongoing enactment for social change at its core. In October 2003 in the USA, the Aspen Institute and the World Resources Institute jointly launched the latest review of postgraduate management education and its response to sustainability. The report cites that half of the 100 business schools surveyed across 20 countries require students to take more than one course with social and/or environmental content. Judith Samuelson, executive director of Aspen Institute's Business and Society Progam, said, 'We've seen positive change this year [2003] and a lot of innovation taking place in selected schools. But the reality is too many MBA students still graduate without an understanding of social impact and management.'[33]

The complexity of ethical, social and environmental impacts is significant. Some have begun to explore this link between how we learn and the type of sustainable development that is created. Two books, launched in December 2003 by William Scott and Stephen Gough, explore the connections between sustainable development and learning.[34] Meanwhile, Waikato Management School in New Zealand (re)launched itself so that 'At the heart of our business is transformation—we exist to inspire fresh understandings of sustainable business success in a connected world.'[35] Meanwhile, the School of Management at the University of Bath continues to pay attention to the way in which individuals can engage in social and environmental leadership when at work, through the structure and processes on the part-time 'Master's in Responsibility and Business Practice'.

The challenges of changing how we educate managers and business people suggests that important attention needs to be placed on the gaps between what managers say they value and what values they use to guide their actions—between their 'espoused theories' and ethical values and the actual theories being used when they act, plan and formulate strategy.[36] How can managers be supported in this challenge? Part of this requires a shift in how we understand education, training and learning.

David Orr, Professor of Environmental Studies and Politics and Chair of the Environmental Studies Program at Oberlin College, has recognised that 'the crisis we face is first and foremost one of mind, perceptions, and values; hence, it is a challenge to those institutions presuming to shape minds, perceptions, and values. It is an educational challenge. More of the same kind of education can only make things worse.'[37]

With many issues on the sustainable development agenda, such as HIV/AIDS and ecological disruption, the call to immediate action is considerable. Meanwhile, many of the ethical questions have a double-edged character of clarity and haziness. An ongoing challenge remains, then, in how to bring the two together in practice. Our experience of teaching has informed us that it is not enough to stand at the front and preach about the importance of doing these things. More often than not, managers seem to be aware of the collapsing fisheries or the impact of business practices on health and labour standards. They also seem to be aware of a variety of both selfish and altruistic reasons to act on these. As Orr suggests, 'our goal as educators is to present a sense of hopefulness to students, and the competence to act on that hope'.[38] In a competition-oriented culture, it seems difficult to know how to enact a set of values in effective ways. For this, we need to create spaces in our busy work for moving variously between reflective observation and conceptualisation and active experimenting. We must recreate forms of education and learning that allow people to gently nurture the questions and dilemmas that they encounter in the midst of their working lives.

2004

Foreword

Jeremy Moon
International Centre for Corporate Social Responsibility[1]

It is a pleasure for the International Centre for Corporate Social Responsibility (ICCSR) to be able to support the fourth Lifeworth Annual Review. The 'World Review' contributions to the *Journal of Corporate Citizenship*, of which this Annual Review is made up, share the ICCSR's interest in detailing and reflecting upon current CSR issues on a global scale. This collected version provides an added service by making this contribution freely and widely available.

The Review raises the challenge of how CSR can move from being mainly constituted by one-off causes and activities to more systematically addressing social threats and opportunities. Readers can expect to be informed, stimulated and challenged.

Introduction

From review to preview—
an agenda for the future of CSR

Jem Bendell and Wayne Visser

The four quarterly *Journal of Corporate Citizenship* World Reviews of 2004, which make up this Annual Review, ranged over significant territory, both literally and figuratively. The coverage was indicative, we think, of the crucial debate that is beginning to emerge about corporate social responsibility (CSR), which acknowledges that the sophistication of stakeholder challenges and corporate responses has gone up a gear, but questions whether CSR itself is too little too late, or even a red herring.

Geographically, the emphasis was strongly on the challenges of corporate citizenship in the developing world, including specific pieces on the Millennium Development Goals (MDGs) and the 'Bottom of the Pyramid' concept about servicing lower-income markets, and CSR in the Pacific Rim, the Middle East, Chile, Nigeria and Russia. We think this focus accurately portrays the current shift in CSR concerns towards the global South, where, despite the scale and urgency of development needs, determining the best way for business to respond to poverty remains extremely complex.

Although the Asian tsunami disaster focused attention on humanitarian relief efforts, which many companies contributed to, it is also encouraging to see corporate leaders engaged in a wider discussion about how normal business influences the poor and disadvantaged around the world and what business models could be more supportive of development.

However, our analysis is that current debates about the opportunities for corporate contributions to the MDGs often lack a full understanding of processes of 'development'. Much of the profitable business with lower-income markets involves products such as mobile phones, not the provision of basic nutrition, sanitation, education and shelter, so the current expansion of profitable business in the global South does not necessarily imply poverty reduction.

In addition, the type of 'development' that is promoted by marketing consumer products to the poor can be questioned, and claims about empowering people by providing means for them to consume cannot be taken at face value. The environmental impacts of changing consumption patterns also need to be looked at, without assuming that such problems will be solved just through technical and financial advancement. And, if more foreign companies do come to serve lower-income markets, we need to assess whether they might displace local companies and increase the resource drain from local economies.

How large corporations might bring their financial, technical and management resources to help local entrepreneurs improve and scale their businesses, and avoid exploitative local middlemen, is important to explore and will become a significant part of the corporate responsibility agenda.

However, exploitative North–South supply chains, tax avoidance and anti-competitive practices are fairly typical of international corporations, undermining their economic contribution to development. These economic issues have been overlooked by mainstream work on corporate responsibility, but this review chronicles those initiatives and debates during 2004 that together suggest such economic issues will become more central in future.

From an institutional perspective, various relationships were critically examined, especially the status and acceptability of partnerships between business and NGOs, on the one hand, and business and the UN on the other.

This examination reflects a sharp rise in the demand for organisations to demonstrate their accountability and transparency, not only business, but NGOs and intergovernmental organisations as well. The ethics of institutional engagement is now centre stage.

Particular issues under the spotlight included activism, climate change, human rights, corruption, globalisation, standardisation, sustainability reporting and taxation. In addition, several industries, and a number of the high-profile multinationals representing them, enjoyed special attention, including the engineering, media and entertainment, mining, and oil and gas sectors. The message here seems to be that the codification of voluntary corporate responsibility activity is advancing apace, but whether it constitutes sufficient progress, or even a desirable approach, remains hotly debated. Which brings us to gauntlet we want to lay down in this Introduction.

We believe that the movement is at a crucial juncture. Companies have climbed the CSR learning curve and are now playing the game like experts. They have reframed the debate into language that they can understand and use without upsetting most of their shareholders, and they have designed policies and programmes that they can implement without having to question their underlying business model.

There seems to be a pervading sense in many CSR circles that there is now business consensus about the most pressing issues in our global society, taking their cues from the MDGs, the Global Compact and other such frameworks. While many of the issues remain difficult to deal with in practice, companies are credited with putting strategies in place for tackling them. Everything, they argue, is going according to plan; hence, there is no need for anything more dramatic, especially not legislation to enforce improved performance. Or is there?

There is another perspective, which enjoys far less airtime. A perspective that says the world is in a deepening crisis of alarming proportions and that the private sector's response, under the guise of CSR, is as effective as placing a band aid on the foot of someone who is haemorrhaging from the head. This alternative perspective, radical as it sounds, nevertheless seems to be confirmed by just about every available statistic on the ecological and social health of our global society.

The question then becomes: is CSR, as it is currently being preached and practised by multinational corporations around the world, actually a red herring? Is it a distraction from the more fundamental transformation (perhaps revolution, even) of the capitalist business model that is needed? And, as CSR becomes an established professional practice, will it take as given that its purpose is to benefit those who employ its professionals, rather than a primary goal of transforming the world?

If so, CSR will have contributed towards a global 'crash and burn' scenario, with growing ecological and social degradation. Such criticism forces those of us who work on corporate responsibility issues, perhaps even identify ourselves as part of a CSR movement or a CSR profession, to reflect on our roles.

Do we have a clear strategy for how we can help solve the big problems of poverty, pollution, abuse and so forth, by working with/in corporates? And, if we think we are helping in small ways, do we have a plan for how to scale up our impacts to address problems that require widespread action, such as climate change?

Without one, might we just be pretending we are helping the planet and its people, while climbing another greasy pole? The risk here is that we all seem remarkably adept at coming up with explanations of our own behaviour and priorities that maintain an appearance of 'ethicalness' . . . at least to ourselves.

We have to find the courage to be self-critical, and explore what we are thinking and doing. It is through this reflexivity that CSR might avoid being complicit in a global 'crash and burn' and become a crucial part of a 'rise and shine' scenario, where the world achieves a greater harmony between its peoples and with ecology. This scenario requires systemic change.

For CSR to help with this systemic change, we need to embrace both idealism and realism. Idealism is important as we must reawaken the values that underscore the CSR agenda, rather than hiding them sheepishly behind commercial arguments for action. A revival of zealous passion and moral belief as a driver of corporate change and an intensity of questioning of the reigning business model is key.

Idealism and realism are often counterpoised, yet we need both if we are to promote systemic change. Idealism should not blind us from awareness of the limits of individual voluntary action. Some realism about markets and the law is essential. The commercial benefits from improved social and environmental performance are patchy, and many companies still make profits by externalising social and environmental costs— a process that is promoted by mainstream financial markets that still focus on short-term value creation.

Given this situation, the current system of governance, regulation and law enforcement is not often sufficient, as international companies can evade accountability through the use of subcontracting and subsidiaries, while also being able to influence the processes of public governance itself, with questionable outcomes.

An idealistic–realistic approach calls us to engage in making CSR a catalyst for systemic change. Consequently, a new agenda for CSR can emerge, with four essential tracks where coalitions need to be built. The first track involves 'changing the baseline' of markets, the driving force behind most business. This will involve coalitions of businesses, financiers, NGOs, governments and others, aimed at changing the rules that govern the basics of capitalism, such as company law, currency flows, property rights, competition, and tax management and executive accountability. Such work will be time-consuming and technical, and may seem too abstract and negative for some. But there are other crucial things to do . . .

The second track involves 'playing the solos' within markets, by pioneering sustainable and just models of enterprise. Social entrepreneurs will help prefigure a new economy by creating businesses and projects that are inherently just and sustainable, including environmental technologies, cooperatives, and even sustainability stock markets. Their own success and their ability to take over the mainstream economy will, however, depend partly on how well the first track is 'changing the baseline'.

To some people, these first two tracks may seem too much like pontificating about macro-economics, on the one hand, or following a fashion for eco-ethical enterprise on the other. They will focus instead on how people continue to be abused, poisoned, evicted, sacked and even killed, because of corporate interests and activities.

Therefore, the third track involves standing alongside and 'singing the chorus' with those negatively affected by current market dynamics. Thus, some will continue to work either with or against large companies to help specific groups of people improve their lot or seek redress: an area where much of the current effort on CSR and corporate accountability is located.

The fourth track involves 'maintaining the beat' within the CSR profession, to maintain its focus on a transformative agenda. This will require preventing it from becoming either solely client-directed and interested only in the goals of its paymasters, or protectionist and primarily interested in regulating access to services in this area. Instead, coalitions will form to help evolve a values-oriented profession, to maintain the commitment that is essential to a transformative movement.

The activities one chooses to engage in will depend on one's particular skills, inclinations and circumstances. But, for CSR to be part of the 'rise and shine' scenario, a four-track agenda is required, with the tracks harmonising to create a powerful music greater than the sum of its parts.

This means that people working in each of the four tracks will need to recognise the value of each and ensure their own work synergises with, rather than undermines, the other tracks. Unfortunately, this is not always the case at the moment, as some people suggest their path is the only right one.

We hope that developing and sharing a vision of how different activities could actually synergise towards creating systemic change will help that vision to become a reality.

1Q2004

January–March

Jem Bendell and Kate Kearins

Heading for divorce?

So, the honeymoon is over. After a decade of increasingly closer relations between business and NGOs, which contributed to the birth of a revitalised concept of corporate social responsibility (CSR), the strains are beginning to show. In the UK, which is seen by many to have been at the forefront of this area, many NGOs are now turning their back on CSR initiatives, or even making them the focus of criticism and campaigns. For example, international development groups such as the World Development Movement, ActionAid, New Economics Foundation, War on Want and Christian Aid are not as active in the Ethical Trading Initiative (ETI), which they all helped to found and which brought them together with companies to work on improving labour conditions in corporate supply chains.

'Key NGOs have now turned their back on the opportunity that [corporate citizenship] represents, to fall back on easy anti-corporate messages that play well to their core constituencies', said Mallen Baker, of Business in the Community, in February 2004.[1] He was commenting after the British charity Christian Aid had made criticism of CSR initiatives the mainstay of its campaign to push for global regulations for global corporations. 'The image of multinational companies working hard to make the world a better place is often just that—an image', said Christian Aid's report *Behind the Mask*, published in January 2004. 'What's needed are new laws to make businesses responsible for protecting human rights and the environment wherever they work', they said, and added that CSR initiatives are used by many companies to undermine progress towards such laws.[2] That some people involved in, or commenting on, initiatives that might be labelled CSR sometimes use their existence to push a neoliberal economic agenda was identified as a key challenge in previous reviews (see the third quarter of 2003), as was the need to see corporate support for, or lobbying against, mandatory mechanisms for improved social and environmental conduct as a key dimension to a company's social responsibility (see the second quarter of 2003).

Some criticised Christian Aid's report for not engaging with the companies it was attacking or not conducting a more systemic analysis of the impacts of CSR. For example, Mallen Baker suggested that, as the report featured just three case studies, even if everything Christian Aid said about those were true, it wouldn't mean that the wider

CSR or corporate citizenship community discourse and practice is defunct.[3] However, Christian Aid is not the only one whose methodology can be criticised. Much academic management research employs case studies to build concepts, arguments and theories, while think-tanks, corporations and consulting firms often use case studies as the basis for positive assessments of the potential and reality of corporate social responsibility and corporate citizenship. The use of case studies must be tempered with the knowledge of their particularity, partialness and, possibly, partiality. Case studies are useful for allowing a richness and depth of understanding, and for their powers of explanation or evocation. However, it is difficult to generalise from a sample of one, or even three. Therefore quantitative studies may add another dimension to our understanding of the nature of corporate responsibility. One person who attempted such work is Professor Richard Marens of California State University. He suggests that, if corporations in the United States have indeed been tending to the interests of their diverse stakeholders, especially over the past 20 years since Ed Freeman published his articulation of the stakeholder concept of management,[4] then it should be reflected in key statistics. However, he notes that nationwide statistics show average wages have declined and working hours increased in America, while employee security and benefits have declined.[5] Considering taxpayers to be a key stakeholder, he notes how corporate taxes have fallen and more public funds been spent on private corporations. In addition to these indicators of corporate impacts on society, we could consider pollution levels. Carbon emissions in the United States have increased by over 15% since 1990; globally carbon emissions have increased over 10% in the past decade. The release of toxic chemicals has fallen, but this can be attributed to the Emergency Planning and Community Right to Know Act of 1986 (which requires companies to register information on their use, storage and release of toxic substances), rather than a voluntary responsibility effort alone.[6] These statistics suggest that, if we leave aside case studies, there is little evidence to suggest that those practices we label CSR or corporate citizenship are having a significant effect on the big picture—as yet.

Christian Aid's criticism of CSR is neither unique nor novel. Many people and groups are 'sceptics', regarding corporate responsibility as old-fashioned public relations (PR) with the aim of distracting society from the need for more effective regulation of corporate activity and transformation to an economic system grounded in the ecological and social realities of the planet. On the other side of the political spectrum there are the critics of corporate responsibility who see it as distracting business managers from securing profits for the owners of corporations. 'From an ethical point of view, the problem with conscientious CSR (as opposed to fake CSR) is obvious: it is philanthropy at other people's expense' said *The Economist*, in an article commenting on the Christian Aid report.[7] Between these negative poles there are people who are fairly evangelical, pragmatic or ambivalent about CSR, as described in Box 3.

To be defensive when criticised is an understandable reaction. However, our hope is we might see more corporate responsibility professionals engaging with critics and sceptics. The critics make it more important for us to be clear on what we believe to be the business case for corporate responsibility; the sceptics make it more important for us to be clear on what we believe to be the people's case for corporate responsibility—in other words, the benefit for society. We need critics and sceptics to help us reflect on our own practice, assumptions and interests, and ensure we are authentic in what we do.

Box 3 VIEWS ON CORPORATE SOCIAL RESPONSIBILITY (CSR)

Critics: anti-CSR, seeing it as distracting business from securing profits. Some are market fundamentalists, believing the pursuit of self-interest will create the greatest social gain. Others see that government has a role to play and CSR can distract us from this.

Evangelicals: pro-CSR, believing there is a win–win relationship between business and society, and that everyone can do well by doing good. The fact there are still problems is a result of people not realising the benefits of CSR.

Pragmatics: pro-CSR, believing that there are some win–wins between business and society but that there are also situations where business needs to be regulated, or rewarded, to ensure socially acceptable performance.

Ambivalents: neither pro- nor anti-CSR, believing that it could be beneficial for some aspects of society and some businesses but that it involves the intrusion of commercial values into the realms of the social and human, so it is worrying.

Sceptics: anti-CSR, believing that it is largely a public relations exercise to further empower business to control the lives of people in the pursuit of profit maximisation, and distracts our attention from the need to regulate corporate power.

We have come a long way since the mid-1990s when business and NGOs were thought to be risking 'sleeping with the enemy'[8] by working with each other, and the turn of the millennium when they were said to be 'getting engaged'[9] and then enjoying a 'honeymoon period' for corporate responsibility'. The word 'honeymoon' comes from the tradition of a married couple drinking fermented honey for a month after their marriage. Might business and NGOs be realising they've been drunk on the hope and novelty of their initial engagement? Could this sobering-up lead to a permanent divorce, with fights in the courts of law and public opinion?

As we suggest above, we hope that conflict will not be the only outcome, but that it might lead to a transformation of the relationship between business and society, and perhaps even a new level of collaboration and dialogue that focuses on how to drive systemic changes in the global political economy.

CSR growing up?

For the business–NGO relationship to gel, its CSR offspring may have to grow up fast and reflect the changes within the business and NGO sectors over the past decade. If we consider development NGOs, the last ten years have seen an increased focus on both rights-based understandings of development, and the systemic causes of maldevelopment. One example of this level of analysis is the *Real World Economic Outlook*, which was published by the New Economics Foundation at the end of 2003.[10] The argument is that economic globalisation has created a situation of debt and deflation. This is because globalisation's great achievement—falling prices for labour, goods and services—will make it more difficult for individuals, households, governments and corporations to repay the debts acquired through financial liberalisation. The *Outlook* argues that ordinary people have been lured into a quagmire of debt and deflation. Worse, a finance-centred economy has led to a dramatic increase in inequality, both within and between countries. Putting finance at the centre of our society 'has proved disastrous for the environment and for billions of people in poor countries. It now poses a threat to people and households in the west, as well as to corporations and governments', says Ann Pettifor, who edited the report.

ANN PETTIFOR: EDITOR OF NEW ECONOMICS
FOUNDATION'S *WORLD ECONOMIC OUTLOOK*

One key aspect to this problem is currency volatility, where over a trillion dollars' worth of different monies are traded on electronic exchanges each day. The ease of making short-term speculative transactions has been held partly responsible for creating currency crises which have increased poverty in various regions—an example being Indonesia where poverty doubled as a result of the East Asian currency crisis.[11] Moreover, the currency markets exert undemocratic pressures at all times, as any negative perspectives from finance companies on the politics of a sitting or prospective government can lead to a devaluation of its currency. Thus there was a run on the Real as Luiz Inácio Lula Da Silva moved toward the Presidency of Brazil.[12] In February 2004, the Swiss NGO Bread For All published a study on the negative effects of currency volatility.[13] What was unusual was that it set out key reasons why there is a business case for companies in various parts of the world, and various economic sectors, to see a reduction in currency volatility. Speaking at the preparatory meeting for the 11th ministerial conference of the UN Conference on Trade and Development (UNCTAD), co-author of the report François Mercier called on progressives within the private sector to engage with civil society in a global dialogue on how to calm currency markets and promote more developmental financial flows to the global South. 'Cooperation, dialogue and partnership between business and civil society has to become more strategic and more systemic if we are to address the root causes of poverty', he said. Given that only the top 20 international banks account for about 80% of global currency

FRANÇOIS MERCIER: CALLING FOR
CALM IN CURRENCY MARKETS

transactions, the vast majority of financial services companies, and other businesses, could constructively engage in an initiative on calming financial volatility.

Two other events in Geneva in the first quarter of 2004 suggested this type of 'new-generation partnership' between business and civil society might be possible in the near future. First, the report of the World Commission on the Social Dimension of Globalisation was published by the UN's International Labour Organisation (ILO) in February 2004. Discussing the governance of globalisation the report highlighted the growing problem of currency volatility, arguing that 'serious defects need to be corrected if we are to attain a fairer and more inclusive pattern of globalization'. However, the report noted that 'progress has been slow and limited' (p. 39). Although it did not elaborate, the reasons are quite clear, as the International Monetary Fund (IMF) has been responsible for driving currency market liberalisation in past decades: the IMF is controlled by the richest nations on Earth, where the banks that benefit from currency speculation are based. Multilateral action would be required to address currency volatility for development objectives, and thus UNCTAD should have a role, yet the secretariat of the UN body were reportedly cautious about acting on this agenda, given the concerns of key donor governments from the West.

Another initiative launched in Geneva in January 2004 suggested that there might be some governmental leadership in this area. Progress towards the UN's Millennium Development Goals (MDGs), which include a target to halve the number of malnourished people by 2015, has stalled, with a fall in bilateral development aid from Northern governments not helping the prospects of success. 'The implementation of those goals must be revitalized', said President Lula Da Silva, at the launch of a fund to combat hunger and poverty. The fund was launched with French President Jacques Chirac, who said government development aid alone could not provide the estimated 50 billion more dollars a year needed to fight poverty. In a joint declaration in January 2004,

LUIZ LULA DA SILVA (LEFT) AND JACQUES CHIRAC: LAUNCH OF A NEW FUND TO COMBAT HUNGER AND POVERTY

the two presidents relaunched the idea of international taxes on arms sales and financial transactions to generate funds to achieve the MDGs.[14] A global partnership is envisaged that will engage governments, the UN system and financial institutions. And the tough issues might not be avoided, as Chirac told journalists after the launch that 'we cannot avoid setting up a system of international taxation'.

Given that the currency markets are often likened to a global casino, bank executives might take inspiration from the moves of the American Gaming Association. Just before Christmas this industry association for US casinos launched a code of conduct for its members to target problems with compulsive gambling. The code includes mandatory training in responsible gambling for new employees, information for gamblers on the probabilities of winning or losing at specific games, and exclusion programmes for known problem gamblers.[15] The world's problem gamblers are the top 20 banks. Whether they can be weaned off their addiction to gambling with currencies, and the lives of billions of people, is another matter.

More dangerous liaisons

Mercier's speech at UNCTAD was given as the organisation considered one of four key themes for its ministerial conference in June 2004: partnerships. This means that UNCTAD is following suit, as other UN organisations and corporations are in the early flush of excitement as their partnerships grow. As 2003 came to a close the UN General Assembly endorsed the Secretary-General's report, *Towards Global Partnerships*, which provides a favourable analysis of this growing trend. However, in the New Year, one former Secretary-General, Boutros Boutros Ghali, called the UN's partnerships with business 'dangerous liaisons'. That was in the foreword to a book funded and co-published by the UN system itself.[16] Report author Ann Zammit argues that current relations between business and the UN put 'development at risk' unless they are fundamentally rethought. Since the UN began working more closely with the private sector there have been a range of concerns and criticisms, sometimes featured in these Annual Reviews, but this extensive critique from within the UN is a significant development. Given the growing concern, one co-author of this review, Jem Bendell, published a paper that reviewed the various criticisms and some possible solutions for the UN's key initiative in this area, the Global Compact.[17] Five key criticisms of the Compact are identified. First, some argue that it is wrong for business with questionable practices to participate in the Compact, that there is little monitoring of their commitments, and that participation can thus diffuse criticism of individual companies. Second, some suggest that the Compact could compound the power of large companies in the global economy, with negative implications for development. Third, that key issues necessary to improving the practice of all corporate actors are being sidelined or undermined, such as macro-economic questions and concerns about mandatory corporate accountability. Fourth, that the Compact is allowing its own agenda to be shaped by business, as well as other parts of the UN, and permitting the organisation's name to be used by some companies to promote their own perspectives and interests. Fifth, that these problems cannot be addressed while the Compact is not itself more accountable to the UN system of agencies and member states.

A range of responses to these challenges are suggested, and a new agenda mapped out that would ensure that the Global Compact addresses the systemic governance problems of the global economy. The paper argues that the Compact would not be necessary if the UN's government delegations truly represented the long-term interests of their peoples and were able to work together on issues of common concern. The assertion is that, with appropriate information on the situation of our planet, people would not choose to be represented in ways that undermine the global sustainable development of humankind. However, for a variety of reasons that relate directly to the power of corporations and global finance, governments do not seem to represent their people's longer-term interests. As governments are hampered in serving 'peoples of the United Nations', freeing the democratic potential of member governments from negative pressures of global finance and transnational corporations should be a core objective of the UN Secretariat's relations with business.

Numbers or stories

When you hit that quadrennial quirk in the calendar, February 29th, what happens to the bottom line—meaning the dominant economic one? Harry Levins, St Louis Post-Dispatch's senior writer asked whether this extra day in the year—equating numerically to almost three-tenths of one per cent of the whole year—would nudge up economic stats.[18] Would it appear not just on the calendar but also on America's bottom line—in its gross domestic product, which measures the value of goods and services produced in the United States? Apparently not: these aberrations get smoothed by the statisticians. Bottom lines—in the financial sense—do have some meaning, however, as there is some agreed state of bottomness: that tell-tale '0' integer between profit and loss. Whether any agreed state of bottomness exists between positive and negative social and environmental impact is far less clear. In 2004, though, all things considered, with an extra day at our disposal, any educated person could conjecture an even greater negative impact on society and the planet. A social construction through and through, the bottom line concept is amenable to considerable stretching, with businesses engaging with their self-proclaimed heroes despite their individual and collective impacts being on the wrong side of the ledger.

The concept of the triple bottom line[19] still has quite a bit of traction in popular understandings of sustainability and sustainable development. At the very least, it reminds punters to include social equity and ecological concerns in the management mix of businesses—and increasingly, though by no means completely, to report on measures of performance other than just financial ones. What the triple bottom line means beyond this is up for debate, however.

On the academic front, Wayne Norman and Chris McDonald published a useful critique of the triple bottom line in Business Ethics Quarterly.[20] The authors remind us that the ideas behind the TBL concept are not new—obligations to stakeholders have long been talked about if not universally accepted; rather, they contend it is the measuring, calculating, auditing and reporting on them that yields an exciting promise. Promise, yes. Fully explicated and easy to implement? No to the first question, and no again to the second, unless the concept of triple bottom line falls prey to being what Norman and McDonald call a 'Good old-fashioned Single Bottom Line plus Vague Commitments to Social and Environmental Concerns'—that is, business-as-usual flavoured with triple-bottom-line rhetoric.

Norman and McDonald point out that there is an implicit claim in the TBL concept that social (and environmental) performance can be measured and reported on in similar ways to financial performance. And that, so doing—that is, buying into social obligations and transparency as key business mantras—adds up to more profitable business in the long run. That these authors—though they are sympathetic with the idea of socially responsible business practice—can have a field day in laying bare the fallacies in these arguments should be obvious. Briefly, as readers will likely be aware, there are all sorts of problems with measuring and monetarising social impacts; and being open about all these issues all the time (if, indeed, possible or seen as desirable by stakeholders) may not necessarily end up ringing the tills.

Taken to the extreme, where can uncritical adoption of flawed concepts lead? New Zealand's *National Business Review*[21] featured three large female bottoms in an article entitled 'The Expanding Triple Bottom Line', lambasting the concept's uncritical uptake and noting that 'pressure to measure up as a good corporate citizen is driving some companies to outlandish acts'. The article cited ailing insurer AMP's announcement that it was going into the tree-planting business to mitigate the effects of its million 550 page information memoranda required to explain the Australian company's split into two. Terry McCrann in Australia's *Herald Sun* was cited responding to the initiative as offsetting the environmental damage done to Australia: 'It would be better for AMP to focus on running the business well and not doing damage to the financial environment of its shareholders'. Uncritical adoption of the TBL takes us full circle—back to providing fodder for critics of corporate citizenship.

However, some enlightened companies—our leading reporters—have fortunately gone beyond the TBL rhetoric, and indeed hardly refer at all to it in their latest reports. The ACCA UK Awards for Sustainability Reporting[22] announced as best in the sustainability reporting category The Co-operative Bank plc, with Shell International as runner-up. The TBL concept is implicit rather than explicit in The Co-operative Bank's *Sustainable Development Partnership Report 2002*[23] (the latest on its website). Translating the TBL elements to 'delivering value, social responsibility and ecological sustainability' as an effective overview, the report focuses more on a partnership approach—'moving forward together', noting the importance of trust and its external ratings in that respect, as well as its impacts on various stakeholder categories. *The Shell Report 2002*[24] (the latest on the Royal Dutch/Shell Group's website) owes more to its historical ties with the proponent of TBL, John Elkington, with economic performance, environmental performance and social performance strongly headlined, and focused around 11 key performance indicators whose lineage is traced, allowing for some comparability between years at least. Beyond that, though, we get contextualised reporting in light of the energy challenge, and what the *Shell Report* calls 'in-depth case studies on some of the most important issues or site level challenges'. This 'qualitative hot spot reporting is important to give a meaningful picture of our performance' and features community development in Nigeria, refineries in South Africa, resettlement at the Nanhai petrochemicals complex, and animal testing.

Andrew Harding, Executive Director of ACCA UK, said they were 'pleased to have received so many strong entries for this year's UK Awards which recognise that sustainability reporting helps all stakeholders to gauge non-financial risk and identify poor performance. If used properly, non-financial reporting also helps organisations to control weaknesses and minimise the risk of ethical misconduct. There is, however, a long way to go. Many more organisations should be reporting in this way and those that do still have room for improvement.'[25] One area highlighted was that there needed to be more disclosure of lobbying positions taken by organisations on key public policy issues, an issue dealt with in previous Annual Reviews.

Indeed, following the theme of room for improvement, we note there are a number

ANDREW HARDING, EXECUTIVE
DIRECTOR OF ACCA UK: THERE ARE
STRONG CONTENDERS FOR THIS YEAR'S
SUSTAINABILITY REPORTING AWARDS

of metaphors present in the discourse around sustainability reporting and in the reports themselves which present sustainability as a learning experience for those businesses embarking upon it, and as what progressive (and progress-oriented) businesses do. The sustainability-as-a-journey metaphor is a potent one that enables businesses to embark on activities that might lead towards enhanced sustainability—or, indeed, diminished unsustainability—but equally might not in the absence of some serious thinking about the concept. Without businesses defining the destination of their respective sustainability journeys, businesses might miss out on the essence of what sustainability could mean for them. For some with an inherently unsustainable business model, perhaps defining sustainability in their case is just too scary as they simply would not be in business any more without substantive and real change. Reporting on the small steps is far easier as we noted above—but whether we will achieve sustainability with multitudes of small steps and without radical and fundamental change is doubtful. Hence, interesting insights can be gained by critically analysing the discourse of corporate sustainability reports in terms of the paradoxes it contains, a project that co-author of this review Kate Kearins is taking forward with fellow New Zealand academics Markus Milne and Sara Walton.

Buzz around the Pacific Rim

Whatever its possible contradictions, the discourse and practice of CSR and corporate citizenship is globalising. In Japan, we have notice of more businesses getting into the sustainability business with the major auditing companies creating centres of speciality, according to the Nihon Keizai Shimbun.[26] Tohmatsu & Co. Ltd, the Japanese member firm of Deloitte ToucheTohmatsu, is to create a department specialising in CSR to be staffed by about 20 experts in areas such as the environment and law. ChuoAoyama Audit Corp has launched a CSR department to oversee environment and risk management on behalf of its corporate clients, while Japan's largest auditing firm, Shin Nihon & Co. Ltd, has established Shinnihon Integrity Assurance Inc.

In February 2004, UN Secretary-General Kofi Annan called on Japanese companies for leadership in citizenship, telling them that business has a key role to play in addressing the world's problems. Japanese companies, he said, are demonstrating ever-stronger leadership in the field of corporate citizenship, and are well placed to enjoy the benefits of 'responsible competitiveness'.

Thirteen Japanese companies had so far signed up to the Global Compact, which aims to create a global ethical framework by embracing universal principles—in the areas of human rights, labour standards and the environment. This number was considered insufficient to reflect the weight of multinational corporations based in the country.

> Today, I call on all Japanese companies and business groups to support the Global Compact by committing themselves explicitly to its principles. Through the active engagement of Japanese companies and other stakeholders, I am optimistic that the Global Compact will provide a useful platform to advance corporate citizenship and help produce a more sustainable and inclusive world economy, so that globalization's benefits can be shared by everyone, including the world's poor.[27]

Also in February 2004, some way south on the Pacific Rim, the St James' Ethics Centre spearheaded the launch of The Corporate Responsibility Index,[28] the benchmarking tool for ranking Australian companies on their responsible business practice, developed in the UK by Business in the Community. The index process will aim to encourage Australia's top companies to show their CSR performance against what is being called a robust framework, developed by business. It follows controversy in previous years over the Reputation Index, which was heavily criticised by business for its methodology. But the controversy appears to have changed, not gone away. Now, it is argued that the index is avowedly 'business-led' with the NGO component less evident—and there are suggestions that 'the rationale of the new index appeared problematic and may be driven by an anti-NGO sentiment in some circles.[29]

Educating for sustainability

Back in New Zealand, the government was trying to turn fantasy into reality, as the success of the film Lord of the Rings meant the country was recognised as home to the beautiful and wild Middle Earth. To nurture a society and economy that would both preserve and complement such natural beauty, the Parliamentary Commissioner for the Environment released See Change: Learning and Education for Sustainability.[30] The report looked at the whole range of educative institutions and activities, from formal education through to religions, the media and the private sector. Looking beyond symptoms and the role of individuals, and focusing on underlying causes and systems, the report attempts to raise the level of debate and stimulate action towards learning to live more sustainably. 'There will be heated debate', claims the Commissioner, Dr Morgan Williams, 'because this learning will challenge strongly held beliefs about our social and economic systems'.[31] Arguing for a paradigm shift, he lays the blame on

> our dominant value systems [which] are at the very heart of unsustainable practices. Making progress towards better ways of living therefore needs to be a deeply social, cultural, philosophical and political process—not simply a technical or economic one. Technical and economic mechanisms will certainly be key parts of the process. However, they will not come into play unless we, as a society, are prepared to openly and honestly debate the ways that our desired qualities of life can be met. That is why there must be a vastly expanded focus on education for sustainability.[32]

MORGAN WILLIAMS, PARLIAMENTARY
COMMISSIONER FOR THE ENVIRONMENT:
PROMOTING SUSTAINABILITY IN NEW ZEALAND

This also seems to be the year for a big emphasis on the role of business school education in meeting this challenge—in publication terms, at least. Greenleaf Publishing's *Teaching Business Sustainability: From Theory to Practice*, edited by Chris Galea, is due out in August 2004.[33] The Wiley journal *Business Strategy and the Environment*[34] is currently calling for papers for a special issue on a similar topic.

The stated rationale for the former is once again the increasing incidence of corporate governance scandals that has brought 'the role of business schools in producing the managers of today—and tomorrow . . . into sharp focus'.[35] *Teaching Business Sustainability* promises to begin to reveal the state of the art in teaching business sustainability worldwide, with a focus on a wide mix of supposedly successful and leading-edge teaching practices and tools. Such approaches share an experiential and often a team-based element, linking theory to practice. The argument for experiential approaches or simulations is that 'whenever possible, educators need to link the learning to the students' immediate and pressing 'real-world' realities [said to apply] equally to undergraduates or high-level executives'.[36]

The book also presents the case for sustainability education requiring holistic and interdisciplinary learning. Interdisciplinarity is often problematic within traditional business school departmental and career structures, let alone in reaching across to our colleagues in ecology, engineering and biology and geography. The co-author of this column has not made herself popular reminding business school colleagues that various physical and social sciences are way ahead of ourselves in considering sustainability matters—and indeed that students from outside the business school are a welcome addition to classes on these topics.

Both the book and the call for papers alluded to do promise some critique. For, after all, we are not there yet with sustainability—and nor most obviously is business. It's what we might consider the mainstream business and the mainstream business school classroom that has to change most radically. The tendency for us to celebrate the leading edge, while healthy in itself, must not be allowed to mask the scale of the task and the wide range of expertise that must be brought to bear in solving the problems before us.

2Q2004

April–June

Jem Bendell and Mark Bendell

Stinging caterpillar

The Palestinian–Israeli conflict is never far from the headlines, but a recent twist in campaign tactics by peace activists and human rights lawyers have made it an issue of corporate citizenship. 'Caterpillar faces an intifada' reported Farhad Manjoo in the online magazine *Salon.com* in May 2004, as various groups targeted 'the manufacturer of the giant bulldozer that Israel uses to demolish Palestinian homes'.[1] Since 1967, the Israeli government has used Caterpillar equipment, including specially armoured D9 and D10 bulldozers to destroy over 7,000 buildings in the West Bank and Gaza Strip, leaving 50,000 men, women and children homeless.[2]

In June 2004, a protest took place outside the head office of the company in Geneva, following protests in the United States and calls to boycott Caterpillar products, which also include branded clothing.[3] Meanwhile, the United Nations Special Rapporteur on the Human Right to Food, Jean Ziegler, wrote to the CEO of Caterpillar, James Owens, asking him about their position on the use of their equipment to destroy Palestinian agricultural resources such as olive groves, greenhouses, and orchards of dates,

JEAN ZIEGLER OF THE UN: QUIZZING
CATERPILLAR ON POTENTIAL COMPLICITY

prunes, lemons and oranges. Ziegler said that allowing the delivery of their bulldozers, 'in the certain knowledge that they are being used for such actions, might involve complicity or acceptance on the part of your company to actual and potential violations of human rights'.[4] This followed a resolution at the Human Rights Commission in April 2004 that condemned the destruction.

The complicity of the company in legal terms is not clear. Various products are used for damaging purposes where the manufacturer is not held legally responsible. For example, cars have killed millions of people, are often designed to drive well beyond speed limits, and their speed is often used as a selling point in advertising; yet the car manufacturers are not (yet) legally liable for deaths and injury caused by speeding. Any case against Caterpillar would probably need to prove that the company designed bull-dozers so they could be armoured to operate in conflict situations, and advertised this adaptability in their sales promotion, while knowing human rights abuses were being carried out with their products. 'Legally, it is difficult to make this case. Morally, how-ever, it is not, and it is to the consciences of the people who manage, work for, and invest in Caterpillar that I appeal', wrote Dr Elizabeth Corrie in May 2004.[5] She is the cousin of Rachel Corrie, who was killed by a Caterpillar bulldozer while protesting the demolition of Palestinian homes in Rafah.

Dr Corrie cited the corporate citizenship policy of the company, which states, 'Cater-pillar accepts the responsibilities of global citizenship' and recognises that Caterpil-lar's 'commitment to financial success must also take into account social, economic, political, and environmental priorities'. It is not just a question of principles, but also profit. The previous month some Caterpillar shareholders expressed concern over 'the actual and potential damage to Caterpillar's international sales and worldwide reputa-tion' and their interest 'in determining if the evidently small amount of revenue derived from these sales outweighs the economic and public relations costs, especially in the United States, Europe and Arab countries'. This is in addition to the risk of costly future legal action, given the trend towards human rights-related corporate litigation.

At the Annual General Meeting in April, Jewish Voice for Peace, a California grass-roots group that advocates an end to Israel's occupation of Palestinian territories, and two other organisations sponsored a shareholder resolution, asking the management to re-examine its sales to Israel. The management recommended that shareholders vote against the proposal, pointing out that 'more than two million Caterpillar machines and engines are at work in virtually every country of the world each day. We have nei-ther the legal right nor the means to police individual use of that equipment.' Cater-pillar's management did not want to set a precedent in relation to Israel, given that its equipment is not only used to build the infrastructures of societies and improve lives but also to destroy homes, forests and rivers, around the world. Many companies do, however, decide to do business only with clients whose social and environmental per-formance they can accept, and this includes not only the purchase of products and ser-vices but also the sale of them, such as the sale of financial services by banks with ethics policies. The potential financial implications of reputational damage may have caused some companies to have responded positively to the campaign on purely commercial grounds. Caterpillar, however, not having been in the corporate responsibility spotlight before, seemed to have a rudimentary understanding of the corporate citizenship agenda. 'We believe any comments on political conflict in the region are best left to our governmental leaders', they said, which illustrates a limited understanding of cor-porate citizenship—one that does not embrace a public role for companies.[6]

In the event, stockholders representing only 4% of Caterpillar shares favoured the resolution, but this percentage met a threshold that allows the groups to reintroduce their resolution in 2005, suggesting that the issue is unlikely to go away. Yet we can ask what if, after a year or maybe many years of campaigning, the company makes a decision on commercial grounds not to sell machines to Israel, then what would this achieve for resolving the Palestinian–Israeli conflict? The government could purchase machines from other foreign, or even domestic, manufacturers. Much energy would have been exerted by peace activists and lawyers and little achieved. When activists have adopted brand-bashing as a tactic in the past it has been a means of increasing media attention on an issue and getting the company to improve the lives of specific workers or communities involved in its operations. Neither of these aims apply in the Caterpillar case, as the conflict already has high media attention, and the company cannot change its operations in ways that will benefit the affected community, only wash its hands of any connection.

Brand-bashing campaigns may seem novel, and create energy and interest, but are counterproductive if they galvanise people into action with no clear strategy for change. If the Caterpillar campaign raises awareness of the wider commercial interests in the Palestine–Israeli conflict, then it might prove helpful. People always make money out of war. The two billion US dollars of military aid, and half a billion US dollars of economic aid, provided to Israel by the US government every year translates into profits for a range of companies and individuals, who have this to lose from a resolution to the conflict.[7] Determining who they are and what influence they have might make the economics of the conflict far clearer. In addition, some companies and individuals make money from producing products and services within the Palestinian occupied territories. The extent to which Palestinians benefit from these commercial activities, or whether they just create vested interests in maintaining the occupation, needs to be understood by any campaign aiming to address corporate complicity in the conflict. Movement on this agenda appears slow, with university divestment campaigns and initiatives such as boycottisraeligoods.org not seeming to have a clear strategy that learns from the history of boycotts about their potential and limits. A key point of leverage might be the Socially Responsible Investment (SRI) community, but initial inquiries suggest that they are not yet considering the reputational risk that could arise from corporate relations with the Palestinian– Israeli conflict.

No movement?

What the Caterpillar campaign, and the attention of a UN Commissioner, may do is increase attention on the issue of corporate complicity with human rights abuses, helping us to regard certain practices not as merely regrettable but as specific human rights violations, which could be prosecuted in the future. What it won't do is help the people in whose name these issues are raised, at least not in the near future.

Considering the bigger picture, the 60th Commission on Human Rights (HCR) in April 2004 was a major failure in the move towards promoting mandatory corporate accountability for human rights. The HCR discussed the recommendations of its Sub-Commission on the role of transnational corporations, including the Draft Norms on the Responsibilities of Transnational Corporations and Other Business Enterprises with Regard to Human Rights. The International Chamber of Commerce (ICC) and International Organisation of Employers (IOE) continued their staunch opposition to the Norms with face-to-face lobbying with government delegations to encourage them to reject the Norms as uncalled for and without legal status. 'If put into effect' the Norms 'will undermine human rights, the business sector of society, and the right to development', they said.[8]

Sir Geoffrey Chandler, who is both a former chair of Amnesty International UK Business Group, and a former Director of Shell International, said that, by attacking the Norms, the 'ICC and IOE bring discredit to their own organisations and do a disservice to their members'. He explained they 'portray a dangerous lack of understanding of the world in which companies operate today and of the risks with which they are confronted'.[9]

GEOFFREY CHANDLER: 'ICC AND IOE BRING
DISCREDIT TO THEIR OWN ORGANISATIONS'

Sune Skadegård Thorsen, Senior Advisor on CSR at Novo Nordisk, commented that 'It has become a tradition for these organisations to oppose any kind of legislation or regulation that limits the behaviour of companies.' Her company is participating in the Business Leaders Initiative on Human Rights (BLIHR), which in April 2004 officially launched a three-year project to look at the business benefits of attention to human rights. Novo Nordisk is joined by ABB, Barclays, Hewlett-Packard, MTV Networks Europe, National Grid Transco, Novartis and The Body Shop International. A number of them are trialling the Norms in their own operations.[10]

The lobbying against the Norms worked, as the HCR resolution on the matter completely rejected the outcome of the process they had initially requested, saying that the document containing the Norms had 'not been requested by the Commission and, as a draft proposal, has no legal standing, and that the Sub-Commission should not perform any monitoring function in this regard'.[11] The HCR decided to request another report on the matter, to be done by the Office of the High Commissioner itself (OHCHR).

Amnesty International tried to put a positive spin on this outcome. 'This is the first time the UN Commission has companies' responsibilities on its agenda', they said. They hoped to save the process by encouraging the OHCHR to build on the progress made by the Sub-Commission. 'Amnesty International expects that the OHCHR will draw on the Norms and their related Commentary as a principal source in the identification and assessment of existing standards in this area.'[12] This is optimistic, given the political pressures that led to the rejection of the existing outputs from the process.

Instead, the drafting of a new report will be less well resourced and conducted by less-experienced and -qualified persons than that prepared by the Sub-Commission, and will be more politically cautious. Some may say they took the matter out of the hands of experts and placed it in the hands of bureaucrats, establishing another process because they did not like the results of the first one.

There are a number of lessons from this. First, it illustrates the success of the two-pronged strategy of some corporations to engage voluntarily with social and environmental issues, with some NGOs and some parts of the UN, and then use the existence of that voluntary engagement to undermine processes towards developing or implementing mandatory rules on their behaviour. The use of lobby groups to further the political interests of specific companies, while somewhat shielding them from negative coverage themselves, is key to this strategy. One organisation argued that Shell International was using the ICC and IOE as a cover for its own aggressive lobbying against the Norms. They reported that Robin Aram, Shell's Vice-President of External Relations and Policy Development, worked with the ICC's Commission on 'Business in Society' to combat the Norms. Aram confirmed that 'From a Shell perspective we don't find the Norms helpful.'[13] Given the prompting to come forward, Shell confirmed its stance against the Norms but said it was wrong 'to imply that because we express our concerns about the draft Norms that in some way undermines or puts into question our commitment to support human rights'.[14] If the commitment is real, then they may have some further way to go in their understanding of how to ensure human rights for all.

A second lesson is the lack of strategy and coordination between mainstream non-governmental organisations (NGOs) and those companies that supported the Norms, to prioritise the lobbying of governmental delegations. Some NGOs working on corporate accountability issues were distracted by and wasted scarce advocacy resources on global meetings, such as the Johannesburg World Summit on Sustainable Development which had no legal power and no implementation structures and therefore were unable to commit sufficient funds to ensure the passage of the legally enforceable Norms. More radical groups working on this agenda spent time preaching to the converted at meetings such as the World Social Forum and European Social Forum. Many NGOs did become involved in the process of deliberating the Norms, but the outcome proves that this was a political issue, not a technical or intellectual debate. Public joint statements to their own communities, and sympathetic yet small media outlets, were not effective. Grandstanding at the Commission itself was too little, too late to make any difference.[15]

Nevertheless, the failure of the Norms may lead to some critical reflection among the corporate citizenship community, and a renewed impetus for coordinating efforts towards systemic change. A paper published by the UN's Research Institute for Social Development (UNRISD) in June 2004 argued that a corporate accountability movement could now be identified, which may lead to that systemic change. *Barricades and Board-rooms* chronicles the failure of various national and international attempts to restrict the growth of corporate power during the 20th century, in order to locate a discussion of recent events.[16] It argues that the growth of a global civil society in the last decades has created a new context, and a new opportunity to address the problems posed by growing corporate power. A range of relations between corporations and civil-society groups is analysed, including the way these have created a renewed emphasis on corporate social responsibility. The paper examines the limitations of voluntary corporate initiatives in addressing systemic problems in the global economy, but suggests voluntary corporate responsibility could be an opportunity if it can lead to the re-channelling of corporate power to address those systemic problems. Thus a new generation of partnerships may emerge, which involve companies collaborating with civil-society groups to push for more appropriate and effective regulation. An example of this was when 15 socially responsible investment organisations with a combined $28.5 billion in assets under management asked the US Congress to support the International Right to Know (IRTK) campaign, which proposes legislation on corporate reporting on social and environmental performance worldwide.[17]

The paper concludes with a discussion of whether accomplishing greater corporate accountability will address the systemic problems with world development. It introduces a concept that looks beyond the corporation and to the accountability of capital itself. This concept of 'capital accountability' arises from reconsidering the obligations that must be placed on the bearers of property rights. The concept is argued to provide an opportunity for common ground to be found among progressives working in the quite separate arenas of corporate accountability, corporate social responsibility and anti-globalisation.

Oil change?

By the Northern summer of 2004 the oil company Shell was hearing criticism of its ethics on many more issues than its questionable lobbying. The company faced multi-million-dollar class-action suits brought by enraged investors, and five legal investigations from, among others, the US Justice Department and the Securities and Exchange Commission. Everything had been called into question and little was clear following the shock announcement earlier in the year that the company had 'lost' one-fifth of its assets, leading to dramatic revisions of its global reserve bookings. Shell now faces question marks over the honesty of its directors, what assets the company actually has (there have been four successive revisions), the company's ability to deliver on corporate social responsibility and even on the veracity of its accounts.[18]

Despite changes in the boardroom and a noticeable shift of tone towards a more contrite approach by admitting its mistakes, the company seemed to be engulfed in the kind of identity crisis that either breaks institutions, or from which they emerge fundamentally transformed. The Shell Chairman Lord Oxburgh—whose appointment followed the departure of three senior managers including the former Chairman Sir Philip Watts—didn't even seem to be sure that Shell should be in the oil business at all: 'No one can be comfortable at the prospect of continuing to pump out the amounts of carbon dioxide that we are pumping out at present . . . with consequences that we really can't predict but are probably not good', Oxburgh told the *Guardian* newspaper.[19]

If Oxburgh's reflective mood signalled that Shell wanted to rethink everything, including its contribution to climate change, what better place to start than its long-criticised Nigerian operations? Nigeria was at the centre of successive reserves booking revisions.[20] Activists and oil-producing communities in the poverty-stricken Niger Delta were unsurprised by the findings of a leaked WAC Global Securities report commissioned by Shell into the depths of their problems, which stated that Shell Nigeria is 'part of Niger Delta conflict dynamics and that its social licence to operate is fast eroding', and that, if events continued as expected, it would be 'surprising' if the company could operate onshore beyond 2008.[21] Shell rejected this suggestion of a move offshore, which communities and environmentalists claimed would leave behind a legacy of pollution, poverty, corruption and communal violence.

The WAC report claimed that militia groups involved in 'bunkering' (theft of oil) were importing rocket-propelled grenade launchers and surface-to-air missiles. Independent observers on the Niger Delta have identified a marked increase in militias since armed gangs were employed by various political groups to rig Nigeria's 2003 election process. There is 90% unemployment among young men in the oil-producing region of the Niger Delta, despite Nigeria being the fourth-largest OPEC producer.

Shell Nigeria was contrite in accepting some of the blame for the mess that oil dependency has created in Nigeria, but its contrition only went so far. 'As part of an industry inadvertently contributing to the problem, we are also determined to help', Emmanuel Etomi, Sustainable Community Development Manager for SPDC (Shell Nigeria) reported on shell.com at the time of the launch of its Nigeria social and environmental reporting for 2003.

Yet the WAC report does not find the role of Shell Nigeria's staff in fostering violence is so inadvertent. 'Instigating violence in the community so that claims based on "force majeure" can be made towards the [Shell Company in Nigeria] has become a business in itself among some contractors.' The clear implication of the report's findings is that—by tacitly approving of what their contractors are doing—Shell Nigeria is part of the problem. 'This logic feeds into an "it's-not-our-fault" mentality that becomes an obstacle to conflict resolution', the WAC authors conclude.[22]

If Shell wanted to find a way out of this mess it has helped to create in Nigeria—rather than be forced into the sea—it could make a start by ending gas flaring, environmentalists said. Alternatives to Shell's practice of burning off natural gas produced along with oil (associated gas) into the atmosphere are to gather it for processing (the purpose of the long-delayed Bonny Liquefied Natural Gas project) or to reinject it into the oil deposit. The Nigerian oil industry is the world's leading practitioner of gas flaring, accounting for about one-fifth of all gas flared in the world. World Bank officials have suggested that gas flaring in the Niger Delta has 'contributed more emissions of greenhouse gases than all other sources in sub-Saharan Africa combined' and that the energy lost is equal to more than half sub-Saharan Africa's thermal-based power generation.

TIM CONCANNON: SHELL NEEDS TO
SHAKE OFF ITS OLD HABITS

An activist who has worked on Nigerian issues since the early 1990s with the Ogoni organisation MOSOP, Tim Concannon, argues the company has a come to a crucial turning point. 'Shell has played an historic role across the globe in creating a culture based on oil, and in fuelling conflicts in places like the Niger Delta. If Shell is serious about being an ethical company, it has to move beyond nice words, glossy brochures and esoteric audit systems. Shell needs to shake off its old habits and begin delivering real answers to these problems.'

Responsible news

Throughout 2004 the responsibility of journalists was, somewhat ironically, a running story in the media. This began with the release of the Hutton Report in the UK, prepared by a government-appointed judge, to inquire into the circumstances surrounding the apparent suicide of the weapons inspector David Kelly. The judge chose to focus on one part of one radio report by the BBC, and (contestably) determined that Kelly had been misrepresented. To many observers' consternation, Hutton prioritised his condemnation of the BBC's professionalism and management structure for allowing and then defending the radio report. Commenting on the Hutton Report, Professor Noam Chomsky suggested that 'the idea that the state—whether hiding itself beyond a judge's robes or not—should even have a voice in whether a journalist's report was "unfounded" is utterly shocking . . . can you imagine an inquiry into whether a press report praising state or corporate power was "unfounded"?'[23] What the row over the BBC's coverage of the lead-up to the invasion of Iraq did was raise a debate about media integrity and independence.

NOAM CHOMSKY: 'THAT THE STATE . . . SHOULD EVEN HAVE A VOICE IN WHETHER A JOURNALIST'S REPORT WAS "UNFOUNDED" IS UTTERLY SHOCKING'

In May, the *New York Times* published an apology for its coverage of the issue of whether Iraq had weapons of mass destruction. They wrote that the 'accounts of Iraqi defectors were not always weighed against their strong desire to have Saddam Hussein ousted. Articles based on dire claims about Iraq tended to get prominent display, while follow-up articles that called the original ones into question were sometimes buried.'[24] The apology itself was somewhat buried on page A10, and not as long as 2003's front-page corrective on Jayson Blair, even though the implications are more significant.

The *New York Times* was not unusual among newspapers in its reporting of the run-up to war, while the approach of television news was often even more questionable. One academic study found that the more commercial television news people watched, the more incorrect they were likely to be about basic facts concerning the war on Iraq. In a major survey of viewers, researchers from the University of Maryland found those who watched the Rupert Murdoch-owned Fox News channel, in particular, were more likely to hold basic misperceptions.[25]

News of the abuse of Iraqi prisoners broke in the Northern spring of 2004, and the *Mirror* newspaper in the UK came under fire for printing pictures of alleged abuse by British soldiers, which turned out to be probable fakes. Yet just as questionable as the *Mirror*'s stance was the rest of the British media, including that of the BBC, who omitted relevant facts in order to argue that the paper and its editor had unfairly slurred soldiers, rather than having been hoaxed. For example, at the time of this row, both Amnesty International and the Red Cross released detailed reports on the abuse of prisoners and killing of civilians by the British army in Iraq.[26]

For its part, the BBC has been looking to address afresh its responsibilities as a broadcaster. At a seminar about the future of BBC journalism prompted by the Hutton Report, in-house *Ariel* magazine reported that John Simpson, the BBC's grandly titled World Affairs Editor, had asked the corporation to appoint a news ombudsman to overview complaints, a system already in place at the *Guardian*, for example. Simpson argued, 'It could be helpful to have an individual who was entirely objective, who looked at everything you damn well said.'[27] This approach rests on sandbanks of assumptions, particularly that objectivity is both possible and desirable, and that issues of responsibility can be addressed by focusing on the work of individual reporters.

JOHN SIMPSON: ASKED
THE BBC TO APPOINT
A NEWS OMBUDSMAN

First, social scientists reveal how 'objectivity' is often really just a particular subjectivity that is widely shared—and that it might be widely shared because it is shaped by powerful systemic forces, such as capitalism, patriarchy or racism.[28] Instead, claims of integrity and validity in one's reporting can be based on one's efforts to be conscious of one's own subjectivity, to reflect on it, question it, and be open about it.[29] Therefore, one would need to consider the influences on one's own perceptions and perspective, especially if those influences act on many people, and so structure society. In addition, as this 'critical subjectivity' does not assume a single truth that can be objectively known, so one's validity and integrity also stems from one's support for pluralising the voices and perspectives on an issue. It is a responsibility toward democratic debate. There is no pot of objectivity at the end of the rainbow, just a colourful spectrum of subjectivities, which must not be dulled by consolidation. The policy implication of this understanding is that we need plural biases in media outlets.

Some social scientists argue that we should not focus our consideration of media responsibilities on individual reporters, editors or managers, as there is a systemic problem affecting media output. Noam Chomsky has argued that, despite the endeavours of committed journalists, the corporate media generally filters the news agenda in five ways. First, the business interests of the owner companies influences reporting. Second, media managers need to please (and certainly not upset) current and potential advertisers. Third, journalists often rely on press releases from organisations with a commercial interest in influencing the media. This reliance has increased as profit objectives restrict the amount of time most journalists have to research stories. Fourth, journalists that rock the boat are liable to professional criticism and sometimes litigation. A fifth filter is a blind acceptance of neoliberal economic ideology, so that many journalists are bemused at, and uninterested in, fundamental critiques of the economic system.[30] These filters help to shape the media profession as a whole, and therefore the activity of non-corporate broadcasters as well.

Most media outlets in the world are run for a profit by corporations, suggesting a systemic bias that militates against a true plurality of voices—which does not just mean a quantity of voices, but qualitatively different voices. In any case, the growth in TV channels, for example, masks how the quantity of voices is in decline: it has been estimated that 40% of all media in the world are controlled by just five transnational corporations.[31] Given these arguments, large media-owning corporations present a social dilemma by their very existence. At the very least, lobbying to enable ever-greater consolidation of media ownership, and undermining of non-commercial media, become issues of corporate irresponsibility. Yet such practices are business-as-usual for many media companies—even to the extent that they *become* the government.

For example, in the US, Michael Powell, whose family has major interests in AOL, chaired the Federal Communications Commission, which controversially proposed new legislation removing restrictions on media ownership.[32] In May 2004, Italian President Carlo Azeglio Ciampi legalised a media reform bill, which facilitated further consolidation. Critics of Prime Minister Silvio Berlusconi claimed this would further increase his already gargantuan power over the means of mass communication in the

SILVIO BERLUSCONI:
INFLUENCES 90% OF ITALIAN TV

country. Berlusconi, Italy's richest man, owns two newspapers and Mediaset, which includes three commercial television stations. The new bill resulted in the chairman of the state media TV company RAI, Lucia Annunziata, resigning in protest at excessive governmental intervention. RAI's chairwoman claimed that this involvement was intended to 'completely destroy the profile of the corporation' which would lead to 'the annulment of every type of autonomy and pluralism'.[33] With this de facto control of RAI, Berlusconi has direct or indirect influence on 90% of Italy's TV output, posing a threat to democratic discourse. Democracy requires a cacophony of birdsong, not the monotonous dirge from a powerful elite.

Broader media responsibilities

Beyond news reporting, the media sector faces a number of responsibility challenges, such as the type and level of advertising, an issue highlighted by the *State of the World 2004* publication, which chronicled the role of advertising industries in driving unsustainable consumption around the world.[34] Other challenges include privacy issues, intellectual property protection, and the nature of media content—films, documentaries, music and so on. The potential of the media sector to influence society in its discussion of public issues was highlighted by the eco-disaster movie *The Day After Tomorrow*. Its release heralded a spike in global media discussion of global warming, as popular television shows and tabloid newspapers discussed the representation and the reality of climate change catalysed by the Hollywood blockbuster; with the Greenland shelf melting, fears of rising tides and plunging temperatures trickled into media outlets not normally preoccupied with the environmental agenda. Interestingly, the film itself was 'carbon-neutral', meaning that the makers invested in tree-planting to offset the carbon emissions involved in producing the film. This reminds us that media companies are not exempt from those issues that face any corporation, such as environmental management, labour rights, and community relations in their own operations and those of their suppliers.

Some small enterprises such as the US TV production firm Lucita,[35] and the UK communications companies Futerra and Ethical Media,[36] have made attention to such issues integral to their business. Ethical Media works for a range of clients in the non-profit sector, and companies engaged in corporate responsibility. 'We only work on projects we believe in', says founding director Marco Kuntze, which he argues creates a better service for clients as it generates a commitment and hence creativity and efficiency. In addition, they seek to conduct their business in line with environmental best

ETHICAL MEDIA'S MARCO KUNTZE:
'WE ONLY WORK ON PROJECTS WE BELIEVE IN'

practice. Kuntze considers he has a growing niche, as various companies begin to consider their responsibilities to society, while the mainstream media and communications industries have yet to engage fully in the CSR agenda (with notable exceptions such as advertising firms like St Luke's).

Fifteen larger media companies in the UK launched a new initiative aimed at correcting this lack of engagement, or at least correcting that impression.[37] Members of the CSR Media Forum include the BBC, ITV, Reuters, Pearson, Trinity Mirror, AOL, Sky, Reed Elsevier and Capital Radio, among others. In April 2004, another member, the Guardian Media Group, released a voluminous social audit, which was generally praised by its assessor. Richard Evans, Director of ethics etc . . . , claims in his auditor's statement that the corporation has been 'remarkably thorough and honest'. Evans urges that the company 'continue with efforts to reduce energy consumption and waste . . . significant improvements can be achieved through raising awareness and improving environmental responsibility amongst the staff'.[38]

RICHARD EVANS OF ETHICS ETC . . . :
PRAISE FOR GUARDIAN MEDIA GROUP

Movement on corporate media responsibility is somewhat overdue, if we consider that over two years ago both SustainAbility Ltd and the UN Environment Programme (UNEP) released reports on media companies, arguing that they were lagging behind other industries.[39] Business in the Community (BitC) reported in 2004 that media companies were some of the least responsive to their survey of performance, and scored low on their index of responsibility.[40] However, the CSR Media Forum feels that the operationalisation of the CSR concept by such groups unfairly labels their companies. It contends that current responsibility questionnaires and indices cohere with retail and manufacturing sectors; these can demonstrate hard, quantifiable changes, such as a reduction in the use of toxic emissions, for example. They argue that the media beast is a different species, requiring different corporate anthropologist to track its movements—its prey, excretions and fertilisations.

It is true that the BitC index, among others, may need upgrading to consider issues that relate to the media sector, such as their advertising policies, programming and or political stances on market liberalisation and ownership consolidation. However, the CSR Media Forum was not making this point. Instead, they argue their role in promoting responsible agendas should be taken into account. Media companies 'occupy a unique position in supporting the democratic process by making information, knowledge and a range of opinions openly available and ensuring the public and private institutions are accountable for their behaviour. This is social responsibility in its highest form and should also be recognised', argues the chief executive of Guardian Media Group, Bob Phillis.[41] Such justifications for the activities of the media in the public sphere recall traditional debates about the role of the press as a fourth estate, acting as a watchdog, or guardian, of the nation. It echoes long-established pluralistic arguments that the press is an alleged safeguard of democracy—it sniffs out stories power elites would rather see buried. The *Guardian* itself, as a non-profit-making trust, may have grounds for such arguments, but they do not apply to the sector as a whole. 'The media' term deployed by Phillis is rather a loose one: the distinctions between serious journalism and more sensationalist mass-market journalism is not made.

Resuscitating the pluralist paradigm to defend media corporations ignores the debates discussed earlier about the filters on corporate media and the problems with greater consolidation of media ownership in the hands of a few companies. It suggests that the capitalistic superstructures on which these media mansions are resting will not be subject to a structural survey, to look for signs of dry rot, subsidence or rising damp. Critical intellectuals could usefully enter into dialogue with media practitioners to open up these foundations, and broaden the agenda to consider the responsibilities that arise from influence over information, communication and knowledge.

There is a risk that these laudable toe-dips into the CSR arena will result in self-legitimisation; while they might result in recycling bins in neon-lit newsrooms, they do not interrogate the very nature of power/knowledge collection, filtering, dissemination and reception. They may confirm existing processes of information production, *confirm* the self-justification of media practitioners, rather than questioning the ideologies, the compromises, and the 'taken for granted' rules of journalistic games.

There is a need for media initiatives on CSR to look at the broader issues and the public policy implications—to consider their corporate citizenship. This is particularly because the media, communications and entertainment industries are so important in shaping society, so social progress will require all companies in this sector to improve their conduct, not just a select few. Yet, rather like responsible parents of good children at a school parents' evening, the more ethically receptive media firms may turn up at CSR meetings; but those least connected to the CSR agenda, those with greater penetration of popular markets, and therefore huge potential to impact on popular consciousness and behaviour change, are, currently, least likely to sign up to CSR fora.

Indications that tangible results may arise from participation in the CSR Media Forum came from Reed Elsevier, the world's largest academic publisher. Once firmly opposed to online open access to its publications, in June 2004 it was reported to have decided to permit academics to put papers accepted for publication in its print and online journals onto the Internet. This could be seen as a socially responsible move, whereas rival publishers felt this was all Machiavellian marketing to defend a business. Some competing publishers have already embraced the open-access model, charging academics to publish papers, then making them available to all online.[42] This approach also has its drawbacks, by introducing a financial barrier to publication, and creating a business model that relies on people wanting to publish, not wanting to read—a potential hazard for quality control. How do we address this challenge in the context of the *Journal of Corporate Citizenship* World Review, where these reviews first appear? Greenleaf initially publishes them only for subscribers to the journal; but it is then made available at the end of every year, free of charge, on the Internet, in collaboration with Lifeworth, the ethical careers company.[43] A collection of these Annual Reviews is what you now hold in front of you.

3Q2004

July–September

Jem Bendell and Kate Ives

Is that sporting?

Mid-way through 2004 there was an explosion of exceptional international sport, with the Athens Olympics in August following swiftly on the heels of the Euro 2004 football championship in Portugal. Tapping into the mass audience and support for these competitions were several events that aimed to promote awareness of social problems evident across the globe and raise money for charitable causes. The fundraiser, Sport Relief in the UK, had raised over £11 million by August 2004, for projects in Guatemala, Tanzania, Uganda, India and Pakistan, as well as the UK.[1]

Sport-related fundraising is not a new phenomenon. Marathons have been particularly successful at motivating thousands of individuals to take part in sport while raising money for charity. Over £134 million has been raised by participants in the London marathon alone since its first race in 1981.[2] However, there is a rise in projects occurring in developing countries financed by sports institutions rather than fans or fundraisers. The biggest players are sporting confederations themselves, such as the Union of European Football Associations (UEFA) and its global guiding force, the Fédération Internationale de Football Association (FIFA).

Both FIFA and UEFA have funded international development organisations since the mid-1990s. UEFA has given CHF 6.1 million to the International Committee of the Red Cross (ICRC) since 1997, of which over CHF 1 million has gone to 'Mine Action'—a project not connected to football, or indeed sport, in any apparent way.[3] Additionally, money raised by the fines imposed on teams in UEFA's Euro 2004 went to ICRC's 'Protect Children in War' campaign.

One project that appears more closely linked to the impacts of sport is FIFA's 'partnership' with UNICEF, for which over a million US dollars has been provided to combat child labour since 1997. However, despite a decade of campaigning by NGOs against the sport industry's role in perpetuating child labour through ignoring or not doing enough about the problem of supply chain management and standard enforcement, it is estimated that, in 2004, 75% of the world's hand-stitched footballs will have been made in Pakistan, notorious for child labour.[4] In response to media attention, FIFA introduced a Code of Conduct in 1996 aiming to protect child labourers, although, by its own admission, only 4% of the world's footballs are covered by this code—the rest having been made in workshops throughout Asia that are not officially contracted to FIFA.[5] Nevertheless, pressure from NGOs on the issue has been consistent against all major sporting bodies. In June 2004, Oxfam, along with the Clean Clothes Campaign and the International Confederation of Free Trade Unions (ICFTU), launched another attack on the International Olympic Committee (IOC) for ignoring its moral and legal responsibility towards workers in factories that produce Olympic merchandise.[6] The report states, '[so] intrinsically linked is the practice of sport with the sports-brands that any taint on the industry's reputation also stains the reputation of the sports institutions. Yet the sporting world—apart from a few exceptions—has done very little to call for change on the part of the sportswear companies.'[7]

Are the contributions of sporting confederations to development organisations a simple response to pressure from civil-society activists, or is it more complex than that? UEFA's motivation for contributing to development projects is given on its website: 'By adopting a flexible and clear charity policy, UEFA is supporting the belief that football should be used as a force for broader benefit within society, using its potential to influence attitudes and behaviour beyond the confines of the stadium.'[8] And its potential to influence is certainly huge. The 31 matches played in Euro 2004 drew some 80 million viewers worldwide, which was over 15% more than the comparative statistics for Euro 2000.[9]

Of course, sport has long been recognised as an activity beneficial to individual development. In addition, scholars and sportsmen alike have connected sport with community development. The link between sport and community development goes back at least as far as the modern Olympic Games. Pierre de Coubertin, founder of the modern Olympics, was just as interested in the promotion of peace among nations.[10] Indeed, if sport transcends cultural barriers, then football as the world's 'beautiful game' is commonly acknowledged as the best barrier-breaker there is. The example of German and British troops briefly laying down their weapons on Christmas Day 1914 for a game of football and a moment of surreal relief from the surrounding chaos reinforces the idea that sport, on account of its universalism, can indeed build bridges between communities in a way that most other cultural activities cannot.[11] But, tragically for all concerned, war continued the following day and the role of sport did nothing to stop it. The question therefore remains: can sport promote peace and development?

Such an idea is in direct opposition to the national or ethnic identity that is central to international or regional competition. One only has to consider the British press in a World Cup year to witness the nationalist fervour that the sport inspires and feeds on. Yet there has been a strange development, because the increased migration of players is, arguably, undermining simplistic nationalist and regionalist sentiment among supporters.[12] When Senegal beat its former colonial master France in the 2002 World Cup, none of its winning squad played for Senegalese local teams—they had all been playing in France in the season preceding the games.

However, the globalisation of sport goes much further than the movement of its players. Football is, after all, big business—in 1999 alone Americans spent a whopping $763 per capita on sporting goods.[13] In a game where supporters become consumers, FIFA's involvement with UNICEF or UEFA's with ICRC could be seen as part of a strategy to expand the future consumer base into countries that have no historical or prior cultural connection with football.

The cultural connection provides interesting fodder for social theorists concerned with cultural hegemony and the globalisation of culture, discussed in the previous quarter.[14] By Gramsci's definition, whereby culture cannot be divorced from ideology and hegemonic status is achieved not through force but through acquiescence and consent, sport is achieving a powerful status. The globalisation of the Olympic Games, in which 'Western' sports undoubtedly dominate, undermines the power of local sports for the sake of those with the biggest mass audience. Moreover, the close association with Western products, and thus values and lifestyle, add to its Westernising influence. In football it is the Western leagues, such as the English Premiership and European Championship that are marketed globally, along with their star players and sponsors' brands. The globalising of Western sports can therefore be viewed as part of a process of marketing to the world those ways of life and aspirations that serve particular commercial (and, perhaps, political) interests.

The irony is that, despite the charitable activity of football institutions, football has become the conduit for a flow of money from poor countries to rich ones. The purchase of Chelsea Football Club by the Russian billionaire Roman Abramovich illustrates this well. Chukotka, the north-eastern province of Russia in which Abramovich is governor, was declared bankrupt in June 2004. Given serious concerns about the way Russian oligarchs came to own previously state-owned corporations, and the low to non-existent levels of tax these companies now pay, one cannot help but wonder whether the $233 million that Abramovich has spent on assembling his star players might have been better spent covering some of the $320 million debts of the poverty-stricken region.[15] Meanwhile, a bid by the Thai Prime Minister Thaksin Shinawatra, and a later offer from Thai media tycoon Paiboon Damrongchaitham, to buy a third of Liverpool Football Club with sums well in excess of £60 million is further testament to this rather odd reverse flow of money as well as the increasing cultural power of Western football clubs.

Compared to these amounts of money, FIFA's and UEFA's attempts to enhance social development seem to fall well short of the desired finishing line. Perhaps it is time for the sports industry to follow calls from civil-society activists as other industries have, and attempt to shift away from philanthropy towards increased accountability of the entire industry.

The oil oligarchs

Roman Abramovich is not the only so-called 'oligarch' under suspicion for the way in which he amassed his fortune. In the spate of privatisations that occurred following the collapse of the USSR in the early 1990s, a small handful of men have made enormous personal profits, largely through buying shares at well below their real value in the previously state-owned oil industry.

Unlike Abramovich, however, some of the others have not escaped the scrutiny of the Russian government for their business activities since then. Mikhail Khodorkovsky, former CEO of the troubled oil giant Yukos, was arrested in October 2003 and, as of September 2004, awaits trial on charges of fraud, embezzlement and tax evasion.

Yukos came under fire for tax evasion and was found guilty of evading nearly $2 billion during 2000. While the company denies the charges, the Russian tax ministry has revealed that Yukos operated a system of transfer pricing through its special-purpose companies in known tax havens such as Gibraltar.

Khodorkovsky, meanwhile, as Russia's richest man (estimated to be worth more than $15 billion according to *Forbes* magazine), is seen by some as a scapegoat for Putin's attack on the oligarchs who were well known for their ties with Yeltsin's government. The fact that the oligarchs are widely seen as criminals by the Russian public is also a convenient vote-winning tactic on Putin's behalf. Khodorkovsky is not shy in his political affiliations and funding of opposition parties, including Putin's biggest rivals, the communists.[16] He also bought the rights to the *Moskovskiye Novosti* newspaper and hired outspoken critics of the Putin government as staff.

However, to dismiss the claims made against Yukos and Khodorkovsky as political manoeuvring on the government's behalf is to dismiss the serious question of the obligations of rich citizens and companies to the country that spawned their wealth, and concern about the legality of corporate financial practices. The involvement of accounting firms such as PricewaterhouseCoopers (PwC) in the scandal is testament not only to the influence of these global organisations but also to their far-reaching influence in terms of accounting practice. As Robert McIntyre, the director of Citizens for Tax Justice, commented in September 2004, '[O]ur accountants have exported their tax-sheltering skills so that even former godless communists can evade taxes just like church-going, red-blooded American corporate chiefs.'[17]

Whether the clampdown on oil oligarchs reveals a return towards a more authoritarian Russia, an endeavour from within the Duma to increase support for the presidency, or a more righteous attempt to stop the flow of money outside of the country along with oil, what can be understood is that Putin's hunting-down of the oligarchs has only just begun.

Digging dirt: BHP Billiton in Chile

Accusations of corporate tax evasion also abounded in Chile. A paper published in a volume by World Economy, Ecology and Development (WEED) examined why most private mining companies operating in that country do not publish financial results or pay taxes.[18] It focused on one company that is regarded as more responsible, because of the fact that it publishes its financial results, pays some tax, and voluntarily supports a variety of social projects. That company is Minera Escondida, the world's largest private copper-mining operation, owned by BHP Billiton. A comparative study of the financial results of Minera Escondida and the state-owned mining company found that the former might not be as responsible as some assume. The central claim is that, by not refining its copper in Chile but selling it as concentrates, mainly to a consortium of refiners related to its ownership structure, the Billiton subsidiary Escondida has fewer earnings than its state equivalent, per ton of copper produced (even after corrections for transport and refining charges). The study asserts that the losses of tax revenue to Chile as a result are between 125 and 212 million dollars a year, from 1998 to 2002. The author Manuel Riesco told us that something must be wrong when 'Chile is providing private companies access to rich mineral deposits at almost no charge at all'.

Earlier in the year the paper's main findings were presented to the president of the special commission of the Chilean Senate that considers the financial practices of the mining industry. The Senate considered that the findings were serious enough to send the study to the taxing agency as well as the mining and finance cabinet ministers. Arguments ensued between the different ministries and senators, with the press reporting the debate. As a result, a new bill, which would establish a royalty on mining exports, was tabled and discussed in Parliament.

That a revised version of the paper was scheduled to be published by the United Nations raised further alarm in BHP Billiton.[19] They commissioned Pontificia Universidad Católica de Chile (PUC) to prepare a study countering the claims made in Riesco's study. Instead of addressing the key claims, the PUC paper showed Escondida to be a greater contributor of taxes than its private competitors, and documented the social and environmental projects that benefit from the company donating of 1% of its pre-tax earnings.[20] This reflects three aspects of CSR that are often used for questionable effect in public discourse. First is the notion that 'best in class' is good enough: if you are better than the rest of your competitors, then you can be regarded as socially and environmentally responsible. Second is that the presence of voluntary projects funded by profits reduces the need to question about how those profits were arrived at. Third is that voluntary positive action negates the need for regulatory innovations. But should CSR initiatives be used in the fight against paying taxes? Or is payment of tax a basic responsibility? In a letter to the chair of UNRISD's board, Jorge Lavandero Illanes of the Chile Senate, Andrés Varela García, President of CENDA (Centre of National Studies on Alternative Development), and Tomás Moulian Emparanza of ARCIS University argued that 'CSR should first consider respect for taxing obligations that exist in countries that host [transnational corporations] as well as, and particularly, respect for the sovereign right of each country to dispose of its natural resources as it considers best.'[21] By September 2004, the legislative initiatives had stalled, with stiff resistance from mining companies: a clear case of the political influence of corporations being a valid concern for corporate citizenship.

Tax justice?

A report of UNRISD's conference on CSR, published in July 2004, quoted Eddie Rich, of the UK Department for International Development, on corporate tax management. The 'biggest contribution that business can make to development is through taxation . . . You have companies spending a lot of time developing codes . . . [while at the same time] employing an army of accountants to try and avoid paying their full social and economic duty in the places where they operate . . . [T]axation is the way that the government and the private sector can start engaging properly—that is the mechanism for partnership.'[22]

Reports in the *Financial Times* in August 2004 suggested that tax was a problem not just for developing countries. Their investigation of companies in various sectors, such as automobiles, pharmaceuticals, retail and banking, suggested that transfer pricing, and moving debts and savings between different countries, is dramatically reducing government tax yields from corporations.[23] For example, the most profitable investment bank in London, Goldman Sachs Group Holdings (UK), whose directors include Lord Browne of Madingley, showed a tax credit of $7 million on pre-tax profits of $665 million. Some might wonder why in Russia the senior management of companies that do not pay tax are threatened with prison whereas, in the UK, they are rewarded with a peerage. The *FT* argued that declining tax revenues from corporations 'is an inexorable consequence of growing foreign direct investment, which produces increased potential for companies to reap the benefits of international tax arbitrage'.[24] This challenges the assumption that FDI is good for economic development and that pursuing it is, by itself, an expression of good corporate citizenship.

In September 2004, economist John Christensen, coordinator of the Tax Justice Network, argued that 'curiously the CSR debate, which has touched on virtually every other area of corporate engagement with broader society, has only recently begun to question companies in the area where their corporate citizenship is most tangible and most important—the payment of tax'.[25] The Network was conceived at the European Social Forum in Florence in November 2002, by a coalition of NGOs, academics, professionals and faith groups, who seek to campaign against aggressive tax practices and harmful tax competition. The Network is engaging with stakeholders in the CSR debate 'to advocate for global policy measures to overcome the systemic faults', says Christensen, that allow transnational corporations to 'run rings around nationally based tax regimes'. The implications for corporate citizenship are clear. 'Unless directors acknowledge that paying taxes is the core of good citizenship they risk losing public

JOHN CHRISTENSEN: CSR HAS
ONLY JUST BEGUN TO FOCUS ON TAX

confidence in their commitment to CSR and will undermine initiatives to tackle global poverty', says Christensen. CSR standards should therefore evolve in this area, to cover such things as 'the publication of all necessary accounting information and the use of profits-laundering vehicles that operate without substantial economic purpose'. He continues that CSR reports should list the countries in which the company trades, how much profit is derived from activities in each of these countries, and where these profits are booked for tax purposes, indicating any special-purpose vehicles that are used, and the extent of tax avoidance arising from the use of 'novel tax planning ideas'.

This would mark a major conceptual shift within the business and accounting worlds. Compelled by the desire for profit maximisation and by a legal principle that asserts that tax payers may organise their affairs so as to pay the least possible tax under the law, tax advisors currently regard tax as a cost of doing business. This resonates with the philosophy of management put forward by the Chicago School. Addressing the issue of anti-competition violations, Professors Frank Easterbrook and Daniel Fischel wrote in the 1980s that company directors should violate rules in pursuit of profit. They argued that rule violations can be seen as 'externalities' and paying the associated fines and penalties is a normal cost of doing business. Evidence from recent US Senate enquiries show that staff in major accounting firms such as KPMG apply this logic to the tax avoidance products they market to clients. In a series of emails released to the enquiry, a senior tax practitioner told colleagues that, even if regulators acted against them, the potential profits greatly exceeded the possible penalties. 'Our average deal would result in KPMG fees of US$360,000 with a maximum penalty exposure of only $31,000', said one email.[26] If the corporate citizenship agenda does not move on this issue, then there may be the political will for government action. The United Nations General Assembly agreed in December 2003 to start the process of forming an inter-governmental commission involving its 191 member countries in developing new anti-avoidance measures.

Ten commandments

At the end of June 2004, the Global Compact Leaders' Summit drew more than 400 corporate executives, government officials and civil-society leaders to the UN headquarters 'for the largest and highest-level gathering ever held at the United Nations'. The Summit adopted a simple statement that 'business should work against corruption in all its forms, including extortion and bribery'.[27] This became a tenth principle of the Compact, to reflect the United Nations convention on this subject. Peter Eigen, Chairman of Transparency International, an international NGO devoted to combating corruption, recalled that, until recently, the world business community regarded corruption as a necessary evil, with some top executives openly defending the practice of bribing foreign firms with a shrug of the shoulder and an offhand remark: 'I hate to do it . . . and I hate all the problems it will cause down the line . . . but I have to.' He said that this had changed and 'there was now a solid consensus behind the need to fight corruption'.

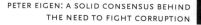

PETER EIGEN: A SOLID CONSENSUS BEHIND
THE NEED TO FIGHT CORRUPTION

One example of possible corruption was particularly topical, given the US presidential campaign. Questions mounted about the involvement of United States oil services company Halliburton in the distribution of US$180 million of allegedly corrupt payments on a $10 billion gas export project in Nigeria made while Dick Cheney headed the corporation—before becoming US Vice-President. The allegations have been the subject of a state investigation in France since October 2003 and in Nigeria and the USA since the beginning of 2004. In 1999, Halliburton's wholly owned subsidiary KBR (Kellogg, Brown & Root), along with three other contractors, made a payment of $51 million to a British lawyer, Jeffrey Tesler. The lawyer confirmed this in a statement to the French investigating magistrate, insisting it was legitimate remuneration for his work as consultant on the gas project.[28] Nice work if you can get it—but was it too good to be true? Lawyers are known to receive ridiculous sums, but even the top earners at firms such as Slaughter & May and Clifford Chance only take home about £1 million a year.

Even at that level of income there are accusations of foul play. The largest legal firms have doubled their revenue in six years, promoting Britain's Law Society to draft a code of conduct for solicitors to discourage them from putting profits before professional ethics. The Society's training chief, Sue Nelson, said there were concerns that 'young lawyers don't have any ethics', yet might it be the case that the ethics of older lawyers, who own the companies, are at fault in pressurising young lawyers to meet unrealistic targets for billable hours? If so, the partners in law firms should be the target of ethics training. Whether you can train a greedy old dog new ethics tricks is another matter—perhaps a topic for further research.[29]

Not many firms of lawyers are participants in the Global Compact. Nor, unsurprisingly, is Halliburton. Participation in the Global Compact suggests an intention to improve one's ethical conduct; the initiative does not address those companies who express no such intent. And those with no such intent are, we might assume, more likely to be engaged in corrupt practices. Thus it is the system of laws, police and courts that appear more pertinent to combating corruption than a voluntary initiative. For example, Halliburton is being investigated in France due to the 1997 adoption of an OECD convention on the 'fight against the corruption of foreign public officials in commercial negotiations' which came into effect in French law in 2000.[30] Companies can be investigated in the US under the Foreign Corrupt Practices Act.

Nevertheless, it is useful for companies to express their commitment against corruption, and the rhetorical power of the Global Compact's ten commandments of corporate citizenship could prove transformative. However, open and honest engagement in the problem of corruption will lead Compact participants to a realisation of the need for greater enforcement mechanisms against those who participate in corruption. 'Relying on companies to disclose information voluntarily has so far failed because they fear being undermined by less scrupulous competitors' argues the campaign Publish What You Pay.

Therefore, to 'work against corruption' as participants are called to do, could imply joining initiatives such as this, which are calling on G7 governments to require transnational resource companies to publish the net taxes, fees, royalties and other payments made in countries where they operate. They call for stock market regulators to require that resource companies report net payments to all national governments as a condition for being listed.[31]

How the Compact relates to the need for irresponsible performance to be discouraged, punished, stopped and redressed, rather than only incentivising and facilitating better performance for those who want this, is an issue that is increasingly recognised by its participants and leaders. This was reflected in a new publication on the Com-

JOHN ELKINGTON: CO-
AUTHOR OF *GEARING UP*

pact, called *Gearing Up: From Corporate Responsibility to Good Governance and Scalable Solutions*, which was launched at the Summit.[32] The report represented a more mature appreciation of the potential and limits of voluntary corporate responsibility, recognising that 'some responsible businesses have scratched the surface of global issues like climate change and HIV/AIDS, but just as many work to maintain the status quo. The efforts of business, in combination with government and civil society, are quite simply being outpaced by the problems.'[33]

Furthermore, the report points to the complicity of many companies in creating the system conditions within which social and environmental problems worsen. 'Where links between companies and government do exist, they are often dominated by regressive lobbying—the automotive industry lobbying against effective action on climate change, for example, or fast food companies lobbying to slow controls on their industry.' The report calls on Global Compact participants to help drive system-level change. Business is generally encouraged to stay out of politics, but the challenge business leaders face is increasingly political. Co-author of the report, SustainAbility Ltd chair John Elkington, said that 'business leaders must align their companies' lobbying with their corporate responsibility activities. They need to help governments to act courageously in such areas as climate change, corruption and HIV/AIDS.' Another co-author, Georg Kell, Executive Head of the Global Compact, said the corporate responsibility movement 'will need to focus on two things simultaneously: achieving critical mass across all industry sectors, and connecting private actions with public policy efforts so that root causes of problems are tackled'.

The report set out a 'Global Compact Challenge', which asks companies to question, among other things, how they can 'help co-evolve wider governance frameworks'. It also suggests that the UN use its 'convening power to foster new thinking on ways in which business can help promote necessary changes in governance and market systems, ensuring adequate representation from developing countries'. The report did not go into the various issues that would need to be addressed to drive system-level change in the global economy. That issue was taken up in another publication launched at the Summit, *Learning to Talk*, where one chapter mapped out a future agenda for the Compact based on a systems view of corporate citizenship, including issues such as currency flows, mandatory corporate accountability, competition law and tax evasion.[34]

Given the growth of the Compact, as well as some criticism, previously chronicled in this column, *Gearing Up* also reported that the Compact is toughening its criteria for participants, requiring all to submit regular communications on progress, and threatening delisting if these are not forthcoming.

Privatised regulation

In July 2004, people were digesting the announcement from ISO, the International Organisation for Standardisation, that it would proceed in developing an 'International Standard for Social Responsibility'. The objective is to produce 'a guidance document, written in plain language which is understandable and usable by non-specialists' and not intended for use in certification.[35]

ISO is an organisation that brings together national standards institutes, such as the British Standards Institution, which are usually membership-based organisations that develop their own standards for business performance. Members are mainly businesses, their trade associations, and specialist 'conformity assessment' firms. Government agencies are also members, and many governments specify a particular standards institute as the nationally recognised institute. ISO has developed over 7,000 voluntary standards on business behaviour. Most are explicitly technical, such as standards on the size of a plug, or the strength of a light bulb, but increasingly they address areas such as quality, environmental management and corporate responsibility.

ISO established an advisory group on corporate social responsibility in early 2003 to help it decide whether to develop standards in this area. The majority of the Advisory Group concluded that ISO should indeed proceed, by developing a guidance document, a step that was backed by the conference.[36] Their recommendation follows significant activity by ISO's national members; standards bodies in Israel, Australia, the UK, France, Spain, Mexico, Malawi, Japan and Austria have developed or are developing CSR management standards or other instruments. This is the latest phase in the evolution of standards bodies, including ISO, away from a narrow technical focus towards one that embraces issues normally deliberated in more public spheres—social and environmental issues. ISO Secretary-General Alan Bryden said that 'the very fact that ISO is being asked to consider the area of social responsibility illustrates the extension of the scope and perception of ISO, from being primarily a technical organisation, quite engaged in a broad range of product and technology areas, to one whose work is now increasingly recognised as having important economic and social repercussions'.

ALLEN BRYDEN: THE ISO HAS IMPORTANT
ECONOMIC AND SOCIAL REPERCUSSIONS

The importance of standards-making in this area should not be underestimated. Although most private standards are not mandatory by law, some of them, such as the

ISO 9000 standards on quality management, have become mandatory for companies that want to trade internationally. Adherence to private standards is often a precondition for the acceptability of products by key consumers and/or distributors. Companies often oblige others to adopt certain policies, not on the basis of formal authority but on the basis of resource dependency, such as when a small firm has to meet the requirements of the company it is supplying. Some insurance companies are requesting compliance with standards to reduce product liability exposure.

Private standards are becoming ever more linked to governmental and intergovernmental regulatory apparatus. In litigation, a company's certification or non-certification to a particular standard is sometimes put forward as evidence of due diligence, or lack thereof.[37] Particularly in Europe, governments are granting some 'regulatory relief' to firms if they have installed, or will install, an environmental management system certified to appropriate standards. For example, the Netherlands introduced a 'framework permit' for pollution, which is more simple than the traditional one. It sets end-goals, and leaves the design of the processes and procedures to the company's environmental management system, which most of the time is one certified to ISO 14001. A cumulative reading of these changes may suggest that private regulation is, if not *de jure*, at least *de facto*, substituting public regulation in determining what characteristics products and production/process methods need to match to be fit for trade. In effect, regulation is being privatised.[38]

Developments at the intergovernmental level are most important for the growing power of private standards, and represent a new stage in this privatisation of regulation, by imposing these private standards on governments. This is occurring through the Technical Barriers to Trade (TBT) agreement, and the General Agreement on Trade in Services (GATS), at the World Trade Organisation (WTO). If a company considers that a particular technical standard in a country is too strict for it to sell products or provide services to consumers in that country, it might lobby its government to bring a case against that country at the WTO. In determining whether the standards in question are 'least trade-restrictive' or not, the people on the WTO dispute resolution panel consider 'relevant international standards'. What constitutes a credible international standard is not mentioned in the agreements, but subsequent triennial reviews of the TBT have specified what they look like in a way that reflects ISO's approach, and codes have been drafted for the conduct of standards organisations, with ISO being nominated by the WTO as the registrar for acceptable organisations. Thus, we have a situation where a company bringing a case at the WTO may have itself helped write the international standard that will then be used to judge the appropriateness of a domestic regulation set by government. There is some dispute as to whether this situation applies directly to the GATS agreement as well, in which case it would mean that domestic regulations on standards of water, education and medical service delivery, among others, would be subordinate to the relevant international private standards.[39]

This is not speculation. At the prompting of transnational water companies, ISO has been developing a standard for 'service activities relating to drinking water supply and sewerage'. According to local US water agencies, which voted against ISO developing this standard, standardisation in this area will facilitate global water privatisation, by giving transnational companies a common standard they can then suggest governments adopt for, and certainly not exceed with, their domestic regulations.[40]

Standards development is not free from manipulation, power struggles and opportunistic behaviour. Standards empower the organisations that decide their criteria and control their administration, monitoring and certification. Those who control standards have power over users, and not all users have the same influence in the process of standard development and administration. Standards affect where profits are made along a value chain. Stefano Ponte therefore argues that, rather than simply being a technical instrument to decrease transaction costs associated with asymmetry of information, they should be viewed as a strategic instrument of value chain coordination. This process not only affects people economically but also physically, socially and environmentally, as the standards involve processes of negotiating to what extent to include negative externalities.[41]

This power of standards to govern trade is one reason to explain the current flurry of activity in different countries to establish CSR standards: to define them in ways that accord with the self-interests of those who define them. In the past there has been concern that standards have been developed in order to deflect social and environmental concern, rather than improve performance. This has been the argument of some NGOs over the ISO 14001 standard, which does not require a specific level of environmental performance but prescribes the type of management system that should be adopted, leaving companies to decide their own goals. Might this be repeated for social issues in the context of a CSR standard? The Chair of the Japanese initiative, Professor Iwao Taka, said their standard would 'be flexible enough to respect cultural diversity'. While

IWAO TAKA: CSR STANDARD WILL RESPECT
CULTURAL DIVERSITY

it is important to ensure that the West's dominance in the CSR agenda, and its problematic effects, is addressed, recourse to cultural diversity has often been used to excuse companies choosing their own labour and human rights standards, not those of the international community. This concern led ISO's Advisory Group to reaffirm the place of UN agencies, such as the International Labour Organisation (ILO), in establishing such standards, and that any new standards or documents from ISO should not undermine this. Indeed, there is a case for ISO advising its national members against any standards development that might contravene this principle.

A fundamental problem remains—democracy. As standards development and assessments are political not technical activities, and are increasingly regulating markets and even regulating how governments can regulate markets, we have to question their lack of democratic mandate to do this. This concern was partly expressed in the Advisory Group's recommendation that 'ISO reviews its processes and where necessary makes adjustments to ensure meaningful participation by a fuller range of interested parties'. ISO has made steps to ensure that participants from the South and from non-commercial groups can participate in the process of developing the standard. However, more opportunities for participation will not be enough, as there are basic problems with the organisational structure of ISO that limit its accountability to the millions affected by its decisions. The basic business model of the organisation has relied on selling copies of its standards—a barrier to full transparency. Its members are themselves all dominated by corporate memberships, and are the only organisations with that decision-making power that is invested in voting rights. In addition, its existing standards, on issues such as certification and accreditation, have been developed in ways that accord with the needs of the conformity assessment industry, which may be contrary to the needs and approaches of other stakeholders. For example, a small NGO with local expertise would not be able or willing to change its practices in order to fit with ISO's standards on certification and accreditation processes. Sidestepping this problem, ISO has decided against developing any standard that could be assessed. Nevertheless, the existing institutional infrastructure of ISO and its members is founded on a commercial and objectivist ideology, undermining its ability to deal with complex and contested social and environmental issues.[42]

One member of the Advisory Group, Gordon Shepherd of WWF International, dissented from the final conclusion, particularly stressing concerns about participation and accountability. In addition, he pointed to how the Advisory Group had been tasked

GORDON SHEPHERD: CONCERNS OVER CSR
STANDARD APPLYING TO NGOs

with looking at *corporate* social responsibility, not that of all organisations, yet ISO was now committing to develop a standard for all organisations. That ISO might issue any instrument or advice with a presumption it could apply to NGOs, while not having explored the vast arena of (highly contested) standards, codes and initiatives on NGO accountability, seems to indicate the problems that can arise from the commercial entrepreneurialism at the heart of private standards bodies. Democratic public policy-making cannot be easily managed by an organisation seeking to sell products and services.

4Q2004

October–December

Jem Bendell and Wayne Visser

Profit from poverty?

From child labour to tropical deforestation, practices in the global South, or the 'developing' world, have been central to Western debate and practice of corporate citizenship during the past decade. However, a company's relationship with the broader issue of international development per se has not been a key focus of mainstream corporate citizenship—until now. 2004 witnessed more corporate activity being framed within the context of promoting international development. This is increasingly being discussed as the way in which business can support the Millennium Development Goals (MDGs).

The UN Development Programme (UNDP) and International Business Leaders Forum (IBLF) suggested in 2003 that that there are three broad reasons why it makes sound business sense to contribute to the achievement of the MDGs: first, investing in a sound environment in which to do business; second, managing the direct costs and risks of doing business; third, harnessing new business opportunities.[1] This latter focus, on business opportunities in the global South, received growing attention as the year progressed.

In December 2004, the World Resources Institute held a conference in San Francisco, titled 'Eradicating Poverty through Profit: Making Business Work for the Poor'.[2] Over 800 people from the private, voluntary and government sectors attended, to hear the latest on the opportunities for corporations to source from or sell to disadvantaged people in ways that improve their quality of life while generating profit. The opening plenary saw C.K. Prahalad of the University of Michigan present this proposition, which is developed in *The Fortune at the Bottom of the Pyramid: Eradicating Poverty through Profits*.[3]

He said that there is an undeveloped and untapped market waiting at the bottom of the world economic pyramid—a market of four billion people who live on less than $2 a day. Prahalad cites case studies of rural electrification in Nicaragua, small-scale construction in Mexico, and salt iodisation in India to show how companies can make money from selling to people who have low incomes, while improving their quality of life. He points to transnational companies such as Unilever, Philips, Hewlett-Packard, DuPont and Johnson & Johnson which have developed new business models and strategies aimed at low-income markets. To achieve this requires rethinking basic

C.K. PRAHALAD: THERE IS AN UNDEVELOPED
AND UNTAPPED MARKET WAITING AT THE
BOTTOM OF THE WORLD ECONOMIC PYRAMID

approaches, such as the approach to pricing. Traditional pricing sums the costs of a production and distribution system and then adds on a profit margin, whereas selling to low-income markets requires determining what people are able to pay, deducting a profit margin, and then working out how to deliver the product within that budget. Prahalad emphasised to *The Economist* that these markets 'need to be built not simply entered'.[4]

He suggests that the biggest barrier to success has been the mentality of managers. These markets have been 'invisible to most large companies', Prahalad argued in *For - tune* magazine,

> because few executives can conceive of a market among people that are poor. Business-people think that the poor cannot afford their products and services, and also assume, naively, that the poor have no use for advanced and emerging technology. In fact, sell-ing to the poor is a uniquely powerful way to achieve breakthroughs in products and management practices. The bottom of the economic pyramid is a sandbox for innova-tion. But you have to understand the rules of the game, which can be startlingly differ-ent from what you are used to.[5]

In his book he writes, 'if we stop thinking of the poor as victims or as a burden and start recognizing them as resilient and creative entrepreneurs and value-conscious consumers, a whole new world of opportunity will open up'.[6]

Central to the argument is that companies are not the only ones that can profit from this new approach to business. The cover of his book contends that, if we 'create the capacity to consume', we are 'delivering dignity, empowerment, and choice—not just products' and thereby promoting 'an inclusive new capitalism'. Some of the case stud-ies in the areas of information technology and banking appear to support this view. The experience of microfinance, in particular, is worth some attention. The problem it addresses is the poor's lack of access to even the smallest loans to support their entre-preneurship. Muhammad Yunus founded the world's largest microcredit programme 30 years ago with the establishment of the Grameen Bank in Bangladesh, which has so far distributed more than $3 billion in loans to the poor since the first $27 loan was granted. A key target beneficiary of this has been women, organised into small groups that share the loan and the commitment to repay it. 'These services not only alleviate poverty and enhance growth, but they also consolidate networks of trust and create opportunities for women', said Beatriz Armendariz de Aghion, a visiting Harvard pro-fessor and microfinance expert.[7]

MUHAMMAD YUNUS: FOUNDER OF THE GRAMEEN
BANK IN BANGLADESH

Microfinance institutions have achieved average repayment rates greater than 95%, which is higher than rates for many more financially powerful debtors. Commercial banks are beginning to profitably enter the sector,[8] and governments are beginning to back it. In November, Princess Basma bint Talal of Jordan hosted a conference on the topic, and endorsed its role in promoting development in an article in the *Jordan Times*.[9] In India, the Finance Minister P. Chidambaram said at a conference of micro-credit recipients that the government wanted more done, as 'only 10 per cent of bank credit goes to small borrowers, who account for 72 per cent of the bank accounts'.[10]

PRINCESS BASMA BINT TALAL OF JORDAN: HOSTED
A CONFERENCE ON MICROCREDIT

The development potential arising from new corporate strategies to serve low-income markets makes this an area of interest for the corporate responsibility community. Both the Sustainable Livelihoods Project of the World Business Council for Sustainable Development (WBCSD) and the UN's 'Growing Sustainable Business (GSB) for Poverty Reduction' initiative have focused on this for some time.[11] But the growing importance of this corporate social opportunity, not just corporate social responsibility, was reflected by Prahalad being given the plenary speech at the second academic conference of the Global Compact's Learning Forum in Philadelphia.

Meanwhile a flurry of articles during 2004 reflected an excitement among sections of the mainstream business press that tackling poverty might be the next big thing. The *Wall Street Journal* reported that the bank Citigroup is courting a new clientele— not the 'ultra-rich' anymore, but the 'unbanked'.[12] *Newsweek International* reported that 'consumer-goods makers are realizing they have only one direction to go for growth: down-market'.[13] Prahalad's publishers were keen to stoke this excitement, arguing that

> the ramifications of this book are just beginning. Globally, this is a movement in the making that will affect everyone and the life of the planet. After all, what company or individual entrepreneur wouldn't want to make money, create successful products and services that no one else has thought of, and save lives and our earth at the same time?

True, it would be difficult to think of anyone who wouldn't want to take part in such a win–win world. The publishers are right to suggest that this theory has legs. One reason is that it is an argument that resonates with the priorities of powerful institutions in society—be they business, government or intergovernmental groups; it holds out hope for current patterns of economic globalisation, by suggesting that big business is key to solving the problems of poverty, not a reason for them. As more effort goes into the compilation of case studies, so this theory may grow from a proposition to a statement of fact about how development works. However, case studies do not *prove* a theory. It is important to critically examine some of the claims being made.

First, we should question whether the concept of profitable business with low-income markets is really evidence of engaging those in poverty. There is a great diversity of incomes in the four billion that are often referred to. Some of the most profitable examples are from the high-technology sectors, with reports of booming cell phone sales across Africa[14] and laptop sales across Asia.[15] Yet what does this say about poverty eradication? Cell phones and IT may have multiplier effects on an economy by facilitating more electronic payments and access to financial instruments for some people, but it is not clear how this benefits the malnourished and those without clean water? The argument that wealth will 'trickle down' does not correspond with the experience of many countries, where economic development has led to wealth gushing up to the rich few. Issues of power in supply chains and patterns of ownership are crucial in determining where incomes accrue.

Second, we can question the type of 'development' that is being promoted. One often-quoted example of a successful bottom-of-the-pyramid product is the work of Unilever's subsidiary in India, Hindustan Lever, in selling shampoo. The company had been focusing on the richer consumers and not looking at how to sell to poorer consumers, who were not able to afford a whole bottle of shampoo. They started producing and marketing single-serving shampoo sachets, which were cheap enough for people, particularly young women, to afford. These examples are presented not only as a way of making money but as a form of empowerment for these women. 'When the poor are converted into consumers, they get more than access to products and services. They acquire the dignity of attention and choices from the private sector that were previously reserved for the middle-class and rich', says Prahalad.[16]

However, is this shampoo story really one of empowerment and dignity? Commenting on the uptake of brand-name shampoos sold in single-serving sachets in Thailand, Nicola Bullard, of the NGO Focus on the Global South in Bangkok, pointed towards the marketing machine that creates the demand.

> Thai TV advertising is an endless parade of beautiful young women with long glossy hair swirling without a care—obviously commercial and chemical shampoos are not only better than traditional or local products, but they also make you more beautiful, richer and more modern. Who can blame the village girls for buying the brightly packaged foaming chemicals when they are subjected to such relentless hair-swirling![17]

Claims about empowering people by providing means for them to consume certain products can not be taken at face value.

Prahalad seems to use positive language about the autonomy and potential of the poor, while at the same time reaffirming their identity as the poor that by definition need to change, with outside help, and to change to become more like that outside 'developed' world. The 'developed' are shown to be able to learn from the poor, but only in terms of technical matters, while 'development' and 'progress' are assumed to be about more 'stuff' being bought and sold. There is an implicit recognition in his work that development is more than consumption, but other issues such as self-esteem are then dealt with in terms of consumption choices. There is a problem with expressing on the one hand a recognition and support for the autonomy and potential of the poor, while on the other assuming their basic aspirations, and not considering how those aspirations are shaped by commercial forces.

The third area of debate concerns the environment. The shampoo sachet example automatically raises questions about the increased amount of packaging and transportation, and the comparative environmental impact in comparison to using locally produced cleaning materials, such as soaps, herbs, lemon and vinegar. It may seem a small issue in comparison to acute environmental problems and global challenges such as climate change, but some analyses of sustainable development suggest that all socioeconomic relations are important and local production and consumption is crucial. The bottom-of-the-pyramid (BoP) thesis assumes a different perspective on sustainable development, where environmental problems can be solved through technical and financial advancement. Stuart Hart, professor at the Johnson School of Management at Cornell University, who was the first academic to conceptualise the BoP, argues that environmental concern is effete to the poor, and 'sustainability requires massive reductions in poverty and that means bringing billions of people into the market economy'. Contrary to this, the rural poor are depending on their immediate environment for survival in ways that richer urban dwellers do not, and express their own environmentalism which is integrated into normal practice.[18]

STUART HART: 'SUSTAINABILITY REQUIRES MASSIVE REDUCTIONS IN POVERTY'

A fourth area about which we need more deliberation is the issue of ownership. Should a more inclusive capitalism mean that there are more capitalists, more owners of production? A problem often identified with foreign companies is that they can dislocate indigenous business and so the profits arising out of local economies are repatriated as profits outside of the community. Mr Japheth Katto, the Capital Markets Authority chief executive officer in Uganda, has said that 'corporate social responsibility should be looking at shareholding to have any relevant meaning for Africa'.[19] It is unclear whether growth of BoP market business models from transnational corporations (TNCs) will promote or undermine local capital ownership. In the meantime, any facilitation of TNC trading with BoP markets by development agencies might even compound current problems with North– South supply chains, tax avoidance and anti-competitive practices that are fairly typical of TNCs.

As work on the BoP grows, these questions will become more important. Some will challenge the fundamental basis of this concept, by pointing out that generating a profit from poverty has been the *raison d'être* of the corporation since their original invention to exploit Europe's colonies. Thus BoP work could be seen as just the latest expression of post-colonial imperialism administered by corporations. That position could find support from the way that business researchers and consultants are currently approaching the BoP issue, with the aim of advising and benefiting the TNCs. For example, one management school study of Unilever's Indian subsidiary looked at how the company learned from their local Indian competitor company, Nirma, about how to sell to poorer markets. This was not so much about 'building markets' but about large foreign-owned companies competing with local companies. In addition, one of the key social development benefits of the local company's operation, employment arising from the use of smaller community-level labour-intensive factories, was *not* copied by Unilever.[20]

There is certainly potential, but more research is required on the BoP concept. Questions such as how large corporations might bring their financial, technical and management resources to help local entrepreneurs improve and scale their businesses, and avoid exploitative local middlemen, are important to address. The potential for large corporations to adapt technology to provide clean fuels, safer and more nutritious foods, medicines and communications to people living in poverty could also be looked at. But the potential negative implications must also be explored, by drawing on a range of intellectual disciplines, such as sociology and anthropology. There is some movement. Within the management discipline, IESE in Barcelona is developing a BoP Learning Laboratory. Coordinator Miguel Angel Rodriguez told us that as 'BoP markets are a multidimensional reality, so diverse vantage points are necessary in order for companies to understand this reality and be able to build the right business models and deliver products and services that satisfy people real needs in a sustainable way'. Interdisciplinarity will be key, but also an approach that is not merely instrumentalist, not merely focusing on what is in this for certain types of business.

With BoP ideas, traditional assumptions of corporations as the enemies, unconscious engines, or ungrateful beneficiaries of development are now being challenged, as corporations are now argued to hold potential as conscious agents of development. This makes the interfacing of management studies and international development studies an important activity to help inform policy and practice in a way that delivers for the majority of the world who live in the global South.

A new generation of activism?

The targeting of companies by activists is not new. Indeed, it is a large part of what shapes the corporate citizenship agenda. The past few months, however, have seen some interesting and potentially significant variations on this theme. The first is an example of activism reaching a new level of sophistication. Max Keiser, former stockbroker and founder of investment activist website KarmaBanque.com, has teamed up with the editor of *The Ecologist* magazine, Zak Goldsmith, to launch a hedge fund which aims to halve the value of Coke's share price to $22 dollars in 12 months from its current value of around $40. The campaign website described the basic formula as 'A 4-way relationship that drains Coke's stock: 1) you boycott, 2) we sell-short, 3) victims of Coke get the profits at the expense of, 4) Coke's shareholders'.[21]

The way it works is that, for every 1,000 new boycotters, Keiser's group of inves-
tors/activists promises to increase the size of the fund by £5,000, with all profits
(minus a 2% processing fee) going to the groups/people who are they claim are the
victims of 'bad' companies. In Coca-Cola's case, the allegations mainly concern labour
oppression and human rights abuses in Columbia and environmental impacts in
India. These issues have been high on agenda of a rolling anti-Coke campaign which
saw protests in various cities in India, the UK and the USA during November and
December 2004. Keiser is also forthright about a bigger issue, which has to do with
the so-called cultural imperialism of America, saying: 'There's general anti-American
feeling out there which is growing all over the world . . . People now associate Coke's
brand with the American brand and they are rejecting it across the globe. The company has never been more vulnerable.'[22]

The targeting of Coke goes beyond mere popular 'anti' sentiment. It has also been
selected because it scores high on KarmaBanque's Boycott Vulnerability Rating (BVR),
which is a measure of which stocks would be most negatively impacted by a boycott.
The BVR is derived in turn from a Boycott Profitability Ratio (calculated by dividing a
company's current market capitalisation by its trailing 12 months of gross sales) and
the Short Interest Ratio (which measures what percentage of a companies stock is held
in short positions). Coca-Cola's BVR is quoted on the website as 4.53, which is regarded
as significant, but by no means the highest. BVR Leaders are listed as Ryanair (10.46),
Microsoft (9.91), Starbucks (7.70), Pfizer (5.96) and Eli Lilly (5.64).[23] Coca-Cola
spokesman Ben Deutsch told Reuters that 'This so-called campaign is based on bla-
tant falsehoods . . . It's unfortunate that anyone would attempt to hurt Coca-Cola
shareholders by waging such an effort without knowing and recognizing the facts.'[24]

Activist concerns about business–society relations also found increasing expression
through 'corporate satire'. December 2004 saw the 20th anniversary of the Bhopal
chemical disaster in India where 3,500 people died because of a chemical leak from a
Union Carbide factory. That company was taken over by Dow Chemical, and on the
anniversary BBC featured an interview with whom it thought was a spokesman for the
company. The 'spokesman' stated that Dow accepted it had a responsibility for the victims and would establish a compensation fund. The BBC had been hoaxed by a group
called 'The Yes Men', who pretend to represent corporate organisations in order to say
what they think those organisations should be saying and doing.[25] The stunt worked
in that it made the anniversary headline news, with some journalists going beyond the
BBC-got-it-wrong story to consider what has happened since the disaster. The fallout
on the chemical industry included a range of voluntary initiatives on environment,
health and safety, and legislation in many states, such as the Community Right to Know
Act in the US. However, as the International Right to Know campaign points out, in
many countries, including in India, communities still do not have legally required
access to information on toxic substances stored or processed in local factories.[26] The
issue was explored in some detail in a report from SustainAbility, launched on the
anniversary, which concluded that corporate liability is, nevertheless, increasing in
many jurisdictions, posing risks which companies should manage by being more
proactive on their societal relations.[27]

'The Yes Men' group was the focus of a documentary of the same name that was
released in cinemas in the Northern autumn of 2004. Another film in the corporate
satire genre was a hit at box offices in Canada. *The Corporation* brought together three

key themes. First, that corporations are so powerful in societies today that they influence almost every aspect of our lives. Second, that they are an invention that protects people from the consequences of their actions, while giving the same rights as individuals to these artificial 'persons'. Third, that they have created an environment that rewards characteristics and behaviours that clinical psychologists define as being those of the psychopath. These themes have been developed previously,[28] but the power of film is to reach a mass audience and to turn this political comment into comedy. Satire has always been a powerful political weapon and 'corporate satire' may be no different. The *Daily Telegraph* said 'it may do for big business what *Jaws* did for sharks'. One of the film's makers released a book to coincide, which provides more detail of the arguments, and ventures some suggested responses to help make the corporation more tame and sane.[29]

Multinationals do sometimes hit back. During October 2004, ExxonMobil was successful in obtaining a court-ordered ban on Greenpeace staging protests against the company anywhere in the US for seven years. The agreement, which Greenpeace has signed, is believed to be the first of its kind involving a US company and a protest group. It is the final outcome of a case filed against Greenpeace after a protest approximately 18 months ago at an ExxonMobil facility in Texas resulted in breaches of the law and damage to the company's property. The judgement covers corporate property, filling stations and any event sponsored by the company or involving company officers. Any breach would bring the automatic risk of fines and imprisonment.

ExxonMobil is quoted on the FT.com website as saying that 'The Greenpeace break-in should not be mistaken as following "the right of non-violent protest" . . . Greenpeace breaks laws not because its members are subject to unjust laws but because Greenpeace has failed by democratic means to get its way.' Sarah Burton, Greenpeace International's legal consultant, counters that 'The US government, not the city or the state, was seeking to curtail the entire organisation. I think this gives quite a clear signal, whether to industry or to others, that people who take direct action are fair game.' While ExxonMobil claims to be 'satisfied' with the judgement, Greenpeace says it will continue its campaign against ExxonMobil within the limits set by the Texas court.[30]

Those who do not appreciate the current trends towards greater focus on business responsibility are also hitting back. One initiative, called CSR Watch,[31] claims to be 'Your Eye on the Anti-Business Movement'. It describes its rationale as follows:

> Businesses are increasingly under attack by the anti-business movement, i.e. social activists operating under the banners of Corporate Social Responsibility (CSR) and Socially Responsible Investing (SRI). These activists threaten businesses, investor interests, jobs and the free enterprise system. This site monitors and comments on the anti-business movement.

Despite developments in CSR over the past years, events in 2004 reminded us that business–society relations remain a contested field. Corporate citizenship and CSR remain essentially contested concepts, like democracy and justice.[32] This reminds us that debates about the meaning of concepts relate closely to debates about their application.[33]

New premium on hot air

The last quarter of 2004 saw climate change hit the headlines, owing to its growing influence on politics and economics. In the past 60 years the Earth's temperature has increased by 0.6°C. Growing concern has not yet registered on the global thermometer, with global emissions of the greenhouse gas carbon dioxide having climbed about 10% since the world leaders were awoken to this threat to humanity at the 1992 Earth Summit in Rio de Janeiro.[34] The media is somewhat immune to these dire portents of pending doom, but Russia's ratification of the Kyoto Protocol in November 2004 provided this 1997 United Nations-brokered accord with the critical mass it needed to enter into force, and sparked a renewed debate about the world's response.[35] From 16 February 2005, the Protocol binds its 36 ratifying countries, representing 61% of the developed nations' greenhouse gas emissions, to specific reduction targets which on average will cut their emissions to 5.2% below 1990 levels by 2012.

This landmark move returns the spotlight to the United States' and Australia's refusal to ratify the Protocol on the grounds that it will be too costly for their economies and that it fails to bind any developing countries to emission reduction targets. The US government, for instance, claims that the treaty would cost nearly $400 billion to implement and result in almost five million job losses.[36] By contrast, the book *Win - ning the Oil Endgame*,[37] by Rocky Mountain Institute's Amory Lovins among others, suggests that their proposed energy strategy for 'profitably breaking oil's stranglehold on our civilization' would save a net $70 billion a year, revitalise key industries and rural America, create a million jobs, and enhance security.

AMORY LOVINS: BREAKING OIL'S STRANGLEHOLD
WOULD ACTUALLY SAVE BILLIONS

The International Energy Agency's *World Energy Outlook*,[38] released in October 2004, reminds us that the Protocol is not in itself enough, with developing-country impacts growing fast. According to the report, world energy demand will grow by 59% by 2030 and fossil fuel energy sources (oil, gas and coal) will supply 82% of that reference case demand, up from 80% in 2002. Two-thirds of the new demand will come from India and China alone, neither of which are signatories to the Kyoto treaty. And China's greenhouse gas emissions, reported to the United Nations for the first time in November 2004, were already 2.6 billion tonnes of carbon dioxide in 1994.[39]

The equity-based counter-argument is that Western countries should pay for the legacy costs that their development has imposed on global society. According to WWF's *Living Planet Report*, also launched in October 2004, the global Ecological Footprint has grown by 70% between 1970 and 2000, of which the energy footprint, dominated by fossil fuels, was the fastest-growing component, increasing by nearly 700% since

1961. Per person energy footprints in 2001 show a fourteenfold difference between high- and low-income countries.[40]

As a result of this insatiable thirst for energy by the developed countries to fuel their own development, today, the US, representing around 5% of the world's population, emits around 25% of global greenhouse gases, which translates into 19 tons of carbon dioxide emissions a person a year, while India, representing around 15% of the world's population, emits only 2% of global greenhouse gases, or 0.8 tons of carbon dioxide a person a year. Similarly, the greenhouse gas generated by one Australian equals that of approximately 20 Indians or 10 Chinese.[41]

Despite Russia's ratification and the entry into force of the Kyoto Protocol, the US has maintained its position that it will strive to achieve President Bush's stated target of an 18% reduction in greenhouse gas intensity by 2012, using a combination of economic incentives and technology investments.[42] Given this emphasis on voluntary action within the world's largest economy, a flurry of reports have been published in the past quarter which show why industry should act, and in many cases how it is already doing so effectively. For instance, The Climate Group has conducted research into the greenhouse gas reductions and associated monetary savings of climate change actions by 22 companies, 13 cities and 10 regional initiatives from Australia, Canada, Europe, Japan, the US and the UK. The report, called *Carbon Down, Profits Up*, finds that five of the companies surveyed have achieved greenhouse gas reductions of 60% or more (DuPont, Alcan, BT, IBM and Norske Canada), with combined savings of over US$5.5 billion.[43]

Other reports released at this time carry a similar theme: *A Climate of Innovation: Northeast Business Action to Reduce Greenhouse Gases* by the World Resources Institute highlights actions of nine diverse northeast-based US corporations (Bristol-Myers Squibb, Citigroup, Eastman Kodak, General Electric, Johnson & Johnson and Pfizer);[44] *US Business Actions to Address Climate Change: Case Studies of Five Industry Sectors* by the Sustainable Energy Institute and Numark Associates describes actions in five US industrial sectors (aluminium, chemicals, electric power, forestry and paper, and pharmaceuticals);[45] and the Annual Review of the Climate RESOLVE Program by the Business Roundtable stresses that 70% of its member companies—drawn from every sector of the US economy—have embraced voluntary actions to address greenhouse gas emissions.[46]

The second reason for climate change being so much in the spotlight was the fact that the European Union's Emission Trading Scheme (EU ETS) was scheduled for its launch on 1 January 2005. The EU ETS affects 12,000 installations across the continent. This follows from the precedent set by the UK Emissions Trading Scheme, which began in March 2002 when 31 organisations voluntarily took on emission reduction targets. As a result of this and other initiatives, according to the New York-based emissions trading firm Natsource, European countries already traded 2.5 million tons of emissions allowances in 2003.[47]

The EU plans to use the ETS as the primary vehicle for achieving its emission reduction targets, thus giving effect to the intentions of the Kyoto Protocol. Recent European Commission studies suggest that this can be achieved at an annual cost of between €2.9 billion and €3.7 billion, which is less than 0.1% of gross domestic product in the EU, compared to costs of €6.8 billion without the ETS.[48]

Not everyone is so optimistic, however. In a report entitled *The European Union Emis-sions Trading Scheme: A Challenge for Industry or Just an Illusion?* Ernst & Young has surveyed 204 European companies to determine their level of preparedness for the EU ETS and found that only 39% believed the EU ETS would achieve its emission reduction targets, with 50% claiming to have dealt with the consequences of emissions trading in detail and 61% having identified measures to reduce emissions.[49] A study by UK-based Enviros Consulting seems to support their scepticism, claiming that, on the basis of allowances allocated to existing facilities covered by the ETS, European industry will be allowed to increase annual carbon dioxide emissions by 5% during the first phase of the scheme (2005–2007) relative to their emissions in 2000.[50] Given the urgent need for absolute reductions in greenhouse gas emissions if we are to reduce climate change, we may question whether the ETS says more about contemporary ideologies and political realities than it does about our collective ability to protect our common security. The UK's Chief Scientist Sir David King has stated that 'climate change is the most severe problem that we are facing today, more serious even than the threat of terrorism'.[51] A trading system where countries could sell their 'rights' to produce weapons of mass destruction to those states that wanted them would not be viewed as a sensible policy response to that particular threat—and, on its own, a trading system does not appear to be a serious attempt to manage the global threat of climate change. It is more difficult to demonise an enemy when that enemy is found within, in one's own assumptions, routines and desires. Yet our future depends on that kind of introspection, especially by the most powerful in society.

SIR DAVID KING: 'CLIMATE CHANGE IS THE MOST SEVERE PROBLEM THAT WE ARE FACING TODAY'

Over and above the issue of whether the EU ETS will meet its targets, the new market in emissions looks set to spark off a new debate about how this affects free trade. For instance, German energy giant EnBW has filed a formal complaint with the commission's competition and environment departments. Independent experts employed by EnBW estimate that the German trading scheme will result in a $1.2 billion competitive disadvantage for the period 2005–2020.[52]

What is not in dispute, however, is that the use of market-based instruments to tackle climate change is mushrooming. According to Natsource, global carbon dioxide trading rose from 29 million tons in 2002 to 78 million tons in 2003 and is expected to double again for 2004.[53] The effect of Russia's ratification has been clear and immediate, with about 670,000 tonnes of carbon emissions traded in the first week of October 2004, according to Point Carbon, compared with the record one million tonnes in September 2004 and fewer than 50,000 tonnes a month earlier in the year.[54]

Apart from a rise in market trading activity, the past quarter saw other manifestations of the trend: Toyota, Sony and 33 other Japanese companies and industry organisations announced plans to establish a US$135 million fund for buying greenhouse gas emission rights from foreign businesses; and Sterling Waterford Securities made public its intention to list instruments derived from carbon credits on the JSE Securities Exchange SA in South Africa.[55] A more tangible move to actually reduce emissions came from the telecoms giant BT, which made the world's biggest purchase of 'green' electricity, saving emissions equivalent to the amount of carbon dioxide produced by over 100,000 cars or 50,000 homes—the size of a small town.[56]

BJØRN LOMBORG: COPENHAGEN CONSENSUS LISTS CLIMATE CHANGE AS THE LOWEST SPENDING PRIORITY

What we shouldn't expect any time soon is consensus within the debate, as two reports make clear. A group of economists, including three Nobel prize winners, brought together under the auspices of the so-called 'Copenhagen Consensus' by controversial environmentalism critic Bjørn Lomborg and asked to prioritise how money should be spent on helping the world's poor, listed climate change as the lowest spending priority of 32 of the most critical global challenges.[57] In contrast, a report called *Up in Smoke?* by the Working Group on Climate Change and Development, a coalition of 18 environmental and development groups, warned of the economic implications of climate change on the world's poor, calling for cuts in emissions of 60–80% on 1990 levels. The report was endorsed, among others, by Nobel Prize winner Archbishop Desmond Tutu, who remarked that climate change is 'detrimental to humanity at large and especially to the most vulnerable of the world's communities'.[58]

Perhaps it is heartening to know that academia is not being left out of the debate. The Imperial College, London, has just launched a leading international, peer-reviewed journal on responses to climate change, called *Climate Policy*. The journal presents a wide range of refereed research and analysis that address the broad spectrum of policy issues raised by the prospect of changes in the global climate.[59]

ARCHBISHOP DESMOND TUTU: CLIMATE CHANGE IS DETRIMENTAL TO HUMANITY AT LARGE

The status quo on sustainability reporting

Corporate sustainability reporting was another area in which several market developments and a fresh batch of research converged over the last quarter of 2004. This
allowed us not only to see how this phenomenon is evolving but also to question the
limitations of its reach and value. In addition, it highlighted the still-raging debate
about the most appropriate format for corporate sustainability reporting, with some
arguing for stand-alone published sustainability reports, others favouring integration
within annual financial reports, and still others claiming that information on corporate websites is sufficient and preferable.

Reflecting the first approach, in November 2004, SustainAbility, the United Nations
Environment Programme (UNEP) and Standard & Poor's launched their joint global
benchmarking report, *Risk and Opportunity: Best Practice in Non-financial Reporting*, in
which 50 of the world's best stand-alone sustainability reports were analysed. Positive
findings included that the average score of the reporters (50%) represented a 70%
increase on scores in 2002, and that 52% of the top 50 reporters were new entrants,
many from the developing countries such as South Africa and Brazil. Also noteworthy was that 94% were using the Global Reporting Initiative (GRI) Guidelines and 78%
included a discussion of external assurance, although their approaches to independent
verification still varied greatly. The biggest challenge, it seems, remains how to link
sustainability and financial issues, with only 6% of the sample able to recognise the
social and environmental risks posed to company balance sheets.[60] Report co-author
John Elkington said,

> Is the glass of non-financial reporting (and wider sustainability reporting) currently
> half full, as enthusiasts might argue, or half empty, as some critics allege? The evidence
> suggests a positive assessment, though there are still major gaps to be closed in the
> linked fields of disclosure, reporting and communication.[61]

This research complemented the findings of another global survey launched earlier
in the year in which the Association of Chartered Certified Accountants (ACCA) and
CorporateRegister.com analysed nearly 5,000 non-financial reports issued since
1990.[62] According to this research, the number of sustainability/non-financial reports
have increased from fewer than 100 in 1993 to more than 1,500 in 2003, with external assurance rising from 17% in 1993 to 40% in 2003. Most reports are environmental in focus (42% in the period 2001–2003) and are published by European companies
(58% in the period 1990–2003). The reporting boom appears to be levelling off globally. Growth in Europe is slowing, North America is static, Japan and Australasia
remain dynamic, and only South Africa shows significant activity in Africa and the
Middle East.

The *2004 KPMG Survey on Integrated Sustainability Reporting in South Africa* was
launched in December 2004, and analysed the disclosure practices of the 154 companies listed on the Johannesburg Stock Exchange's All Share Index. Overall, 64% of the
companies were found to have been providing some level of sustainability data within
their public reports. Twenty-two companies (14%), of which the majority reside in the
Resources and Financial Services sectors (nine and six, respectively), produce independent 'Stand-alone' reports, while a further 77 companies (50%) produce 'Combined'
reports, whereby the companies provide some level of sustainability reporting within

their annual financial reports.[63] Meanwhile, in December 2004, Deloitte & Touche also announced Dreher Breweries as the winner of its Green Frog Award 2004 for environmental reporting in Central and Eastern Europe.[64]

The second approach to sustainability reporting was given a boost in the UK by the government's use of Clause 13 of the Companies (Audit, Investigations and Community Enterprises) Act to make the first reporting standards for a mandatory Operating Financial Review (OFR). Under the government proposals, announced in November 2004, quoted companies will be required to prepare a statutory OFR for the first time for financial years beginning on or after 1 April 2005. Crucially for the sustainability reporting agenda, the new proposals specify that the review: 'shall include information about the employees of the company and its subsidiary undertakings, environmental matters and social and community matters'; and 'shall include analysis using financial and other key performance indicators, including information relating to environmental matters and employee matters'.[65]

CTN Communications' *2004 CSR Online Survey* launched in October 2004 put the third approach to sustainability reporting formats under the spotlight, examining the Internet disclosure practices of FTSE companies. Its findings show that 98 of the FTSE 100 and 131 of the FTSE 250 companies include CSR information on their website and 81 and 59 respectively include a full report. On the other hand, 121 companies (2 FTSE 100 and 119 FTSE 250) make no mention of CSR at all on their websites.[66]

In terms of developments in the sustainability reporting framework itself, the GRI remains the leading facilitative organisation, with over 600 companies having registering their use of the Sustainability Reporting Guidelines with the GRI secretariat by November 2004. October saw the beginning of a round of multi-stakeholder consultation to innovate the Guidelines and aspects of the overall reporting framework. Innovations in the next generation of the Guidelines ('G3') will aim at broadening the uptake of the GRI Framework, both in geographic terms and total numbers, and deepening the level of consistency among existing GRI-based reports.

Meanwhile, work continues in parallel on various GRI sector supplements and other guidance documents. Specifically over the last quarter, the consultation period on the draft Boundaries Protocol ended and two GRI publications were launched—the *High 5! Handbook*, which is GRI's publication for SMEs (small and medium-sized enterprises) on sustainability reporting, and a linkage document to help businesses assess and report how their activities are contributing to the achievement of the Millennium Development Goals (MDGs). The latter claims to build on the UNDP and IBLF resource document, mentioned earlier, by suggesting indicators from the GRI Guidelines that can help businesses to measure and communicate their contributions.[67]

2005

Foreword

Jules Peck
Global Policy Advisor, WWF [1]

I'm told that 2005 was a good year for wine. I'd say it's also been a good year for maturing the debate about the role of corporations in society.

The bitter taste of Enron, Parmalat and other corporate scandals, and the strong flavour of popular systemic critiques in the book *No Logo* and the film *The Corporation* have fermented more creative thinking on how to resolve the clash between financial and social pressures on companies.

For instance, in 2005 the oil giant BP began teaching its customers about their carbon footprints while at the same time calling on government and other companies to do more to solve climate change and support those companies that are taking action.

Major financial institutions such as HSBC, Allianz and others have been calling on their peers to engage with sustainability. At events throughout the year, such as the EU corporate responsibility conference, the clarion call is now much the same from NGOs, investors and companies—'it's the market stupid'.

Thoughtful people in all sectors recognise the need to change the frameworks within which business operates, in order to make responsible and sustainable activities more financially viable. Despite this emerging consensus, many governments seem deaf to it and the implications for public policy, and afraid to act in case they upset their friends in stale trade associations such as the Confederation of British Industry.

Some will remain cynical of corporate motives but others detect a change in the old 'regulate or deregulate' debate. Sophisticated companies are recognising that they cannot shift their business models to more sustainable ones without the support of government, consumers and investors. This Annual Review describes how the cutting edge of corporate citizenship is now about working with those three groups to engineer the business case for sustainability and create new market opportunities.

True leadership will come from refocusing efforts from communicating in sustainability reports read only by specialists, to speaking the right language to these key audiences. It will come through transparent and accountable third-generation lobbying[1] of governments, encouraging them to re-engage and recognise the need to step in to address market failures. It will come from empowering consumers to become part of the shift to sustainable consumption (and thus sustainable production) through responsible marketing and advertising.

And it will come from innovative ways to engage with investors so that they give companies more free rein to act in the longer-term interests of people and planet. This challenge requires professionals in all sectors to see beyond the walls of their organisations and work together on generating systemic change. In this review, Jem Bendell highlights how some executives are beginning to express such 'transcending leader-ship'. The review also describes how many people and organisations are not transcending narrow self-interests, being trapped in cellars of separative thinking and short-termism. If Milton Freedman was right that companies are unable to be moral, then we need to reinvent them and the rules that define them so that they can be.

We would do well to revisit Adam Smith's sentiments on morals and markets to rethink what it really is we ultimately want—increased economic growth or maximum well-being? If the latter is the case, then we also need to question whether our current political and economic systems and their operators are up to the job. As Bendell says in this review, if we want to change the way business does business, we have to change the way money makes money. As such, working to create greater 'capital accountability' must become a central part of future efforts at systemic change, within the corporate responsibility arena.

Transforming capitalism to a system that enables prosperity in harmony with each other and the planet is the greatest challenge of our time. Today, companies are the most pervasive and persuasive communicators and have a key role to play in this great transition towards a sustainable society. Corporate executives urgently need to innovate in how they use their influence and show moral leadership. The stories and analysis in this review will hopefully encourage us all to engage with this task with greater maturity and, perhaps, a youthful fizz. After all, can there be anything more invigorating than playing a part in the most important challenge of our time?

Introduction

The generation of transcending leadership for transforming capitalism

Jem Bendell

In 2005, another Jem, prettier than me and with a better voice, had a hit singing 'Who are they, where are they, how could they know all this? I'm sorry, so sorry, I'm sorry we do this'. It was about four months before I actually paid any attention to the lyrics, such is my low expectation of modern pop.

I had thought 'Live 8' was as good as it gets with the social conscience and commentary of our contemporary stars. But the success of singers such as Jack Johnson in 2005 suggests that singing about the human condition is back in fashion. One of my favourite tracks of his reflects our complicity in supporting the mass media we experience: 'It was you, it was me, it was every man, we've all got the blood on our hands. We only receive what we demand and if hell is what we want, then hell is what we'll have.'

This awareness that we co-create the systems we live in, and that we all have a hope, however stifled, to work on what matters for something greater than ourselves, has been at the heart of Lifeworth's agenda since 2001. Achieving a synergy between our 'life' in terms of its true nature and purpose, and our 'worth' in terms of our ability to earn a living, is embodied in the name we chose.

When this Annual Review was first published, it marked our fifth anniversary, and as such provides a broader analysis and prognosis than previous Annual Reviews. In so doing, it reflects a new confidence of knowledge and purpose within people in some of the business, public policy and academic networks we engage with. This confidence arises from a new sense of urgency, greater experience, and self-discovery. One reason for the sense of urgency is that environmental problems have fast moved from prediction to reality, while the rate of damage is increasing rapidly with industrialisation in the East. The stubbornness of poverty in the face of numerous international commitments to make a difference, including the Millennium Development Goals, adds to this sense that widespread results must come now.

In addition, the contemporary emphasis and initiative on voluntary corporate responsibility is now a decade old, with 2005 being the tenth anniversary of Ken Saro-Wiwa's execution in Nigeria, which added to the public outcry over the oil company Shell at the time. Participants in and observers of voluntary corporate responsibility initiatives have had some time to understand the potential and limitations of this area. With this experience, the commercial difficulties of making companies and markets more sustainable and responsible are more widely known. As Jules Peck argues in the Foreword to this review, 'Sophisticated companies are recognising that they cannot shift their business models to more sustainable ones without the support of government, consumers and investors.'

Whereas this argument used to lead to business people passing the buck, now it is leading them to explore how they may be able to engender that support from government, consumers and investors. They are exploring how to act together to cultivate a business case for sustainable behaviour, in order to create systemic change in society. It is this approach that guides the new strategy of the corporate responsibility team at one of the sponsors of this Annual Review. Another reason for the new confidence of knowledge and purpose may relate to self-discovery.

People who work on corporate responsibility can be regarded as a social movement, and a new profession. As a profession, it is very new, and there are no professional institutes for corporate responsibility practitioners that have the support and participation of large numbers of those practitioners. Professional culture, identity and purpose are still evolving. Many people came from not-for-profit backgrounds, and many started in this field as young professionals. Consequently, people have been learning how to act and behave in this new profession, and cautious about expressing themselves fully. They have been on a journey of self-discovery.

Now, with some years under their belt, many people have greater confidence in their more fundamental assessments of situations and in expressing their views. This new confidence is leading to more assertive work that aims at larger transformations of organisations and societies than have been attempted within the corporate responsibility arena in the past. In 2005, a range of activities suggested that more of us are not prepared to merely tinker with the edges of corporations and capitalism and instead will work toward systemic transformations. The growing focus on responsible lobbying responds to the need to reconfigure the relationship between business and government in order for government to intervene for longer-term commercial and societal interests and not be swayed by short-term expediency of certain companies and industries.

The greater popularity of concepts such as 'social entrepreneurship' and 'authentic business' reflects the desire of people to work in ways that are good for humanity, rather than merely being less bad. The rapid advances with collective action in the financial sector to change its integration of social and environmental value also reflect a growing desire to change the basic framework conditions that companies and their executives have to operate within.

Ultimately, this may lead to a fundamental rethinking and eventual reordering of the rights and duties of capital. Certainly, the private financial sector looks set to become the focus of more NGO campaigns and projects. We may be on the cusp of a 'capital turn' in civil society that will have as significant effect on business as the 'corporate turn' of civil society in the early 1990s, when NGOs began engaging business more energetically. Individual people, acting together, are creating these changes. That may seem so obvious, but the implications can be overlooked.

One implication is that we need to know the nature and action of such people, to learn from them, to nurture them and to inspire others to become like them. One characteristic is that they are all crossing boundaries, whether organisational or cultural, to try new ways of working to serve wider society. 'Crossing a threshold' is one concept that the etymological study of the origins of the word 'leadership' suggests. 'Marking a path' is another.

The topic of leadership is well established in the fields of business and organisational behaviour and therefore provides a useful frame for understanding and communicating the qualities of those who are marking a path towards a sustainable and just society by crossing the thresholds of organisations, industries, countries, cultures and generations. Traditionally, analysts and educators on corporate leadership have assumed that it involves leading people towards the goal of their employer, the company.

Mark Gerzon of the Mediators Foundation describes this as a focus on 'leadership within borders', when what the world needs is 'leaders beyond borders'. This means people who can see across borders created by others, such as the borders of their job, and engage others in dialogue and action to address systemic problems. We can call this 'transcending leadership'. It is a form of leadership that transcends the boundaries of one's professional role and the limits of ones own situation to engage people on collective goals. It is a form of leadership that transcends a limited conception of self, as the individual leader identifies with ever greater wholes.

As Albert Einstein wrote,

> the human being experiences oneself, one's thoughts and feelings as something separated from the rest—a kind of optical delusion of our consciousness. This delusion is a kind of prison for us, restricting us to our personal desires and to affection for a few persons nearest us. Our task must be to free ourselves from this prison by widening our circle of compassion to embrace all living creatures and the whole of nature in its beauty.'[2]

Ultimately, transcending leadership is a form of action that transcends the need for a single leader, by helping others to transcend their limited states of consciousness and concern and inspire them to also lead for the common good. Writing about organisational learning and change, Peter Senge argues that to create change in organisational systems requires leadership qualities that arise from an awareness of systems and one's own connectedness to those.[3] This is even more the case for the challenge of societal learning and change, as it requires an understanding of interorganisational relations and whole social, economic, political, economic and cultural processes.

Therefore, people who move beyond organisational and personal transformations to leading societal transformation are praised as 'Alchemists' by David Rooke and Bill Torbert, in an article for the *Harvard Business Review*.[4] Perhaps the best modern example of transcending leadership is Mohandas Gandhi, who aroused and elevated the hopes and demands of millions of Indians and whose life and personality were enhanced in the process. He called on us to understand our connectedness to 'all that lives', and identify with ever greater wholes.

The transcending leaders of today are not necessarily charismatic figures in positions of institutional authority. There is often a mistaken assumption that leadership is about being a boss. Today's transcending leaders are those who cross boundaries to influence society for the better, and operate at all levels of organisation or none. When I think of people who exhibit these qualities, I do not think of senior people within the United Nations system, with which much of my work was during the period covered by this volume.

Instead I think of people such as James Gifford, who came to the UN as an intern and quietly developed a responsible investment initiative that is helping shift trillions of dollars of assets behind the sustainability transition. Or Alisa Clarke, who created a network of UN staff and consultants to promote revitalisation and reform of the UN system from the bottom up, by focusing on the importance of personal values in one's profession. I think of Mike Zeidler, who created an Association of Sustainability Practitioners to support people who seek to transform organisations towards sustainability through their work.[5] And I think of Bill Zhang, who has been helping the sustainability movement in China to grow. All are quietly acting for the collective.

In 2005, another transcending leader I had the privilege to know passed away. His achievement in building institutions yet not being very bothered about his or others' 'position power', his interest in crossing boundaries and experimenting with the new, and his commitment to social change, made Richard Sandbrook someone I deeply respected. Jonathon Porritt wrote in the *Guardian*,

> the essence of this extraordinary person lay in his irrepressible humanitarianism. Though he loved to poke fun at all and sundry, deliberately cultivating a world-weary scepticism to strip away self-importance and cant wherever he met it (especially among his colleagues), his heart never stopped beating for the world's oppressed.[6]

The strength of his legacy embodies the ultimate goal of transcending leadership. Our challenge today is to cultivate these qualities in each other: to learn ways of achieving states of connection, and ways of implementing our compassion. There are skills to learn, experiences to hear about and niches to find. In 2005 a variety of organisations did useful work in this regard. The Oxford Leadership Academy[7] and Shambhala Authentic Leadership Institute[8] continued to help top executives to tune in to their desire to serve society. The Society for Organisational Learning continued to expand outside the United States and bring more people into a dialogue about systemic change.[9] Forum for the Future and LEAD completed their first cross-cultural and cross-sectoral leadership development programme.[10]

All these initiatives are helping to inspire the leadership needed for global social change. In business, and particularly in the field of corporate responsibility, transcending leadership translates into engaging all relevant stakeholders in collective action to change market frameworks to make responsible and sustainable enterprise more financially viable. It involves employing those business functions that communicate with stakeholders, such as public affairs, investor relations, human resources, supply chain management, marketing and advertising, in pursuit of systemic change. Recognising that capitalism is the larger system within which we operate, transforming capitalism to a sustainable and just means of socioeconomic organising is the key challenge for real business leaders.

Our own work at Lifeworth these past five years focused on this goal of corporate executives playing a role in systemic change. We have pursued it, rather limitedly, through research, strategy and policy advice, writing and educating, especially in the area of cross-sectoral relations and dialogue, as well as through life coaching, and providing career and recruitment consulting in the corporate responsibility field. Our understanding has been that much of the emphasis in the professional services field focuses on the organisation—not on the person within it or the system around it.

We believe that the most important work today is both deeply personal and highly systemic. People need to find ways of succeeding in their organisations, by transforming those organisations to succeed in societies, by transforming those societies to succeed in the world. More simply: people need to be able to serve the world while not bankrupting their organisation or getting the sack! After five years we are now planning to take our work to another level.

Therefore in 2006 we are co-creating a study circle on 'Consciousness, Leadership and Humanity'. This circle is open to anyone who seeks to cultivate this 'transcending leadership' in their organisation or through their work, and who can contribute substantively to a process of elucidating the principles, purpose and practices of such leadership, including how to cultivate and sustain it. The project will be open source, with all intellectual outputs made freely available.

I hope you find this Annual Review helpful. It both reviews and embodies the new confidence of a profession and movement that arises out of an awareness of serving something greater than itself. I hope that 2005 comes to be remembered as a time that began the generation of 'Transcending Leadership for Transforming Capitalism'. Now that would be worth singing about.

1Q2005

January–March

Jem Bendell and John Manoochehri

Professionalisation: a new approach required

In January 2005, the International Organisation for Standardisation announced the establishment of a group to develop a global standard on social responsibility. The ISO Working Group on Social Responsibility had its first meeting in March 2005 in Salvador, Brazil, establishing a workplan culminating in the issue of standardised guiding principles for the field of social responsibility. This represents an ISO reference for the business community to match its weights, measures, standardised grades of aluminium, and 15,000 other global standards. The development of this standard is the latest step in the growing 'professionalisation' of CSR service provision in the corporate social responsibility (CSR) and corporate citizenship fields.

In addition to the development of standards for management practice, there are increasing moves to standardise the practice of those working in this field. At the end of 2004, AccountAbility and the International Register of Certified Auditors (IRCA) came together to launch the world's first individual certification scheme in the field of sustainability assurance. The so-called 'Certified Sustainability Assurance Practitioner Program' will help auditors—both internal as well as external to companies—provide quality assurance to sustainability reports.

This initiative came hard on the heels of a new CSR Academy in the UK, which developed a 'CSR Competency Framework' for managers.[1] This outlines a set of core characteristics that CSR managers should exhibit, and is intended to help managers improve their practices both within the specific CSR profession and also in other specialisms where business–society issues are relevant. This is because 'in today's business environment,' says Andrew Dunnett of CSR Academy, 'managers across the business require the skills and competencies to take into account an increasing range and complexity of factors relating to the financial, environmental and social implications of business operations.'[2]

History teaches us of the mixed blessing when individuals and organisations come together to establish, improve and ultimately protect a profession. On the positive side, they provide the opportunity for people to share knowledge and expertise and maintain standards through peer review. They also provide a form of guarantee for consumers of professional services that the provider is of a certain standard, with particular

ANDREW DUNNETT OF CSR ACADEMY:
PROMOTING THE 'CSR COMPETENCY
FRAMEWORK' FOR MANAGERS

training, qualifications and experience. However, this social benefit from professions and professional associations is not without its kickback. 'Professions strike a bargain with society in which they exchange competence and integrity against the trust of client and community, relative freedom from lay supervision and interference, protection against competition as well as substantial remuneration and higher social status', commented the sociologist Rueschemeyer, some 20 years ago.[3] A body of work on the sociology of professions demonstrates that the definition of what is professional training, qualification, experience and practice is not just a technical exercise.

Some see professionalisation less as an issue of quality and more one of self-interest. 'All professions are conspiracies against the laity', wrote George Bernard Shaw in 1906. Today many regard the development of professions as projects of occupational closure. This means making it more difficult to get into the profession, thereby restricting supply of a service and driving up prices and remuneration. Professions can therefore play a role in perpetuating class divisions,[4] which could become a key issue for professionalisation in the area of business–society relations. Further, professionalisation of the CSR domain is likely to filter out the more creative wavelength of idea generation, to challenge fast-moving changes and weigh them with new administrative burdens, and to insulate itself from voices critical of the mainstream.

The history of professions also raises issues about the relationship of CSR and government. Professionals, whether accountants, doctors or others, have been found to seek and maintain the judgement domain and indeterminacy of their professional task as a way of empowering their members, and also restricting external interference.[5] Thus professions seek a certain amount of independence from the state in order to carry out their activities; yet they need the state to give them a monopoly to protect their activities.[6] As the issue of public policies on CSR becomes more developed in subsequent years, so the relationship of the CSR profession to regulatory processes will become increasingly important. Evidently, the increasingly professionalised CSR community has a lot to lose by being actually critical of either its client base or regulatory masters.

Given that questions of organisational accountability are central to debates and initiatives on CSR and corporate citizenship, the accountability of CSR professionalisation must become a key issue. Who should CSR standards development be accountable to? CSR practitioners? Or their intended beneficiaries? Can we assume that their intended beneficiaries are not only their clients but those affected by their clients' activities? If so, what opportunities for meaningful participation in CSR professional standards development can those constituencies really have? CSR professionalisation could learn well from the history of professions, as well as innovating a new conception of professional identity, where the professional serves not only the client but a set of principles that speak directly to the need for a more sustainable and just world. The establishment of the Association of Sustainability Practitioners[7] in 2005 is one attempt to encourage such an orientation among professionals in this field.

Rethinking intellectual property

The responsibility of software companies towards society has not been high on the agenda of the corporate social responsibility community, perhaps because the environmental and social impacts of production appear to be very low, while the value added to society appears pretty high. When such companies as Microsoft appear in the corporate responsibility press it is often about traditional corporate philanthropy, involving their donation of products or services to specific educational projects.

However, information technology (IT) companies sit at the nexus of two of the most important changes to capitalism today, which should make them a key focus for future work on corporate responsibility issues. On one side is a key technological development in contemporary capitalism—cheap IT—while on the other side is the international protection of intellectual property, which is probably the most important regulatory development in capitalism of our time, as it extends private property rights into new areas. The allocation of private property rights as opposed to collective use rights, and the responsibilities and obligations of those people or organisations that enjoy such property rights, is a key political question at the heart of capitalism. When the nature and allocation of private property rights are being negotiated, as is the situation with intellectual property today, it reveals to us the way 'property' is an inherently political concept concerning a balancing of private and collective interests. As this balancing of the private and collective interests is a key theme in most corporate social responsibility and citizenship debate, we might reasonably expect developments in the nature and allocation of property to appear.

The responsibility of pharmaceutical corporations who hold patents to crucial drugs for diseases such as AIDS has been the focus of some attention over the last few years. Most corporate responses have been in the form of cutting prices and in some instances relaxing their patents, to improve access to medicines in the global South. However, the key issue of what constitutes the responsible use of corporate power in shaping the regulatory regime on intellectual property remains relatively undebated and unresolved. Recent events in the IT sector make this question even more urgent to explore, and bring IT companies more firmly into the corporate responsibility spotlight.

A significant development came in February 2005, when the European Parliament rejected unanimously a draft Directive to introduce patenting for software.[8] The issue had been in play since moves in 1997/98 by the European Patent Office to institutionalise patents for software design, and on the negotiating table since a draft Directive was proposed in 2002.[9] The issue of patenting of software is just one of the intellectual property (IP) issues facing the information and communications technology (ICT) sector that have implications for public benefit, and thus can be considered in the context of corporate responsibility.

IP is legally defined under three headings: copyright, patents and trademarks. Patent coverage is generally more restrictive than copyright because, while copyright restricts re-use of a particular *piece* of creativity, a patent, in IP terms, is the equivalent of protecting a whole *style* of creativity. So, taking language as a hypothetical example, copyright covers a particular text; but patenting would cover a whole style of formatting, or genre of writing, or a certain use of grammar or punctuation. And, thus, applied to software, patents could close down a wide range of potential creativity, bringing all sorts of software developments within the scope of concepts of 'similarity' in both 'operation' and 'effect', and thus under the control of patent holders.

What is at stake here in practical terms? A huge amount for both business and society. Arriving on the software scene has been open source software, with Linux, the desktop/server operating system, at the head of the charge. But the terrain in which these newcomers are emerging is not smooth, and is getting bumpier: the open-source movement is in serious danger of being tripped up not so much by questions of quality or compatibility (issues with open-source software that are now being overcome, partly through backing by computing giants such as Sun and IBM) but by questions over IP. If software patents are set up in Europe, the open-source movement might have its scope for software development badly curtailed; and Linux users are already being sued for illegally using, within the Linux software code, supposedly copyrighted proprietary code.

In 2004, Microsoft was bidding to install its software on the 14,000 desktops of the Munich municipal government. After eventually offering a 35% discount on the original US$40 million bill and sending its senior management to meet the Mayor, the Munich government chose Linux, the freely available, no-licence-required open-source operating system for its desktop machines. Why was this important enough for Microsoft to offer such reductions? By going with Linux, the Munich contract was a watershed in the transition to the desktop machine of Linux, out from its ghetto in back-office servers to the mainstream via the desktop machines of a municipal government—a market where Microsoft's dominance has been hitherto unassailable.[10]

Nevertheless, the switch to Linux was nearly scuppered by the threat of messy IT patent lawsuits. Munich put its transfer to Linux on hold while it waited for a clarificatory ruling from the EU Commission over whether its shift to open-source would put it in regulatory difficulties should the then-current draft Directive on software patents have come into force; and leave it moreover with software to which updates would be only patchy and infrequent (since those updates would themselves be subject to patent disputes). In the end, Munich proceeded before receiving guidance—and Mayor Christian Ude told the Commission that it should scrap the software patents law in any case.[11]

Although the patent issue is at bay, at least in Europe, Linux is having a rougher ride in terms of copyright. Much of the crisis with Linux over copyright has arisen due to the company SCO, which claims that Linux uses some of its code (code for the parent system of Linux which SCO owns) illegally. And is therefore it is suing the biggest corporate users and vendors of Linux for colossal sums—firms such as IBM, Daimler-Chrysler and computer companies such as Novell and Red Hat. The first sign of the strength of SCO's case, however, was revealed in 2004 when a judge dismissed most of its case against DaimlerChrysler before a trial even commenced.[12] IBM, the biggest mainstream convert to Linux, having invested hundreds of millions of dollars in developing it for its machines and clients, has attempted to obtain a similar dismissal in its own case against SCO.[13] What may be working against SCO's claim that Linux has pirated code that it owns is its unwillingness to say which bits of code these actually are.

SCO's legal campaign poses difficult questions for Microsoft. This is because of allegations from open-source advocate Eric Raymond, who analysed a leaked SCO email, that 'at least a third of SCO's entire market capitalization' comes from Microsoft.[14] Despite various denials and clarifications, a significant commercial link exists.[15] The question this raises is whether or not Microsoft's seeming association with SCO is a legitimate way to interact with its competitors. It also raises the issue of what is a responsible use of corporate power on issues as fundamental as determining the scope and nature of private property rights.

The probability of legal action, and its success, is not the same as the potential for legal action and it is the latter that concerns large corporations making long-term software decisions. Microsoft's Steve Ballmer, speaking late in 2004 in India,[16] focused on the likelihood of continuing IP difficulties as the main risk posed for those in Asia deciding to adopt Linux. That copyright concerns are threatening the access of the global South to the software they need for their development is a concern, and the role of corporations in this situation should be a focus of corporate responsibility, especially given the increasing attention on corporate contributions to economic development in the South.

MICROSOFT'S STEVE BALLMER,
INTELLECTUAL PROPERTY RIGHTS WILL
CAUSE DIFFICULTIES FOR THE GLOBAL
SOUTH ADOPTING LINUX

The main theoretical argument for the protection of software IP goes that properly protected IP is an incentive to perform ever better in a competitive environment: if you won't get any more from making even better products, because you can't protect the return on that investment, why make the products better? The fact that Linux is so successful without anyone having being paid to write its code suggests that this issue is open to debate. In addition, without serious competitors, protected IP becomes a licence to print money. The ethics of arguing about the need to 'protect return on investment from the competitive environment'—when there is no competitive environment—are problematic. In the absence of competition, the inevitable state of affairs is that profits are vastly in excess of investment—as they are in the case of Microsoft's products, running at up to 400% profit in some cases[17]—and that prices remain high with no incentive to come down. Poorer regions of the world should not be denied the opportunity to participate in development based on office and home computing; but, at current prices, they are.

Growing pressure from open-source technology and piracy led to Microsoft offering in February to sell its XP operating system at half-price across China, for a short

MICROSOFT SENIOR VP AND CEO OF EUROPE,
MIDDLE EAST AND AFRICA, JEAN-PHILIPPE
COURTOIS: BRINGING INFORMATION
TECHNOLOGY TO JORDAN

period.[18] Microsoft has also responded to the 'digital divide' by rolling out a range of educational projects. Also in February, Microsoft senior vice president and chief executive officer of Europe, Middle East and Africa (EMEA) Jean-Philippe Courtois officially opened the Regional School Technology Innovation Center in Jordan, and announced Microsoft's collaboration with United Nations Development Fund Women's e-Village Initiative, to bring IT to educational centres across the country. 'Microsoft's alliance with the Jordanian Government is an extension of our broader commitment to help individuals, communities and nations in the Middle East region gain access to the technology, tools, skills and innovation they need to realize their full potential', said Mark East, Microsoft EMEA Senior Director of Education.[19]

The benefits of helping women to learn IT skills and have access to IT resources could be significant. However, is the best way of developing a sustainable IT sector in countries such as Jordan to set people on a path of using proprietary software, rather than the free alternatives? One often-heard criticism of voluntary corporate responsibility initiatives is that they are part of a ploy to distract attention from systemic challenges by diffusing conflict. The business model of proprietary software companies appears inherently problematic for sustainable development, and so a true embracing of responsibility would be to look at how to change that business model.

Although Microsoft is a special case, other companies whose core business is based on digital IP protection could do well to engage in dialogue about the future of intellectual property. Security is so readily bypassed by the armies of crackers in the programming community, and files are so readily transferred online—often by 'centreless' peer-to-peer networks which cannot just be shut down—that some solution other than conventional IP enforcement may become commercially necessary, in addition to being more socially beneficial.

Rupert's rights

Beyond the realm of software, companies involved in information and communications technologies have been pushing for the introduction of new property rights. One example is 'The Draft Treaty on the Protection of Broadcasting Organisations', being negotiated at the World Intellectual Property Organisation (WIPO).[20] The proposed treaty aims to extend new rights to broadcasting organisations. This is not a category of society widely considered to be threatened by rights violations: in 2004 Rupert Murdoch's News Corporation had amassed total assets of approximately US$53 billion.[21]

The treaty would give such broadcasters, cablecasters and, under the US proposal, webcasters a range of new rights, and substantially expand both the scope and duration of currently recognised rights for broadcasting organisations.

The US National Association of Broadcasters (NAB) and the Association for Commercial Television (ACT) in Europe argue that new rights are a necessary measure to defend against 'signal theft', whereby a broadcast of a public event, for example, is picked up by a third party who re-broadcasts it. Lawyers for the Digital Media Association (DIMA) (whose members include AOL, FullAudio, RealNetworks and Yahoo!) are arguing for the new protections to also include webcasters.

The extent of the re-broadcast problem remains open to debate. In addition, the draft treaty goes much further than signal protection, covering what happens when a signal has been received and stored. Such proposals could enable treaty broadcasters to restrict the distribution of material that is not copyrightable, is in the public domain or is made freely available by its creator. David Tannenbaum of the Union for the Public Domain argues that, while 'broadcasters have convincingly argued that the passage of this treaty will boost their profits', they have yet to show why the effort to create entirely new rights to the broadcasting stream is either economically necessary or desirable, particularly when balanced against its costs to society at large—such as restrictions on access to knowledge and encroachment on the public's rights to fair use.[22]

DAVID TANNENBAUM OF THE
UNION FOR THE PUBLIC
DOMAIN: BROADCASTERS HAVE
YET TO SHOW WHY NEW RIGHTS
ARE NECESSARY OR DESIRABLE

The draft treaty itself provides no justification for its existence in terms of the public interest. Thiru Balasubramaniam of the Consumer Project on Technology told us that social and development goals do not readily occur to most participants in the WIPO committee that is drafting the treaty. That such issues are not a concern, let alone the top priority for WIPO, is highly problematic. As a UN agency, WIPO's work should be in support of the UN Charter, to advance peace and social progress. However, WIPO has struggled to understand its work in that context, and a coalition of 14 developing countries have called for the development dimension to be incorporated into the core of WIPO's mandate.[23] Others have questioned the impartiality of its secretariat, pointing to evidence that they have been pressurising governments to back the new treaty. 'It appears that the tail is wagging the dog', said Robin Gross of IP Justice. The institutional interests of WIPO and its closeness to industry may be key factors, which raises questions about appropriate corporate influence over intergovernmental institutions.[24]

As mentioned earlier, the nature of property rights, their potential extension, the social obligations of bearers of property rights, as well as the responsibilities of those who infringe such rights, should all be central to debates about corporate–society relations. Thus, the role of corporations in influencing the definition and regulation of private property should be a key focus for those concerned with corporations using their power more responsibly, for public as well as private benefit. However, a review of various online corporate social responsibility newsletters and magazines in the past months indicates that this has yet to emerge. Nevertheless, it is only a matter of time before companies such as News Corporation, Microsoft and Yahoo! will need to consider more closely how the worldwide extension and consolidation of their property rights will impact on society, become more transparent about their political activities, and engage with their critics.

Is it good to talk?

The mobile phone industry is another sector that, in conventional CSR areas of environmental impact and social responsibility, scores as high as the computing and software sectors as an industry of concern. Indeed, it is hailed as a sector that can catalyse social and economic development across the global South. But how *safe* is the technology? Is electromagnetic radiation a hidden pollutant? Debates in the UK during 2005 highlighted continuing concern about the relationship between science, politics, business and human health.

At the start of 2005, the UK Health Protection Agency (HPA) issued updated guidance to the 2000 report of the National Radiological Protection Board (NRPB)—the 'Stewart Report'. 'Within the UK, there is a lack of hard information showing that the mobile phone systems in use are damaging to health . . . a precautionary approach to the use of mobile technologies should continue to be adopted . . . limiting the use of mobile phones by children remains appropriate as a precautionary measure.'[25] So that's clear then: Mobiles are safe. But use them with caution.

SIR WILLIAM STEWART, HEAD OF THE UK
HEALTH PROTECTION AGENCY: REPORT WAS
NON-COMMITTAL ON RISKS

The report carries no specific limit for the age group of 'children' considered particularly at risk, but this did not stop one UK newspaper headlining its report on the updated study: 'No mobiles for under-nines, study says'[26] on the basis of ad hoc comments made by the head of the HPA, Sir William Stewart, at the press conference. Indeed the original Stewart Report was notably non-committal not just on the age of 'children' whose access to mobiles should be restricted, but also on what 'caution' really means in relation to the use of a mobile phone. Recommending 'shorter calls', as it did, is hardly a scientific breakthrough; and its other concrete recommendation, to use an 'approved hands-free set'[27] was contradicted by its own finding that no approved hands-free sets exist: 'The regulatory position on the use of hands-free kits and shields is unclear and the only information available to the public appears to be that supplied by their manufacturers.'[28]

The NRPB seems, in fact, to have overturned the conventional understanding of the 'precautionary principle', in that, rather than finding evidence for the safety of mobile technology, it states that mobiles are not known to be unsafe—but suggests 'caution' in any case. This may have gone unnoticed by the mobile-safety campaigners,[29] who point to more traditional interpretations—in which the burden of proof is on those wanting to implement a new technology, not on those against it. Perhaps the most important fact driving the NRPB's position is what the original Stewart report unashamedly stated: 'The use of mobile phones and related technologies will continue to increase for the foreseeable future.'[30] Which really *is* clear: there is nothing we can do.

So who *is* driving the debate on mobile phone safety? The mobile phone networks, who on this issue now speak with one carefully honed voice—the media-savvy Mobile Operators Association (MOA)—immediately 'welcomed' the Stewart update.[31] Ditto the equally organised Mobile Manufacturers Association, emphasising specifically how NRPB has 'reaffirmed the absence of any scientific evidence of adverse health effects from wireless communications technologies particularly mobile phones'. Regarding the 'other end' of the mobile safety debate, the masts (or base stations), the MOA reminded us in February 2005 that the NRPB had stated 'there is no scientific basis for establishing minimal distances between base stations and areas of public occupancy'. And in their Corporate Social Responsibility reports for 2003/2004 both mmO$_2$ and Vodafone discussed these issues. Jim Stevenson, O$_2$'s Community Relations Manager, said 'we are building a lot less now than three years ago, but the level of community consultation is far greater today'.[32] The focus in its report is on the provision of reassurance and early information to the communities concerned. Vodafone, on the other hand, is more assertive in its dismissal of the scientific basis for community concerns over health. 'Based on current scientific review, there is no evidence of an impact on human health when electromagnetic fields (EMF) exposure levels are below internationally recognised guidelines', it stated.[33] So, as far as the mobile companies are concerned, caution notwithstanding, it's all systems go.

But these assertions by the mobile phone companies serve to amplify the inconsistency embedded in the Stewart report: that, if phones are safe, why is there any need to exercise 'caution'—indeed take any notice of the Stewart recommendations at all? Or, put in terms of the precautionary principle, if companies are aware that risks may emerge at a later stage, why are they not hesitating to put up masts and marketing their products with that risk in mind, rather than moving forward as though there will never be any health issues emerging from mobile telephony. The 'caution' that manufacturers are enacting amounts to either various forms of 'consultation', before doing what they plan, or leaving it to the consumers to decide their own fate. On the question of children's particular risk of exposure to electromagnetic radiation, the MOA confirmed in February simply that: 'the operators reviewed their marketing policies to ensure they do not actively market mobile phones to the under-16s', and the MMA explicitly passed the buck to parents, saying 'we believe that it is an issue of parental choice whether children should be provided with a mobile phone'.[34] And, in submitting a planning application near a school, the limit of their responsibility, according to the MOA is merely to follow governmental guidance and, in their own words, to 'provide evidence to the local planning authority that they have consulted the relevant body of the school or college as required by the guidance'.[35]

However calm the MOA and MMA are—and thus all the operators and handset manufacturers—about the issue of health, it refuses to go away. One claim, from the burgeoning mobile health action community but with strong scientific backing, is that the NRPB is, perhaps wilfully, measuring the wrong impact (studying only heating effects of microwave radiation, but not other effects, on the body).[36] Crucially, a Swedish/European study released in October 2004, with the strongest scientific credentials,[37] suggested that, for users with more than ten years of regular mobile use, there was a clear link to cancers in the ear—acoustic neuroma—on the side of the head at which users normally held their phones. While the NRPB and mobile operators responded to a previous Swedish study, pointing out flaws,[38] they have notably failed to comment in depth on this latest Swedish study. And new health scares keep emerging—another concern, on the basis of a Hungarian study from 2004, is that mobile use reduces sperm count.[39]

There has in the past been some indication of too close a link between the scientific research community and the mobile operators—for example, that NRPB funded 'independent' research from an adviser to Orange.[40] It remains the case that the main body funding 'independent' research on mobile phones and health, the Mobile Telecommunications and Health Research Programme (MTHR), is very considerably funded by the mobile industry itself.[41] Whether this arrangement implements the recommendation in the first Stewart Report that a 'substantial research programme should operate under the aegis of a demonstrably independent panel'[42] is open to question; the mobile safety campaigners are not convinced.[43]

Nevertheless, many scientists with knowledge of the issues are becoming decreasingly convinced of just how safe mobile phones and masts are. Only in March 2005 was research released suggesting that, finally, hands-free sets could be proved to reduce radiation reaching the head—if used with a ferrite bead that absorbed emissions from the cable itself. Lawrie Challis, head of the MTHR, was unequivocal: 'there is no evidence yet that mobile phones are harmful to health but people have not been using them long enough for us to be sure . . . Using a ferrite bead effectively reduces emissions to the head to zero but as yet manufacturers do not put them on hands-free kits . . . I am not sure why, but I wish they would . . . you would think they would like to promote it.'[44] And the response from Michael Milligan of the MMF? 'I agree they can have an impact. But the bigger issue is that mobile phones are tested to comply

LAWRIE CHALLIS, HEAD OF THE MTHR:
THERE IS NO EVIDENCE YET THAT
MOBILE PHONES ARE HARMFUL

with standards and have been passed safe.'[45] So, finally, we have a split between the UK scientific establishment on 'caution'—and the manufacturers. Stewart himself has been critical of the extent to which the manufacturers are using a reverse of the precautionary principle (i.e. doing nothing until danger is proven). 'We said in the report that it's not possible to say categorically that there are not health effects. But what has come out from the industry is that mobile phones are safe', he said.[46]

The validity of the mobile phone industry's response to these issues through stakeholder dialogues is under question. At a MOA stakeholder meeting in 2004, at which government, industry and civil society stakeholders were present, many concerns were raised about processes of consultation. Some claimed that 'industry representatives often refuse to attend public meetings, and that this leaves communities feeling angry and disempowered' and that 'it was felt by some that the public get very frustrated that operators appear to be "judge and jury" on the health issue . . .'[47]

Other methods have been employed to understand stakeholder concerns. Vodafone commissioned a 'perception survey' from MORI in 2003 to assess public views of mobiles and mobile safety. That found 'the public believes that network operators are not taking the [radiation and health] issue seriously enough'.[48] Vodafone's response to this, as per its 2003/2004 Group CSR report[49] is that its 'role is to support independent research and explain the findings in plain language so that our customers have the information they need to make their own decisions on mobile phone use'. The message from the phone companies is that stakeholder engagement is not about listening to customers—it's about telling them everything's okay, according to the science. This is far from real dialogue—the irony being that phone companies might have something to learn about how to talk properly.

'It's important to abide by what the science tells us', said British Prime minister Tony Blair responding to a question on the subject of phones and sperm counts, in parliament.[50] Apparently, the science isn't telling us anything definitive either way. But if the trend of evidence, as the Swedish study on acoustic neuroma seems to imply, points to the pragmatic conclusion that mobile phone radiation does increase cancer risk, the deeper question is what anyone can or will do, and who will take the rap if things go wrong. The scientific community—led by Stewart and Challis—is starting to distance itself from the industry's calm. However, governments are making so much money from mobiles (the 3G licence auction brought in a staggering £22.5 billion to the UK government), they are not likely to want to slow the mobile juggernaut. If the evidence ever becomes overwhelming, it would appear that it will then be too late either to undo society's reliance on mobiles or to prevent a welter of health symptoms from arising due to long-term mobile use. If the precautionary approach ends up meaning everyone for themselves, then the mobile users themselves will end up being the scapegoats.

Whole-systems change

The cases of mobile telephony and intellectual property in software and broadcasting illustrate the importance of regulation in shaping the market for new technologies and therefore the impact of such technologies on society. They highlight how the corpo-

rate influence on regulatory developments is a central question for corporate responsibility. The lack of engagement by the CSR community on these issues also highlights
its limited engagement on the rules of the game—the system conditions that shape
the environment within which corporations operate. However, during 2005 the need
for 'whole-systems change' in global capitalism, and the role of corporate leaders in
helping this, began to be more widely discussed.

'Whole-systems change' means changing the factors that shape what all agents
within that system do. In the context of companies, this means changing those factors
that shape what economic actors do, so that all behave in a sustainable and accountable manner. In January 2005, the introduction to the previous Annual Review, originally published by Lifeworth, called on CSR professionals to make their work 'a catalyst
for systemic change', and outlined different paths that would together constitute a
transformative CSR agenda (see page 217). Then the magazine *What is Enlightenment?*
ran a special feature on 'The Business of Saving the World', which chronicled a nascent
leadership among some business executives, aiming 'to transform the systems that
govern global enterprise'.[51]

In the article Nike's Darcy Winslow identifies two system conditions that need to be
tackled for all companies to be made more responsible. 'One is government: a lot of
laws that are in place right now do not give financial incentive to do things differently
in future. The other is Wall Street. At the end of the day, the shareholders and Wall
Street are what keep corporations moving in the direction they are moving in.'[52] A few
months earlier her company was the feature of an article in the widely read *Harvard
Business Review*. In it Simon Zadek, CEO of the UK-based institute AccountAbility,
chronicled the bumpy route Nike has travelled towards more responsible business
practices. Organisations learn in unique ways, Zadek contends, but they inevitably pass
through five stages of corporate responsibility, from defensive ('It's not our fault') to
compliant ('We'll do only what we have to') to managerial ('It's the business') to strategic ('It gives us a competitive edge') and, finally, to what he describes as 'civil' ('We need
to make sure everybody does it').[53] This highest stage has strong resemblance to a
whole-systems change approach.

Frank Dixon of Innovest Social Investors has noted that 'the traditional CSR movement has been focused on improving corporate environmental and social performance
(i.e.: reducing pollution, making safe products, taking good care of employees, acting
responsibly in developing countries, etc.). This has prompted great improvement, but
much more is needed to achieve sustainability. The missing element of sustainability
is system change.'[54] In the *What Is Enlightenment?* article he described Innovest's 'Total
corporate responsibility (TCR)' approach to rating companies as one that 'recognises
that economic and political systems essentially force firms to be irresponsible and
unsustainable by not holding them fully accountable for negative impacts on society.
TCR encourages firms to work proactively with others to achieve system changes that
hold them fully accountable.'[55] TCR therefore suggests a new mind-set for business.
Rather than seeing itself as one entity operating independently from the rest of society, business would see itself as being part of one interconnected system. It would give
priority to the good of the overall system, and in so doing ensure its own prosperity.
However, the TCR approach recognises the realities of today's marketplace and suggests that firms take practical, incremental, profit-enhancing actions that improve
internal CSR performance as well as promoting system change. Other initiatives explic-

itly talking about systems change are the Global Transitions Initiative (GTI)[56] and Corporation 20/20, which asks the question, 'What would a corporation look like that was designed to seamlessly integrate both social and financial purpose?' In 2005 it continued its search by convening various experts to develop principles for the future corporation.[57] It is a major task, and whether it is able to provide some answers to systemic issues about the nature of property and profit, and then how to actually achieve the needed whole-systems change, is still to be seen.

The earlier discussion of corporate influence over governance on basic issues such as property rights and consumer safety illustrates that there is much work to be done for a systemic view to actually impact significantly on the global political economy. The most famous meeting of corporations and politicians, the 2005 World Economic Forum, showed little evidence of a shift towards awareness of systemic problems and thus system-change solutions. WEF's recommendations for global priority-setting attended to some serious issues: poverty, equitable globalisation, climate change, education, the Middle East.[58] However, the recommendations were then wedded to the usual neoliberal economic world-view of greater corporate activity being of benefit to all regions, including the poorer, and the limited role of governments in facilitating corporations' contributions by ever-'freer' international trade'.[59]

Perhaps we will require many more personal transformations before global transformations become possible. As the journalist for *What is Enlightenment?* put it, 'only as business leaders begin to fully embrace the truth of our unity and interdependence will they demand accountability from each other to change these powerful global systems'.[60]

The nature of this transformation, and the type of leadership it may inspire, was something increasingly discussed during 2005, and is returned to in this report. (See 'The living dead' on page 320.)

2Q2005

April–June

Jem Bendell

China changes everything

The view that China poses particularly difficult challenges for corporate citizenship is widespread in both the academic and practitioner communities engaged in these issues. Concerns are expressed on both social and environmental issues. A report by the US-based NGO Worldwatch Institute reported that China's spectacular economic boom is inflicting a terrible toll on the environment.[1] China is in the middle of the largest rural migration in human history, with millions of its people leaving for the cities. About 240 million Chinese people are now in the consumer class, buying the types of goods and services that most people in Western nations purchase. While that number is the same as in the United States, it represents only 19% of the total Chinese population, and so growing demand is likely. The World Bank reported that China's economy was growing by 8.3% in 2005.[2]

With factories multiplying and car ownership surging, cities' air quality has plummeted. Sixteen of the 20 most polluted cities in the world are in China. The number of Chinese workers suffering from pneumoconiosis, which causes lung damage due to the inhalation of toxic materials and dust, was over half a million in 2001, of whom 140,000 have died.[3] Meanwhile, scores of rivers have dried up in northern China over the past 20 years, with more than 75% of river water not suitable for drinking or fishing. The damage to the environment is not restricted to China's borders, with the Worldwatch Institute highlighting the country's growing ecological footprint around the world. 'China is becoming the sucking force, taking raw materials from across the planet, because it alone doesn't have the resources it needs to sustain its growth', said Lisa Mastny, the director of the research project. China's increasing consumption has been cited as one of the factors driving up global prices on a range of products, from oil to wheat. In April the figures on Chinese steel production told of a 25% increase in one year, depleting iron ore stocks so fast that there could soon be shortages.[4] Aside from the ecological impact of resource extraction, China is now the second-largest emitter of carbon dioxide after the United States, adding to the difficult challenge of addressing climate change. Raising the alarm about China does not reduce the need for rich Northern countries to act. As much of China's resource consumption and pollution is driven by its export industries, its ecological footprint is heavier due to carry-

ing the West on its back. Nevertheless, the ecological implications of a resource-rav-
enous China make initiatives in the North something of a sideshow in the unfolding
planetary sustainable development drama. Consequently, those global corporations
and financial institutions that are seeking to address systemic challenges to future
value, such as climate change, need to assess how they are influencing the way Chinese firms fill their appetite for resources.

Aside from environmental issues, China also continues to pose challenges for companies on a range of social issues. Given its totalitarian political system, truly independent trade unions and NGOs are hard to find in mainland China. This social landscape
has limited the ability of workers and communities to articulate their views effectively
if they differ from those of business executives and Party officials. Chinese labour law
does not incorporate international standards on freedom of association, for example,
which is part of most voluntary labour standards.[5]

Voluntary efforts by foreign companies to ensure that Chinese suppliers meet basic
labour standards have been hampered by this problematic legal and social context. In
April 2005, more evidence of Chinese factories faking records and coaching workers
in how to answer auditor questions came to light.[6] Eight out of nine Chinese toy suppliers investigated in a report by Fair Trade Center and SwedWatch were in breach of
both national legislation and international conventions on workers' rights. They
argued that seven of these suppliers had systematically been cheating during social
audits. The International Council of Toy Industries is now working on a global initiative to tackle these problems but, according to the report, this initiative is not addressing the underlying causes.[7] For five years it has been known that, to be effective, social
auditing requires active participation and ownership of standard setting, monitoring,
verification and corrective action implementation by independent representatives of
the workers themselves.[8] Without change to the social and legal context in China it
will be difficult for companies to responsibly source from there.

In 2005, there was evidence of growing domestic concern about the social and environmental challenges arising from Chinese industrialisation. The human face of ecological recklessness appeared in April when thousands of villagers rioted in eastern
China after two of about 200 elderly women protesting against factory pollution died
during efforts to disperse them.[9] Historically, the vocal NGOs have mainly been based
in Hong Kong. For example, in April the Justice and Peace Commission of the Hong
Kong Catholic Diocese urged people to write to the Chinese Premier Wen Jiabao over
conditions in coal mines.[10] In mainland China, NGOs are beginning to articulate the
views of people who are being affected by current developments. In April 2005, an
NGO was formed to rally all Chinese people against worsening pollution. The All China
Environment Federation, which includes government officials, other environmental
and social organisations, enterprises and ecologists, claims it will serve as a bridge
linking the public and the government to rally society to fight China's worsening pollution.[11]

Meanwhile, the Shenzhen-based Institute of Contemporary Observation (ICO),
China's most visible labour rights organisation, won a sustainability award from Shell
China and the *Beijing Economic Observer*. ICO's Director Dr Liu Kaiming believes that
ICO's success in 2005 is a signal that labour issues are perceived as more important
than before. The major factors leading to the award were ICO's training, education and
activities for workers. In the short term, ICO plans more training on infectious dis-

ICO DIRECTOR LIU KAIMING: LABOUR
ISSUES ARE MORE IMPORTANT

eases, such as AIDS, and will be working with young migrant workers (15–18 years old) who travel to Guangdong looking for work.[12]

A critical media has been recognised as key to creating incentives for greater voluntary corporate responsibility. Therefore, government restrictions on reporting in China pose some difficulties for effective information exchange and dialogue about corporate practices. Western-based companies such as News International and Yahoo! have been criticised for agreeing to restrictive media regulations in order to access the Chinese market. Even within this context, questions of corporate responsibility have begun to appear in Chinese media. In April the *New Beijing News* published an article arguing that China's rich lack social responsibility. It said the rich seek status purely in terms of financial wealth rather than on any social or moral grounds.[13] Meanwhile some media commentators have begun to suggest that greater corporate responsibility is an opportunity for business.[14] To highlight the success that can be had, *China Enterprise News* ran a story on the China People's Electric Appliance Group, which over the past few years has received more than 100 awards from local, provincial and central governments for its corporate responsibility.[15]

Not a lost cause?

Faced with the China challenge, some practitioners, analysts or advocates of corporate citizenship may lose hope in the potential of voluntary business action. However, evidence in 2005 suggests that it would be wrong to assume that Chinese business and government are irrevocably opposed to improving the social and environmental impacts and contributions of business. A WWF survey on China and the environment suggests that some of China's biggest and most important companies are intent on improving environmental standards and practices. All of the companies that participated in the survey said protecting the environment was important, with more than half indicating that it was part of their company's core values. The survey reported that 22% of respondents are implementing tougher environment standards than are legally required, with 13% calling for even stricter mandatory rules.[16]

Some opinion leaders in the Chinese business community have begun calling for greater action. In April 2005, Dr Xu Zhiming, Chairman of the Hong Kong General Association of International Investment, appealed to Chinese entrepreneurs to be more socially responsible.[17] Meanwhile, speaking on behalf of 23 food corporations in Beijing, the general manager of the Yili Group, Liu Haichun, stated that the industry would actively advocate CSR and improve the industry's reputation.[18] Companies are undertaking numerous voluntary projects to improve their impacts. For example, the Hang Seng Bank has launched an e-Statement Tree Planting Scheme in Hong Kong, whereby the bank will pay for one tree to be planted for every ten paper statements that are avoided by its customers using e-statements instead.[19]

Another area where business is beginning to be proactive is HIV/AIDS. In May the People's Republic of China Ministry of Health and Merck Co., Inc. announced their plan to establish a public–private partnership to fight HIV/AIDS. The Merck Company Foundation will support the $30 million programme which includes education, prevention, care and treatment. The partnership represents the largest of its kind in China and will be launched later in 2005 in the Liangshan Prefecture in Sichuan Province. Trevor Neilson, executive director of the Global Business Coalition (GBC), said that 'China's HIV/AIDS epidemic is starting to move from high-risk groups to the general population. Merck's commitment to tackle HIV/AIDS among drug users and sex workers presents a unique opportunity for China and shows that companies don't need to shy away from HIV/AIDS prevention programmes in countries where the epidemic is still centred on these groups'.[20] The following week the GBC announced that another 26 companies were taking steps to implement non-discrimination policies for HIV/AIDS for their China-based employees. These moves have come after Chinese Vice Premier Madame Wu Yi's call on companies to take action to stem the growing HIV/AIDS epidemic.[21]

This initiative reflects the government's growing awareness of novel social challenges that are arising from rapid changes in Chinese society. On the environmental front, some sections of the government are recognising the damage that is being caused to its people, and is enforcing legislation. It has, for example, introduced strict fuel-economy standards for new cars, and passed a renewable-energy law that sets ambitious targets for using wind and solar energy.[22] Meanwhile the State Environmental Protection Administration (SEPA) has demanded that Chongqing, Shenyang, Wuhan, Xi'an and Harbin regulate material waste producers, make greater efforts to enforce related laws, build an orderly recycling system of sensitive material wastes, and gain experience that can be used to develop a nationwide solution to the environmental problems caused by sensitive material wastes.[23] SEPA is particularly concerned with reducing the use of persistent organic pollutants (POPs), and implementing the Stockholm Convention on POPs.[24] There has also been some movement on social issues, illustrated by the Shenzhen government fining 22 enterprises for not paying back wages and worker insurance.[25] In April 2005, a factory owner in Shandong was punished for hiring workers under 17 and working them 15 hours per day, a form of abuse that the government has not policed effectively in the past.[26] In his blog on corporate responsibility, ERM's director of CSR services in China, Mark Eadie, reported in May that, as the government works on China's 11th Five Year Plan, 'it is looking increasingly likely that sustainable development aspirations and objectives will be put into the central planning process'.[27]

There are some indications that Chinese society is beginning to respond to its social and environmental challenges, and so Western companies may not be able to claim that such matters are beyond their control and responsibility in that country. Indeed, in April 2005, the tables were turned when Guo Wencai from the All China Federation of Trade Unions criticised the lack of responsibility from Western companies. He said that 'some (foreign) enterprises, with Wal-Mart being representative, turned a blind eye to China's trade union laws and set very negative examples during the country's unionizing effort'.[28]

There are also indications that the assumption—that demand for Chinese products from other parts of Asia is not sensitive to concerns about sustainable development— may also be questioned. Japan, in particular, has experienced something of an environmental awakening in the last ten years. This was illustrated by the Japanese electronics company Sony announcing tough environmental tests for more than 4,000 Chinese electronics manufacturers. This is a result of the electronics giant adopting a new Green Partner programme for environmental management systems. The influence of Europe in this environmental initiative is apparent, as one of the reasons for Sony's action is to ensure it meets standards set by the European Union on electronics products. About 3,000 of the manufacturers are expected to fail Sony's test and be threatened with dropping off its supplier list unless they can improve.[29]

The dramatic impacts of industrialisation in China and the rest of East Asia on their own peoples and environments, as well as the impact on the global environment, and the increasing importance of the region for the future supply to, and sales of, major transnational corporations, makes the region of central importance for future work on corporate citizenship. It was this context that led to the creation of 'CSR Asia' at the start of the year. Founded by Richard Welford of the Corporate Environmental Governance Programme (CEGP) at the University of Hong Kong and Stephen Frost of the South East Asia Research Centre (SEARC) at the City University of Hong Kong, CSR Asia provides information, research, training and analysis of CSR issues in the Asia Pacific region. It has offices in Hong Kong and Shenzhen and plans to expand further around the region.[30]

The importance of the region to the future of the world is so great that more of the world's best minds on sustainable development are needed to apply themselves to the necessary sustainability transition in Asia. Currently, corporate and governmental responses to sustainable development in the region are insufficient, as they generally seek to add on social and environmental issues to a dominant paradigm of economic development, which necessitates greater consumption and pollution. That model of economic development is a psychological hangover from colonialism, as it is based on a perspective of human nature and social progress that arose from European societies. Sustainable development requires us to reconceive human well-being beyond the merely material, and therefore reconfigure the processes that create resource demands as well as those that shape how such demands are met. Given the philosophical history of Asia, especially the holistic notion of the individual as existing in connection with all of that lives, as reflected in many Buddhist, Jain, Hindu and Taoist teachings, sensitivity to collective and environmental needs should not be intellectually foreign to Asians. The scale and urgency of the challenge makes it important that these philosophies are recalled. The future of human civilisation will be determined in Asia. In its present it holds the seeds of the world's destruction; in its past it has the seeds of its salvation.

Nike says time to team up

In 2005 Nike returned to reporting on its social and environmental practices after a couple of years of silence due to legal concerns. The sports and clothing company is very important to countries such as Vietnam, where it is the largest private-sector employer with more than 50,000 workers producing shoes through subcontractors.[31] Nike's new report makes sobering reading, as it describes widespread problems in Asian factories. The company said it audited hundreds of factories in 2003 and 2004 and found cases of abusive treatment in more than a quarter of its South Asian plants. For example, between 25% and 50% of the factories in the region restrict access to toilets and drinking water during the workday. The same percentage deny workers at least one day off in seven. In more than half of Nike's factories employees work more than 60 hours per week. In up to 25%, workers refusing overtime were punished. Wages were below the legal minimum at up to 25% of factories.[32]

For the first time in a major corporate report the details of all the factories were published. The report was significant for this transparency and being so candid about the problems that workers for Nike still face, and therefore the challenges that remain for the management. The NGOs working on these issues know that Nike is not alone in facing such problems. Indeed, they realise that the company has invested more in improving conditions than many of its competitors. Studies of voluntary corporate attempts at improving labour standards in global supply chains have suggested that they are delivering widespread improvements, and instead new approaches are needed that engage governments, NGOs and local businesses.[33]

This realisation has led to a new strategy from Nike. In May 2005, Nike's Vice President of Corporate Responsibility, Hannah Jones, told delegates at the Ethical Trading Initiative (ETI) conference that, whereas the company had previously been looking into how to solve problems for themselves, now they are exploring how to create systemic change in the industry. She explained that 'premium brands are in a lonely leadership

NIKE'S VP OF CORPORATE RESPONSIBILITY, HANNAH JONES: CONSUMERS ARE NOT REWARDING US FOR IMPROVED SOCIAL PERFORMANCE

position' because 'consumers are not rewarding us' for investments in improved social performance in supply chains. Like other companies, they have realised that the responsibility of one is to work towards the accountability of all. Consequently, one of Nike's new corporate citizenship goals is 'to effect positive, systemic change in working conditions within the footwear, apparel and equipment industries'. This involves the company engaging labour ministries, civil society and competitors around the world to try to raise the bar so that all companies have to attain better standards of social and environmental performance. One example is its involvement in the Multi-

Fiber Arrangement (MFA) Forum to help countries, unions and others plan for the consequences of the end of the MFA.

This strategy is beyond what many consultants, media commentators and academics currently understand. By claiming to be an advance in thinking, an article in *The Economist* in May 2005, by the worldwide managing director of McKinsey & Company, illustrated the limits of current consulting advice. It suggested that seeking good societal relations should be seen as both good for society and good for profitability. 'Profits should not be seen as an end in themselves,' suggested Ian Davis, 'but rather as a signal from society that their company is succeeding in its mission of providing something people want.'[34] However, those who have experience working in this field for some years, including Nike, realise that, however we may wish to talk about the compatibility of profits with people and planet, the current societal frameworks for business are not making this a reality. The implication is that we have to make this so by changing those frameworks.

The key strategic shift for Nike's management is that they no longer regard the company as a closed system. Instead, they understand its future depends on the way customers, suppliers, investors, regulators and others relate to it. Their challenge is to reshape the signals being given out by those groups to itself and its competitors, so that the company can operate in a sustainable and just way, which is also financially viable.

Nike's experience is pertinent to other companies, whose voluntary efforts are failing to address the root causes of the problems associated with their industry. Unilever, for example, was criticised by ActionAid for profiting from worsening conditions for workers on plantations.[35] Falling prices have led to plantations laying off workers and wages going unpaid—a trend that has seen a consequent increase in attacks against owners and managers. Apply a systems view to the situation would suggest that Unilever reconsider how it influences the global political economy that is driving down prices for tea.

The challenge is not only one of strategy but also leadership. Traditionally, analysts and educators on corporate leadership have assumed that it involves leading people towards the goal of their employer, the company. In May 2005, an article on leadership in Conference Board Canada's *Organizational Performance Review* quoted the thoughts of leaders from World War II and the Korean War.[36] This reflects what Mark Gerzon describes as a focus on 'leadership within borders', when what the world needs is 'leaders beyond borders'.[37] This means people who can see across borders created by others, such as the borders of their job, and reach across such borders to engage others in dialogue and action to address systemic problems. We could call this 'transcending leadership', which was alluded to by James McGregor Burns, in his pathbreaking book *Leadership*,[38] and is being developed by organisations such as the Shambhala Institute, who speak of 'authentic' leadership. It is a form of leadership that transcends the boundaries of one's professional role and the limits of one's own situation to engage people on collective goals. It is a form of leadership that transcends a limited conception of self, as the individual leader identifies with ever-greater wholes. It is a form of leadership that transcends the need for a single leader, by helping people to transcend their limited states of consciousness and concern and inspire them to lead.

Perhaps the best modern example of transcending leadership is Gandhi, who aroused and elevated the hopes and demands of millions of Indians and whose life and personality were enhanced in the process. It is an irony of our times that this anti-imperialist who chose to spin his own cloth could be an inspiration for the future direction of executives in large companies sourcing clothes from factories across Asia. Gandhi called on us to understand our connectedness to 'all that lives', and identify with ever-greater wholes. There is a lesson here for Nike and others. The apparel sector is an open system, and so wider issues of trade flows, governance, media, financial markets and politics impact on the potential of the sector, and thus Nike, to become sustainable and just. Without changes to the financial markets, Nike may find its efforts are in vain.

Changing money

In 2005, more people working in the corporate citizenship field began to express a belief that, in order to change the way business does business, we have to change the way money makes money. Greater focus is now on the role of the financial markets as the origin of, and therefore potential solution to, social and environmental problems. In the UK a variety of campaigning organisations including Amnesty International, Greenpeace, People & Planet and WWF joined together to launch FairShare, a campaign to mobilise UK pension fund owners to put pressure on their trustees, fund managers and ultimately the companies they invest in to behave in a responsible and sustainable manner.[39] The year 2005 witnessed a greater level of activity in the financial services sector, including a range of collaborative initiatives. In April, the group Just Pensions published a 'trustee toolkit' to help UK pension scheme trustees to understand more about responsible investment and how they might integrate it into their scheme's long-term investment strategy.[40] Denmark's National Pension Fund announced that it would work with the Ethical Investment Research Service (EIRIS) to help it invest responsibly.[41] Meanwhile, investors started to report more clearly on their screening, indexing, engagement, voting and government lobbying activities. For example, the asset manager of Insight Investment [the asset management arm of the HBOS Group] reported on its engagement with 62 companies on governance and corporate responsibility issues, representing 11% of its clients' holdings.[42]

Some institutional investors are recognising that major problems such as AIDS, climate change and poverty actually pose threats to long-term business success, and to combat them will require all companies to respond, not just a few companies that seek an ethical profile. Many investing institutions such as pension funds are so large that they own a broad cross-section of an economy, and so many of the costs externalised by some companies in their portfolio are picked up by other companies in the same portfolio, thereby impacting negatively on the value of the fund as a whole. For example, a steel company's likely success at securing an import tariff to protect its domestic market would be assessed favourably by many fund managers, and so that form of political lobbying activity would be incentivised by the stock market. However, the result of this may be to increase the price of steel thereby reducing the profitability of steel-using companies in the same portfolio, and so reducing wealth overall. A systems view of the situation would look at which individual corporate behaviours are likely to support longer-term value creation in the economy as a whole, without nega-tively impacting on that company in the short term, and then incentivise those, not for an immediate return to that company but a longer-term return to a wider set of stocks. Currently, most fund management still involves an assessment of individual compa-nies that is based on an atomistic not systemic mind-set: a company is assessed purely in terms of its own prospects (mostly in the near term).

As 'universal owners', Professor James Hawley of Saint Mary's College argues that institutional investors should be taking a lead to change the way their assets are man-aged, and redefine what it means to exercise fiduciary duty to include a broader range of factors.[43] A whole-systems theory of value and valuation would take into account a company's influence and reliance on the well-being of the whole world economy. A number of initiatives signpost what may emerge in the future as this theory of value develops. Frank Dixon of Innovest Social Investors has developed a new approach to assessing the social and environmental performance of companies which focuses on the political activities of companies and thereby 'encourages firms to proactively work with others to achieve system changes that hold them fully accountable'.[44] Another signpost is the launch of the Enhanced Analytics Initiative (EAI), where asset managers and asset owners with over €380 billion Assets Under Management (AUM) are actively supporting better sell-side research on extra-financial issues concerning society, the environment and corporate governance. They have committed to allocate individually a minimum of 5% of their respective brokerage commission to sell-side researchers who are effective at analysing material extra-financial issues and intangibles.[45]

One of the most significant initiatives is the development of the UN Responsible Investment Principles, covering the central importance of more active ownership and assessment of extra-financial issues in enhancing conduct of fiduciary duty.[46] Far-sighted fiduciaries looking after trillions of dollars of assets are engaged in this initia-tive, and many have also backed the Carbon Disclosure Project and the Extractive Industries Transparency Initiative, both of which encourage more corporate reporting on extra-financial issues.

Committed individuals in these investment institutions are beginning to lead beyond the borders of individual companies, and beyond their own short-term inter-ests. There is, however, some way to go. More engaged ownership can help address the social and environmental challenges of our time when the owners are pension funds with far-sighted fiduciaries. However, the average US mutual fund turns over its portfolio once every ten months, and consequently the more influence these myopic money flows exert on corporate boards the more difficult it may become for CEOs to lead their companies towards sustainability. The challenge such CEOs must meet is to reach across borders, to their competitors, to civil society, to far-sighted investors, and to governments, to build a critical mass of support for a fundamental transformation of the basic principles of our economy—property rights and their related obligations.

There is a deep simplicity to the surface complexity of malaise we see around the world today. This is because there is an initial system condition or trigger that creates a cascading fractal of social fracturing, by putting anti-social pressures on financial firms, to put anti-social pressure on CEOs, to put anti-social pressures on suppliers, communities, governments and, ultimately, 'all that lives'. That initial condition is this: the ability for people to demand an increase in their personal repository of power (i.e. financial capital), without being accountable to those who are affected by that demand.

Financial capital is one expression of property rights. Property rights are one form of human rights. The premise of most human rights thinking is that we enjoy rights so long as our exercise of a right does not infringe on the ability of others to enjoy theirs. By assuming that the numbers in our accounts will rise, without having any concern for how this is achieved, we are abrogating ourselves of the basic obligations that come with human rights. By demanding that our financial property increases we are creating situations that lead to the infringement of others' human rights (and even our own). If we believe in democracy, then it cannot be left up to the powerful to decide if they are responsible or not, or if they are carrying out their obligations or not. Instead, we must focus on the governance of capital by those who are affected by it—a concept dubbed 'capital accountability' by this author in a report for the UN Research Institute for Social Development (UNRISD).[47] An economy based on this concept of property would be one where owners of capital could invest only in activities that are accountable to those affected by them. Nick Robins, head of SRI at Henderson Global Investors, and author of the forthcoming *Imperial Corporation*, told me that demands for capital accountability will become greater as people realise that 'ultimately you cannot hold

NICK ROBINS: 'YOU CANNOT HOLD
CORPORATIONS TO ACCOUNT UNLESS YOU
HOLD CAPITAL TO ACCOUNT'

corporations to account unless you hold capital to account'. Drawing on Adam Smith's incisive critique of the irresponsibility of that iconic corporation of the 18th century, the East India Company, Robins argues the corporation's capacity for genuine wealth creation continues to be marred by design flaws. To remedy these, Robins proposes that the corporate privilege of limited liability needs to be matched by a legal duty of care to do no harm to people or the environment in the pursuit of profits for shareholders.

Work in progress

'I believe that the inequality between the rich and the poor is what causes the ills of the world—environmental deterioration, crime, drugs, terrorism.' So spoke the billionaire founder of eBay. It might have been 1 April 2005, but Jeff Skoll was dead serious during his speech at Oxford University.[48] He continued that 'social entrepreneurs work to decrease that inequity, bringing in new ideas to leverage small amounts of resources into something that creates a great amount of good. A great social entrepreneur is someone who makes a difference at scale, who doesn't just affect a small number of people, but who shifts the entire landscape.' Skoll was speaking at an event that

JEFF SKOLL: 'A GREAT SOCIAL
ENTREPRENEUR IS SOMEONE . . .
WHO SHIFTS THE ENTIRE
LANDSCAPE'

carries his name: the 2005 Skoll World Forum on Social Entrepreneurship, which was organised by Saïd Business School's Skoll Centre for Social Entrepreneurship.[49]

The centre is backed by the Skoll Foundation, whose mission is to advance systemic change to benefit communities around the world by investing in, connecting and celebrating social entrepreneurs. Along with the Ashoka, Schwab and Avina foundations, it is helping to promote the 'new heroes' that are making the world a better place. They use the term 'social entrepreneur' to describe professionals in private or non-governmental sectors who are pioneering new approaches to social and environmental problems. The Schwab Foundation describes social entrepreneurship as 'about applying practical, innovative and sustainable approaches to benefit society in general, with an emphasis on those who are marginalized and poor'. It defines a social entrepreneur as 'a pragmatic visionary who achieves large scale, systemic and sustainable social change through a new invention, a different approach, a more rigorous application of known technologies or strategies, or a combination of these'.[50] Such social entrepreneurs can work within and transform large organisations to make them more socially beneficial, or create their own organisations that provide solutions to social challenges.

ANTHONY HOPWOOD, DEAN OF
OXFORD UNIVERSITY'S SAÏD
BUSINESS SCHOOL: 'SOCIAL
ENTREPRENEURS ACT AS THE
CHANGE AGENTS FOR SOCIETY'

The Dean of Oxford University's Saïd Business School, Anthony Hopwood, explains that 'just as entrepreneurs have changed the face of business, social entrepreneurs act as the change agents for society, seizing opportunities others miss and improving systems, inventing new approaches and creating sustainable solutions to change society for the better'.[51]

At the conference the recipients of the 2005 Skoll Awards for Social Entrepreneurship were announced. One of these was the Rugmark Foundation USA, which has been working since 1994 to eliminate child labour in carpet manufacturing.[52] In Nepal, Pakistan and India, the organisation monitors factories, certifies carpets made without child labour, and rescues and educates child labourers. In consumer countries, it seeks to create market preference for certified rugs. Imports of certified rugs now represent 1% of the US market, and with help from Skoll, Rugmark Foundation USA hopes to increase the market share of certified rugs to 5% by 2007. Another recipient is the Appropriate Technologies for Enterprise Creation (ApproTEC) which since 1991 has been developing and promoting technologies that can be used to run profitable small-scale enterprises.[53] Working in developing countries in Africa, ApproTEC introduced low-cost, people-powered irrigation pumps that enable farmers to grow more crops and sell produce in the dry season, when prices are high and supply is low. Since its inception, ApproTEC reports it has helped farmers start 36,000 new businesses in Kenya, Tanzania and Mali that collectively generate more than $38 million in new profits and wages per year.

Ashoka Foundation's Olivier Kayser argues that one of the most powerful things they do for people, beyond providing financial support, is giving them a sense of common identity as social entrepreneurs.[54] This reminds us of how concepts are powerful in shaping our lived realities. The way the concept of 'social entrepreneurship' is defined is therefore an important process. Some understand it in a more narrow sense, to describe the practice of those involved in 'social enterprise', which is viewed as 'those businesses with primarily social objectives whose surpluses are principally reinvested for that purpose in the business or in the community'. That is the definition offered by the Sustainable Enterprise Research Group (SERG) at the Management School of Liverpool John Moores University in the UK. They continue that it is 'an umbrella term for a range of alternative business models, which combine civic engagement and public service with wealth creation'.[55] It is certain that the burgeoning activity of alternative companies involved in fair trade, community-based or organic production warrants more research, and that larger corporations that seek to be more responsible should not be grouped together with them as 'social enterprises'. However, individuals with the attitude and skills to successfully innovate and implement new approaches to social challenges can work in all social and organisational settings, and their common characteristics invite definition, investigation and support.

How is the management academe responding to this phenomenon? 'Social entrepreneurship is a growing international trend and increasingly business educators are incorporating the discipline into their core curricula', argues Anthony Hopwood. Yet his university is one of the few that have made research and teaching on social entrepreneurship a priority. The US is where the management academe have engaged most with social entrepreneurship, although in many cases it has meant a rebranding of existing work on the non-profit sector. For example, emerging out of its work on non-profit-sector management, Harvard University has established the Social Enterprise Initiative, which regards 'social enterprise' as encompassing 'the contributions any individual or organization can make toward social improvement, regardless of its legal form (nonprofit, private, or public-sector)'.[56] The Association to Advance Collegiate Schools of Business, an international accrediting agency, lists 28 other schools that report programmes in social entrepreneurship, including Columbia, Stanford, Duke and Yale.[57] Much impetus for work in this area is coming from students themselves.

Students of the National University of Singapore, for example, have created the Social Entrepreneurship Forum, which convenes every year.[58] In New Zealand the stu-

dent-led University of Auckland Entrepreneurship Challenge 2005 called for applications from social entrepreneurship projects.[59] The largest example of a student-led initiative is 'Net Impact', which seeks to 'shape the future of business by fostering a
network of new-generation leaders who are committed to using the power of business
to improve the world'. Headquartered in San Francisco, with more than 100 local
groups in cities and graduate schools around the world, it now involves more than
11,000 members.[60] Amlan Saha, co-founder of the Net Impact chapter in the Haute
École de Commerce (HEC) in France, told us that, 'if a business school is lagging behind
in providing education on social entrepreneurship, it is often students affiliated to the
Net Impact network who organise seminars, which once tried, are often incorporated
into the curriculum. It's a student movement for more powerful and progressive business education.'

Intellectual development in this area is limited, perhaps because those most interested in it want to do something rather than just write about it. Ashoka publishes the
journal *Changemakers*[61] which provides useful information in a journalistic style. The
Schwab Foundation collaborates with the Spanish business school IESE to publish a
case studies series, which, although useful, focuses on describing success and therefore serves as advocacy material.[62] In 2003 Stanford started the first academic journal
dedicated to the subject, the *Stanford Social Innovation Review*, which also presents
fairly functional and uncritical analysis of the area.[63] The Liverpool University
researchers are editing a special issue of the *Journal of Social Economics* which will also
add to thinking in this area.[64] However, despite a few papers describing the development of this concept,[65] it remains under-researched and under-theorised. One reason
may be because it poses a challenge to the traditional research disciplines in management studies. There is certainly valuable interdisciplinary research, theorising, publishing and educating to be done on social entrepreneurship in general.

The growing interest in social entrepreneurship is driven by a questioning of traditional business practices on the one hand, and traditional forms of charity on the other.
Changes to their funding environment have pushed some non-profit organisations to
look at potential market-based models of social change. Growing interest in the potential commercial opportunities to be found in providing products and services to the
world's poor is another factor. In 2005, the Shell Foundation made a splash on this
topic with its report 'Enterprise Solutions to Poverty'. Using a series of case studies in
Africa and India, the Shell Foundation explains how multinationals operating in developing countries can apply non-financial assets—such as their convening power, networks and management acumen—to the problems of poverty.[66] A book by Stuart Hart
broadened this 'base of the pyramid' concept, to suggest that business leaders should
engage with the world's really difficult problems as they could find profitable business
models in providing practical solutions.[67] The rise of this concept in the management
studies academe was illustrated by IESE's development of a learning laboratory on the
base-of-the-pyramid concept.[68]

IESE's focus is on large international corporations. However, John Elkington, who
is writing a book on social entrepreneurship, told me that the old economy of large
consuming and controlling organisations will eventually die off and seeds of the future
economy are being planted by socially and environmentally conscious entrepreneurs
who are starting their own companies. This view recalls the concept of 'creative destruction' first articulated by Joseph Schumpeter in 1942: 'Capitalism . . . is by nature a

form or method of economic change and not only never is but never can be station-ary . . .' wrote Schumpeter. 'The fundamental impulse that sets and keeps the capital-ist engine in motion comes from the new consumers, goods, the new methods of production or transportation, the new markets, the new forms of industrial organiza-tion that capitalist enterprise creates.'[69] An example of this process comes from per-sonal computing. The industry, led by Microsoft and Intel, destroyed many mainframe computer companies—but, in doing so, entrepreneurs created one of the most impor-tant inventions of this century.

Evolutionary biologist and social commentator Elisabet Sahtouris uses the metaphor of the butterfly to reflect the hope that the coming transformation will create some-thing more beautiful than the current economic order. 'In metamorphosis, within the body of the caterpillar little things that biologists call imaginal discs or imaginal cells begin to crop up in the body of the caterpillar. They aren't recognized by the immune system so the caterpillar's immune system wipes them out as they pop up. It isn't until they begin to link forces and join up with each other that they get stronger and are able to resist the onslaught of the immune system, until the immune system itself breaks down and the imaginal cells form the body of the butterfly.' Sahtouris says this 'is a beautiful metaphor for what is happening in our times. The old body is going into meltdown while the new one develops. It isn't that you end one thing and then start another. So everybody engaged in recycling, in alternative projects, in communal liv-ing, in developing healthier systems for themselves and each other is engaged in build-ing the new world while the old one collapses. Its collapse is inevitable. There is no way around that.'[70]

This social butterfly takes Schumpeter's view of creative destruction to a new level, for, if its cells are new types of entrepreneur, its body will be a new form of economic system.

3Q2005

July–September

Jem Bendell

Money talks . . . but will it listen?

Since 1998, when up to 60,000 people formed a human chain in Birmingham during the G8 meeting in England that year, the mass mobilisations of people protesting at international summits have helped to make capitalism a point of popular political debate. This 'counter-globalisation' movement has prompted us to question whether our economic system is functioning for the collective good or creating such inequality and ecological destruction that it is leading humanity to ruin. Since 1998 inter-governmental summits have been organised in more secure locations, where the protesters have little chance of disrupting the meeting. Consequently, the question for many people interested in mass public mobilisation, as part of a counter-globalisation movement, has been 'where to go from here'.

In July 2005, the 'Make Poverty History' campaign and associated 'Live 8' musical events marked a new stage in social activism around these summits. Coordinated NGO action in the build-up to the summit, combined with initiative by UK Chancellor Gordon Brown, meant that the world's media expected an announcement on what the G8 leaders would do to improve their role in the aid, trade and debt situation of the global South.

UK CHANCELLOR GORDON
BROWN: MAKING MOVES
ON DEBT RELIEF

The way that celebrity involvement dominated the message broadcast around the world was a concern for some. The message became one of charity not justice, with the powerful men of the world asked to help the unfortunate rather than being challenged to correct their own countries' involvement in oppressive trading and financial relations with poor countries. The movement on trade issues was non-existent, and the debt cancellation deal was not comprehensive.

Nevertheless, the G8 leaders did agree to write off 100% of the debts of 18 countries that were owed to the IMF and World Bank, and to require those countries to agree to measures that would reduce corruption, but not require them to adopt other reforms that would amount to interference in their domestic political processes. This achievement represented the culmination of a number of forces, including the seven years of protests at these international summits.

The agreement does not, however, end the rich countries' abuse of the South through its odious debt claims. It is still to be seen whether some countries will fund debt cancellation by diverting money from their aid budgets—robbing Peter to pay Paul. Debt still stands at US$2.5 trillion, much of which has been paid for many times over, in cash, as well as in the lives of children denied medical care and education as a result. The West's moral debt remains unpaid.

The biggest problem with the debt cancellation agreement, one that development NGOs did not highlight clearly at the time, but which is relevant to the corporate citizenship agenda, is that the majority of the developing-country debts are owed to private financial institutions and are therefore not covered by the G8 agreement. In Latin America, for example, 63% of their external debts are to the private sector, and only four of the continent's countries will benefit from the G8 debt cancellation initiative.[1]

These bonds of poverty and exploitation are known in the financial world as 'emerging-market debt', and have been one of the best-performing asset classes since 2000. When Switzerland and other countries cancelled their government-held debts in the 1990s, the net debt repayments from developing countries didn't actually fall, as those countries were then in a better position to service other debts, owed to creditors such as the World Bank and private institutions. So, although the G8 politicians could express their joy that thousands of children in sub-Saharan Africa will be able to get an education because of debt cancellation, it is shareholders and fundholders that are the immediate winners of government debt cancellation, as poor countries will be better able to service their private debts. No wonder, then, that emerging-market debt prices spiked in the weeks following announcements about deals on debt, along with the shares of banks such as UBS.

So what have these 'secret winners' of the G8 actually done to help alleviate the debt crisis? Through the 'London Club' process they have rescheduled debts, reactively, when a country has reached such difficulty they have to suspend payments, and then on really expensive terms. Worse, the private financial institutions and their associations, such as the Washington-based Institute of International Finance (IIF), have blocked efforts to get an arbitration process set up for all debts to be looked at in terms of their legitimacy. We should remember that a quarter of the loans making up the current debt stock were lent to dictators. Not encumbering new democracies with the debts of the regime they have replaced was a good enough argument for the US and UK to cancel Iraq's debts accrued under Saddam Hussein; but they do not wish to recognise this as a matter of principle.

The lack of leadership from the banks on the debt crisis is understandable when you consider their role in lubricating the processes that led to it. Capital flight from developing countries has been a key factor in balance-of-payments problems. An estimated US$11 trillion is held in tax-haven banks by highly wealthy individuals, costing the world's governments about US$255 billion a year in lost tax revenue. Currency speculation at over a trillion dollars a day is also a major problem, destabilising currencies so that there is a mismatch between loans priced in rich-country currencies and repayments in domestic currencies. The world's top 20 banks account for 80% of this currency speculation, making a huge profit from a trade that helps no one and contributes to debt crises.

In 2005 the private financial sector in rich countries lobbied hard for regulatory changes in poor countries that would do little to address these problems, and their own culpability in the current and future odious debts of the developing world. Their efforts led to a declaration from the G8 on the importance of progress in the developing world liberalising its financial sector, and a commitment to attaining commitments by the Hong Kong ministerial of the World Trade Organisation. There is no proven development benefit from such liberalisation, and many developing countries doubt the benefits of capital liberalisation. In fact, countries who have not liberalised their financial sectors, such as Malaysia, China and Chile, have managed to ride out financial crises affecting their regions. Corporate lobbying for blanket liberalisation of financial sectors is, therefore, irresponsible.

With the message of the 2005 G8 protests having been so managed by celebrities and mainstream NGOs, protesters may now consider that protesting at these summits has run its course, and turn their attention elsewhere. Many of the people who protested on the streets at the Birmingham G8 summit saw G8 governments and institutions such as the World Bank and IMF to be mere servants of a system of unfettered profit-seeking. The system itself has to change, not its functionaries. This thinking was illustrated by the mass protest in the UK that followed the 1998 G8, which was called 'Stop the City' and targeted London's financial district. With government debt cancellations the banks are now in the hot seat on debt. Therefore, in answering the question 'where to next?', the counter-globalisation movement may once again turn its attention to the private financial institutions. Reports on the conclusions of the counter-Summit suggested that such a shift in focus is likely.[2]

A report in September from Christian Aid gave an indication of this shift in focus toward the questionable impact of private banks in international development. The charity attacked offshore tax havens and the banks that use them, estimating that tax evasion and offshore banking secrecy costs third-world governments up to US$500 billion a year in lost revenues. The report's author, Andrew Pendleton, said the UK government had a particular responsibility. 'Of the world's 72 tax havens, 35 are British territories or Commonwealth members. Tackling global evasion will take a lot of international cooperation, but it would be fitting for Britain to take the lead.'[3]

Are the banks and investors ready for growing critical attention from civil society? Many currently consider their social responsibility is sufficiently addressed by having a recycling programme in headquarters, employee volunteering, more sophisticated risk assessments, and a few extra product lines for niche markets, called ethical or socially responsible investment funds. HSBC has gone further than most in addressing its own in-house impacts on the environment, committing itself to carbon neutrality.

Some have also begun to address issues more central to their core business of providing financial services. For example, Barclays has given an account of its efforts to improve its consumer and corporate lending practices, and promote financial inclusion, in its *Corporate Responsibility Report* for 2004.[4] A number of banks have also begun addressing the impacts of their lending practices, through the Equator Principles. HSBC's *Corporate Social Responsibility Report* for 2004 reported for the first time the number and value of transactions approved and the number of transactions declined through applying the Equator Principles.[5] A number of initiatives in the institutional investment arena (see 'Changing money' on page 299), are also indicating that the sustainable development dimension to normal fund management practices are beginning to be looked at. However, some of the greatest impacts of the financial sector on sustainable development could involve Southern-country debts, capital flight and tax avoidance, hedge funds, and currency speculation. It is not surprising that these areas are left unaddressed by most financial institutions, because finding socially and environmentally beneficial ways of conducting these activities appears to be a difficult challenge, perhaps impossible. Some prodding from activists may make this challenge an unavoidable one, and usher in a new paradigm in responsible finance, which addresses the core activities on banks and investors.

The power of the private financial institutions in shaping the policies of the G8 reminds us clearly that money talks. As the counter-globalisation moves its attention towards those same financial institutions, we will find out whether money can listen.

Feeling peaky about oil?

One thing the G8 did manage to agree was a common statement on climate change, which was recognised as a 'serious long-term challenge' for the entire planet. The original draft communiqué had said 'our world is warming', reflecting the fact that global ambient temperatures have risen 0.6°C in the past 60 years, and each of the last 25 years have been the hottest on record.[6] However, this reality was uncomfortable for the administration of US President G.W. Bush, and they had the G8 text watered down, in similar ways to their influence on the UN summit in September.[7]

Despite the ostrich impression of some world leaders, the realities of climate change demanded attention during 2005, with spiralling demand for oil, increasing oil prices, severe weather events, droughts and economic implications being felt worldwide.

In August 2005, the price of oil bumped up against $70 a barrel. This was not just an anomaly due to political instability or speculation, with Goldman Sachs predicting that oil prices could move to $100 a barrel in the near future. Instead, major changes in supply and demand have been affecting the price of oil. Key to growing demand has been the industrialisation of large countries such as China. It had already increased its oil consumption by 11% in 2004, becoming the second-largest oil consumer after the United States. The other side to the price equation is supply. Overall discoveries of oil peaked in the 1960s, with just one new barrel of oil being discovered today for every four that is consumed. New extraction techniques and new discoveries may keep things going, but estimates of the oil peak, when supply won't keep up with demand, range from between 2006 and 2020. A global peak in production is not the same thing as oil running out, as large amounts of oil will still be pumped after that point, but on an unavoidably declining basis. Although debates about the end of oil may have a '70s retro feel to them, given the last time an oil shock hit the world, this time the evidence suggests that we are arriving at the beginning of that end.[8]

The impact of past and present consumption of oil continued to be felt during 2005, but this time in ways that made the global media. Changing weather and seasons had already been disrupting people's lives in China, the Pacific, and Peru.[9] Poor monsoon rains had hit agriculture in India, reducing economic growth.[10] However, the hurricanes in the United States were broadcast to the world, and led many to discuss the implications of climate change. It was the region's worst hurricane season in history, with the weather authorities running out of names for the number of storms. Although meteorology is complex, this upturn in storm activity was consistent with predictions based on current patterns of climate change. The impact of Hurricane Katrina on the thinking of some in the US was clear. Wal-Mart CEO Lee Scott said he had had an epiphany on climate change and the wider environmental challenge. 'We should view the environment as Katrina in slow motion,' he said. 'This used to be controversial, but the science is in and it is overwhelming.' Wal-Mart announced it will invest $500 million a year in new environmental technologies, including renewable energy systems.[11]

The business implications of climate change continued to unfold during 2005. Lloyd's Insurers announced that Katrina would probably cost it over US$2 billion. Allianz, the giant German financial services group, released a report jointly with WWF, which reported that weather-related disaster costs are currently rising at 2–4% a year, with premiums rising to meet the costs. It called for a 60–80% reductions in global emissions by 2050. Meanwhile, prices for carbon allowances rose sharply in the middle of the year, up from €12 a tonne in April 2005 to almost €29 by July. One reason is the EU's reduction of allowances to some countries, but another important reason is the rising price of natural gas, which has led more electricity companies to source energy from coal, which is proving cheaper, despite the carbon charges due to its greater production of CO_2.[12] This again raises concerns that the carbon trading system may do little to reduce carbon emissions. The limited geographical application of the system to Europe also raises questions about its effectiveness: some companies, including Norsk Hydro and Corus, have said they may move their factories abroad to mitigate high fuel costs and carbon charges.[13]

Despite concern about the competitiveness implications of action on climate change, Nick Robins of Henderson Global Investors argues that there are many opportunities 'for those who understand the dynamics of the coming carbon crunch and invest in industries of the future'.[14] In light of this, KLD Research and Analytics Inc. has launched the Global Climate 100 Index, the first investor index comprising companies focusing on solutions to global warming. The CEO of the world's largest company, GE, Jeff Immelt, announced his conviction that 'green is green', making reference to the colour of the US dollar, and that his company 'plan to make money' from investing $1.5 billion in environmental technologies. It is estimated that the world market for environmental goods and services is already worth around £270 billion.[15]

Not all companies can find easy win–win solutions to the carbon crunch. The airline industry faces a particular challenge. In July 2005, a coalition of UK airlines, airports, aircraft manufacturers and air navigation operators began working on the

'Sustainable Aviation' initiative to increase fuel efficiency by 50% by 2020 compared with 2000 levels, and seek to enter the EU's Emission Trading Scheme. Environmental groups pointed out that a threefold increase in the volume of air flights in the next 30 years is being planned for by the industry. It is difficult to see how voluntary corporate action on reducing the volume of passenger sales is possible, and so the challenge appears to be one for government.

The inevitability of major changes arising from the carbon crunch is making more investors hungry for good information on the risks and opportunities faced by their portfolios. Henderson Global Investors has worked with Trucost to create a way of measuring companies' carbon emissions relative to their earnings.[16] Henderson's Nick Robins said that, if companies had to pay the UK government estimate of the economic damage done by a tonne of carbon, about £20 a tonne, then more than 12% of the FTSE 100's earnings would be at risk. He explained that more disclosure of carbon emissions is essential for investors. 'Carbon is set to become a critical factor in business strategy, influencing the pattern of corporate acquisitions and divestments, for example. There should be no surprise when the first carbon-driven profits warning is issued. For investors, getting standardized comparable carbon data from companies is now imperative.'[17]

In a new book on the future of capitalism, Jonathon Porritt called for concerted action between government, business and civil society to address the systemic challenge of climate change and sustainable development more broadly. 'It is critical that politicians the world over stop flirting with renewables as "an interesting little niche" and start investing in them as if our future depended upon them—which, indeed, it does.'[18] Porritt notes that renewables will not substitute oil like for like, and so societies will need to adapt in more profound ways. Agriculture, energy, manufacturing and transportation will all be impacted in ways that require shifts in how we under-

JONATHON PORRITT: CALLING FOR CONCERTED ACTION BETWEEN GOVERNMENT, BUSINESS AND CIVIL SOCIETY

stand and meet our needs. For example, although more hybrid cars will be useful, they will not play a role in meeting personal mobility needs, without a major change in those needs, and options to fulfil them through non-carbon-emitting forms of transport. A fundamental questioning of current concepts of personal and societal progress is necessitated by the environmental challenge. In the past decade many environmentally aware people have become skilled professionals in government, business and elsewhere, and focused on achieving incremental or small-scale changes. This has lead to a death of vision, according to Michael Schellenberger and Ted Nordhaus writing in *Grist Magazine*. 'Those of us who call ourselves environmentalists have a responsibility to examine our role and close the gap between the problems we know and the solutions we propose', they wrote. It appears that, with environmental problems moving from prediction to reality, a renewed moral conviction and transformative vision may arise from the environmental movement in the coming years, with implications for the corporate citizenship agenda, and beyond.[19]

Ten years on

At the other end of the hydrocarbon value chain, oil companies were receiving a mixed press for their impact on the communities under which much of their resources are drawn. In Nigeria, communities in the oil-producing Niger Delta went to court to try to stop 'gas flaring'—the burning off of gas during the production of crude oil. Natural gas is released during the extraction of crude oil, and it is estimated that this flared gas from Nigeria could be pumping 35 million tonnes of carbon dioxide and 12 million tonnes of methane into the atmosphere annually. The gas flaring has been linked to local acid rain, and poor health in the region. Shell announced earlier in the year that it would not be able to capture the gas so as to stop the flaring by 2008, as required by the government. Meanwhile, accusations continued that oil companies in the region are supporting local militia in order to quell an uprising and protect their oil operations.[20]

This is reminiscent of the situation ten years previously, which brought Shell's operations in Nigeria into the international spotlight. On 10 November 1995 nine Nigerians, who claimed that the regime of dictator Sani Abacha and Royal Dutch/Shell were complicit in oppressing the Ogoni tribe, were executed. Their leader was the charismatic writer and activist Ken Saro-Wiwa, and at the trial before his death he pointed

KEN SARO-WIWA: PAID THE
ULTIMATE PRICE FOR HIS ACTIVISM

the finger at Shell, and called for an international boycott of the company. That boycott spread to three different continents, and the impact on the company helped spark the contemporary corporate responsibility movement. It demonstrated that civil society had grown and become internationally connected, had turned its attention to the malpractices of companies, that consumers had become aware of the power and therefore responsibility of large corporations, and that their abuses in the global South would no longer go unnoticed.

Nevertheless, ten years on, the jury is still out on Shell, the oil industry, and the usefulness of voluntary corporate responsibility more generally. At its 2005 annual meeting, activist shareholders circulated the third alternative Shell report, called *Lessons Not Learned*, which argues that, despite commitments made in previous years, Shell still disregards the environment and the rights of the people living near its operations in many parts of the world.[21]

Amnesty International published a report that focused on a number of other oil companies operating in Africa. Amnesty argued that agreements signed by Exxon-Mobil and other companies with the governments of Chad and Cameron requires these governments to give priority to the oil company interests over and above the interests of those living in the vicinity. The organisation said that there had already been abuses in these areas with farmers displaced and refused compensation, and the agreement threatened further human rights problems for the local population.[22]

Meanwhile the government of Chad has taken steps to report on its anti-corruption efforts in the oil industry. An Oversight Committee (Collège de Contrôle et de Surveillance des Revenues Pétroliers) appointed by the Chadian government has detailed the findings of its first inspection of the implementation of projects financed by Chad's 2004 oil revenues. According to the World Bank, 'publication of this report is a demonstration of the Chadian government's commitment to the transparency of its oil revenue management'. However, the World Bank also expressed its concern with some of the report's findings, which suggest there is some way to go.[23] This effort toward greater transparency of the use of revenues derived from the oil industry is one response to the outcry in 1995 about Saro-Wiwa, as it attempts to address the financial incentives that have fuelled government corruption and oppression.

The Extractive Industries Transparency Initiative (EITI) is the broad inter-governmental effort tackling this challenge. It has now gained the support of most major multinationals, and the government of Nigeria is playing a leading role. At the G8 Business Action for Africa Summit, African firms also expressed their support for EITI and other initiatives that fight against corruption in their home countries.[24] If EITI is successful, regimes such as the Abacha dictatorship will be far more difficult to maintain, and the allure of dictatorial power in such countries could wane.

The current government of Nigeria points to increasing foreign investment, such as US$150 million from Coca-Cola, as a sign that it has turned away from its past of corruption and mismanagement. Although that particular investment came in for some criticism from some Nigerian NGOs in July 2005, due to various concerns about water, pollution, labour rights and nutrition, the argument that Africa needs invest-

SHELL CEO JEROEN VAN DER VEER:
IMPORTANT TO TACKLE POVERTY IN
AFRICA

ment not just charity was made clearly by a range of corporate leaders, the G8 and the New Partnership for Africa's Development (NEPAD).

Interestingly, given the history described above, a foundation established by Shell has been taking a lead in this arena. The Shell Foundation announced a $100 million fund to address the lack of finance and business skills for small African businesses. In addition, the Foundation announced a project with retailer Marks & Spencer, where the Foundation will invest US$1 million in local flower- and fruit-growing enterprises that are involved in the retailer's supply chain.[25] The Chief Executive of the Royal Dutch/Shell Group, Jeroen van der Veer, said that it is important for the company, and others like it, to explore how to tackle poverty in Africa through their everyday business operations, although he argued that government has a key role to play in providing a context for local economic development.[26]

The political bottom line

oil companies were also in the spotlight in 2005 for lobbying on climate change. Exxon-Mobil, for example, was criticised for influencing US energy policy in ways that undermine action on carbon emissions.[27] Corporate influence over political processes is a key concern of critiques of globalisation, and has featured in previous Annual Reviews. The scale of lobbying is significant. In 2004 alone, the collective invoices of Washington lobbyists were likely to have exceeded $3 billion. In Europe an estimated 15,000 lobbyists represent a €60–90 million industry, but no comprehensive figures are available as disclosure takes place only on a voluntary basis. [28] The Alliance for Lobbying Transparency and Ethics Regulation–EU has argued that 'The enormous influence of corporate lobbyists undermines democracy and all too frequently results in postponing, weakening or blocking urgently needed progress in EU social, environmental and consumer protections.'

In addition to corporate lobbying, corporate political contributions became a growing concern for investors during 2005. Responding to pressure from faith-based shareholders prior to their annual general meetings, pharmaceutical companies Johnson & Johnson and Schering–Plough agreed that they will account for and publicly disclose on their websites an annual list of corporate political contributions. This was a success for the Interfaith Center on Corporate Responsibility (ICCR), which coordinated a series of resolutions on this issue at Merck & Co., Abbott Laboratories, Wyeth and Eli Lilly. Major funds backed the resolutions, including the New York State Common Retirement Fund, the US's second-largest public pension fund. Margaret Weber of the Adrian Dominican Sisters, who filed a primary filer with Schering–Plough, explained that 'companies need to be held accountable to their shareholders for their political activism'.[29]

Meanwhile, in the UK, the issue of corporate lobbying became central to the corporate responsibility debate in the late Northern summer of 2005. Friends of the Earth UK published a report in July that condemned the UK's largest trade association, the Confederation of British Industry (CBI), for routinely exaggerating the costs of environmental regulation and falsely presenting its anti-regulatory position as if it has consensus support across the business community.[30] The report, 'Easy Listening', details instances such as CBI lobbying on the EU's Emission Trading Scheme leading to the government increasing the UK's greenhouse gas allocation by 20 million tonnes per year. The report challenges the CBI's negative view of regulation and says good legislation would drive innovation and investment.[31] The environmental group's executive director, Tony Juniper, said 'there is little evidence to back up the CBI's mantra that regulation damages UK competitiveness. Time and again, they have exaggerated the costs of regulation and ignored the benefits. It's time the Government started to demand

FRIENDS OF THE EARTH UK'S TONY JUNIPER:
THERE IS LITTLE EVIDENCE THAT REGULATION
DAMAGES UK COMPETITIVENESS

hard evidence from the CBI and started listening to other, more progressive business voices.' His argument was endorsed by the chairman of the Environmental Industries Commission, representing almost 280 companies working in the environment sector, Adrian Wilkes. He said 'scare-mongering by polluting industries regularly exaggerates the costs of pollution control, making the Government back-pedal on environmental protection'.[32]

Historically, trade associations have pursued the collective interests of their members either by restricting government involvement in their members' affairs, or encouraging intervention where it could create or protect markets. The sustainable development challenge requires a new paradigm from trade associations, where they pursue the longer-term strategic interests of their members by attending to the problems of free-riders. Unfortunately, the level of dialogue at an International Labour Organisation conference of employers' organisations in Geneva in October did not suggest that this new paradigm is imminent, with negative implications for the ability of this world body to play an effective role in the corporate citizenship agenda.

Consequently, some companies have been breaking ranks with the reactionary positions of many trade associations, and lobbied the political process for socially beneficial innovations. Examples include Electrolux supporting producer responsibility on electrical goods, and Marks & Spencer's support for more legislation on the use of chemicals.[33] Companies are also taking collective action where there is none from traditional trade associations. A group of large corporations including BAA, BP, Cisco Systems and HSBC have publicly petitioned governments for more action on climate change. In a letter arguing for more government leadership, they wrote that 'the private sector and governments are caught in a "Catch 22" situation . . . Governments tend to feel limited in their ability to introduce new policies for reducing emissions because they fear business resistance, while companies are unable to take their invest-ments in low carbon solutions to scale because of lack of long-term policies.'[34]

In the September issue of the journal *Business Strategy and the Environment*, three key reasons were identified for this broadening of the corporate citizenship agenda to include political action: first, the growing criticism of the ability of voluntary corporate responsibility initiatives to deliver social and environmental benefits; second, the increasing awareness and targeting of corporate political activities by NGOs; and, third, a realisation among certain corporate executives and financiers that, without changes to public policies, an individual company's own voluntary responsibility may not deliver sufficient commercial returns and government may need to intervene to pun-ish the laggards.[35] That the voluntary corporate responsibility policy community in the UK is grappling with the implications of this shift of attention to the 'political bottom line' was illustrated by three new publications.

The Institute of Business Ethics published its analysis of the issue[36] and then Sus-tainAbility and WWF published results of their analysis of how 100 of the world's largest companies report on their lobbying practices.[37] In September 2005, the Institute of Social and Ethical Accountability (AccountAbility) followed up with a publication that suggested a framework for corporate management of this issue.[38] Each of the reports discussed issues of the transparency of political influence, stakeholder consultation and communication in the development of political positions, the level of coherence between political influence and espoused business policies, and the content of the political influence in relation to wider social or environmental standards.

Transparency is a key focus for SustainAbility and WWF. 'Until this "black box" of lobbying is comprehensively opened up, allowing the interface between private busi-ness and governments to be more transparent and better understood, trust—which has been flagging for many years—will remain elusive.'[39] However, AccountAbility was ambiguous on the importance of greater transparency. One of its arguments against transparency relates to practicality. It noted that 'lobbying is by its very nature an informal process and thus often opaque'.[40] As Mallen Baker illustrated in a column on the topic, 'the quiet word at a charity event, the brief conversation in the Wimble-don enclosure . . . will always take place and be unrecorded'.[41] This is not, however, reason for not making more political influence transparent where it is possible to do so. Another argument put forward against transparency was that lobbyists do not want it: 'many lobbyists argue that transparency and effectiveness in lobbying are some-times incompatible, given the variable timescales, informality and inherent confiden-tiality of their profession', AccountAbility wrote.[42] Some might question the reason-ing that because a profession does not want something it is not worth pursuing. The third reason was that transparency was not, in itself, enough. 'Transparency and responsibility are not the same thing. For example, many people would disapprove of a company lobbying against restrictions on tobacco sales to minors, even if done openly and acceptably within a country's legal framework.'[43] Oddly, this is exactly the reason why transparency is important, to allow such conflict to be surfaced, and hopefully, eventually resolved through various processes of engagement. Nevertheless, Account-Ability did propose transparency as an important part of its framework for responsi-ble lobbying.

WWF, SustainAbility and AccountAbility highlighted the importance of engaging stakeholders on corporate lobbying positions. The aggregates company Lafarge is one large corporation that engages stakeholders in public policy discussions.

AccountAbility, however, also expressed doubts that stakeholder consultation would prove effective in this area. 'There is an inherent difficulty in defining a process standard which would make both corporate lobbyists and their clients happy, while at the same time assuaging the concerns of those with opposing viewpoints on substantive issues.'[44] Given that AccountAbility's main work in the last ten years has been the proposition of best practice for stakeholder dialogue, through AA1000, this suggestion that a process standard involving transparency and consultation is not a sufficient solution is notable.

The AccountAbility report moves beyond these caveats to make the argument that the consistency between a company's political activities and its expressed values is the most important issue. This responds to the fact that a key reputational risk for corporations arises from claims of hypocrisy. The easiest target for campaigners is where a company's stated values are directly contravened by the objectives and conduct of its lobbying. This consistency could not be judged by external audiences, including auditors, if there is no transparency. SustainAbility and WWF therefore propose a framework that integrates transparency and consistency. They rated companies from the provision of no information, through to basic, developing, systematic and integrated reporting. Over 51 companies achieved at least a basic rating and a handful of corporate reports, including those from BASF, BP, Chevron, Dow, Ford, General Motors, GlaxoSmithKline and HP, provided more detailed information. However, the report still identified what was considered inconsistency between lobbying positions and corporate policies on sustainable development. For instance, 'while Ford and General Motors may have high levels of transparency and a growing sophistication in reporting their lobbying activities, they still actively resist controls on greenhouse gas emissions via sponsorship of their industry trade group'.[45]

AccountAbility noted that consistency is not a sufficient criterion for making lobbying 'responsible', as highlighted by their mention of tobacco lobbying, above. The involvement of the United Nations Global Compact in co-publishing the report meant that the role of international standards on human rights and the environment would have to be addressed. Therefore, within the concept of consistency or coherence, AccountAbility includes consistency with 'universal values' as well as internal policies and codes. Similarly, implicit in the SustainAbility–WWF position is that some objectives of corporate lobbying are better or worse—they favour lobbying that they consider supports governments protecting human rights and the environment. What neither report considered was who decides what is the best way of enacting a 'universal value', realising human rights, or protecting the environment. To return to the issue discussed at the beginning of this column, who should decide that financial-sector liberalisation is the best way to increase the realisation of the universal values embodied in the covenant on economic, social and cultural rights? Or that water privatisation is the best solution for watershed management?

This brings us to the question of why particular views are held, arguments are made, and whose views and arguments become the rules of society. These are questions of democratic governance. The meaning of democracy was not discussed in detail in any of the three reports, with only short comments that lobbying is one aspect of freedom of expression, and therefore central to democracy, but that some consider the growing volume of corporate lobbying is a threat to democracy. A key reason why corporate political activities are more contentious today is because of concerns about the abuse of power. Therefore, the challenge is how to ensure the democratic governance of markets for the public interest; and any serious discussion of corporate lobbying must engage with concepts and mechanisms of democracy.

It is a fundamental misunderstanding of democracy to defend corporate lobbying on the grounds of freedom of expression. Powerful organisations have freely expressed their opinions throughout the ages in systems of feudalism, monarchy, corporatism and fascism. Democracy is about self-governance, and therefore communication by the governed with the mechanisms of governance needs to be equitable. The problem is that organisations with large resources have more opportunity to influence; to craft their messages in ways that resonate; and communicate them at the right times, more often. This means that people with more resources have their interests more effectively put to government, which is a challenge to democratic governance. Arguments for lobbying to be more internally consistent will not address this problem. Instead, the challenge is to find ways of ensuring more diverse communications with government.

These reports illustrate how the epistemic community of corporate responsibility consultants and promoters usually looks at social challenges in a way that puts companies at the centre of the analysis, and in terms of what is possible to be done voluntarily by individual companies. Although it is useful to explore potential management tools or define what constitutes voluntary best practice, if this establishes a paradigm where the notion of democratic governance or the role of regulation are not appreciated, then the process can be counter-productive.

The ignoring, or active dismissing, of the role of regulation in addressing the challenge of corporate lobbying ignores the impacts of one of the most significant regulatory moves on transparent government in the recent history of the UK. The Freedom of Information of Act came into force in 2004, and, in the first six months, one in ten voluntary organisations surveyed reported that it had already used the Act. Ashridge Management School and the National Council of Voluntary Organisations (NCVO) reported that 'more than 20,000 organisations have plans to make requests about government relationships with companies. The Act could therefore have an enormous impact on the political lobbying activities of companies'.[46] The level of enquiries for information may mean that all communications will be routinely logged on the Internet, leading to an unprecedented new level of transparency.

Currently, the debate within the corporate responsibility community has not seriously questioned why we should look at responsible lobbying. There exists a confusion between identifying a financial argument as a mechanism for achieving a principled goal, and the financial argument being seen as the goal. Some have assumed that the reason to promote 'responsible' lobbying is to protect business from reputational damage. Others have listed a range of public policy issues on which they wish to see action as the objective, such as moves on climate change or international trade negotiations. However, the goal of the responsible lobbying agenda needs to become broader: to be the promotion of democratic governance. This would involve the creation of more democratic patterns of lobbying rather than a few more strands of lobbying we like, and less of that which we don't like, depending on who 'we' happen to be. This perspective suggests that the most responsible forms of corporate lobbying would be those aimed at encouraging governments to adopt new regulations on the conduct of politicians and civil servants, to ensure that policy processes are less influenced by corporate lobbying, and instead to invest in mechanisms of active pluralism where the voices of the under-represented and weaker groups in society are sought out. The Freedom of Information Act is one example.

Key to this notion of responsible lobbying is the use of one's power to help empower others, and ultimately to address systemic power imbalances. Currently very few companies are actually lobbying for systemic changes. One example is the Co-operative Financial Services (CFS) in the UK. It has worked with the CORE campaign, a coalition of NGOs, to advocate mandatory ethical and environmental reporting in the UK, and has called for the establishment of key performance indicators as the basis of materiality questions in the UK's Operating Financial Review (OFR). By supporting mechanisms that would provide various stakeholders with more rights to information and more requirements on managers to respect those stakeholders, CFS is addressing a systemic issue.

KATE KEARINS: MANAGERS
NEED TO ADDRESS THE
SYSTEMIC PROBLEMS OF THE
GLOBAL ECONOMY

This is a small step towards addressing broader power imbalances through corporate lobbying. As Professors Kate Kearins and Jem Bendell contended , in 'The Political Bottom Line', managers will need to 'address the systemic problems of the global economy and the compromised independence of communities and governments. If this happens then broader issues may appear on the horizon of management—the independence of democratic processes and the media, and the negative social impacts of currency speculation, tax management and evasion.'[47]

4Q2005

October–December

Jem Bendell and Shilpa Shah

The living dead

The popular depiction of today's office worker as highly stressed, struggling to get ahead in the rat race of today's cut-throat corporate world is a familiar one. Yet the key concepts in a book at the top of the UK business list in November 2005 were boredom, time-wasting and apathy. *The Living Dead,* by *Times* columnist David Bolchover,[1] turns notions of time management and striving to maintain a work–life balance inside out— its aim is to 'unearth the last taboo': that a large proportion of office workers do not actually do very much work at all. Offices across the public and private sectors around the world are argued to be filled with workers whose talents and energies are being wasted, as employees spend their time pretending to work hard instead of actually doing so.

Statistics such as '14.6% of US workers admit to surfing the Internet for non-work related items *constantly*', presented in support of this perturbing phenomenon, may elicit a nod of identification from those workers who while away their employers' time playing Internet games at their desk. The international popularity of Dilbert cartoons[2] and *The Office*, a UK 'mockumentary' parodying workplace dynamics, reflects the element of identification that many people feel with their own working lives—work is not a meaningful activity that engages our skills and motivation but a often a façade of productivity that must be paid lip-service to between the hours of 9 am and 5 pm.

Research by the Chartered Institute of Personnel and Development (CIPD)[3] in the UK uses the concept of a 'psychological contract' between individual employees and organisations to describe the unspoken agreement based on mutual trust and fairness that exists in addition to legal contracts. Good-quality supervisory leadership and appropriate human resources policies are considered key to ensuring that this contract is upheld, bringing about high levels of employee satisfaction and performance. A survey published in November 2005[4] studied the 'organisational DNA' of 50,000 companies worldwide and came to the conclusion that around 70% of businesses have 'unhealthy' organisational cultures, where poor relations between staff led to low levels of efficiency. It also found that low-level employees were more able to diagnose unhealthy practices than senior management. Bolchover's book aims to catalyse an improvement in middle-management practices, to bridge the gap between the rosy vision of efficiency held by senior management and the reality at many office desks.

The issue of effective leadership is important, but problems undermining meaningful employment and work satisfaction can run deeper than being undervalued and overlooked by an 'invisible' manager. A survey[5] of 15,000 workers worldwide found that one-quarter of US and Brazilian, one-third of British and 40% of French employees are indifferent to their work and the success of their employer. A job pays the bills for these people, but disengagement from the goals of their efforts means that the activity that consumes one-third to one-half of their waking life is compartmentalised, separated from pursuits that bring meaning and value into our existence. Consequentially, low energy levels, depression and reliance on alcohol and other drugs are on the increase. A 2004/2005 study by the British Health and Safety Executive[6] suggests that depression or anxiety caused by stress, or perhaps underwork, account for an estimated 12.8 million reported lost working days per year in the UK—more than double the levels of 1990.

Neil Crofts, founder of the website www.authenticbusiness.co.uk and author, argues that this dissatisfaction with our working lives is a symptom of the disharmony between the objectives of the current individualistic, hard-hearted form of capitalism in which we operate in and the well-being of the planet and its people. In the *Authentic Business* November 2005 newsletter, Crofts presents health problems associated with work, smoking and overeating, and also social and ecological degradation on a community and global level, as *self*-harm carried out on an individual and collective scale. Whether they keel over from working 70-hour weeks or sit idly playing com-

NEIL CROFTS: THE 'AUTHENTIC SELF', IS THE BUILDING BLOCK OF A MORE JUST GLOBAL EXISTENCE

puter Solitaire, millions of people are conforming to society's expectations regarding the acquisition of increasing levels of material wealth, even if the process is at direct odds with self-fulfilment, maintaining close family relationships and the ecological well-being of the planet. Cycles of self-harm are argued by Crofts to be propelled by a lack of confidence in ourselves and each other, resulting from a false separation between what we value and what we feel we must do with our lives.

Mohandas Gandhi famously said that 'you must be the change you want to see in the world'. The 'authentic self', to use Croft's term, is argued to be the building block of a more just, safer, happier global existence. Central to the concept is our confidence in our own judgements of the world we perceive around us—if the factors influencing our decision-making are based mainly on norms and expectations shaped by families, communities and the media, we may not be following paths that promote our psychological and physical well-being and, consequently, the well-being of the planet. Accepting that all that glitters is not gold is easy. But stepping back and realising that, even if it is gold, it is no big deal requires a good deal of confidence in your own judgement and in your capabilities to find happiness elsewhere. Our blinkered system of material wealth-chasing has successfully taught us how to be employees, bosses and shoppers. Those who want to live, work, eat and travel without harm to others or the environment have to step out of this cushioned comfort zone and simply be *human* again.

The suggestion that uncovering our 'authentic' selves will enable us to both be happier and also interact more harmoniously with each other and the planet invites us to believe that the 'true' human nature is cooperative and loving. This essential 'human nature' has been debated for centuries by different religious traditions, with many Oriental philosophies suggesting that our spiritual nature is an evolving one, from one reincarnation to the next, while Abrahamic religions include a concept of 'original sin'. However, Oriental philosophies suggest that our true nature, once freed from the illusions of the material world that creates a sense of separation in individuals, is a connected expression of the whole. For some, the implication of this is that there is no separate self, and we are inventing one, whereas others consider the authentic self is a 'higher' self, where all physical, mental and spiritual aspects of our existence are harmonious with the whole. Some strands of thought in Abrahamic religions, such as some Sufism, also stress the oneness of humans with a universal God as the original situation. In this sense, an authentic self would have a relationship with 'God'. Therefore both Oriental and Abrahamic traditions provide some encouragement for the view that we have a natural capacity for being 'good' towards each other. Other insights into human nature, from evolutionary biology to post-structural sociology, raise some difficult questions. Mainstream evolutionary biologists' assumptions about the inevitable spread of selfish genes is problematic if we consider how cooperative and even altruistic behaviour may have helped some communities outperform others.[7] Sociological and psycho-sociological insights into the social construction of identities raise the possibility that there is no 'un-socialised' self that can be discovered, just different socially constructed views of who we tell our 'selves' we are. However, such theoretical positions are difficult to test, and instead some focus attention on helping people to recognise processes of socialisation that may be influencing their own sense of self and who this helps or hinders and, by doing this, helping them to free themselves from those processes—if they so decide. Efforts by Crofts and others to help people discover their authentic selves resonate with efforts at 'consciencisation' pioneered with the poor in Latin America some decades ago,[8] and their work can be regarded as developing a 'pedagogy of the oppressed oppressor'.

Some will be suspicious of the notion that work within a capitalist system characterised by exploitation in order to generate profits can allow the expression of the authentic self at all. In an attempt to bridge the gulf between the authentic self and meaningful work centred on the 'bottom line', Croft's book *Authentic Business*[9] defines such an organisation as built on a purpose *beyond* profit, that is 'profoundly held' and that is socially and/or environmentally positive. The decision-makers in such a business still aim to generate profit, but must foster integrity between communication and action and act on the basis of principles, not just jumping on bandwagons. It is argued that these businesses will boast high levels of efficiency and employee motivation; 'everyone working in an authentic business lives and breathes what the company stands for'. British companies Innocent Drinks and Yeo Valley Organic are two of the given examples of successful 'authentic' businesses. These are also described as 'social enterprises' by some commentators, indicating some overlap in the concepts, and the search for appropriate terminology to describe and understand people who seek to make a positive difference through working in the private sector.

'Corporate social responsibility' and 'corporate citizenship' are often discussed in terms of issue areas such as child labour or deforestation, or business functions such as marketing or public affairs. However, at the root of the movement of professionals that coax companies to perform better in these areas is people's search for a more meaningful way of work—as part of a more meaningful way of life. By engaging this system in order to change it, these professionals risk imbibing its values as our own and beginning to see their work merely in terms of reports, projects and promotions, and becoming a new breed of 'living dead'. This means the development and implementation of effective processes for reawakening and reaffirming the values of professionals working in this area will be essential to the success of voluntary corporate responses to sustainable development.

Las noticias

The first week of November 2005 saw riots and protests at the Argentine coastal town of Mar del Plata, host to the fourth Summit of the Americas. Negotiations for the creation of a Free Trade Area of the Americas (FTAA), which would establish a free trade bloc covering 34 countries stretching from Alaska to Tierra del Fuego in southern Argentina, collapsed as a trend of increasing political assertiveness in the region meant that key players such as Argentina and Brazil refused to agree to the conditions.

The economic and political landscapes of the region are already shaped by important sub-regional groupings such as NAFTA (North American Free Trade Agreement), the recently negotiated CAFTA (Central American Free Trade Agreement), MercoSur, a grouping of Argentina, Brazil, Chile, Uruguay and Paraguay, and a number of bilateral agreements with the US. Those who protested against the proposed FTAA argue that the majority of these existing free-trade mechanisms have largely worsened socioeconomic conditions in many countries in the region, often to the benefit of the US economy. This indicates the views of a significant proportion of the population, according to a survey by the regional polling organisation Latinobarometro which was reported by *BusinessWeek* in November 2005, showing that 61% of Latin Americans have little or no trust in the US government's intentions toward the region.[10]

Latin American countries account for 9 of the top 20 of the latest United Nations (UN) Human Income and Poverty Index,[11] suggesting the region is becoming increasingly affluent. However, such statistics conceal the huge inequalities existing between the countries, and within them, as decades of colonial legacies, civil war, financial instability and positioning as the US's 'back yard' during the Cold War have left scars on the resource-rich nations. According to the UN,[12] 43% of the population of

Latin America are poor, with approximately half of that number living in slums, and a quarter living on less than a dollar a day. The region's forests provide nearly one-quarter of the world forest cover and protect systems rich in biodiversity, but the rate of deforestation, often at the hands of business, is one of the highest in the world at an annual 0.48%.

Well-publicised cases such as Coca-Cola in Colombia, Parmalat in Brazil and sweat-shop labour in Mexican export processing zones have highlighted problems of worsening job security, lower wages and poor health and safety conditions for workers. As in many low-income regions, key aspects of voluntary corporate responsibility, such as regular reporting on non-financial activities, stakeholder engagement and codes of conduct, are not widely recognised or engaged with. However, according to Antonio Vives, head of the Inter-American Development Bank (IADB)'s Corporate Responsibility programme, corporate responsibility in Latin America is 'on the verge of take-off'.[13]

Over 400 business representatives, academics, government representatives and members of civil society from 22 different countries attended the IADB's third annual conference, held in Santiago, Chile. Discussions based around the main theme of 'Who is responsible for responsibility?' explored the roles of the private sector and other actors in developing a more formal, integrated model of CSR for Latin America. A rating of the eight largest countries in the region found Chile to be the most 'ethical' place for business, while poorer countries such as Peru and Colombia scored much lower.[14] An OECD report released in November, detailing case studies of good corporate governance practices in Latin America, hailed Peruvian mining company Buenaventura and Brazilian electricity company CPFL Energia among those who have been found to be complying with CSR standards issued by the OECD and other international organisations.[15]

Participants at the IADB conference argued that these examples of best practice were not indicative of the real status of CSR across a region in which small and medium-sized enterprises (SMEs) account for 95% of firms, employing 40–60% of the population of each country.[16] Religion and altruism were argued to be the main drivers of a more mainstream tradition of ad hoc corporate philanthropy and ethics in these smaller indigenous businesses. Now demand for more embedded, strategic CSR practices, based on the Anglo-American 'business case' model is being voiced.

Some civil-society organisations are sceptical of the applicability of a CSR model created in the West. The region is home to the World Social Forum (WSF) movement, founded to help forge more horizontal links between social movements across the world. The annual meetings of the WSF are held as an alternative to the World Economic Forum (WEF) meetings in Davos, Switzerland. The instrumental rationale of CSR as strategic management practice limits the scope for addressing concerns and critiques of many social movements and is unlikely to be welcomed by vocal NGOs that are wary of big business but supportive of the principles of participatory democracy and social justice.

The Red Puentes network, comprising 31 voluntary organisations working to catalyse an improvement in corporate governance in Latin America, argues that any CSR model for the region must be based on the 'perspectives, visions, rights and needs of the civil societies in which the corporations operate'.[17] They argue that SMEs largely have good local knowledge and links with the communities in which they operate. The call on large, and often foreign-owned, corporations to maintain international standards of social and environmental protection and also to involve civil society in their decision-making to help develop a model of CSR that is genuinely suited to the needs of this vast, diverse region.

Beyond barriers

The UNDP Human Development Report for 2005[18] reported the continual marginalisation of low-income countries in the international trading system. Of the $9 trillion that is generated from world exports, the amount that goes to sub-Saharan Africa, with a population of 689 million, is less that half of that which goes to Belgium, which has a population of 10 million. This skewed trading system supports sizeable profits for corporations at the top of the value chain, who control access to high-value markets. Such corporations have an interest in the rules guiding international trade, as do anti-poverty campaigners who see current rules as barriers to systemic change. After failing to achieve a significant commitment on the issue of trade from the G8 in July 2005, the attention of campaigners and lower-income countries turned to the sixth World Trade Organisation (WTO) Ministerial in Hong Kong, in December 2005.

Last year (2005) marked the 10th anniversary of the WTO. Its creation was originally promoted at a meeting of the World Economic Forum (WEF) and the agreements on services and intellectual property were drafted at the behest of international telecommunications and pharmaceutical industries.[19] This history, ongoing corporate lobbying, and the questionable impacts of trade liberalisation on sustainable development over the past decade, lead many to question the WTO's role. One argument made in favour of the WTO is that it allows multilateral negotiation of trade rules, which gives low-income countries more power than in bilateral or plurilateral negotiations with rich countries. Another is that those negotiations should take into consideration the specific needs of low-income countries so that trade agreements give them 'more time to adjust, greater flexibility, and special privileges'.[20] However, the disparity in both participation in negotiations and ability to use permitted economic sanctions upon dispute resolution means that the WTO can reinforce existing power differentials. A lack of progress in delivering significant changes to richer-country subsidies and barriers that are called for by many lower-income countries undermines the claim for the WTO to have a 'development' agenda. Although the deadline for negotiations of this Doha 'development' round was the end of 2005, a conclusive decision—which requires the unanimity of all 149 member states—was not arrived at, ensuring that the round continues during 2006.

During the WTO meeting, Hong Kong witnessed scenes typical of international trade summits, such as the previous month's FTAA, with street battles between protestors and police, as barriers protected the conference-goers. This Ministerial was considered

PASCAL LAMY OF THE WTO: END OF SUBSIDIES BY
2013 WOULD MOVE NEGOTIATIONS FORWARD

by those within the barriers to be a greater success than the Cancún meeting two years previously, which had ended without agreement. Pascal Lamy, the director-general of the WTO, said that an agreement to end rich countries' subsidising of agricultural exports by 2013 would help with concluding the round and moving negotiations forward.[21] However, some activists called the agreement a failure for the poor. Steve Tibbett from ActionAid said: 'the WTO has served up a diet of peanuts, waffle and fudge'[22] as richer countries continued to push for access to low-income-country markets and stronger rights for their companies while refusing to rapidly reduce their subsidising of agricultural exports. Some commentators argued that the new economic heavyweights India and Brazil helped ensure a resolution to the talks by putting pressure on low-income countries. In addition, a new procedure of plurilateral negotiations was agreed, whereby groups of countries would enter into future negotiations. This is an attempt to speed along future negotiations, in a way that may further undermine the multilateral character of the process.

STEVE TIBBETT OF ACTIONAID: 'THE WTO
HAS SERVED UP A DIET OF PEANUTS,
WAFFLE AND FUDGE'

The agreement reached in Hong Kong was perhaps most important for the staff of the WTO themselves. Due to greater scrutiny from global civil society and better bargaining power from low-income countries, their organisation was in gridlock, and faced with becoming the slow lane of liberalisation, as bilateral and regional trade agreements proceeded at pace. With new allies emerging in the big economies of Brazil, Russia, India and China, the agricultural subsidies issue set aside, for now, and the difficulties of multilateral negotiating reduced through the adoption of new procedures, the WTO is now back in business, to coordinate new agreements on areas such as the liberalising of financial services.

To begin new rounds of liberalisation when existing experience of liberalisation has been so mixed is not a sensible form of international cooperation. A paper by the Trade Union Advisory Committee to the Organisation for Economic Cooperation and Development (OECD)[23] published in the build-up to the Hong Kong Ministerial argued that the agreements under discussion would add to greater income insecurity and lower opportunities for decent work in low-income countries. Some barriers, it appears, are useful. As discussed in the review of the previous quarter, the development effect of liberalising financial services is questionable, and so it is not responsible for private financial institutions to lobby for it. If agreements are reached in finance, tourism and other sectors, it will further the imbalance between internationally agreed and protected rights and freedoms of large corporations and their obligations to the people they affect through their operations. Voluntary initiatives such as the UN Global Compact and the OECD Guidelines for Multinational Enterprises are pointed to by some as an effective response to this imbalance. However, the absence of independent monitoring of corporate activity and the ineffective means for those affected by poor conduct to raise their concerns and secure change have rendered these initiatives insufficient in the eyes of some civil-society groups. A 2005 report by an international coalition of NGOs monitoring the effectiveness of the OECD guidelines[24] found that 'there is no conclusive evidence that the Guidelines have had a positive, conclusive impact' on large corporations' operations.

Meanwhile the WEF's latest report on global governance reported that, although some progress was being made on poverty alleviation, the environmental situation is bad and getting worse, noting that 'no serious frameworks are in place to ensure the integrity of ecosystems', while there has been a 'retreat on human rights' during the year, with growing 'restrictions on freedom from torture and freedom of expression'.[25] Taken together, these findings remind us how the world urgently needs more effective mechanisms to protect people and their environments. This must involve intergovernmental organisations that can enforce both corporate and governmental compliance with existing human rights, labour rights and environmental standards, and ensure these are not overridden by trade rules agreed by government delegations that respond mostly to the interests of their export lobbies. Just as corporations once called for the creation of an organisation like the WTO, so responsible corporations could today join a call for intergovernmental organisations with the necessary bite to protect the social and environmental sub-structure of functioning markets—people's rights and resources. To support this vision of a new phase of intergovernmental cooperation a new leadership consciousness in business executives will be required. This involves seeing across the barriers of one's company, sector, country and culture, and seeing the system within which one exists, how one contributes to systemic flaws, and how to begin helping change those flaws. Enacting this 'transcending leadership', described in the previous quarter, in the area of trade rules, poses a challenge for corporate responsibility executives, as it requires engaging with public affairs and government relations departments, to promote more intelligent and responsible lobbying (see 'The political bottom line' on page 314). Breaking down the internal barriers within large companies is a key skill for this form of leadership.

Responsible competitiveness

The domestic policy implications of falling trade barriers are that a country and its people must seek to be 'competitive' in international markets. In some countries this has created a downward pressure on environmental and social regulations, as well as on taxation, leading to reduced government provision of basic welfare services. In December 2005, the election of the left-wing Evo Morales in Bolivia illustrated a growing trend across Latin America to reject the competition-driven vision advanced by most centrist and right-wing politicians. Continuing protests at intergovernmental summits, and growing attendance at the world and regional Social Forums which advance a different approach to national and international governance, suggest that those who advocate the current trajectory of globalisation are in need of a new story to convince the masses of its merits. That story may emerge with the concept of 'Responsible Competitiveness', advocated by AccountAbility.

EVO MORALES: HIS ELECTION SYMPTOMATIC
OF THE REJECTION IN LATIN AMERICA OF
MARKET-BASED IDEALS

Accepting that seeking international competitiveness is the dominant policy orientation of many governments, AccountAbility states that 'the challenge is to evolve a responsible basis on which competitiveness is achieved'. Responsible competitiveness 'means markets where businesses are systematically and comprehensively rewarded for more responsible practices, and penalised for the converse'.[26] The role of government in guiding the achievement of responsible competitiveness is recognised as 'being responsible sometimes does and sometimes does not pay . . . While the growing significance of intangible assets has created opportunities for leveraging responsible business practices, the intensification of competition and the short-termism of investors constrain such practices.'[27] The challenge they therefore identify is how governments can intervene to improve business social and environmental performance in a way that adds to rather than reducing international competitiveness.

In a report launched at the Global Compact event in Shanghai, in November, AccountAbility pointed to instances where governments are promoting corporate responsibility as an international competitiveness issue. The report highlights the challenge of the end of the textiles quota system, the Multi-Fiber Arrangement, to countries from Cambodia to Lesotho that cannot compete internationally on price with China. This challenge has led them to explore whether adherence to labour and environmental standards might offer an effective non-price competitive advantage. As a result, Cambodia has signed an agreement between producers, 'brand' customers, labour unions and international agencies such as the World Bank to help its achievement of labour standards. Meanwhile, Chile is reported as actively exploring whether raised social and environmental standards might offer their fruit and wine exports an edge in international markets. The Canadian government is aiming to make 'brand Canada' one of quality, including social and environmental quality, in order to develop agricultural exports.

The idea that nations have reputations that are important to market demand for products or services from their nations is not new, and illustrated by Singapore construction firms advertising their national origin at building sites across South-East Asia.[28] Could social responsibility be an important enough factor for reputation to influence competitiveness and, therefore, government policy? If so, could it be important enough in enough countries to influence sustainable development? The report tackles the first question with the introduction of two indices.

The 'National Corporate Responsibility Index (NCRI)' is an attempt to measure the state of corporate responsibility across 80 countries, covering key factors such as levels of corruption, businesses' adoption of environmental management, and the state of corporate governance. Nordic countries rank highest, with four appearing in the top five and Finland scoring highest. South Africa is the highest-ranking emerging economy (excluding eastern and central Europe), followed by Korea, Chile, Malaysia, Costa Rica and Thailand. The second index, the Responsible Competitiveness Index (RCI) incorporates the NCRI as one more variable in the World Economic Forum's Growth Competitiveness Index (GCI).

Ranking people, organisations or countries is always a useful way of stimulating debate, and these indices also offer a way of testing the proposition that widespread corporate responsibility in a country adds to that country's competitiveness. 'There is a significant correlation between the competitiveness of a country and its corporate responsibility level. This might indicate that . . . corporate responsibility can fuel country competitiveness', states the report.[29] Press releases on the report did not use the conditional tense, yet methodological difficulties may make this a premature claim. The validity of some of the regression analysis can be questioned, as when one index partially incorporates another there is a likely correlation between the two. This is the case with correlations between the RCI and either the NCRI or GCI, as the RCI incorporates the others, to a degree decided by the researchers.

As the report notes, correlation does not mean causation. Correlations can be influenced by other factors such as the cultural assumptions of researchers and the data they use. This is especially the case in an area such as this, where researchers are quantifying intangible issues. Deciding what constitutes 'corporate responsibility' is as much a cultural and political challenge as it is a technical one. For example, the existence of a corporate sustainability report could be regarded as evidence of a negative impact on sustainable development as much as an indicator of corporate responsibility, given that companies with large-scale environmental or social impacts are more likely to publish this information. An indicator such as the number of ISO 14001 certifications may depend on the international connectedness of a country, and the availability of assurance services, both of which may be due to the level of economic development of a country rather than the state of its business–society relations.

Indicators of corporate performance on issues of public importance, rather than processes of voluntary engagement with those issues, is important if we are to explore any relationship between beneficial business–society relations in a country and its competitiveness, and the NCRI could be improved in this area. The NCRI includes the factors comprising the context for business–society relations, such as regulations and the vibrancy of civil society. However, a researcher's culture influences what they consider indicative of this external context, such as the number of 'NGOs' in a country. This figure may be as much an indicator of a liberal political system, formalised social economy and retreating state as one of healthy community organising, and so the number of NGOs may correlate directly with economic development, not business responsibility. In addition, the weighting given to various issues from freedom of association to carbon emissions is a subjective one. For instance, some may argue Costa Rica should not rate so highly given that trade unionism has been effectively undermined in that country. Both the issues and the way one assesses performance on them are political as much as scientific endeavours.

Aside from these methodological challenges, what potential might responsible competitiveness have for encouraging government leadership on corporate responsibility? This may depend on the relationship between country-branding and practice, and the importance to a country's economy of those trades sensitive to responsibility issues in comparison with those that are not. On the former, there is sometimes a tenuous link between a country's brand and its performance on related issues. Returning to the example of Costa Rica highlights this. The award-winning 'Costa Rica—no artificial ingredients' campaign to promote tourism occurred at a time when it was the highest per capita importer of agrochemicals in the world. If a public's perception is that the existence of wilderness constitutes a country's 'greenness', rather than ecologically conscious forms of production and human settlement, then the potential of a country's green branding to influence government promotion of sustainable business may be limited. Another example of the disjuncture between rhetoric and reality is the Canadian agricultural ministry marketing the country as a source of high-environmental-quality products, whereas unlike many countries it allows genetically modified crops to be grown and does not require product labelling of GM content. In Europe 3,500 municipalities are no-grow zones for GM, with only two in Canada in 2005.[30] This example raises the question of whether a concern for the value of a 'responsibility brand' in some product areas is enough to drive changes in government policy.

The answer to this question will depend on which commercial sectors have the most influence over government policy. A country's environmental services industry could benefit immeasurably in both domestic market size and international branding from more government intervention on greenhouse gas emissions, for example, but other energy-heavy sectors can actively resist such action. This situation reminds us that as industries are so different it may not be possible to argue that a whole country's economy can be more or less competitive due to overall corporate responsibility. The varying importance of different social responsibility issues to consumer behaviour also undermines any general claim about responsible competitiveness. An issue such as pesticide residues in food may be much more important to a consumer than social aspects of the product, due to his/her own health concerns. If performance on a responsibility issue has an impact on the quality of the product or service, then it is likely to be a more important factor influencing market demand than those issues that do not. This also makes any generalised claims about the impact of corporate responsibility on market demand difficult to justify.

Greenwashing globalisation?

What are the implications for global sustainable development? Sean de Cleene, of the African Institute of Corporate Citizenship, suggests that 'the future for countries like Malawi is in niche markets, and perhaps improved social and environmental performance can be value added—the market will pay a premium for something that meets people's values'.[31] This highlights the opportunities that can be seized by some, but also the limitedness of niche responsible markets, so that only some countries will be able to serve such markets.

As responsible competitiveness depends on differentiating one country from another as being more or less responsible, it is not something that all governments can aspire to. The international branding opportunity for Costa Rica and Canada may be one that resonates with an interest in sustainability, but what of the brand opportunity for Mexico or China? The limitedness of 'responsible markets', especially those that pay premiums rather than requiring responsible production for no extra cost, means that a 'responsibility race' is improbable. Given that many social and environmental issues, such as climate change, disease and terrorism, can not be addressed without action in all parts of the world, the moves of some governments to seek and secure trade with responsible markets may be beneficial for those involved in the near to medium term, but not deliver the scale of changes required.

To accept the 'competitiveness' discourse as a starting point for government policy to promote sustainable development is problematic, for three reasons. First is the environmental cost of increasing transportation and associated pollution if increasing international trade. For example, the Canadian agricultural ministry's encouragement of a perceived green brand for its products in places such as Mexico will not have a net positive environmental impact when we consider the transportation involved. Second is the issue of risk. Managing risk to incomes and resource flows is an important aspect of sustainable development. To the degree that international trade diversifies income and resource flows, it can reduce the potential damage from disruption to specific flows, such as a failed harvest; but, if it leads to increased dependence on specific markets, as well as cheap energy for transportation, then it increases the risk to the dependent community. The third problem with the competitiveness discourse concerns scale, in that it overplays the importance of international trade to the well-being of a people and their economy. The majority of trade in most countries is domestic, not foreign. That the interests of a minority of economic actors in a country involved in exports should determine government policy is questionable.

Despite these theoretical and methodological weaknesses of the proposition that global sustainable development can be enhanced by country-level responsible competitiveness strategies, the popularity of the concept grew in 2005 and is likely to continue to do so in the coming years. This is because it offers a more refined story for proponents of current patterns of economic globalisation.

Until now, the 'political brand proposition' of the dominant players in the global economy has been that more trade is good for all, and can be promoted by removing trade barriers, protecting foreign-owned property, liberalising financial markets, restricting government policy freedoms and privatising public assets. This 'Washington Consensus' is increasingly seen to have failed to deliver sustainable development. A new story is being sought to give a social justification for global capitalism. There-

fore, responsible competitiveness may become global capitalism's new brand proposition, telling us—the consumer of political ideas—that a neoliberal free-trade agenda
will not eat us up in a competitiveness race, but that it is compatible with our well-
being, so long as governments help companies become more responsible and market
themselves as such.

Some may question what it says of our moral character that our integrity and welfare, as communities and nations, has to become the stuff of sales pitch to others. At
the heart of responsible competitiveness is a capitulation to the idea that our welfare
must be commodified and commercialised so it is functional to selling ourselves, in
order for us to have the means to continue looking after our welfare. Has the market
mentality become so omnipotent that we must now conceive of public goals in terms
of marketing?

Responsible competitiveness is not a sufficient conceptual framework for government action on business–society relations, and could greenwash globalisation. Rather
than the well-being of humanity being pursued only through market logics, another
approach is required: one that recognises how a global market requires global rules on
matters of human dignity and welfare. Just as some companies no longer assert that
their social responsibility is helping them to compete, and are beginning to call for
government regulation, so governments need to recognise the dilemma posed by competitiveness pressures, and work towards more effective intergovernmental regulation.

Whatever one's perspective on the global economy in general, and responsible competitiveness in particular, this discussion highlights that the field of corporate citizenship is a political one. As a site of what sociologist Ulrich Beck calls 'sub politics', the
debates and initiatives in this field constitute a battleground of ideas which is shaping
the ideology of our time. Some professionals that work in this field may understand
these political processes and engage to counter the historical forces of capital, race and
gender that shape the current hegemonic view. Whether their efforts are counter-hege-
monic depends on the effects of their work as much as their motivations. Other professionals may not be so aware and act as channels for the re-production of hegemonic
discourse. In explaining their rationale for responsible competitiveness, Account-
Ability appeals to those with power by pointing to threats to their hegemony, identifying 'two risks': 'corporate responsibility being discredited for delivering too little' and
'the drive for international competitiveness being challenged for creating unacceptable negative externalities'.[32] On paper, therefore, the authors of the AccountAbility
report act in defence of hegemony. Whether this is the personal intention, or will prove
to be the effect, is in question. Many professionals engaged in corporate responsibility are seeking to engage with the centres and flows of power in society to direct them
towards progressive outcomes. This raises the question of whether a progressive outcome necessarily involves reducing that power, or whether a more responsible, perhaps more 'authentic' or 'civil', exercise of power is possible. The goal of 'transcending
leadership', discussed at different points during this Annual Review, requires actual-
ising this more responsible form of power. Understanding power and its responsible
use is probably the bedrock question underlying much work on corporate citizenship
today.

About the contributors

Désirée Abrahams believes that growth in the CSR movement is evidence of the groundswell of global support for responsible business practices. Within CSR, Désirée has been interested in the international regulation of companies and wrote *Regulating Corporations: A Resource Guide* (UNRISD, 2004) and *Regulations for Corporations: A Historical Account of TNC Regulation* (2005). Committed to working with companies to advance their human rights due diligence, she currently works at the International Business Leaders Forum, as Human Rights Impact Assessment Project Manager. Désirée was a Research Assistant at the United Nations Research Institute for Social Development (UNRISD) when she contributed to this volume.

Jem Bendell believes it is important to integrate insights from diverse social, political and organisational arts and sciences into strategy, learning and evaluation processes by those who seek to contribute to, and benefit from, the systemic transformation of markets to promote global wellbeing. For over 12 years Dr Bendell has worked on corporate responsibility as a campaigner, researcher, writer, educator, advisor and entrepreneur. He helps create innovative corporate responsibility initiatives, such as the Marine Stewardship Council and the Authentic Luxury Network. Director of Lifeworth Consulting, his clients include UN agencies, leading NGOs, universities and business, in over a dozen countries. An Adjunct Associate Professor of Management, he is advising Griffith Business School in Australia to become a leading sustainability business school in the Asia Pacific. With over 50 publications, this is Dr Bendell's third book. His current focus is the potential of global marketing and global finance to promote a movement towards global well-being. His next book is *Higher Ends: Sustainable Luxury Management*. See www.jembendell.com and www.lifeworth.com.

Mark Bendell believes that academic writing needs to be understandable by, and enter into dialogue with, the world outside of academe. Dr Bendell has been Senior Lecturer at Chester University, UK, for several years, and has published on corporate social responsibility in works such as 'Facing Power' (in Stephen May [ed.], *Communication and Corporate Social Responsibility* (Oxford University Press, 2007); additional published areas include identity politics and questions of representation.

Tim Concannon is a writer and a researcher for campaigning organisations including Friends of the Earth. He founded the Stakeholder Democracy Network to support the voices and action of Southern communities on their corporate responsibility concerns; see www.stakeholderdemocracy.org.

Paul Gibbons is Chairman of Future Considerations, a small consultancy in London and Madison that works with the top leaders of Global 100 companies on groundbreaking leadership development work and sustainability. See www.futureconsiderations.com.

Kate Ives works at AccountAbility in the UK. Prior to that Kate worked with Care International, on business partnership. At the time of contributing to this volume Kate was a Research Assistant at the United Nations Research Institute for Social Development (UNRISD) in Geneva, working for its programme on markets, business and regulation. See www.unrisd.org and www.accountability.org.uk.

Kate Kearins is keen to prompt the next generation of business leaders to think more holistically about business impacts and responsibilities—and to be clear about what they are and are not doing in the name of sustainability. Professor Kearins has been teaching and researching in the business and sustainability area for 15 years. As Professor of Management at Auckland University of Technology in New Zealand, she worked with Jem Bendell on a contribution to this volume, among other projects. For further information, see www.aut.ac.nz/schools/business/business_research/management/professor_kate_kearins.htm.

John Manoochehri has a degree in Sanskrit from the University of Oxford, and is working on a PhD with the Centre for Environmental Strategy, University of Surrey (UK) and at the Royal Institute of Technology, Stockholm, as Associate Research Fellow. After leaving the United Nations Environment Programme (UNEP), he acted as Special Advisor to the Stockholm Environment Institute to help design a programme on sustainable production and consumption, and has a range of strategy consulting clients, including the Eden Project and Carbon Neutral. See www.johnmanoochehri.net.

Jeremy Moon is Professor and founding Director of the International Centre for Corporate Social Responsibility and Deputy Director of Nottingham University Business School, UK. He won a *Beyond Grey Pinstripes* European Faculty award for preparing MBAs for social and environmental stewardship in 2005. He is a Fellow of the Royal Society for the Arts. He is co-editor of *The Oxford Handbook of CSR* (Oxford University Press, 2008) and co-author of *Corporations and Citizenship* (Cambridge University Press, 2008).

Jules Peck spent his formative years climbing through trees and hedges exploring the natural world in Gloucestershire and Herefordshire, UK. He now lives with his wife outside Bath and is still doing quite a lot of the same. Jules was for two years Director of UK Conservative Party leader David Cameron's Quality of Life Policy Group, advising the Party on well-being and environment issues. A committed Citizen, he has spent the past 20 years advising business, NGOs and government institutions on sustainability issues and well-being. In a varied career, Jules has worked on environmental issues in Brussels at the EC, in the US and EU in marketing and public affairs roles with a number of companies, and internationally for WWF as a Global Policy Adviser. A regular public speaker and published author, Jules is also a trustee and board member of a number of charities and not-for-profit initiatives. He is a strategic counsel on Edelman UK's advisory board. Jules is also joint founder, with John Grant, of Arkism. Jules's recent publications include: *Blueprint for a Green Economy* (Quality of Life Policy Group, 2007), *Let Them Eat Cake* (WWF, 2006) and *Hope and Glory* (Green Ventures, 2008). For further information, see www.citizenrenaissance.com.

Rupesh Shah seeks to use a process of action research to look into the engagement between powerful actors as part of a transition for sustainable development and the emergence of a participatory worldview. Dr Shah is a freelance action researcher, working on projects in India and the UK. At the time of contributing to this volume, he was working with the New Academy of Business, a progressive management education charity founded by Anita Roddick.

Shilpa Shah believes that global justice issues should be talked about in a way that inspires solutions and is accessible to all. Ms Shah has pioneered work engaging black and minority ethnic and faith groups on climate change and provides training for environmental organisations keen to become more inclusive in their work. She works for Friends of the Earth UK, working alongside communities suffering environmental injustice, as a Rights and Justice campaigner. At the time of contributing to this volume, Shilpa was the coordinator of the Akashi Project; see www.akashi.org.uk.

Wayne Visser believes that CSR needs to adapt or die; hence his energies are directed to promoting CSR 2.0 (the new evolution of CSR). A former strategy analyst for Cap Gemini and Director of Sustainability Services for KPMG in South Africa, Dr Visser is now CEO of CSR International and Senior Associate of the University of Cambridge Programme for Industry in the UK. He is the author/editor of five books on CSR, including *The A to Z of Corporate Social Responsibility* (John Wiley, 2007) and, most recently, *Making a Difference* (VDM, 2008). At the time of contributing to this volume, Wayne was completing his PhD in CSR. For further information, see www.waynevisser.com and www.csrinternational.org.

Mark Young has worked with London-based leadership consultancy Future Considerations since 2002. He specialises in leadership development, organisational change, facilitation of complex challenges and working with organisations to embed sustainable development in their strategies and cultures. Mark facilitates senior teams, cross-sectoral groups and long-term leadership programmes in Europe, North and South America, India and his native South Africa. His clients include Cadbury, the Carbon Trust, HSBC, KPMG, Shell, Anglo American, UNIDO and several government organisations. Mark was previously Organisational Development manager of Procter & Gamble South Africa, where he worked on organisational change and diversity. See www.futureconsiderations.com.

Endnotes

Introduction

1 Noam Chomsky and Edward Hernan (1994) described how the corporate media filtered the news agenda in five ways. First, the business interests of the owner companies influenced reporting. Second, media managers needed to please (and certainly not upset) current and potential advertisers. Third, journalists often relied on press releases from organisations with a commercial interest in influencing the media. Fourth, journalists that 'rocked the boat' would be liable to professional criticism and sometimes litigation. A fifth filter was a blind acceptance of neoliberal economic ideology, so that many journalists were bemused at, and uninterested in, fundamental critiques of the economic system.

2 The belief in giving a free hand to foreign investors was not always so dominant. In the 1960s and 1970s some 22 less-commercialised countries passed legislation controlling international corporate activities, while the nationalisation of foreign corporations reached a peak in the 1970s. Regional agreements such as the Andean Pact imposed controls on incoming investors. In 1974 the United Nations set up the Centre on Transnational Corporations (UNCTC) following a report of the 'Group of Eminent Persons' convened by the UN Economic and Security Council. This led to the development of a 'Draft Code of Conduct on TNCs', which set out a framework for regulation. Much of the work of the UNCTC was to provide training and advice to developing-country governments on negotiation strategies *vis-à-vis* TNCs. The work of the UNCTC was suspended under pressure from certain UN-member governments (Jenkins 2000).

3 British government advisers at the time, such as Anthony Giddens, and ministers such as Hilary Benn, argued that evidence suggested liberalisation was good for poverty reduction. At that time, though, their assertions could only have been based on one highly questionable study for the World Bank. David Dollar and Aart Kraay (2002) compared countries considered to be 'globalisers' with those considered to be 'non-globalisers' and argued that trade liberalisation promoted economic growth and that economic growth promoted poverty reduction. However, Rodrik (2000) explained how the authors included and excluded countries and statistics in ways that created the correlation to support their argument. He undertook the same analysis and found that there was no evidence that countries with more open economies experienced higher growth rates and greater poverty reduction.

4 Some theorists attempt to bridge the divide between 'new' and 'old' social movements. For example, if one recognises that every fundamental need that was not sufficiently satisfied is a sign of poverty, then there are many different forms of poverty, and the view that cultural identity is the key motivating factor can be reconciled with the position that deprivation is the key factor (Max-Neef 1992; Veltmeyer 1997).

5 The term 'economic democracy' is already used to describe some other concepts and approaches, and is often used to speak in unspecific terms about economic reform.

1Q2001

1 Charles Leadbeater, *The Weightless Society* (Texere/LLC, 2000).
2 www.ceres.org, accessed March 2001
3 www.viatru.com, accessed March 2001 [link no longer active]
4 mc.diageo.co.uk, accessed March 2001 [link no longer active]
5 WTO heads for Qatar', BBC News, 30 January, 2001; news.bbc.co.uk/hi/english/business/newsid_1144000/1144362.stm, accessed March 2001.
6 K. Naidoo, in *e-CIVICUS* 104 (13 February 2001).

7 F. Fukuyama, *The End of History and the Last Man* (Penguin, 1993).
8 Tellus Institute, 'Do Voluntary Mechanisms Work?'; tellus.org/publications/files/Michigan_Vol_Mech_Exec_Sum.pdf, accessed January 2009.
9 Secretary-General's address to World Economic Forum, 29 January 2001; www.unis.unvienna.org/unis/pressrels/2001/sg2772.html, accessed January 2009.
10 Halina Ward, Royal Institute for International Affairs, 'Governing Multinationals: The Role of Foreign Direct Liability', February 2001; www.earthscape.org/p1/wah03, accessed January 2009.
11 Since writing the 2001 Review, the Cape plc case has been settled out of court. More information on the Lords' ruling on the case is available at www.leighday.co.uk/news/news-archive/leigh-day-co-recover-a3150-000-for-south-african, accessed January 2009.
12 UK Home Office, 'Reforming the Law on Involuntary Manslaughter: The Government's Proposals', May 2000; www.homeoffice.gov.uk/documents/cons-2005-corporate-manslaughter/2000-cons-invol-manslaughter.pdf?view=Binary, accessed January 2009.
13 At the time of writing, the Supreme Court ruled that it will not prevent the case against Shell from going forward.
14 samoa.saigon.com, accessed March 2001; Vietnam Labor Watch, 'Report on the Working Conditions of Vietnamese Workers in American Samoa', www.vlw.org, accessed March 2001; and Sweatshop Watch, www.sweatshopwatch.org, accessed March 2001 [link no longer active].
15 www.nikebiz.com, accessed March 2001

2Q2001

1 'Helping People with One Click: TIME Partners with Charitable Website Netaid.Org to Help Victims of the Epidemic', 4 February 2001; www.timewarner.com/corp/newsroom/pr/0,20812,668447,00.html, accessed January 2009.
2 www.msf.org/petition, accessed June 2001
3 'South Africa vs the Drug Giants: A Challenge to Affordable Medicines', Oxfam Policy Papers, February 2001.
4 South African business leaders estimate that HIV/AIDS will have a massive effect on the local economy. With 4.7 million South Africans infected with HIV and 1,500 more being infected daily, urgent intervention from the private sector and the government is needed, business leaders say. Companies may have to train three people for every job, as the death toll from AIDS is expected to reach 500,000 annually by 2008.
5 GSK reports it is the only company currently involved in research and development for both prevention and treatment of all three top-priority diseases of the WHO: malaria, tuberculosis and HIV/AIDS.
6 www.gsk.com/community/downloads/facing_the_challenge.pdf, accessed January 2009
7 www.business-in-environment.org.uk, accessed March 2001; www.mori.com, accessed June 2001
8 Jem Bendell (ed.), *Terms for Endearment: Business, NGOs and Sustainable Development* (Greenleaf Publishing, 2000).
9 www.ftse4good.com
10 'Ilisu activists damn Protocol at Balfour Beatty AGM', Lycos News, 2 May 2001.
11 www.waldenassetmgmt.com, accessed March 2001; www.socialfunds.com, accessed June 2001
12 www.calvertgroup.com, accessed June 2001
13 www.wri.org, accessed March 2001; www.calvert.com, accessed June 2001
14 Christian Aid, 'The Regulatory Void: EU Company Involvement in Human Rights Violations in Sudan', May 2001.
15 www.burmacampaign.org.uk, accessed June 2001
16 www.accountability21.net/aa1000series, accessed January 2009
17 www.globalwitness.org, accessed June 2001
18 US State Department, Bureau of Democracy, Human Rights, and Labor; www.state.gov, accessed June 2001.
19 www.novo.dk, accessed June 2001

20 www.iisd.ca/linkages/unepgc/20sess, accessed June 2001

21 See Section XIV of 'Environmental Cooperative Agreement between Wisconsin Electric Power Company and Wisconsin Department of Natural Resources'; www.dnr.state.wi.us/org/caer/cea/ecpp/agreements/wepco/agreements/final/finalagreement.pdf, accessed January 2009.

22 www.iccwbo.org, accessed June 2001

23 www.corpwatch.org, accessed June 2001

3Q2001

1 www.corpwatch.org, accessed September 2001

2 'Boxy but Good', *Grist*, 28 August 2001; www.grist.org/news/daily/2001/08/28/good/index.html, accessed January 2009.

3 www.nam.org, accessed September 2001

4 'Why it Pays to be Green', US News, 6 August 2001.

5 www.emission55.com, accessed September 2001

6 'ExxonMobil fights back, *Guardian*, 18 June 2001; www.guardianunlimited.co.uk/globalwarming/story/0,7369,508478,00.html, accessed January 2009.

7 www.hillandknowlton.com, accessed September 2001

8 US PIRG, www.pirg.org, accessed September 2001

9 www.lifeworth.com, accessed September 2001

10 www.siricompany.com, accessed September 2001

11 www.unepfi.net, accessed September 2001

12 www.business-minds.com, accessed September 2001

13 www.respecteurope.com, accessed September 2001

14 V. Haufler, 'Public Role for the Private Sector: Industry Self-regulation in a Global Economy', Washington, DC: Carnegie Endowment for International Peace, 2001; www.carnegieendowment.org/publications/index.cfm?fa=view&id=679&prog=zgp&zoom_highlight=Virginia+Haufler+, accessed January 2009.

15 'The NGO–Industrial Complex', *Foreign Policy*, July/August 2001: 56-65.

16 D.F. Murphy and J. Bendell, 'Partners in Time? Business, NGOs and Sustainable Development' (Discussion Paper 109; UNRISD, 1999).

17 R. Jenkins, 'Corporate Codes of Conduct: Self-Regulation in a Global Economy' (UNRISD Technology, Business and Society Programme, Paper 2, April 2001).

18 Knowledge Resource Group, Business Partners for Development, 'Endearing Myths, Enduring Truths: Enabling Partnerships between Business, Civil Society and Government' (2001; www.globalknowledge.org/gkps_portal/view_file.cfm?fileid=376, accessed January 2009).

19 The Copenhagen Centre website, accessed September 2001

20 www.who.org, accessed September 2001

21 www.ethicalperformance.com, accessed September 2001

22 Ralph G. Steinhardt, 'Litigating Corporate Responsibility', www.globaldimensions.net/articles/cr/steinhardt.html, accessed January 2009.

23 For example, corporate-citizenship@yahoogroups.com

24 www.eoa.org, accessed September 2001

25 www.iccr.org, accessed September 2001

26 Deborah Leipziger, *SA8000: The Definitive Guide to the New Social Standard* (Financial Times/Prentice Hall, 2001).

27 Human Rights Watch, 'Egypt. Underage and Unprotected: Child Labor in Egypt''s Cotton Fields', January 2001; www.hrw.org/reports/2001/egypt, accessed January 2009.

28 www.unglobalcompact.org

4Q2001

1 'Boeing profits rise but layoffs loom', BBC News, 19 October 2001; news.bbc.co.uk/hi/english/business/newsid_1607000/1607211.stm, accessed December 2001.

2 'Redundancies: Are Corporations Making Unethical Excuses?', *Reputation Impact* 1 (November 2001): 3.

3 www.busrep.co.za, accessed December 2001 [link no longer active].

4 UNAIDS, 'HIV/AIDS in Africa' press kit.

5 *Business Respect: CSR Dispatches*, 3 November 2001; www.mallenbaker.net/csr/nl/16.html, accessed December 2001.

6 ' "New World Order" may turn out to be world interconnectedness', SRINews.com, 12 October 2001; www.srinews.com/article.cgi?sfArticleId=685, accessed December 2001.

7 List of Global Action against the WTO; www.nadir.org/nadir/initiativ/agp/free/qatar/index1, accessed December 2001.

8 H. Anheier, M. Glasius and M. Kaldor, *Global Civil Society 2001* (Oxford University Press, 2001).

9 Peter Sinton, 'Crisis of conscience: Corporations are finding social responsibility boosts the planet and the bottom line', SFGate, 22 November 2001; www.sfgate.com/cgi-bin/article.cgi?file=/chronicle/archive/2001/11/22/BU100478.DTL&type=business, accessed December 2001.

10 www.ethicalcorp.com, accessed December 2001

11 www.christian-aid.org.uk, accessed December 2001

12 www.attac.org, accessed December 2001

13 'Nike releases first corporate responsibility report', CSRwire, 15 October 2001; www.csrwire.com/article.cgi/786.html, accessed December 2001.

14 CSR Network Limited, *The State of Global Environmental and Social Reporting: The 2001 Benchmark Survey* (CSR Network Ltd, 2001).

15 *Business Respect: CSR Dispatches*, 1 December 2001; www.mallenbaker.net/csr/nl/18.html, accessed December 2001.

16 'Impact on Society: Business in the Community's New CSR Reporting Website'; www.mallenbaker.net/csr/CSRfiles/iosreporting.html, accessed December 2001.

17 'Partnership with Yukos Oil', UNOPS, 12 October 2001.

18 David Henderson, *Misguided Virtue: False Notions of Corporate Social Responsibility* (Hobart Paper, 142; Institute of Economic Affairs, 2001).

19 'Curse of the Ethical Executive', *The Economist*, 15 November 2001; www.economist.com/finance/displayStory.cfm?Story_ID=863487, accessed December 2001.

20 Milton Friedman, *Capitalism and Freedom* (University of Chicago Press, 1962): 133.

21 P. Dobers and P. Cerin, 'What does the "Dow Jones Sustainability Group Index" tell us?', *Eco-Management and Auditing* 8.3 (2001): 123-33.

22 George Soros, *The Crisis of Global Capitalism* (Public Affairs, 1998).

23 www.iii.co.uk, accessed December 2001

2002: Foreword

1 www.futureconsiderations.com

1Q2002

1 'When the Numbers Don't Add Up', special report on 'The Trouble with Accounting', *The Economist* 362.8259 (9 February 2002): 67-70.

2 ILBF (International Business Leaders' Forum), 'Selling Sustainable Success: A Guide to Corporate Responsibility for Consulting and Professional Services Firms' (ILBF, 2002).

3   'Pinstripe Protestors: Activists are learning to use the capitalist system', *Business Respect: CSR Dis - patches* 24 (23 February 2002); www.mallenbaker.net/csr/nl/24.html#Anchor-Pinstripe-63255, accessed March 2002.

4   David F. Murphy and Jem Bendell, *In the Company of Partners* (Policy Press, 1997).

5   Jem Bendell (ed.), *Terms for Endearment: Business, NGOs and Sustainable Development* (Greenleaf Publishing, 2000).

6   Pabst Brewing Company, 'Letter from the President', web.archive.org/web/20021107031943/ http://www.pabst.com/president/120701.asp, accessed March 2002.

7   Quoted in *Business Respect: CSR Dispatches* 19 (15 December 2001).

8   tobacco.who.int, accessed March 2002

9   www.bat.com, accessed March 2002

10 Credit Suisse/First Boston, 'International Tobacco Marketing Standards: New Standards Create Consistent, Responsible International Marketing Practices', September 2001; web.archive.org/ web/20030426025452/http://www.ash.org.uk/html/advspo/pdfs/csfb.pdf, accessed February 2009.

11 *Sunday Times*, 20 January 2002.

12 www.ft.com, accessed March 2002

13 www.new-academy.ac.uk, accessed March 2002

14 www.narmada.org/gcg/gcgindex.html, accessed March 2002

15 Madeleine Bunting, 'Grassroots Gamine: Arundhati Roy is a thrilling political icon who represents the coming of age of feminism', *Guardian*, 7 March 2002; books.guardian.co.uk/news/articles/ 0,6109,663274,00.html, accessed March 2002.

16 www.thejakartapost.com, accessed March 2002

17 www.itglwf.org, accessed March 2002

18 www.global-unions.org, accessed March 2002

19 www.empresa.org, accessed March 2002

20 www.teriin.org, accessed March 2002

21 web.archive.org/web/20011007132424/http://www.new-academy.ac.uk/unv.htm, accessed February 2009

22 web.archive.org/web/20021204214227/http://bizspirit.com/business/index.html, accessed February 2009.

23 www.spiritinbusiness.org, accessed March 2002

2Q2002

1   Joseph Nocera, 'System Failure: Corporate America has lost its way. Here's a road map for restoring confidence', *Fortune*, 24 June 2002, web.archive.org/web/20021203153927/http://www. fortune.com/indexw.jhtml?channel=artcol.jhtml&doc_id=208314, accessed February 2009; 'T h e Wickedness of Wall Street', *The Economist*, 6 June 2002, www.economist.com/displayStory.cfm? Story_ID=S%27%29H%28%2AQA%2F%24%200%204%0A, accessed June 2002; 'Restoring Trust in Corporate America: Business must lead the way to real reform', *BusinessWeek*, 24 June 2002, www.businessweek.com/magazine/content/02_25/b3788001.htm, accessed June 2002.

2   Nocera, *op. cit.*

3   pewforum.org, accessed June 2002

4   *BusinessWeek*, 24 June 2002; www.businessweekeurope.com.

5   US Securities and Exchange Commission, 'Commission Formally Proposes Framework of a Public Accountability Board', press release, 20 June 2002; www.sec.gov/news/press/2002-91.htm, accessed June 2002.

6   *Business Respect: CSR Dispatches* 32 (16 June 2002).

7   www.sharedcapitalism.org, accessed June 2002 [link no longer active]

8   www.tesco.com, accessed June 2002

9   *BusinessWeek*, 24 June 2002; www.businessweekeurope.com, accessed June 2002.

10 'If Only CEO Meant Chief Ethical Officer', *BusinessWeek*, 13 June 2002; www.businessweek. com/bwdaily/dnflash/jun2002/nf20020613_9296.htm, accessed June 2002.

11 news.ft.com, accessed June 2002

12 www.eyenetwork.co.uk

13 www.new-academy.ac.uk, accessed June 2002

14 Ryan Underwood, 'Radicals for Responsibility', *Fast Company*, May 2002; web.archive.org/web/20021209184206/http://www.fastcompany.com/feature/02/haas.html, accessed February 2009.

15 www.csreurope.org, accessed June 2002

16 *Building Partnerships: Cooperation between the United Nations and the Private Sector* (United Nations, Department of Public Information, 2002; https://unp.un.org/Details.aspx?pid=11925, accessed February 2009).

17 www.unicttaskforce.org, accessed June 2002

18 www.vaccinealliance.org, accessed June 2002

19 *UNRISD News* 23 (2002); www.unrisd.org, accessed June 2002.

20 United Nations Environment Programme, 'Industry as a Partner for Sustainable Development: Compilation of Executive Summaries', 2002; web.archive.org/web/20050913070501/http://www.uneptie.org/outreach/wssd/docs/sectors/final/ex_summ-english.pdf, accessed February 2009.

21 United Nations Environment Programme Division of Technology, Industry and Economics, 'The state of the planet is getting worse but for many it's still "business as usual" ', press release, 15 May 2002; web.archive.org/web/20030319062959/http://www.uneptie.org/outreach/wssd/docs/PR-ENG.pdf, accessed February 2009.

22 United Nations Environment Programme, 'Industry as a Partner for Sustainable Development: Tourism', 2002; web.archive.org/web/20030403055122/http://www.uneptie.org/outreach/wssd/docs/sectors/final/tourism.pdf, accessed February 2009.

23 United Nations Environment Programme, 'Industry as a Partner for Sustainable Development: Aviation', 2002; web.archive.org/web/20040806174749/http://www.uneptie.org/outreach/wssd/docs/sectors/final/aviation.pdf, accessed February 2009.

24 *Ibid.*: 31-32.

25 United Nations Environment Programme, 'Industry as a Partner for Sustainable Development. Ten years after Rio: the UNEP assessment', 2002; web.archive.org/web/20030319115036/http://www.uneptie.org/outreach/wssd/docs/global/UNEP_report-english.pdf, accessed February 2009.

26 Luke Eric Peterson 'Dusted-off trade treaties ensure there is no such thing as a free riot', *Guardian*, 6 May 2002; www.guardian.co.uk/Archive/Article/0,4273,4407944,00.html, accessed June 2002.

27 www.basd-action.net, accessed June 2002 [link no longer active]

28 www.wbcsd.org, accessed June 2002

29 www.foe.co.uk, accessed June 2002

30 'Business regulation should not stifle enterprise, BASD chief says'; basd.free.fr/docs/speeches/20020304_holmes.html, accessed February 2009.

31 www.basd-action.net, accessed June 2002 [link no longer active]; www.wbcsd.org, accessed June 2002

32 www.sustain-online.org, accessed June 2002

33 Halina Ward, 'Corporate Accountability in Search of a Treaty? Some Insights from Foreign Direct Liability', Briefing Paper, May 2002; www.chathamhouse.org.uk/publications/papers/view/-/id/56, accessed February 2009.

34 www.worldmonitors.com, accessed June 2002

35 www.worldmonitors.com, accessed June 2002

36 'The Role of Multinational Corporations in Economic and Social Development of Poor Countries', transcript of John Browne's speech to Harvard University on 3 April 2002; www.ethicalcorp.com/NewsTemplate.asp?IDNum=206, accessed June 2002.

37 Heather Stewart, 'Poor miss out as rich nations cream off their trade', *Guardian*, 30 April 2002; www.guardian.co.uk/Archive/Article/0,4273,4404211,00.html, accessed June 2002.

38 www.wdm.org.uk, accessed June 2002

39 WBCSD, 'Partnerships in Practice: Industry, Fresh Water and Sustainable Development', April 2000.

40 www.wbcsd.org, accessed June 2002

41 John Vidal, Charlotte Denny and Larry Elliott, 'Secret documents reveal EU's tough stance on global trade', *Guardian* 17 April 2002; www.guardian.co.uk/Archive/Article/0,4273,4395615,00. html, accessed June 2002.

42 Patrick Lannin, 'EU plays down "leaked" trade plans, greens angry', 18 April 2002; www. planetark.org/dailynewsstory.cfm/newsid/15527/story.htm, accessed June 2002.

43 Nick Mathiason, 'WTO chief targets multinationals', *Observer*, 16 June 2002; www.observer.co.uk/ business/story/0,6903,738106,00.html, accessed June 2002.

3Q2002

1 John Weiser and Simon Zadek, 'Conversations with Disbelievers: Persuading Companies to Address Social Challenges', in S. Zadek, *Tomorrow's History: Selected Writings of Simon Zadek, 1993–2003* (Greenleaf Publishing, 2000): 229-36.

2 Full text of 'Where Next for Corporate Social Responsibility?' from the *Public Affairs Newsletter* is available at www.jembendell.com.

3 'The Case for Defense Stock Investing'; web.archive.org/web/20021208175829/http://vicefund. com/aerospacedefense.html, accessed February 2009.

4 www.vicefund.com, accessed September 2002

5 www.reuters.com, accessed September 2002

6 Jonathan Duffy, 'Coffee: Spilling the beans on quality', BBC News Online, 24 September, 2002; news.bbc.co.uk/1/hi/uk/2275774.stm, accessed September 2002.

7 Oxfam, 'Mugged: Poverty in your Coffee Cup' (Oxfam International, 2002; www.oxfam.org.uk/ resources/papers/downloads/mugged.pdf, accessed February 2009).

8 'Domini Social Investments backs Oxfam's "Coffee Rescue Plan" ', 18 September 2002; www. domini.com/about-domini/News/Press-Release-Archive/Coffee_PR_9-02.doc_cvt.htm, accessed September 2002.

9 Jem Bendell (ed.), *Terms for Endearment: Business, NGOs and Sustainable Development* (Greenleaf Publishing, 2000).

10 ILO, 'Sustainable Agriculture in a Globalised Economy' (ILO, September 2000; www.ilo.org/ public/english/dialogue/sector/techmeet/tmad00/tmadr.htm, accessed September 2002).

11 'The World's 10 Most Valuable Brands', *BusinessWeek*, 5 August 2002; www.businessweek.com/ magazine/content/02_31/b3794033.htm, accessed September 2002.

12 UNICEF, 'UNICEF, McDonald's® and Ronald McDonald House Charities® team up to raise funds for children', press release, 19 July 2002; web.archive.org/web/20021015001629/http://www. unicef.org/newsline/02pr45McD.htm, accessed February 2009.

13 Patrick Butler, 'Unicef in McDonald's link row', *Guardian*, 3 August 2002; society.guardian. co.uk/fundraising/story/0,8150,768404,00.html, accessed September 2002.

14 www.un.org, accessed September 2002

15 *Ibid.*

16 web.archive.org/web/20021217221918/http://www.transnationale.org/anglais/fiches/-1105426268. htm, accessed February 2009

17 www.unglobalcompact.org, accessed September 2002

18 Interview, *Daily Summit*, 25 August 2002; www.dailysummit.net/says/interview250802.htm, accessed September 2002.

19 Terry Macalister and Paul Brown, 'Earth summit agenda "hijacked": Big business is wielding its influence to water down plans for tighter regulation, says aid group', *Guardian*, 9 August 2002; www.guardian.co.uk/worldsummit2002/story/0,12264,771692,00.html, accessed September 2002.

20 'Business regulation should not stifle enterprise, BASD chief says'; basd.free.fr/docs/speeches/ 20020304_holmes.html, accessed February 2009.

21 web.archive.org/web/20021206034525/http://www.johannesburgsummit.org/html/documents/ summit_docs.html, accessed February 2009

22 www.basd-action.net, accessed September 2002 [link no longer active]

23 'Whose Responsibility?', *Daily Summit*, 28 August 2002; www.dailysummit.net/writes/article280802.htm, accessed September 2002 .

24 'Business', *Daily Summit*, 12 September 2002; www.dailysummit.net/archives/cat_business.shtml, accessed September 2002.

25 www.unhchr.ch/Huridocda/Huridoca.nsf/TestFrame/396b1b56d0124306c1256bdc0038bcfa?Opendocument, accessed February 2009

26 *Statement in Support of the Draft Human Rights Principles and Responsibilities for Transnational Corporations and Other Business Enterprise*, IBLF, 2002. Full text available at www.jembendell.com.

27 *Joint Views of ICC and the IOE on the Draft Human Rights Principles and Responsibilities for Transnational Corporations and other Business Enterprises*, 30 July 2000. Full text available at www.jembendell.com.

28 *Human Rights Principles and Responsibilities for Transnational Corporations and other Business Enterprises: An Intervention by Klaus N.I. Leisinger, Novartis Foundation*, July 2002. Full text available at www.jembendell.com.

29 'Business sets the record straight on corporate accountability pre-Summit'; basd.free.fr/docs/articles/20020807_holme.html, accessed February 2009.

30 'White Papers Ease Regulatory Fears', *Ethical Performance* 4.4 (September 2002).

31 europa.eu.int, accessed September 2002

32 Tracey Swift and Simon Zadek, 'Corporate Responsibility and the Competitive Advantage of Nations' (The Copenhagen Centre/AccountAbility, 2002; www.copenhagencentre.org/corprespnations2002.pdf, accessed February 2009).

33 Steve Hilton, 'A Tale of Two Launches: The UK CORE Bill and "Publish What You Pay"', Ethical Corporation, 17 July 2002; www.ethicalcorp.com/NewsTemplate.asp?IDNum=294, accessed September 2002.

34 www.ey.com, accessed September 2002

35 *Ibid.*

36 'Corporations sued over apartheid', BBC News, 9 August, 2002; news.bbc.co.uk/1/hi/world/americas/2183739.stm, accessed September 2002.

37 Jim Lobe, 'US court okays Unocal rights suit', *Asia Times*, 21 September 2002; www.atimes.com/atimes/Southeast_Asia/DI21Aeo1.html, accessed September 2002.

38 Elliot Schrage, 'Analysis: A Long Way to Find Justice', Ethical Corporation, 2002; web.archive.org/web/20021121151830/http://www.ethicalcorp.com/printtemplate.asp?idnum=336, accessed February 2009.

39 www.indiaexpress.com, accessed September 2002.

40 The Copenhagen Centre, 'Ethnic Minority Employment through Partnership: Towards a Model of Good Practice', 2002; www.copenhagencentre.org/ethnicminority.pdf, accessed February 2009.

41 www.hsbc.co.uk, accessed September 2002

42 *Ibid.*

43 'Report by UN rights expert notes rise in racism, xenophobia and anti-Semitism', UN Newsletter, 24 August 2002; www.unic.org.in/News/2002/nl/nl24Aug2002.html#7, accessed September 2002.

44 'Discrimination is Everybody's Business', web.archive.org/web/*/http://www.respecteurope.com/eng/news_e.html#Durban, accessed February 2009.

45 www.ethnicmajority.com/consumer_news.htm, accessed September 2002

4Q2002

1 afr.com, accessed December 2002

2 Roger East, 'Faith in the City', *Green Futures* 37 (2002); www.forumforthefuture.org/greenfutures/articles/601260, accessed February 2009.

3 'Financing the Future: The London Principles of Sustainable Finance'; www.forumforthefuture.org/node/978, accessed February 2009.

4 Nick Robins, 'Turning the Worm', *Green Futures* 37 (2002); www.forumforthefuture.org/greenfutures/articles/601262, accessed February 2009.

5 'Principles of Islamic Banking', *Nida'ul Islam* magazine; www.usc.edu/dept/MSA/economics/nbank1.html, accessed December 2002.

6 David Boyle, 'Islam or Rust?', *Green Futures* 37 (2002); www.forumforthefuture.org/greenfutures/articles/601263, accessed February 2009.

7 web.archive.org/web/20021201170942/http://www.irti.org/conf002.htm, accessed February 2009

8 United Nations Security Council, *Final Report of the Panel of Experts on the Illegal Exploitation of Natural Resources and Other Forms of Wealth in the Democratic Republic of Congo*, New York, 16th October 2002; http://193.194.138.190/Huridocda/Huridoca.nsf/e06a5300f90fa023802566870o518ca4/5e423385c10ae294c1256b1100505218/$FILE/N0132354.pdf, accessed December 2002.

9 See e.g. Stakeholder Democracy Network, 'Coded Words: A Critical Assessment of the Voluntary Approach to Achieving Corporate Accountability', Lewes, UK, October 2002.

10 'Footsie firms caught up in Congo looting probe', *Independent on Sunday* (UK), 27 October 2002.

11 www.forrestgroup.com, accessed December 2002.

12 'Belgium searches ING bank unit in Congo probe', Reuters, 8 November 2002.

13 'Mr Mahmoud Kassem, Chairman of the Panel of Experts on the Illegal Exploitation of Natural Resources and Other Forms of Wealth of the Democratic Republic of the Congo', United Nations daily press briefing, 25 October 2002, New York.

14 Patricia Feeney, 'Making Companies Accountable: An NGO Report on Implementation of the OECD Guidelines for Multinational Enterprises by National Contact Points', Rights and Accountability in Development (RAID), Oxford, UK, November 2002.

15 'NGOs Cautiously Welcome the Launch of Kimberley Process', Interlaken: Global Witness, 5 November 2002; ActionAid, blood diamonds campaign; Martin Plaut, ' "Blood diamonds" polished off', BBC News Online, 5 November 2002; news.bbc.co.uk/1/hi/world/africa/2406407.stm, accessed December 2002.

16 www.wrapapparel.org, accessed December 2002

17 *Ibid.*

18 www.gmies.org.sv, accessed December 2002

19 M. Prieto and J. Bendell, 'If You Want to Help Us Then Start Listening to Us! From Factories and Plantations in Central America, Women Speak out about Corporate Responsibility' (New Academy of Business, December 2002).

20 Miriam Jacobs and Barbara Dinham (eds.), *Silent Invaders: Pesticides, Livelihoods and Women's Health* (Zed Books, 2003).

21 'Batalla por Nemagón se traslada a EE.UU.', *La Prensa*, 15 December 2002; www-ni.laprensa.com.ni/archivo/2002/diciembre/15/nacionales/nacionales-20021215-10.html, accessed December 2002.

22 www.bananalink.org.uk, accessed December 2002

23 www.itanica.org, accessed December 2002; see also www.cawn.org, accessed December 2002

24 EarthRights International, 'In Defense of the Alien Tort Claims Act', 2002; web.archive.org/web/20031224075200/http://earthrights.org/news/atca.shtml, accessed February 2009.

25 Human Rights Watch, 'US/Indonesia: Bush Backtracks on Corporate Responsibility', New York, 7 August 2002.

26 International Labor Rights Fund, 'Show Solidarity with Acehnese Detainees', Washington, DC, 22 November 2002; web.archive.org/web/20031026185003/http://www.laborrights.org/urgent/aceh1122.htm, accessed February 2009.

27 Eveline Lubbers (ed.), *Battling Big Business: Countering Greenwash, Front Groups and Other Forms of Corporate Deception* (2002, www.evel.nl/pandora/bbb.htm).

28 Friends of the Earth, 'CBI Told to Stop Lobbying against Planet', press release, 24 November 2002.

29 USCIB, 'Overdoing precaution can stifle innovation and growth, world business body says', press release, 9 December 2002; www.uscib.org/index.asp?documentID=2387, accessed December 2002.

30 www.iccwbo.org, accessed December 2002

31 Larry Elliott and Charlotte Denny, 'US wrecks cheap drugs deal: Cheney's intervention blocks pact to help poor countries after pharmaceutical firms lobby White House', *Guardian*, 21 December 2002; www.guardian.co.uk/international/story/0,3604,864071,00.html, accessed December 2002.

32 web.archive.org/web/20031226143842/http://www.sustainability.com/programs/janus/default.asp, accessed February 2009

33 Darcy Frey, 'How Green Is BP?', *New York Times*, 8 December 2002; www.nytimes.com/2002/12/08/magazine/08BP.html?tntemail0, accessed December 2002.

34 Geoffrey Lean, 'They came. They talked. And weasled. And left', *Independent*, 8 September 2002; web.archive.org/web/20030710233813/http://www.independent.co.uk/story.jsp?story=331352, accessed December 2002.

35 web.archive.org/web/20031224031134/http://www.ippr.org.uk/research/index.php?current=28&project=129, accessed February 2009

36 Roger Cowe and Jonathon Porritt, 'Government's Business: Enabling Corporate Sustainability', Forum for the Future, November 2002; web.archive.org/web/20040930001607/http://www.forumforthefuture.org.uk/uploadstore/governments_business.pdf, accessed February 2009.

37 Xavier Font and Jem Bendell, *Standards for Sustainable Tourism for the Purpose of Multilateral Trade Negotiations* (World Tourism Organisation, 2002).

1Q2003

1 World Economic Forum, 'Responding to the Leadership Challenge: Findings of a CEO Survey on Global Corporate Citizenship', January 2003; www.weforum.org/pdf/GCCI/Findings_of_CEO_survey_on_GCCI.pdf, accessed March 2003.

2 UNI, '2003 Summary of Annual Learning Forum Meeting, In Depth', 27 January 2003; www.union-network.org, accessed March 2003.

3 'Global Compact Policy Dialogue 2002: Business and Sustainable Development. 2nd Meeting, Paris, 17–18 June. Summary Outcome', www.unep.fr/scp/compact/dialogue/2002/pdf/Dialogue2002-ParisReport.pdf, accessed February 2009.

4 A. Wilson and C. Boasson, 'Exploring Business Dynamics: Mainstreaming Corporate Social Responsibility in a Company's Strategy, Management and Systems' (CSR Europe/E&P/Ashridge, 2002).

5 www.danone.com, accessed March 2003

6 'Organizational Development', University of California–San Francisco, 30 August 2002; web.archive.org/web/20030426044341/http://ucsfhr2.ucsf.edu/training/info.shtml?x=195, accessed February 2009.

7 www.futureconsiderations.com, accessed March 2003

8 www.lead.org, accessed March 2003

9 www.globalegacy.com, accessed March 2003

10 www.lead.org, accessed March 2003

11 www.shell.com, accessed March 2003

12 'PricewaterhouseCoopers—Ulysses: An Intercultural Approach to Leadership Development for Sustainable Business', CSR Europe, web.archive.org/web/20031013131308/http://www.csreurope.org/whatwedo/default.asp?pageid=411, accessed February 2009; 'Project Ulysses: Experiencing Tajikistan', PricewaterhouseCoopers, www.pwcglobal.com/Extweb/career.nsf/docid/845EF7B4CEE08824CA256BF8001123CB, accessed March 2003.

13 Joseph Jaworski, *Synchronicity: The Inner Path of Leadership* (Berrett-Koehler, 1996).

14 Peter Senge, *The Fifth Discipline: The Art and Practice of the Learning Organization* (Currency Doubleday, 1990, 1994).

15 web.archive.org/web/20030429195443/http://www.pegasuscom.com/globalinst/glbllearn.html, accessed February 2009

16 web.archive.org/web/20030421015020/http://www.pegasuscom.com/globalinst/index.html, accessed February 2009

17 Bob Doppelt, *Leading Change toward Sustainability: A Change-Management Guide for Business, Gov**ernment and Civil Society* (Greenleaf Publishing, 2002).

18 Andy Law, *Experiment at Work: Explosions and Experiences at the Most Frightening Company on Earth* (Profile Books, 2003).

19 *Independent*, March 2003: Features: 19, 20.

20 S.H. Appelbaum, D. Hebert and S. Leroux 'Empowerment: Power, Culture and Leadership: A Strategy or Fad for the Millennium?', *Journal of Workplace Learning: Employee Counselling Today* 11.7 (1999): 233-54.

21 Nick Cohen, 'With a Friend Like This . . .', *Observer*, 7 April 2002; www.observer.co.uk/comment/story/0,6903,680100,00.html, accessed March 2003.

22 Richard Allen, '100 Esso Stations Targeted in Protest against Conflict with Iraq', *Evening Standard*, 24 February 2003: 4.

23 Neil King, 'US Quietly Soliciting Bids for Rebuilding Postwar Iraq', *Dow Jones & WSJ*, 10 March 2003; Randeep Ramesh 'The War Dividend', *Guardian*, 13 March 2003, www.guardian.co.uk/Iraq/Story/0,2763,913219,00.html, accessed March 2003; Robert Bryce, 'Cheney is still paid by Pentagon contractor', *Guardian*, 12 March 2003, www.guardian.co.uk/international/story/0,3604,912426,00.html, accessed March 2003.

24 'Latest Legal Advice on War', *Guardian*, 14 March 2003; www.guardian.co.uk/letters/story/0,3604,913965,00.html, accessed March 2003.

25 Richard Perle, 'Thank God for the Death of the UN', *Guardian*, 21 March 2003; www.guardian.co.uk/comment/story/0,3604,918764,00.html, accessed March 2003.

26 Simon Zadek, 'The Road from Here', *Ethical Corporation*, February 2003.

27 Jem Bendell (ed.), *Terms for Endearment: Business, NGOs and Sustainable Development* (Greenleaf Publishing, 2000).

28 Marc Lopatin, 'Big Business Still Dodging the Tax Issue', *Observer*, 12 January 2003; observer.co.uk/business/story/0,6903,872940,00.html, accessed March 2003.

29 Securities and Exchange Commission, 'SEC sues former and current Qwest employees for fraud', press release, 25 February 2003; www.sec.gov/news/press/2003-25.htm, accessed March 2003.

30 Merrill Lynch, 'Merrill Lynch reaches agreement in principle with SEC staff regarding Enron issues', press release, 2003.

31 National Association of Securities Dealers, 'NASD fines J.P. Morgan for sharing in profits from hot IPOs', 20 February 2003.

32 Reed Abelson and Jonathan D. Glater, 'New York will sue two big drug makers on doctor discount', *New York Times*, 13 February 2003, www.nytimes.com/2003/02/13/business/13DRUG.html, accessed March 2003; www.transparency.org, accessed March 2003.

33 Sophie Arie, 'British drugs giant in Italian bribery investigation', *Guardian*, 13 February 2003; www.guardian.co.uk/international/story/0,3604,894332,00.html, accessed March 2003.

34 *Business Respect: CSR Dispatches* 49 (9 February 2003); www.mallenbaker.net/csr/nl/49.html, accessed March 2003.

35 www.transparency.org, accessed March 2003

36 Georg Kell, 'The Global Compact: Origins, Achievements, Challenges', *Ethical Corporation*, 25 February 2003; www.ethicalcorp.com/content.asp?ContentID=403, accessed March 2003.

37 Alfred Mbogora, Researchers to Business, 'Fighting Poverty is Good for You', PANOS, Dar es Salaam, February 2003.

38 *Business Respect: CSR Dispatches* 47 (12 January 2003).

39 *Business Respect: CSR Dispatches* 51 (9 March 2003); www.mallenbaker.net/csr/nl/51.html, accessed March 2003.

2Q2003

1 *Multinational Monitor* 23.12 (December 2002).

2 www.britishamericantobacco.com, accessed June 2003

3 www.burmacampaign.org.uk, accessed June 2003

4 www.foe.co.uk, accessed June 2003

5 *BAT Social Report 2001/2002*

6 *Ibid.*

7 J. Mackay and M. Eriksen, *The Tobacco Atlas* (World Health Organization, 2002; www.who.int/bookorders/anglais/detart1.jsp?sesslan=1&codlan=1&codcol=15&codcch=512, accessed February 2009).

8 www.philipmorrisinternational.com, accessed June 2003; www.britishamericantobacco.com, accessed June 2003

9 www.philipmorrisusa.com, accessed June 2003

10 RJ Reynolds, 'Two of nation's top cigarette manufacturers sue California for misuse of tax funds', press release, 2 April 2003; web.archive.org/web/20030628162824/http://www.rjrt.com/NR/NRreleases_rjrtview.asp?DocId=413, accessed February 2009.

11 www.usdoj.gov, accessed June 2003

12 Alan Boyd, 'Future Hazy for Success of Tobacco Pact', *Asia Times*, 3 June 2003; www.atimes.com/atimes/Asian_Economy/EF03Dk01.html, accessed June 2003.

13 *Ibid.*

14 M. Baker, 'Bringing Corporate Lobbying into the Light', *Business Respect: CSR Dispatches* 57 (1 June 2003); www.mallenbaker.net, accessed June 2003.

15 Word Health Organisation, 'World Health Assembly adopts historic Tobacco Control Pact', press release, 21 May 2003; www.who.int/mediacentre/releases/2003/prwha1/en, accessed June 2003.

16 UNECE, 'Governments Reach Agreement on New United Nations Treaty on Pollution Information Disclosure', press release ECE/ENV/03/P01, Geneva, 31 January 2003.

17 Halina Ward, 'Legal Issues in Corporate Citizenship', paper prepared for the Swedish Partnership for Global Responsibility' (London: IIED, 2003).

18 *International Right to Know: Empowering Communities through Transparency* (IRTK Campaign; Washington, DC, 2003).

19 FoE-NL, 'BP violating OECD Guidelines: Friends of the Earth Netherlands files complaint against oil company BP', Friends of the Earth Netherlands, Amsterdam, 29 April 2003.

20 FoE-NL, 'Using the OECD Guidelines for Multinational Enterprises: A Critical Starterkit for NGOs', Friends of the Earth Netherlands, Amsterdam, 2003.

21 TUAC, 'A Users' Guide for Trade Unionists to the OECD Guidelines to Multinational Enterprises', Trade Union Advisory Committee, Brussels, 2003.

22 FoE-UK, 'Shell boss exposed for lobbying against accountability', press release, 15 May 2003.

23 ACCA, *ACCA UK Awards for Sustainability Reporting 2002: Report of the Judges* (The Certified Accountants Educational Trust, 2003).

24 OECD, *OECD Guidelines for Multinational Enterprises* (OECD, 2000).

25 Keith Alcorn, 'Investment funds tell drug companies to improve treatment access for poorest countries', 25 March 2003; www.aidsmap.com/news/newsdisplay2.asp?newsId=1976, accessed June 2003.

26 *Business Report*, South Africa, 20 May 2003, www.busrep.co.za, accessed June 2003.

27 *Business Report*, South Africa, 3 May 2003, www.busrep.co.za, accessed June 2003.

28 *Business Report*, South Africa, 27 April 2003, www.busrep.co.za, accessed June 2003.

29 *Business Report*, South Africa, 28 April 2003, www.busrep.co.za, accessed June 2003.

30 *Business Report*, South Africa, 18 May 2003, www.busrep.co.za, accessed June 2003.

31 *Business Report*, South Africa, 24 April 2003, www.busrep.co.za, accessed June 2003.

32 *Business Report*, South Africa, 30 April 2003, www.busrep.co.za, accessed June 2003.

33 Naomi Klein, 'Bush to NGOs: Watch your mouths', *Global and Mail*, 20 June 2003; www.globeandmail.com, accessed June 2003.

34 SustainAbility, '21st Century NGO: Playing the Game or Selling Out? International study reveals that more NGOs are shifting from confrontation to collaboration', press release, 26 June 2003; www.sustainability.com, accessed June 2003.

35 See e.g. A.C. Hudock, *NGOs and Civil Society: Democracy by Proxy?* (The Polity Press, 1999); and David Hulme and Michael Edwards (eds.), *NGOs, States and Donors: Too Close for Comfort?* (St Martin's Press, 1996).

36 Marina Ottaway, 'Corporatism Goes Global: International Organizations, NGO Networks and Transnational Business', *Global Governance*, September 2001.

37 David C. Korten, *The Post-Corporate World: Life after Capitalism* (Berrett-Koehler, 1999).
38 J. Richter, *Holding Corporations Accountable: Corporate Conduct, International Codes, and Citizen Action* (Zed Books, 2001).
39 *Business Ethics* 17.1 (Spring 2003).
40 www2.bitc.org.uk, accessed June 2003
41 www.reputex.com.au, accessed June 2003; and 'Australia: Rows break out over promised Corporate Responsibility Index', *Business Respect: CSR Dispatches* 54 (10 April 2003); www.mallenbaker.net/csr/CSRfiles/page.php?Story_ID=909, accessed June 2003.
42 www.nottingham.ac.uk/business/iccsr, accessed June 2003
43 www.kpmg.co.za, accessed June 2003

3Q2003

1 www.equator-principles.com/principles.shtml, accessed September 2003
2 Steve Lippman, 'Banking on Change' (Trillium Asset Management, August 2003; web.archive.org/web/20031205021206/http://trilliuminvest.com/pages/news/news_detail.asp?ArticleID=276&status=CurrentIssue, accessed February 2009).
3 'NGO Collective Analysis of the Equator Principles', Focus on Finance, 2003; web.archive.org/web/20031015232408/http://www.financeadvocacy.org/mod.php?mod=userpage&menu=3&page_id=9, accessed September 2003.
4 www.wbcsd.org, accessed September 2003
5 UK Social Investment Forum, 'Collaborative investor engagement enters new era', press release, 5 August 2003; web.archive.org/web/20041213121436/http://www.uksif.org/Z/Z/Z/lib/2003/08/05-press-collab/index.shtml, accessed February 2009.
6 Sarah Boseley, 'Investors pressure drug firms on pricing', *Guardian*, 25 March 2003; www.guardian.co.uk/aids/story/0,7369,921361,00.html, accessed September 2003.
7 UNCTAD, *World Investment Report 2003*, 4 September 2003; www.unctad.org, accessed September 2003.
8 United Nations, 'UN human rights body approves guidelines for multinational corporations', press release, 13 August 2003; www.un.org/apps/news/story.asp?NewsID=7991&Cr= commission &Cr1=rights, accessed September 2003.
9 'Adoption of UN human rights Norms for companies a welcome step forward', Amnesty International, 13 August 2003; web.amnesty.org/library/Index/ENGPOL300132003, accessed September 2003.
10 To view the final text of the United Nations Norms on business and human rights, go to www1.umn.edu/humanrts/links/norms-Aug2003.html (accessed September 2003).
11 BBC World Service, London, 'Newshour', 13 August 2003, 4:00 pm; web.archive.org/web/20040117114252/http://www.uscib.org/%5cindex.asp?documentID=2729, accessed February 2009.
12 Letter to Louise Fréchette, Deputy Secretary-General of the United Nations, from Jeremy Hobbs, Oxfam International, Amnesty International, Lawyers' Committee for Human Rights and Human Rights Watch, 7 April 2003; web.archive.org/web/20060919191533/www.humanrightsfirst.org/workers_rights/wr_other/joint_ltr_UN_040703.pdf, accessed February 2009.
13 'GC clarifies relation to Norms adopted by Sub-Commission on Promotion and Protection of Human Rights', 13 August 2003; www.unglobalcompact.org, accessed September 2003.
14 BBC World Service, *op. cit.*
15 'Guidelines on Cooperation between the United Nations and the Business Community', issued by the Secretary-General of the United Nations, 17 July 2000; www.un.org/partners/business/otherpages/guide.htm, accessed September 2003.
16 'Towards Global Partnerships: Enhanced Cooperation between the United Nations and All Relevant Partners, in Particular the Private Sector', Report of the Secretary-General, 18 August 2003.

17 Oliver Balch, 'A Question of Answerability', *Guardian*, London, 1 September 2003; www.guardian. co.uk/globalisation/story/0,7369,1033380,00.html, accessed September 2003.

18 Jem Bendell, 'Civil Regulation: A New Form of Democratic Governance for the Global Economy?', in J. Bendell (ed.), *Terms for Endearment: Business, NGOs and Sustainable Development* (Greenleaf Publishing, 2000): 239-54.

19 See Terry Macalister, 'Shell opens its books in Nigeria', *Guardian*, 20 June 2003; www.guardian. co.uk/business/story/0,3604,981193,00.html, accessed September 2003.

20 The plan envisions ending 'a condition of increased dependency on foreign powers that do not always have American interests at heart' by creating 'deep water offshore exploration and production in the Atlantic Basin, stretching from offshore Canada to the Caribbean, Brazil and West Africa', National Energy Policy Development Group, *Reliable, Affordable, and Environmentally Sound Energy for America's Future* (US Energy Department, 17 May 2001; www.netl.doe.gov/ publications/press/2001/nep/nep.html, accessed September 2003).

21 Julian Borger, 'US to lock Africa in a military embrace', *Guardian*, 10 July 2003; www.guardian. co.uk/guardianweekly/story/0,12674,995361,00.html, accessed September 2003.

22 Rory Carroll, 'Bush begins his African odyssey today, but is he there to plunder or provide?', *Guardian*,7 July 2003; www.guardian.co.uk/international/story/0,3604,992914,00.html, accessed September 2003.

23 Rory Carroll, 'Troops seize power in oil rush', *Guardian*, 17 July 2003; www.guardian.co.uk/ international/story/0,3604,999584,00.html, accessed September 2003.

24 UK Department of International Finance and Development, 'Report of the Extractive Industries Transparency Initiative (EITI) London Conference', London, 17 June 2003; web.archive.org/web/ 20031206062659/http://www.dfid.gov.uk/News/News/files/eiti_draft_report.htm, accessed February 2009.

25 See Charlotte Denny, 'Short warns of oil boycott over African corruption', *Guardian*, 11 February 2003; www.guardian.co.uk/business/story/0,3604,893077,00.html, accessed September 2003.

26 Terry Macalister, 'US oilmen fight Blair on transparency', *Guardian*, 18 June 2003; www.guardian. co.uk/business/story/0,3604,979676,00.html, accessed September 2003.

27 Denny, *op. cit.*

28 See Andrew Osborn, 'UK accused of giving in to oil firms', *Guardian*, 13 June 2003; www.guardian. co.uk/business/story/0,3604,976461,00.html, accessed September 2003.

29 See Macalister, 'Shell opens its books . . .', and Christian Aid, 'The need for legally binding regulation of transnational corporations', London, February 2001; web.archive.org/web/ 20031222172001/http://www.christian-aid.org.uk/indepth/0202tnc/transc.htm, accessed February 2009.

30 See Susan Hawley, 'Turning a Blind Eye: Corruption and the UK Export Credits Guarantee Department', The Corner House, Sturminster Newton, UK, June 2003; web.archive.org/web/ 20031008142459/http://www.thecornerhouse.org.uk/document/summary/correcgd.html, accessed February 2009.

31 See Michael Peel, 'Nigeria urged to combat fraudulent transactions', *Financial Times*, 21 November 2002.

32 Conal Walsh, 'Companies snub "clean up your act" call', *Observer*, 29 June 2003; politics.guardian. co.uk/green/story/0,9061,987469,00.html, accessed September 2003.

33 UK Department of Trade and Industry, *Modern Company Law for a Competitive Economy: Final Report* (DTI, July 2002, web.archive.org/web/20030919193752/http://www.dti.gov.uk/cld/final_ report, accessed February 2009).

34 UK Department of Trade and Industry, *The Operating and Financial Review Working Group on Mate - riality* (DTI, 27 June 2003, web.archive.org/web/20031116201346/http://www.dti.gov.uk/cld/ ofrwgcon.pdf, accessed February 2009).

35 Simon Zadek and Mira Merme, 'Redefining Materiality: Practice and Public Policy for Effective Corporate Reporting' (AccountAbility, 2003).

36 See Wilfried Lütkenhorst, 'Corporate Social Responsibility and Developing Country SMEs' (UNIDO, June 2003).

37 Linda Greenhouse, 'Nike free speech case is unexpectedly returned to California', *New York Times*, 27 June 2003.

38 On writ of certiorari to the Supreme Court of California, no. 02-575 Nike, Inc., *et al.*, Petitioners v. Marc Kasky, J. Stevens, concurring, Supreme Court of the United States, 26 June 2003; reclaimdemocracy.org/nike/stevens_concurrence.pdf, accessed September 2003.

39 Statement by Nike, Inc. on Today's Procedural Decision by the US Supreme Court in First Amendment Case, press release, 26 June 2003; www.nikebiz.com, accessed September 2003.

40 Jeff Milchen and Jeffrey Kaplan, 'Saving Corporations from Themselves?', 27 June 2003; reclaimdemocracy.org/nike/nike_court_case_oped_6272003.html, accessed September 2003.

41 www.fairlabor.org, accessed September 2003

42 Adam Liptak, 'Free Speech: Nike move ends case over firms' free speech', *New York Times*, 13 September 2003.

43 www.fairlabor.org, accessed September 2003

44 Quotes from Russell Mokhiber and Robert Weissman, 'Nike gets a pass', 23 September 2003; www.corporatecrimereporter.com, accessed September 2003.

45 www.workersrights.org, accessed September 2003

46 From Mokhiber and Weissman, *op. cit.*

47 See William A. Schabas, *An Introduction to the International Criminal Court* (Cambridge University Press, August 2001): 81, n34; and: Geoffrey Robertson QC, *Crimes against Humanity: The Struggle for Global Justice* (Penguin Books, 2000): 522.

48 See Philippe Sands, 'Our troops alone risk prosecution', *Guardian*, 15 January 2003; www.guardian.co.uk/comment/story/0,3604,874908,00.html, accessed September 2003.

49 See Ian Black, 'Genocide court sets sights on Congo conflict', *Guardian*, 17 July 2003; www.guardian.co.uk/international/story/0,3604,999527,00.html, accessed September 2003: 'He said the court could only intervene if the Congo courts were unable to deal with the crisis. A new government took office in June and it was unclear whether it would prosecute suspected war criminals in Ituri [. . .] He said the fighting appeared to be fuelled by the exploitation of the area's natural resources. Some reports cited links between companies in Africa, Europe and the Middle East and atrocities in Congo. Organised criminal groups from eastern Europe were also said to be involved'. See also 'Firms face "blood diamond" probe', BBC News Online, 23 September 2002, news.bbc.co.uk/1/hi/business/3133108.stm, accessed September 2003; and 'Coalition for the International Criminal Court' website: www.iccnow.org.

50 Ian Black and Ewen MacAskill, 'US threatens Nato boycott over Belgian war crimes law', *Guardian*, 13 June 2003, www.guardian.co.uk/international/story/0,3604,976449,00.html, accessed September 2003; and Amnesty International *et al.*, 'The Belgian law of Universal Jurisdiction gets a second wind', Brussels, 19 July 2002, www.unobserver.com/layout5.php?id=256&blz=1, accessed September 2003.

51 Andrew Osborn, 'Belgium may revive Sharon war crimes case', *Guardian*, 17 January 2003; www.guardian.co.uk/international/story/0,3604,876385,00.html, accessed September 2003: 'There will be a special clause designed to deter "legal tourists". A filtering mechanism will be created to weed out cases which are purely political or propagandist in nature. "We will put up a filter for those cases which are not linked to Belgium . . . to allow for a speedier dismissal of purely political complaints which don't have anything to do with genocide or war crimes and which are often lodged as propaganda", said Vincent Van Quickenborne, a Liberal senator.'

52 meetings.aomonline.org/2003/submissions/theme.html, accessed September 2003

53 Guy Holburn and Richard Vanden Bergh, 'Influencing Agencies through Legislatures', presented at Academy of Management, Seattle, 2003.

54 web.archive.org/web/20030605180424/http://divisions.aomonline.org/one, accessed February 2009

4Q2003

1 'Tougher Law against Women Harassment Proposed', *Dawn Internet Edition*, 17 October 2003; www.dawn.com, accessed December 2003.

2 www.cwfa.org, accessed December 2003

3 'Get the firm out of here, US families lobby says', *Times Online*, 10 October 2003; www.timesonline.co.uk, accessed December 2003.

4 Andrew Adamides, 'Public Anger at FCUK Campaign', *Cyprus Mail*, 27 November 1998; www.hri.org/news/cyprus/cmnews/1998/98-11-27.cmnews.html#06, accessed December 2003.

5 T. Reichart, *The Erotic History of Advertising* (Prometheus Books, 2003).

6 See www.snopes.com/business/market/springmaid.asp, accessed December 2003, for a copy of the advert.

7 web.archive.org/web/20031206081448/http://www.springs.com/corporateinfo/ourbrands/springmaid.html, accessed February 2009

8 'Business Not Yet Playing Its Role in the Fight against AIDS: Business survey finds big gaps in business response to, and understanding about, HIV/AIDS', 1 December 2003; www.weforum.org/en/media/Latest%20Press%20Releases/PRESSRELEASES248, accessed February 2009. World Economic Forum Report, *Business and HIV/AIDS: Who Me?* www.weforum.org/pdf/Initiatives/GHI_BusinessAIDSWhoMe_WAD.pdf, accessed December 2003.

9 Jem Bendell, 'Waking Up to Risk? Corporate Responses to HIV/AIDS in the Workplace' (UNRISD Programme Paper, 2003; www.unrisd.org, accessed December 2003).

10 Rosalind Pollack Petchesky, *Global Prescriptions: Gendering Health and Human Rights* (Zed Books, 2003).

11 Nick Mathiason, 'Companies "undermining global fight against HIV"', *Observer*, 16 November 2003; observer.guardian.co.uk/business/story/0,6903,1085899,00.html accessed December 2003.

12 Global Business Coalition on HIV/AIDS, '2003 Awards for Business Excellence'; web.archive.org/web/20030915185040/http://www.businessfightsaids.org/pdf/2003_Awards_for_Business_Excellence.pdf, accessed February 2009.

13 The Global Fund, 'Seven major companies commit to co-investment to expand community HIV/AIDS programs using corporate infrastructure', press release, 3 December 2003; www.theglobalfund.org/en/pressreleases/?pr=pr_031203, accessed February 2009.

14 *International Symposium on HIV/AIDS Workplace Policies and Programmes in Developing Countries*, Berlin, 1–3 June 2003, Working Group 4, 2 June 2003, Draft Discussion Results; Group 4: 'Reaching Out to Families and Communities'.

15 'Oxfam America President Raymond Offenheiser answers Pfizer's latest response to Oxfam's Cut the Cost Campaign'; www.pfizer.com, accessed December 2003.

16 'Oxfam's Response to Open Letter from Hank McKinnell, CEO of Pfizer, to Oxfam Supporters', 29 July 2003; web.archive.org/web/20031210185041/http://www.oxfamamerica.org/advocacy/art5757.html?backresults=TRUE, accessed February 2009.

17 World Trade Organisation, 'Intellectual Property: Decision removes final patent obstacle to cheap drug imports', press release, 30 August 2003; www.wto.org/english/news_e/pres03_e/pr350_e.htm, accessed December 2003.

18 Naomi Klein, 'Bush's Aids "gift" has been seized by industry giants', *Guardian*, 13 October 2003; www.guardian.co.uk/comment/story/0,3604,1061634,00.html, accessed December 2003.

19 Médecins Sans Frontières, 'Flawed WTO drugs deal will do little to secure future access to medicines in developing countries', press release, 30 August 2003.

20 *Op. cit.*

21 www.oneworldtrust.org, accessed December 2003

22 'NGOs Assess the Millennium Development Goals', *NGLS Roundup* 105 (July 2003); www.unsystem.org/ngls/documents/pdf/roundup/RU105mdg.pdf, accessed December 2003.

23 www.csmworld.org/index.htm, accessed December 2003

24 www.undp.org/mdg, accessed December 2003

25 www.origoinc.com, accessed December 2003

26 J. Wei-Skillern and B. Battle Anderson, 'Nonprofit Geographic Expansion: Branches, Affiliates, or Both?' (HBS working paper; Social Enterprise Series, 27; 2003). See also Carla Tishler, 'The Growth of the Social Enterprise: Q&A with Jane Wei-Skillern', Harvard Business School Working Knowledge, 6 October 2003; www.hbsworkingknowledge.hbs.edu/pubitem.jhtml?id=3697&t=nonprofit, accessed December 2003.

27 'The Underpinning: Essential Elements That Make Social Enterprise Work', *Guardian*, 2 November 2003; society.guardian.co.uk/regeneration/story/0,7940,1076697,00.html, accessed December 2003.

28 'Social enterprise sector set to make big impact', *Co-operative News*, 24 September 2003; web. archive.org/web/20040317055834/http://www.thenews.coop/details.php?id=191, accessed February 2009.

29 R.W. Evans, 'The Rise of the Abdroids', in R.A. Shah, D.F. Murphy and M. McIntosh (eds.), *Some thing to Believe In. Creating Trust and Hope in Organisations: Stories of Transparency, Accountability and Governance* (Greenleaf Publishing, 2003): 98-103.

30 *CSR and Development: Towards a New Agenda*, UNRISD conference, Geneva, 17–18 November 2003; www.unrisd.org, accessed December 2003.

31 www.etikk.no/kalender.php?id=80, accessed February 2009

32 A. Crane and D. Matten, *Business Ethics: A European Perspective. Managing Corporate Citizenship and Sustainability in the Age of Globalization* (Oxford University Press, 2003).

33 www.accountability.org.uk, accessed December 2003

34 W. Scott and S. Gough (eds.), *Sustainable Development and Learning: Framing the Issues* (Taylor & Francis, 2003); W. Scott and S. Gough (eds.), *Key Issues in Sustainable Development and Learning: A Critical Review (Book of Readings)* (Taylor & Francis, 2003).

35 www.mngt.waikato.ac.nz, accessed December 2003. See also Shah, Murphy and McIntosh (eds.), *op. cit*: 104-107.

36 C. Argyris and D. Schon, *Theory in Practice: Increasing Professional Effectiveness* (Jossey-Bass, 1974).

37 www.oberlin.edu, accessed December 2003

38 Marci Janas, 'Ancestry and Influence: A Portrait of David Orr', 17 September 1998; www.oberlin.edu/news-info/98sep/orr_profile.html, accessed December 2003.

2004: Foreword

1 Professor **Jeremy Moon** is Director, International Centre for Corporate Social Responsibility, Nottingham University Business School, Nottingham, UK. University Business School's International Centre for Corporate Social Responsibility (ICCSR) was founded in 2002. It has established an international reputation for its teaching programmes and for the quality of its academic research. ICCSR staff teach on undergraduate and postgraduate courses including an MA in CSR and the first and only MBA in CSR. The ICCSR also provides PhD supervision and offers a small number of scholarships for all these courses. More information on ICCSR is available at www.nottingham.ac.uk/business/ICCSR.

1Q2004

1 M. Baker, 'Behind the Mask: How Christian Aid got it wrong on corporate responsibility', *Ethical Corporation*, February 2004.

2 Christian Aid, 'Behind the Mask: The Real Face of Corporate Social Responsibility', 21 January 2004; web.archive.org/web/20041209185020/http://www.christianaid.org.uk/indepth/0401csr/index.htm, accessed February 2009).

3 Baker, *op. cit.*

4 E. Freeman, *Strategic Management: A Stakeholder Approach* (Pitman, 1984).

5 R. Marens, 'Where's the Beef? Lessons from "the Macro Invisibility of Stakeholder Management" ', paper presented at Academy of Management, Seattle, 2003.

6 *International Right to Know: Empowering Communities through Transparency* (Washington, DC: IRTK Campaign, 2003).

7 'Two-Faced Capitalism: Corporate social responsibility is all the rage. Does it, and should it, make any difference to the way firms behave?', *The Economist*, 22 January 2004.

8 J. Bendell and F. Sullivan, 'Sleeping with the Enemy? Business–Environmentalist Partnerships for Sustainable Development. The Case of the WWF 1995 Group', in R. Aspinall and J. Smith (eds.), *Environmentalist and Business Partnerships: A Sustainable Model?* (The White Horse Press, 1996): 3-33

9 D.F. Murphy and J. Bendell, 'Getting Engaged: Business–NGO Relations on Sustainable Development', in R. Starkey and R. Welford (eds.), *The Earthscan Reader in Business and Sustainable Development* (Earthscan Publications, 2001).

10 A. Pettifor (ed.), *Real World Economic Outlook 2003* (New Economics Foundation, 2003).

11 C. Weller and A. Hersh, 'The Long and Short of it: Global Liberalisation, Poverty and Inequality' (Technical Papers, 40; Economic Policy Institute, 2002; nw08.american.edu/~hertz/fall2002/Weller%20on%20Globalization%20and%20Poverty.pdf, accessed March 2004).

12 L. Beck, 'Election Dysfunction', *Brazzil*, August 2002; accessed at www.brazzil.com/p20aug02.htm, accessed March 2004.

13 F. Mercier and J. Bendell, 'The Business Case for Financial Stability: A Global Dialogue with Business', Bread For All, February 2004.

14 'France, Brazil relaunch "Lula fund" to tax arms sales and fight poverty', Channel News Asia, 31 January 2004; web.archive.org/web/20040821233810/http://www.channelnewsasia.com/stories/afp_world/view/68822/1/.html, accessed February 2009.

15 *Business Respect: CSR Dispatches* 68 (21 December 2003).

16 A. Zammit, *Development at Risk: Reconsidering UN–Business Relations* (UNRISD and the South Centre, 2004).

17 J. Bendell, 'Flags of Inconvenience? The Global Compact and the Future of the United Nations' (ICCSR Research Paper Series, No. 22-2004; Nottingham University).

18 H. Levins, 'Take a Look at Leap Year's Bottom Line', *Miami Herald*, 28 February 2004.

19 J. Elkington, *Cannibals with Forks: The Triple Bottom Line of 21st Century Business* (Capstone Publishing, 1997).

20 W. Norman and C. McDonald, 'Getting to the Bottom of 'Triple Bottom Line', *Business Ethics Quarterly*, 2003.

21 N. Stride, 'The Expanding Triple Bottom Line', *National Business Review*, Auckland, 24 October 2003: 18-19.

22 Association of Chartered Certified Accountants (ACCA), 'Global Accountancy Body Awards UK Voluntary Reporters', press release, 24 February 2004; web.archive.org/web/20051221073053/http://www.acca.org.uk/news/releases/1099682?session=ffffffeffffffffc28288ca40426c7d4852a6332b51fa0bfa71aee1ecbdbceb, accessed February 2009.

23 The Co-operative Bank, 'Sustainable Development Partnership Report 2002'; web.archive.org/web/20040805005659/http://www.co-operativebank.co.uk/ethics/partnership2002/pr/index.html, accessed February 2009.

24 Royal Dutch/Shell Group, 'The Shell Report 2002'.

25 ACCA, *op. cit.*

26 *Business Respect: CSR Dispatches* 71 (29 February 2004).

27 *Ibid.*

28 www.ethics.org.au/our_services/projects/corporate_responsibility_index, accessed March 2004

29 'Australian CR Index drops NGO raters', Ethical Corporation, 25 February 2004; www.ethicalcorp.com/content.asp?ContentID=1705, accessed March 2004

30 www.pce.govt.nz/work_programme/reports_by_subject/all_reports/sustainable_development/see_change, accessed February 2009

31 Parliamentary Commissioner for the Environment, 'Education for sustainability to bring about a sea change in society', Wellington, 15 January 2004; www.pce.govt.nz/news/media_releases/education_for_sustainability_to_bring_about_a_sea_change_in_society, accessed February 2009.

32 Report preface, p. 5; pce.govt.nz.customer.onesquared.net/reports/allreports/1_877274_12_7.shtml, accessed February 2009.

33 C. Galea (ed.), *Teaching Business Sustainability: From Theory to Practice* (Greenleaf Publishing, 2004).

34 www3.interscience.wiley.com/cgi-bin/jabout/5329/Society.html, accessed March 2004

35 www.greenleaf-publishing.com/productdetail.kmod?productid=64, accessed February 2009

36 *Ibid.*

2Q2004

1 F. Manjoo, 'Caterpillar faces an intifada', *Salon.com*, May 2004; archive.salon.com/tech/feature/2004/05/13/bulldozers/index_np.html, accessed June 2004.

2 CAT Proposal 5: Stockholder Proposal re: Sale of Equipment to Israel and Caterpillar Response (2004); web.archive.org/web/20040324184855/http://www.cat.com/about_cat/investor_information/_proxy_materials/pdf/2004_notice_and_proxy.pdf, accessed January 2009, p. 34.

3 www.catdestroyshomes.org, accessed June 2004

4 J. Ziegler, letter dated 28 May 2004.

5 E.W. Corrie, 'The Crisis in Rafah: Caterpillar Should Do the Right Thing, Now', 19 May 2004; www.counterpunch.org/corrie05192004.html, accessed June 2004.

6 See Simon Zadek, *The Civil Corporation: The New Economy of Corporate Citizenship* (Earthscan Publications, 2001) and Jem Bendell (ed.), *Terms for Endearment: Business, NGOs and Sustainable Development* (Greenleaf Publishing, 2000) for discussion of public policy aspects of corporate citizenship, described as 'third generation' and 'radical', respectively.

7 S. Lasensky, 'How Foreign Aid Serves the National Interest', *Buffalo News*, 16 March 2003.

8 IOE and ICC, 'Joint Views of the IOE and ICC on the Draft "Norms on the Responsibilities of Transnational Corporations and Other Business Enterprises with Regard to Human Rights"' (2004); www.business-humanrights.org/Links/Repository/179848/link_page_view, accessed February 2009.

9 G. Chandler, 'Response to the Joint Views of the International Chamber of Commerce (ICC) and International Organisation of Employers (IOE) on the United Nations Human Rights Norms for Companies' (2004); web.archive.org/web/20041011222817/http://209.238.219.111/Chandler-response-to-IOE-ICC-April04.htm, accessed February 2009.

10 Respect Europe, 'Business Leaders' Initiative on Human Rights', 20 April 2004; web.archive.org/web/20040808005350/http://www.bitc.org.uk/news/news_directory/human_rights.html, accessed February 2009.

11 OHCHR, 'HCHR Resolution 2004/116 on Responsibilities of Transnational Corporations and Related Business Enterprises with Regard to Human Rights' (Geneva, 2004).

12 Amnesty International, 'Economic Globalization and Human Rights: Corporate Responsibility Breakthrough at the UN Human Rights Commission', 2004; web.archive.org/web/20041205010102/http://web.amnesty.org/pages/ec-unnorms-eng, accessed February 2009.

13 Corporate Europe Observatory (CEO), 'Shell Leads International Business Campaign against UN Human Rights Norms', *CEO Info Brief*, March 2004; web.archive.org/web/20040810013935/http://www.corporateeurope.org/norms, accessed February 2009.

14 Shell International, 'Comment by Shell International on the Article by Corporate Europe Observatory, "Shell Leads International Business Campaign against UN Human Rights Norms"' (2004); web.archive.org/web/20041126070706/http://209.238.219.111/Comment-Shell-International.htm, accessed February 2009.

15 'Statement of Support for the UN *Human Rights Norms for Business*', to be delivered at the 60th Session of the Commission on Human Rights, 15 March–23 April 2004, Geneva; web.amnesty.org/library/Index/ENGIOR420052004?open&of=eng-398, accessed June 2004.

16 Jem Bendell, 'Barricades and Boardrooms: A Contemporary History of the Corporate Accountability Movement' (Programme Paper 13, UNRISD, 2004; www.unrisd.org, accessed June 2004).

17 www.irtk.org, accessed June 2004

18 See Christian Aid, 'Behind the Mask: The Real Face of Corporate Social Responsibility', pp. 25-26; Human Rights Watch, 'The Price of Oil', ch. 8; Michael Peel, 'Deep Well of Troubles in Nigeria', *Financial Times*, 9 June 2004. In the 2003 auditors' report on Shell Nigeria's CSR work—recently published on the Shell website—KPMG and others remark: 'We are unable to form a conclusion on SPDC's CD [Community Development] project activity.' The auditors point out that 'the CDMIS [Community Development Management Information System] used as the basis for compiling project activity included in this report has significant control weaknesses that impact on data integrity' (SPDC, *People and Environment Report 2003* [Port Harcourt, Nigeria; www.shell.com/static/nigeria/downloads/pdfs/annualreport_2003.pdf, accessed June 2004]).

19 David Adam, 'Oil Chief: My Fears for Planet', *Guardian*, 17 June 2004; www.guardian.co.uk/uk_news/story/0,3604,1240496,00.html, accessed June 2004.

20 Carola Hoyos and Michael Peel, 'Nigeria had raised concerns over Shell oil reserves', *Financial Times*, London, 15 April 2004; Carola Hoyos and Michael Peel, 'Nigeria holds the clue to the groups wrongly booked reserves debacle', *Financial Times*, 24 April 2004.

21 WAC Global Services, 'Peace and Security in the Niger Delta: Conflict Expert Group Baseline Report', Working Paper for SPDC Lagos, December 2003; Karl Maier, 'Shell "Feeds" Nigeria Discord, May End Onshore Work', Bloomberg, 10 June 2004.

22 WAC Global Services, *op. cit.*, p. 29.

23 Chomskychat, 29 January 2004; www.zmag.org, accessed June 2004.

24 'The Times and Iraq', *New York Times*, 26 May 2004; www.nytimes.com/2004/05/26/international/middleeast/26FTE_NOTE.html?8dpc, accessed June 2004.

25 Steven Kull, 'Misperceptions, the Media and the Iraq War', University of Maryland's Program on International Policy Attitudes (PIPA), 2003; web.archive.org/web/20041012224109/http://www.pipa.org/OnlineReports/Iraq/Media_10_02_03_Report.pdf, accessed February 2009.

26 See 'Red Cross report details alleged Iraq abuses', Agencies, *Guardian*, 10 May 2004; and Rory McCarthy, 'Amnesty details killing of civilians by British soldiers', *Guardian*, 11 May 2004.

27 *Guardian*, 3 June 2004, p. 8.

28 See e.g. M.F. Belenky *et al.*, *Women's Way of Knowing: The Development of Self, Voice and Mind* (HarperCollins Basic Books, 1986); and P. Reason and H. Bradbury (eds.), *Handbook of Action Research* (Sage, 2001).

29 P. Lather, 'Fertile Obsession: Validity after Poststructuralism', *Sociological Quarterly* 34.4 (1993): 673-93.

30 N. Chomsky and E. Hernan, *Manufacturing Consent: The Political Economy of the Mass Media* (Vintage, 1994).

31 A. Simms, T. Bigg and N. Robins, *It's Democracy Stupid. The Trouble with the Global Economy: The United Nations' Lost Role and Democratic Reform of the IMF, World Bank and the World Trade Organi - zation* (New Economics Foundation, 2000).

32 'New row over US Media Control', BBC News, 20 August, 2003; news.bbc.co.uk/1/hi/business/3169073.stm, accessed June 2004.

33 *Independent*, 5 May 2004, p. 22.

34 Worldwatch Institute, *State of the World 2004*; www.worldwatch.org/press/news/2004/01/07, accessed June 2004.

35 www.lucita.net, accessed June 2004

36 www.ethicalmedia.com, accessed June 2004

37 Jo Confino, 'Communication with Care', *Guardian*, 15 March 2004; www.guardian.co.uk/print/0,3858,4879684-112841,00.html, accessed June 2004.

38 www.guardian.co.uk/socialaudit, accessed June 2004

39 SustainAbility/WWF-UK, 'Through the Looking Glass: Corporate Responsibility in the Media and Entertainment Sector' (SustainAbility/WWF-UK, 2004; www.sustainability.com/researchandadvocacy/reports_article.asp?id=139, accessed February 2009). See also United Nations Environment Programme, *Good News and Bad: The Media, Corporate Social Responsibility and Society* (UNEP, 2002).

40 M. Baker, 'The Media and Social Responsibility', *Business Respect: CSR Dispatches* 70 (1 February 2004); www.mallenbaker.net/csr/CSRfiles/page.php?Story_ID=1210, accessed June 2004.

41 Confino, *op. cit.*

42 *Guardian*, 3 June 2004, p. 23.

43 See www.lifeworth.net, accessed June 2004

3Q2004

1 sportrelief.com, accessed September 2004

2 'The London Marathon: A History'; marathon-run.com/history.htm, accessed September 2004.

3 web.archive.org/web/20040923142525/http://www.uefa.com/uefa/aboutuefa/AssistanceProgrammes/charity, accessed February 2009

4 www.globalmarch.org, accessed September 2004

5 *Ibid.*

6 Oxfam, Clean Clothes Campaign and ICFTU, *Play Fair at the Olympics: Respect Workers' Rights in the Sportswear Industry* (Oxfam, 2004).

7 *Ibid.*, p. 47.

8 web.archive.org/web/20040923142525/http://www.uefa.com/uefa/aboutuefa/AssistanceProgrammes/charity, accessed February 2009

9 Rick Horrow, 'The Business of Soccer: Futbol, MLS, the Grass Roots Future', CBS Sports News, 29 July 2004; cbs.sportsline.com/general/story/7535307, accessed September 2004.

10 www.olympic.org/uk/passion/museum/permanent/index_uk.asp, accessed September 2004

11 'The Christmas Truce', 20 November 2004; www.firstworldwar.com/features/christmastruce.htm, accessed September 2004.

12 J. Magee and J. Sugden, 'The World at Their Feet: Professional Football and International Labour Migration', *Journal of Sport and Social Issues* 26.4 (2002): 421-37.

13 Mark Mitchell, Robert Montgomery and Sheila Mitchell, 'Do-It-Yourself Investing in Sport-Related Firms', *Sport Journal* 6.1 (2003); www.thesportjournal.org/article/do-it-yourself-investing-sport-related-firms, accessed February 2009.

14 See A. Ingham, in R. Giwianotti, *Sport and Modern Social Theorists* (Palgrave Macmillan, 2004): ch. 1.

15 'Chukotka goes bankrupt', Pravda, 15 June 2001, web.archive.org/web/20041031233858/http://english.pravda.ru/main/2001/06/15/7803.html, accessed February 2009; 'Abramovich region found bankrupt', BBC News, 21 May 2004, news.bbc.co.uk/1/hi/world/europe/3735971.stm, accessed September 2004.

16 'Profile: Mikhail Khodorkovsky', BBC News, 16 June 2004; news.bbc.co.uk/go/pr/fr/-/1/hi/business/3213505.stm, accessed September 2004.

17 Robert McIntyre, 'The Facilitators', *American Prospect*, September 2004.

18 cenda.cep.cl, accessed September 2004

19 Manuel Riesco, 'Pay Your Taxes! Corporate Social Responsibility and the Mining Industry in Chile'. The version of the paper, to be published by UNRISD, is available at: cep.cl/UNRISD/UNRISD_CSR/Mining_CSR_Chile.doc, accessed September 2004. UNRISD also planned to publish a précis of the debate stimulated by the paper and the issues it raises about CSR and research.

20 Gustavo Lagos Cruz-Coke and Marcos Lima Aravena, ' "Pay Your Taxes": Faulty Calculations or Ideological Prejudice?', Pontificia Universidad Catolica de Chile, Engineering Faculty, Mining Center, May 2004; cep.cl/UNRISD/UNRISD_CSR/References/Dimes_Diretes/PUC.doc, accessed September 2004.

21 Letter to Emma Rothschild, July 2004.

22 United Nations Research Institute for Social Development (UNRISD), 'Corporate Social Responsibility and Development: Towards a New Agenda?', Conference News (UNRISD, 2004; www.unrisd.org, accessed September 2004): 5.

23 John Plender and Martin Simons, 'How Transfer Pricing Threatens Global Tax Revenues', *Financial Times*, 21 July 2004.

24 John Plender, 'How Companies Keep Tax Low within the Law', *Financial Times*, 20 July 2004.

25 John Christensen, 'Fast and Loose: The Chicago Legacy', Article 13; www.article13.com/A13_ContentList.asp?strAction=GetPublication&PNID=1040, accessed September 2004.

26 *Ibid.*

27 'Corporate Leaders at Global Compact Summit Pledge to Battle Corruption', UN-DPI, 25 June 2004; www.unglobalcompact.org, accessed September 2004.

28 *Africa Confidential* 45.18 (10 September 2004); www.africa-confidential.com, accessed September 2004.

29 Robert Verkaik, 'Lawyers face curbs over "profits before ethics": New rules for solicitors as client charges spiral to £9bn', *Guardian*, 31 August 2004.

30 Eric Decouty, 'A Nigerian Contract at the Heart of a Corruption Affair', *Le Figaro*, 20 December 2003; www.globalpolicy.org/nations/launder/regions/2003/1220heart.htm, accessed September 2004.

31 www.publishwhatyoupay.org, accessed September 2004

32 UN Global Compact and SustainAbility, 'Gearing Up: From Corporate Responsibility to Good Governance and Scalable Solutions' (2004; www.unglobalcompact.org/docs/news_events/8.1/gearing-up.pdf, accessed February 2009).

33 'CSR Hits Limit, Report Concludes', press release, 24 June 2004; www.unglobalcompact.org, accessed September 2004.

34 J. Bendell, 'Flags of Inconvenience? The Global Compact and the Future of the United Nations', in M. McIntosh, G. Kell and S. Waddock (eds.), *Learning To Talk: Corporate Citizenship and the Development of the UN Global Compact* (Greenleaf Publishing, 2004): 146-67.

35 International Organisation for Standardisation, 'ISO to go ahead with guidelines for social responsibility', press release, 29 June 2004; www.iso.org, accessed September 2004.

36 International Organisation for Standardisation, 'Recommendations to the ISO Technical Management Board', ISO/TMB AG CSR N32 (2004); www.iso.org, accessed September 2004.

37 K. Webb, *Voluntary Codes: Private Governance, the Public Interest and Innovation* (Carleton University, 2002).

38 B. Arts, 'Non-State Actors in Global Governance: A Power Analysis', paper presented at the ECPR Joint Sessions, Edinburgh, 28 March–2 April 2003.

39 J. Bendell and X. Font, 'Which Tourism Rules? Green Standards and GATS', *Annals of Tourism Research* 31 (January 2004): 139-56.

40 Pacific Institute, *International NGO Network on ISO* (brochure; Pacific Institute, 2002).

41 Stefano Ponte, 'Standards and Sustainability in the Coffee Sector: A Global Value Chain Approach', paper prepared for the Sustainable Commodity Initiative, International Institute for Sustainable Development, Geneva, 2003.

42 This is documented in the case of social auditing in J. Bendell, 'Towards Participatory Workplace Appraisal: Report from a Focus Group of Women Banana Workers' (Occasional Paper; New Academy of Business, September 2001; www.new-academy.ac.uk/publications/keypublications/documents/workplaceappraisal.pdf, accessed September 2004).

4Q2004

1 J. Nelson and D. Prescott, 'Business and the Millennium Development Goals: A Framework for Action' (International Business Leaders Forum, 2003; web.archive.org/web/20041226035905/http://www.iblf.org/csr/csrwebassist.nsf/content/f1d2b3aad4.html, accessed February 2009).

2 povertyprofit.wri.org, accessed December 2004

3 C.K. Prahalad, *The Fortune at the Bottom of the Pyramid: Eradicating Poverty through Profits* (Wharton School Publishing, 2004).

4 'Profits and Poverty', *The Economist*, 19 August 2004.

5 C.K. Prahalad, 'Why Selling to the Poor Makes for Good Business', *Fortune*, 3 November 2004.

6 Prahalad, *The Fortune at the Bottom of the Pyramid*, p. 1.

7 'Global Microentrepreneurship Awards will promote small business in conjunction with UN's "Year of Microcredit" campaign', *PRNewswire*, 9 November 2004.

8 *Ibid.*

9 Basma bint Talal, 'Microfinance offers the poor a way out of poverty', *Jordan Times*, 18 November 2004.

10 'Government to ensure higher bank loans to poor through SHGs', *Business India*, New Delhi, 30 October 2004.

11 WBCSD, 'Finding Capital for Sustainable Livelihoods Businesses: A Finance Guide for Business Managers', July 2004; www.wbcsd.org/includes/getTarget.asp?type=DocDet&id=6557, accessed December 2004.

12 Mitchell Pacelle and John Lyons, 'Citigroup courts a new clientele: Mexican workers. Once focused on the ultrarich, it now eyes the "unbanked"', *Wall Street Journal*, 27 July 2004.

13 Mac Margolis, 'Profit and the Poor. Consumer-goods makers are realizing they have only one direction to go for growth: down-market', *Newsweek International*, 19 July 2004.

14 Andy Reinhardt, 'Nokia's Goal: Cell-Phone Planet', *BusinessWeek*, 7 September 2004; www.businessweek.com/technology/content/sep2004/tc2004097_3567.htm, accessed December 2004.

15 Rajesh Jain, 'The next computing Kumbh mela', *Business Standard*, 25 August 2004.

16 Prahalad, *The Fortune at the Bottom of the Pyramid*, p. 22.

17 Nicola Bullard, 'Four billion poor hold key to the future of capitalism', March 2001; www.focusweb.org/publications/2001/Four_billion_poor_hold_key.htm, accessed December 2004.

18 R. Guha and J. Martinez-Allier, *Varieties of Environmentalism: Essays North and South* (Earthscan Publications, 1997).

19 'Uganda: Business told that social responsibility means local shareholders', *Business Respect: CSR Dispatches 71* (29 February 2004).

20 B. Ellison and D. Moller, *A Foot in the Door: Hindustan Lever breaks into the mass market* (case study prepared for MBA, IESE, University of Navarra, Barcelona, 2002).

21 www.karmabanque.com, accessed December 2004

22 Paul Marinko, 'Campaign aims to hit Coke where it hurts', *Guardian*, 25 November 2004.

23 www.karmabanque.com, accessed December 2004

24 'Hedge fund targets Coke for devaluation', *Washington Post*, 25 November 2004.

25 www.theyesmen.org, accessed December 2004

26 www.irtk.org, accessed December 2004

27 SustainAbility, 'The Changing Landscape of Liability: A Director's Guide to Trends in Corporate Environmental, Social and Economic Liability' (SustainAbility, 2004; www.sustainability.com/researchandadvocacy/reports_article.asp?id=180, accessed February 2009).

28 For example, see J. Bendell, 'Psychos in Suits: American CEOs in need of (an) Asylum', *Open Democracy*, August 2002; www.opendemocracy.net, accessed December 2004.

29 J. Bakan, *The Corporation: The Pathological Pursuit of Profit and Power* (Constable, 2004).

30 Jonathan Birchall, 'Activists' Hands Tied for Seven Years', FT.com, 24 October 2004; news.ft.com, accessed December 2004.

31 www.csrwatch.com, accessed December 2004 [link is no longer active]

32 J. Moon, 'Corporate Social Responsibility: An Overview', in *International Directory of Philanthropy* (Europa Books, 2002).

33 W.E. Gaille, 'Essentially Contested Concepts', in *Proceedings of the Aristotelian Society* 66 (1956): 187-98.

34 *State of the World 2003* (Worldwatch Institute).

35 See, for example, coverage on www.csrwire.com, www.ethicalcorp.com and www.wbcsd.org.

36 'Bush outlines alternative plan to Kyoto Protocol', *UN Wire*, 15 February 2002; www.unwire.org, accessed December 2004.

37 A. Lovins, E.K. Datta, O. Bustnes, J. Koomey and N. Glasgow, *Winning the Oil Endgame: Innovation for Profits, Jobs and Security* (Rocky Mountain Institute, 2004; www.oilendgame.org, accessed December 2004).

38 International Energy Agency, *World Energy Outlook 2004* (International Energy Agency, 2004; www.worldenergyoutlook.org, accessed December 2004).

39 'China publishes greenhouse gas emissions', *Point Carbon*, 10 November 2004; www.pointcarbon.com, accessed December 2004.

40 WWF, *Living Planet Report 2004* (WWF, 2004; www.wwf.org.uk, accessed December 2004).

41 R. Sherman, 'Climate Change Politics Emission Trading: The Next Diplomatic Struggle', *Global Dialogue* 3.3 (December 1998).

42 'Bush to unveil alternative global warming plan', *CNN*, 14 February 2002; www.cnn.com, accessed December 2004.

43 The Climate Group, 'Carbon Down, Profits Up', 30 August 2004; www.theclimategroup.org/assets/TCG_Emissions%20Charts%2004.pdf, accessed February 2009.

44 World Resources Institute, *A Climate of Innovation: Northeast Business Action to Reduce Greenhouse Gases* (World Resources Institute, 2004; www.wri.org, accessed December 2004).

45 Sustainable Energy Institute, 'US Business Actions to Address Climate Change: Case Studies of Five Industry Sectors', Sustainable Energy Institute and Numark Associates, 2004; www.s-e-i.org/ISR.asp, accessed December 2004.

46 'Every Sector, One RESOLVE: Survey Results and Annual Report', *Business Roundtable*; www. businessroundtable.org, accessed December 2004.

47 'Natsource reports significant increases in greenhouse gas trading in 2004', *Natsource*, 9 June 2004; www.natsource.com, accessed December 2004.

48 'EC redoubles defence of Kyoto and emissions trading', *Carbon Ventures News*, February 2004; www.carbonventures.com, accessed December 2004.

49 Ernst & Young, 'The European Union Emissions Trading Scheme: A Challenge for Industry or Just an Illusion?', 2004; www.ey.nl, accessed December 2004.

50 'Enviros Consulting paper highlights emissions could rise under the EU ETS', *Enviros Consulting*, 30 September 2004; www.enviros.com, accessed December 2004.

51 Steve Connor, 'US climate policy bigger threat to world than terrorism', *Independent*, 9 January 2004.

52 'EnBW takes legal action in Luxemburg against German implementation of emission trading', EnBW press release, 27 September 2004; www.enbw.com, accessed December 2004.

53 'Natsource reports significant increases in greenhouse gas trading in 2004', *Natsource*, 9 June 2004; www.natsource.com, accessed December 2004.

54 WBCSD, 'Carbon trading in Europe triples since Russian move on Kyoto', 12 October 2004; www. wbcsd.org, accessed December 2004.

55 UNEP, 'Carbon-credit trading set for launch in SA', *The Environment in the News*, 12 October 2004.

56 'BT's Green Switch Over', *Better World* (BT publication) 1 (November 2004); www.btplc.com, accessed December 2004.

57 Copenhagen Consensus, *Copenhagen Consensus: The Results*, 2004; www.copenhagenconsensus. c o m, accessed December 2004.

58 Working Group on Climate Change and Development, 'Up in Smoke?' (New Economics Foundation, 2004; www.neweconomics.org, accessed December 2004).

59 www.earthscan.co.uk/?tabid=480, accessed February 2009

60 Sustainability, UNEP and Standard & Poor's, *Risk and Opportunity: Best Practice in Non-financial Reporting* (Sustainability/UNEP/Standard & Poor's, 2004; www.sustainability.com, accessed December 2004).

61 www.sustainability.com, accessed December 2004

62 ACCA and Corporate Register, 'Towards Transparency: Progress on Global Sustainability Reporting 2004' (ACCA/Corporate Register, 2004).

63 KPMG, '2004 KPMG Survey on Integrated Sustainability Reporting in South Africa' (KPMG, 2004; www.kpmg.co.za, accessed December 2004).

64 Deloitte & Touche, 'Deloitte names Dreher Breweries Winner of the 2004 "Green Frog" Award', 16 November 2004; www.deloitte.com, accessed December 2004.

65 'Operating and Financial Review (OFR)', UK Department of Trade and Industry, May 2004; web. archive.org/web/20041111091403/http://www.dti.gov.uk/cld/financialreview.htm, accessed February 2009.

66 CTN Communications, '2004 CSR Online Survey'.

67 UNDP and IBLF, 'Business and the Millennium Development Goals: A Framework for Action', 2003; www.undp.org/business/docs/mdg_business.pdf, accessed December 2004.

2005: Foreword

1 www.wwf.org.uk

2005: Introduction

1 SustainAbility, 'Influencing Power: Reviewing the Conduct and Content of Corporate Lobbying', 19 July 2005; www.sustainability.com/researchandadvocacy/reports_article.asp?id=317, accessed February 2009.
2 Quote altered from gender-specific language.
3 Peter M. Senge, *The Fifth Discipline* (Century Business, 1992).
4 David Rooke and Bill Torbert, 'Seven Transformations of Leader', *Harvard Business Review*, April 2005.
5 www.asp-online.org, accessed February 2009
6 Jonathon Porritt, 'Richard Sandbrook: Bold environmentalist who forged links between campaigners and big business', *Guardian*, 16 December 2005; www.guardian.co.uk/obituaries/story/0,3604,1668531,00.html, accessed February 2009.
7 www.oxfordleadership.com, accessed February 2009
8 www.aliainstitute.org/institute, accessed February 2009
9 www.solonline.org, accessed January 2006
10 www.forumforthefuture.org, accessed January 2006

1Q2005

1 www.csracademy.org.uk, accessed March 2005
2 A. Dunnett, 'Embedding CSR is the key to better performance', *Ethical Corporation*, November 2004.
3 D. Rueschemeyer, 'Professional Autonomy and the Social Control of Expertise', in R. Dingwall and P. Lewis (eds.), *The Sociology of the Professions* (Macmillan, 1983): 38-58.
4 T. Johnson, 'The Profession in the Class Structure', in R. Scase (ed.), *Industrial Society: Class, Cleavage and Control* (George Allen & Unwin, 1977).
5 N. Harding and J. McKinnon, 'User Involvement in the Standard-setting Process: A Research Note on the Congruence of Accountant and User Perceptions of Decision Usefulness', *Accounting, Organizations and Society* 22.1 (January 1997): 55-67.
6 E. Krause, 'Professional Group Power in Developing Societies', *Current Sociology* 49.4 (July 2001): 149-75.
7 www.asponline.org, accessed March 2005
8 'EU software patent law faces axe', BBC News, 17 February 2005; news.bbc.co.uk/1/hi/technology/4274811.stm, accessed March 2005.
9 'Software Patents in Europe: A Short Overview'; swpat.ffii.org/log/intro/index.en.html, accessed March 2005.
10 B. Acohido, 'Linux took on Microsoft, and won big in Munich', *USA Today*, 13 July 2003; www.usatoday.com/money/industries/technology/2003-07-13-microsoft-linux-munich_x.htm, accessed March 2005.
11 Jo Best, 'LiMux project moving again', ZDNet UK, 13 August 2004; news.zdnet.co.uk/software/applications/0,39020384,39163519,00.htm, accessed March 2005.
12 Linda Rosencrance and Todd R. Weiss, 'SCO Loses a Round in Court', *Computerworld*, 26 July 2004; www.computerworld.com/softwaretopics/os/linux/story/0,10801,94766,00.html accessed March 2005.
13 'IBM Timeline: SCO Group v. International Business Machines, Inc.', Groklaw, www.groklaw.net/staticpages/index.php?page=20031016162215566, accessed March 2005.
14 'Halloween X: Follow The Money', Open Source Initiative, 3 March 2004; Steven Vaughan-Nichols, 'Leaked Memo Revives SCO–Microsoft Connection Furore', *eWeek*, 4 March 2004, www.eweek.com/article2/0,1759,1542915,00.asp, accessed March 2005.
15 Chris Preimesberger, 'Analysis: Microsoft, SCO have a lot more explaining to do', *News Forge*, 8 March 2004; web.archive.org/web/20050921042511/http://trends.newsforge.com/trends/04/03/08/0457259.shtml, accessed February 2009.

16 'Microsoft's Ballmer warns Asia against use of Linux', *India Times Infotech*, 19 November 2004; infotech.indiatimes.com/articleshow/928080.cms, accessed March 2005.

17 'Microsoft's money machine revealed', *Inquirer*, 16 November 2003; www.theinquirer.net/?article=12694, accessed March 2005.

18 J. Chen, 'Microsoft cuts prices on China's market', *Shanghai Daily News*, 18 February 2005.

19 Microsoft, 'Progress on Microsoft Digital Inclusion Programmes in Jordan enables citizens to realise economic goals', press release, 22 February 2005; www.microsoft.com/middleeast/press/presspage.aspx?id=200522, accessed March 2005.

20 WIPO, 'Revised Consolidated Text for a Treaty on the Protection of Broadcasting Organizations, Standing Committee on Copyright and Related Rights', Twelfth Session, Geneva, 17–19 November 2004; www.wipo.int/edocs/mdocs/copyright/en/sccr_12/sccr_12_2.doc, accessed March 2005.

21 'Corporate profile', News Corporation; www.newscorp.com/investor/index.html, accessed March 2005.

22 Carolyn Deere, 'WIPO broadcasting treaty discussions end in controversy, confusion', Intellectual Property Watch, 22 November 2004; www.ip-watch.org/weblog/index.php?p=10&res=1024_ff&print=0, accessed March 2005.

23 www.cptech.org, accessed March 2005

24 Deere, *op. cit.*

25 Health Protection Agency, 'Documents of the NRPB, Vol. 15 No. 5'.

26 Mark Oliver, 'No mobiles for under-nines, study says', *Guardian*, 11 January 2005; www.guardian.co.uk/mobile/article/0,2763,1387812,00.html, accessed March 2005.

27 'Summary and Recommendations', para. 6.75; www.iegmp.org.uk/report/summary.htm, accessed March 2005.

28 *Ibid.*, para. 6.88.

29 Tetra Watch, 'New research'; www.tetrawatch.net/science/mthr.php, accessed March 2005.

30 'Summary and Recommendations', para. 1.2.

31 Mobile Operators Association, 'UK network operators welcome NRPB advice on mobile phones and health', 11 January 2005; www.mobilemastinfo.com/media/news/11_01_05.htm, accessed March 2005.

32 'mmO₂ Corporate Responsibility Report 2004'; web.archive.org/web/*/http://www.mmo2.com/cr2004/downloads/7630_CORE_REPORT.pdf, accessed February 2009.

33 Vodafone Group plc, 'Corporate Social Responsibility Report 2003/04', www.vodafone.com/etc/medialib/attachments/cr_downloads.Par.39964.File.dat/CSR_Report_2003-04_VF-GROUP_20050802.pdf, accessed February 2009.

34 Mobile Manufacturers Forum, 'Mobile Phones and Health 2004', www.mmfai.org/public/docs/eng/MMF%5FViewpoint%5FNRPB%2Epdf, accessed March 2005.

35 Mobile Operators Association, 'Comment on certain issues raised in NRPB Mobile Phones and Health 2004 Report and media coverage', 1 February 2005; www.mobilemastinfo.com/media/issue_statements/01_02_05.htm, accessed March 2005.

36 www.cogreslab.co.uk, accessed March 2005

37 'Acoustic neuroma linked to mobile phone use', Study in Sweden', web.archive.org/web/20050406035518/http://www.sweden.se/templates/SISResearchNews_ _ _ _10209.asp, accessed February 2009; Federica Castellani, 'Mobile phone risk revealed', News@Nature.com, 14 October 2004, web.archive.org/web/20050923063838/http://www.nature.com/news/2004/041011/pf/041011-11_pf.html, accessed February 2009.

38 www.nrpb.org, accessed March 2005 [link no longer active]

39 Lucy Sherriff, 'Mobile phones rot your balls', *The Register*, 28 June 2004, www.theregister.co.uk/2004/06/28/mobile_ball_rot, accessed March 2005; Sarah Boseley, 'Mobiles cut sperm count, says report', *Guardian*, 28 June 2004, www.guardian.co.uk/print/0,3858,4957960-103690,00.html, accessed March 2005.

40 Jay Griffiths, 'TETRA', *Ecologist*, October 2004; www.starweave.com/jays, accessed March 2005.

41 Mobile Operators Association, 'Mobile phone science review welcomed by industry', 14 January 2004; www.mobilemastinfo.com/media/news/14_01_04.htm, accessed March 2005.

42 Independent Expert Group on Mobile Phones, 'Report of the Group (The Stewart Report)', para 5.270; www.iegmp.org.uk/report/index.htm, accessed March 2005.

43 Tetra Watch, 'New research'; www.tetrawatch.net/science/mthr.php, accessed March 2005.

44 'Bead "slashes mobile radiation" ', BBC News, 25 January 2005; news.bbc.co.uk/1/hi/health/4203077.stm; accessed March 2005.

45 *Ibid.*

46 Lester Haines, 'Mobile phone industry in radiation risk rap', *The Register*, 13 September 2004; www.theregister.co.uk/2004/09/13/mobile_raditation_controversy [sic], accessed March 2005.

47 T. Greulich and R. Kemp, 'Stakeholder Roundtable. Mobile Phones, Base Stations and Health: The Current State of the Issue', Galson Sciences Ltd, 23 December 2004; www.mobilemastinfo.com/planning/stakeholder-roundtable-report-0303c_2vi.pdf, accessed February 2009.

48 Vodafone, 'Mobile Handsets and Health'; www.vodafone.com, accessed March 2005.

49 Vodafone Group plc, 'Corporate Social Responsibility Report 2003/04'.

50 *Hansard*, 14 July 2004, Column 1406; www.publications.parliament.uk/pa/cm200304/cmhansrd/cm040714/debtext/40714-02.htm, accessed February 2009.

51 E. Debold, 'The Business of Saving the World', *What is Enlightenment?* 28 (March–May 2005): 82; www.wie.org, accessed March 2005.

52 *Ibid.*, p. 88.

53 Simon Zadek, 'The Path to Corporate Responsibility', *Harvard Business Review*, 1 December 2004; harvardbusinessonline.hbsp.harvard.edu/b02/en/common/item_detail.jhtml?id=R0412J, accessed March 2005.

54 F. Dixon, 'Total Corporate Responsibility: Achieving Sustainability and Real Prosperity', *Ethical Corporation*, December 2003; www.ethicalcorp.com, accessed March 2005.

55 Debold, *op. cit.*, p. 89.

56 www.gtinitiative.org, accessed March 2005

57 web.archive.org/web/20051217102728/http://forums.seib.org/corporation2020, accessed February 2009

58 World Economic Forum, 'Global Town Hall Report', 26 January 2005; www.weforum.org/pdf/AM2005/Global_Town_Hall.pdf, accessed March 2005.

59 World Economic Forum, 'Closing Plenary: What We Should Do in 2005', 30 January 2005; web.archive.org/web/20050328233004/http://www.weforum.org/site/knowledgenavigator.nsf/Content/_S13543?open&event_id=1204&year_id=2005, accessed February 2009.

60 Debold, *op. cit.*, p. 89.

WR19 2Q05

1 Stefan Lovgren, 'China's Boom Is Bust for Global Environment, Study Warns', *National Geographic News*, 16 May 2005; news.nationalgeographic.com/news/2005/05/0516_050516_chinaeco.html, accessed June 2005.

2 www.csr-asia.com, accessed June 2005

3 www.csr-asia.com, accessed June 2005

4 www.csr-asia.com, accessed June 2005

5 *Worker's Daily*, 19 April 2005.

6 www.csr-asia.com, accessed June 2005

7 'Easy to Manage: A Report on the Chinese Toy Workers and the Responsibility of the Corporations'; www.fairtradecenter.se, accessed June 2005

8 TPWA report.

9 www.csr-asia.com, accessed June 2005

10 www.csr-asia.com, accessed June 2005

11 www.csr-asia.com, accessed June 2005

12 Brian Ho, 'ICO wins sustainability award', *CSR Asia* 1 (Week 14); www.csr-asia.com, accessed June 2005.

13 Reported by csr-asia.com, 17 April 2005 (accessed June 2005).

14 China View, 'Corporate Social Responsibility in China', 13 May 2005; news.xinhuanet.com/english/2005-05/13/content_2952742.htm, accessed June 2005.

15 18 April 2005.
16 www.panda.org, accessed June 2005
17 Xinhua, 25 April 2005.
18 Xinhua, 23 April 2005.
19 www.csr-asia.com, accessed June 2005
20 Global Business Coalition on HIV/AIDS, 'Global Business Coalition on HIV/AIDS (GBC) applauds Merck's new commitment to HIV/AIDS prevention in China', press release, 11 May 2005; www. aegis.com/news/bw/2005/BW050506.html, accessed June 2005.
21 Global Business Coalition on HIV/AIDS, '26 companies of the Global Business Coalition on HIV/AIDS (GBC) announce immediate commitments to fight AIDS in China', press release, 17 May 2005; www.aegis.com/news/pr/2005/PR050535.html, accessed June 2005.
22 Worldwatch Institute, *Vital Signs 2005*.
23 www.csr-asia.com, accessed June 2005
24 www.csr-asia.com, accessed June 2005
25 www.csr-asia.com, accessed June 2005
26 *Worker's Daily*, 18 April 2005.
27 singleplanet.blogs.com, accessed June 2005 [link no longer active]
28 www.csr-asia.com, accessed June 2005
29 www.csr-asia.com, accessed June 2005
30 www.csr-asia.com, accessed June 2005
31 www.csr-asia.com, accessed June 2005
32 www.csr-asia.com, accessed June 2005
33 BSR and PwC, 'Public Sector Support for the Implementation of Corporate Social Responsibility (CSR) in Global Supply Chains: Conclusions From Practical Experience', December 2004; www. ifc.org/ifcext/economics.nsf/AttachmentsByTitle/Implementation+of+CSR+in+Global+Supply+ Chains/$FILE/Implementation+of+CSR+in+Global+Supply+Chains.pdf, accessed February 2009.
34 Ian Davis, 'The Biggest Contract', *The Economist*, 26 May 2005.
35 *Business Respect: CSR Dispatches* 82 (16 May 2005); www.mallenbaker.net/csr/nl/82.html, accessed June 2005.
36 Jeffrey Gandz, 'Leadership Character and Competencies', *Organizational Performance Review*, Spring/Summer 2005 (Conference Board Canada).
37 M. Gerzon, *Leaders beyond Borders* (2004); www.mediatorsfoundation.org, accessed June 2005.
38 J.M. Burns, *Leadership* (Harper & Row, 1978).
39 www.fair-share.org.uk, accessed June 2005
40 Cassandra Higgs and Helen Wildsmith, *Just Pensions Responsible Investment Trustee Toolkit* (2005 edn); web.archive.org/web/20051104224210/http://www.uksif.org/J/Z/Z/lib/2005/04/jp-trtk/ index.shtml, accessed February 2009.
41 EIRIS, 'Denmark's national pension fund to invest ethically', press release, 12 April, 2005; www. asria.org/news/press/1113363416, accessed June 2005.
42 www.insightinvestment.com, accessed June 2005
43 J.P. Hawley and A.T. Williams, 'The Emergence of Fiduciary Capitalism', *Corporate Governance* 5.4 (1997).
44 F. Dixon, 'Total Corporate Responsibility: Achieving Sustainability and Real Prosperity' (2003); www.ethicalcorp.com, accessed June 2005.
45 www.enhancedanalytics.com, accessed June 2005
46 UNEP Finance Initiative, 'Principles for Responsible Investment'; www.unepfi.org/work_ programme/investment/principles, accessed June 2005.
47 J. Bendell, 'Barricades and Boardrooms: A Contemporary History of the Corporate Accountability Movement' (Programme Paper 13; UNRISD, 2004; www.jembendell.com/books.html, accessed February 2009).
48 'Jeff's Remarks at 2005 SASE Award Celebration'; www.skollfoundation.org/media/published_ works/jskoll/040105.asp, accessed June 2005.
49 www.sbs.ox.ac.uk/skoll, accessed February 2009
50 www.schwabfound.org/sf/SocialEntrepreneurs/index.htm, accessed February 2009
51 *Ibid.*
52 www.rugmark.org, accessed June 2005

53 www.approtec.org, accessed June 2005 [link no longer active]
54 Personal communication with the author.
55 cwis.livjm.ac.uk, accessed June 2005 [link no longer active]
56 www.hbs.edu/socialenterprise, accessed June 2005
57 www.aacsb.edu, accessed June 2005
58 web.archive.org/web/20050814232713/http://seforum.com.sg, accessed February 2009
59 'Social entrepreneurship a new focus', University of Auckland, 11 March 2005; web.auckland.ac.
    nz/uoa/about/news/articles/2005/03/0007.cfm, accessed February 2009.
60 www.netimpact.org/displaycommon.cfm?an=1, accessed June 2005
61 www.ashoka.org/changemakers, accessed February 2009
62 www.schwabfound.org/sf/Publications/Cases/index.htm, accessed February 2009
63 www.ssireview.com, accessed June 2005
64 www.emeraldinsight.com/Insight/viewContainer.do?containerType=Issue&containerId=23777,
    accessed February 2009
65 See J. Roper and G. Cheney, 'The Meanings of Social Entrepreneurship Today', *Corporate Gover -
    nance* 5.3 (2005): 95-104; J. Gregory Dees, 'The Meaning of 'Social Entrepreneurship'' ' (Stanford
    University; www.fntc.info/files/documents/The%20meaning%20of%20Social%20Entreneurship
    pdf [*sic*], accessed February 2009).
66 'Read the report that got debate started: Opportunities and Challenges for the International Devel-
    opment Community and Big Business', Shell Foundation; web.archive.org/web/200606271754
    25/http://www.shellfoundation.org/index.php?newsID=222, accessed February 2009.
67 Stuart Hart, *Capitalism at the Crossroads: The Unlimited Business Opportunities in Solving the World's
    Most Difficult Problems* (Wharton School Publishing, 2005).
68 www.iese.edu/cat/Research/CentersandChairs/Centers/CBS/Eventosyactiv/LabAprendizaje/
    IndiceBOP.asp, accessed February 2009
69 J. Schumpeter, *Capitalism, Socialism and Democracy* (Harper, 1975 [1942]): 82-85.
70 'From Mechanics to Organics: An Interview with Elisabet Sahtouris', *Insight and Outlook*, 1999;
    www.scottlondon.com/insight/scripts/sahtouris.html, accessed June 2005.

3Q2005

1 J. Bendell and François Mercier, 'Balancing Acts: Swiss Money in Latin America and Latin American Money in Switzerland' (Bread For All [BFA] Background Paper, 2005; www.bfa-ppp.ch/eng/
   IMG/pdf/BFA_Balancing_Acts_June_2005.pdf, accessed February 2009).
2 S. Shah, 'Counter Cultures', *Ethical Corporation*, July 2005: 33-34.
3 *Business Respect: CSR Dispatches* 6 (18 September 2005).
4 www.personal.barclays.co.uk/BRC1/jsp/brcucontrol?task=file&site=pfs&fileName=/PFS/A/Content/
   Files/report_2004.pdf, accessed February 2009
5 www.hsbc.com/1/PA_1_1_S5/content/assets/csr/csr_summary_report_2004.pdf, accessed February 2009
6 www.worldwatch.org/pubs/vs/2005, accessed September 2005
7 Juliet Eilperin, 'US Pressure Weakens G-8 Climate Plan: Global-Warming Science Assailed',
   Washington Post, 17 June 2005; www.washingtonpost.com/wp-dyn/content/article/2005/06/16/
   AR2005061601666_pf.html, accessed September 2005.
8 R. Heinberg, *The Party's Over: Oil, War, and the Fate of Industrial Societies* (New Society Publishers,
   2003).
9 M. Lynas, *High Tide* (Flamingo, 2004).
10 www.csr-asia.com, accessed September 2005
11 '21st Century Leadership', Wal-Mart; web.archive.org/web/20051226203215/http://
    walmartstores.com/GlobalWMStoresWeb/navigate.do?catg=463, accessed February 2009
12 www.pointcarbon.com, accessed September 2005
13 B. Schiller, 'Greenhouse Gas Pressure', *Ethical Corporation*, July 2005: 9-10.
14 Nick Robins, 'The Coming Carbon Crunch', *Ethical Corporation*, July 2005: 8.

15 Friends of the Earth UK, 'The CBI: Big claims, little evidence says Friends of the Earth', press release, 20 July 2005.

16 www.trucost.com, accessed September 2005

17 Robins, *op. cit.*

18 J. Porritt, *Capitalism as if the World Matters* (Earthscan Publications, 2005): 62.

19 Michael Schellenberger and Ted Nordhaus, 'The Death of Environmentalism: Global Warming Politics in a Post-environmental World', *Grist*, 2005; www.grist.org, accessed September 2005.

20 Richard Abdy, 'Flare Up in Nigeria', *Ethical Corporation*, July 2005; www.ethicalcorp.com/content. asp?ContentID=3775, accessed September 2005.

21 'Shell faces community rebellion at its annual meeting: Oil giant's neighbours demand justice', Friends of the Earth International, 27 June 2005; web.archive.org/web/20051230231555/http:// www.covalence.ch/index_uk.php?varNav=menu_ac_uk.php&news=1&varContenu=actualite/news_ uk.php&varssNav=menuss_ac_uk.php&id_titre=53, accessed February 2009.

22 *Business Respect: CSR Dispatches* 86 (18 September 2005).

23 *Ethical Insight* 23 (10 August 2005).

24 news.bbc.co.uk, accessed September 2005

25 Terry Macalister, 'Shell and M&S plan trade aid for Africa', *Guardian*, 5 July 2005; www.guardian. co.uk/business/2005/jul/05/fairtrade.hearafrica05, accessed September 2005.

26 J. van der Veer, 'The Role of the Private Sector in a Changing Africa', 5 July 2005; www.wbcsd.org/ includes/getTarget.asp?type=DocDet&id=16011, accessed September 2005.

27 A. Revkin, 'Former Bush aide who edited reports is hired by Exxon', *New York Times*, 15 June 2005.

28 WWF, 'One company two faces?', 19 July 2005; www.wwf.org.uk, accessed September 2005.

29 ICCR, 'Johnson & Johnson and Schering–Plough to publicly disclose all political contributions: Religious investors score two victories in reform effort as four other pharmas face shareholder resolutions demanding transparency', New York, 7 April 2005; www.iccr.org/news/press_ releases/pr_jnj0040705.htm, accessed September 2005.

30 Friends of the Earth UK, *op. cit.*

31 Friends of the Earth, 'Easy Listening: Why the Government Needs a New Playlist Featuring More than the CBI's Old Favourites. A Research Summary', 2005; www.foe.co.uk/resource/reports/ easy_listening.pdf; and Friends of the Earth, 'Hidden Voices: The CBI, Corporate Lobbying and Sustainability', 2005; www.foe.co.uk/resource/reports/hidden_voices.pdf, accessed September 2005.

32 Friends of the Earth UK, *op. cit.*

33 M. Baker, 'Corporate Lobbying: Rising Up the CSR Agenda', *Ethical Corporation*, 7 July 2005.

34 'Corporate Leaders Group on Climate Change', Letter to UK Prime Minister Tony Blair, 27 May 2005; www.cpi.cam.ac.uk/pdf/Letter%20to%20PM%202005%20Final.pdf, accessed February 2009.

35 Jem Bendell and Kate Kearins, 'The "Political Bottom Line": The Emerging Dimension to Corporate Responsibility for Sustainable Development', *Business Strategy and the Environment* 14.6 (2005): 372-83; www3.interscience.wiley.com/cgi-bin/fulltext/112134425/PDFSTART, accessed September 2005.

36 D. Lascelles, *The Ethics of Influence: Political Donations and Lobbying* (IBE, 2005).

37 SustainAbility and WWF, 'Influencing Power: Reviewing the Conduct and Content of Corporate Lobbying' (SustainAbility/WWF; www.sustainability.com/insight/scalingup-article.asp?id=317, accessed September 2005).

38 AccountAbility and United Nations Global Compact, 'Towards Responsible Lobbying' (Account-Ability, 2005).

39 SustainAbility and WWF, *op. cit.*: 11.

40 AccountAbility and United Nations Global Compact, *op. cit.*: 45.

41 Baker, *op. cit.*

42 AccountAbility and United Nations Global Compact, *op. cit.*: 45.

43 *Ibid.*: 45.

44 *Ibid.*: 45.

45 SustainAbility and WWF, *op. cit.*: 3.

46 M. Gitsham, C. Gribben and B. Pratten, *Called to Account: The Impact of the Freedom of Information Act* (Ashridge and NCVO, 2005).

47 Bendell and Kearins, *op. cit.*

4Q2005

1 D. Bolchover, *The Living Dead: Switched Off, Zoned Out—The Shocking Truth About Office Life* (Capstone Publishing, 2005).

2 See www.dilbert.com, accessed December 2005.

3 CIPD, 'Managing the Psychological Contract', May 2003, rev. January 2006; www.cipd.co.uk/subjects/empreltns/psycntrct/psycontr.htm?IsSrchRes=1, accessed January 2006.

4 Booz, Allen, Hamilton, 'A Global Checkup: Diagnosing the Health of Today's Organisations', 2005; extfile.bah.com/livelink/livelink/151679/?func=doc.Fetch&nodeid=151679, accessed December 2005.

5 ISR, 'The vast majority of Britons enjoy their work', press release, 4 August 2005; www.isrsurveys.com/pdf/media/Britons_pressrelease0805.pdf, accessed December 2005.

6 www.hse.gov.uk/statistics/sources.htm, accessed December 2005

7 E. Sahtouris and W. Harman, *Biology Revisioned* (North Atlantic Books, 1998).

8 P. Freire, *Pedagogy of the Oppressed* (Seabury Press, 1973).

9 N. Crofts, *Authentic Business: How to Create and Run Your Perfect Business* (Capstone Publishing, 2005).

10 Geri Smith, 'Why Latin America Scorns Uncle Sam', *Business Week*, 21 November 2005; www.businessweek.com/bwdaily/dnflash/nov2005/nf20051121_6027.htm?campaign_id=nws_insdr_nov24&link_position=link10, accessed December 2005.

11 UNDP, *Human Development Report 2005*; http://hdr.undp.org/en/reports/global/hdr2005, accessed February 2009.

12 UN, *The Millennium Development Goals Report*, 2005, unstats.un.org/unsd/mi/pdf/MDG%20Book.pdf, accessed December 2005.

13 Notas del SELA, 'Latin America: Development Banking on Responsible Business'; www.sela.org/news_gen.asp?dd=23&mm=8&aa=2005#12, accessed December 2005.

14 Management and Excellence, 'Ranking and Study: For Executives, SRI Funds, Analysts, Researchers Doing Business in Latin America . . .', September 2005; www.management-rating.com/archivo/M&E%20Latin%20America%20Ethics%20Country%20Report%20Brochure.pdf, accessed December 2005.

15 IFC and OECD, 'Case Studies of Good Corporate Governance Practices: Companies Circle of the Latin American Corporate Governance Roundtable', November 2005; www.oecd.org/dataoecd/19/56/35659591.pdf, accessed December 2005.

16 Antonio Vives, 'Social and Environmental Responsibility in Small and Medium Enterprises in Latin America' (Inter-American Development Bank, October 2005; idbdocs.iadb.org/wsdocs/getDocument.aspx?DOCNUM=1580939, accessed February 2009).

17 Red Puentes, 'Vision and Proposals of the Red Puentes Network Regarding Corporate Social Responsibility in Latin America', November 2005; web.archive.org/web/20061007161251/http://www.redpuentes.org/recursos/docs_redpuentes/redpuentesingles/Attachment00018460/Red+Puentes+Civic+agenda+English.pdf, accessed February 2009.

18 hdr.undp.org/en/media/HDR05_chapter_43.pdf, accessed February 2009

19 J. Braithwaite and P. Drahaus, *Global Business Regulation* (Cambridge University Press, 2000).

20 WTO, 'Principles of the Trading System'; www.wto.org/english/thewto_e/whatis_e/tif_e/fact2_e.htm, accessed December 2005.

21 K. Bradsher, 'Trade officials agree to end subsidies for agricultural exports', *New York Times*, 19 December 2005.

22 Larry Elliott, 'Lamy calls on Blair to broker trade deal', *Guardian*, 19 December 2005; business.guardian.co.uk/story/0,16781,1670285,00.html, accessed December 2005.

23 OECD, 'Submission by TUAC to the Trade Committee: Trade Union Statement on the Agenda for the Sixth Ministerial Conference of the World Trade Organisation (WTO)', 14 October 2005, TD/TC/CSO/RD(2005)3; www.olis.oecd.org/olis/2005doc.nsf/LinkTo/td-tc-cso-rd(2005)3, accessed December 2005.

24 OECD Watch, 'Five Years On: A Review of the OECD Guidelines and National Contact Points', September 2005; www.foei.org/en/publications/pdfs/pagesfiveyears.pdf/view, accessed February 2009.

25 World Economic Forum, 'Global Governance Initiative: Annual Report 2006'; www.weforum.org/pdf/Initiatives/GGI_Report06.pdf, accessed February 2009.

26 AccountAbility, 'Responsible Competitiveness: Reshaping Global Markets through Responsible Business Practices' (AccountAbility, 2005): 3, 4.
27 *Ibid.*: 3.
28 *Bangkok Post*, 3 January 2006.
29 AccountAbility, *op. cit.*: 9.
30 CNW Group, 'Yes to GMO-free zones say 58% of Canadians and 62% of PEI residents', March 2005; web.archive.org/web/20060617234940/http://www.newswire.ca/en/releases/archive/March2005/30/c9910.html, accessed February 2009.
31 AccountAbility, *op. cit.*
32 *Ibid.*: 3.

Thematic index

This is an index of industry *sectors*, corporate responsibility *topics*, organisational *functions*, featured *persons* and *organisations*, to help you navigate this volume. The industry *sectors* are based on the international classification benchmark, with some combinations and additions to include non-commercial sectors. The organisational *functions* are those most typically identified by management schools. The corporate responsibility *topics* are adapted from the topic headings identified in the 2008 draft of the ISO 26000 standard. Some of those headings are combined and some are added, such as 'fair taxation', 'fair supplier relations' and 'employee ethics'. The topics are identified in the way they present themselves to management. Often the reviews discussed economy-wide issues, such as trade regulation and global governance, and the way those issues relate to a company is through the management's 'political involvement'. Definitions for the specific terms used in this index can be found online in a 'glossary of terms' at www.lifeworth.com.*

Functions

Accounting, auditing or verification   106-108, 118-20, 166-68, 168, 174-76, 183-84, 221-24, 225-27, 235-37, 245-46, 247-49, 252-55, 268-69

Administration and operations   160-62, 201-204, 235-37, 243-45, 312-14

Communications   61-65, 153-55, 164-66, 168, 170-71, 172-74, 184-86, 200-201, 219-21, 249-52, 268-69, 286-89, 292-94, 306-309, 314-19

Direction, strategy or planning   67-70, 118-20, 163-64, 210-11, 240-42, 289-91, 297-99, 299-301, 320-23

Evaluation or review   83-85, 252-55, 268-69

Finance   50-51, 97-98, 118-20, 166-68, 168, 221-24, 230-32, 246-47, 247-49

Human resources   60, 71-72, 76-77, 116-17, 121-22, 160-62, 162-63, 163-64, 279-81, 320-23

Innovation or design   61-65, 79-81, 256-61, 281-84

IT   281-84

Legal   81-82, 151-53, 168, 197-98, 232-35, 281-84, 284-86, 314-19

Programme, project or account management   312-14

Purchasing or supply   58-60, 112-14, 133-35, 149-51, 170-71, 243-45, 297-99

Research   198-99, 208-10, 228-29, 301-305, 328-30, 331-32

Sales   61-65, 221-24, 230-32

Organisational functions not discussed in this volume are 'specialist practice', such as a medical professional, and 'public service', such as diplomacy, military or law enforcement. General staff within other specialist sectors, such as the clergy, have been categorised as either 'operations' or 'communications'.

* This thematic index was prepared with the help of Lifeworth Associate Sandy Lin.

Sectors

Key sectors not discussed in this volume are 'Biotechnology', 'Utilities', 'Specialised consumer services', 'Real estate', 'Recycling or disposal', 'Household or leisure goods', and 'Forestry or paper'. All of these are discussed in World Reviews in the *Journal of Corporate Citizenship* subsequent to 2005.

Topics

Key topics not discussed in this volume are 'Humanitarian support', 'Nutrition', 'Consumer awareness' and 'Conservation'. All of these are discussed in World Reviews in the *Journal of Corporate Citizenship* subsequent to 2005.

Persons

Organisations

Companies, NGOs, educational establishments, government departments. It also includes treaties, accords, campaigns, legislation, journals and newspapers.

For Product Safety Concerns and Information please contact our EU
representative GPSR@taylorandfrancis.com Taylor & Francis Verlag GmbH,
Kaufingerstraße 24, 80331 München, Germany

Printed and bound by CPI Group (UK) Ltd, Croydon, CR0 4YY
12/05/2025
01866950-0001